AMERICAN PENOLOGY

THOMAS G. BLOMBERG
KAROL LUCKEN

AMERICAN PENOLOGY

A HISTORY OF CONTROL

ENLARGED SECOND EDITION

ALDINETRANSACTION
A DIVISION OF TRANSACTION PUBLISHERS
NEW BRUNSWICK (U.S.A.) AND LONDON (U.K.)

Library of Congress Catalog Number: 2009043020
ISBN: 978-0-202-36334-9
Printed in the United States of America

Library of Congress Cataloging-in-Publication Data

Blomberg, Thomas G.
    American penology : a history of control / Thomas G. Blomberg and Karol
Lucken. -- 2nd ed.
        p. cm.
    Includes bibliographical references and index.
    ISBN 978-0-202-36334-9 (alk. paper)
        1. Prisons--United States--History. 2. Punishment--United States--
History. I. Lucken, Karol. II. Title.

HV9466.B55 2010
365'.973--dc22

                                                        2009043020

Contents

Acknowledgments

We wish to thank William Bales, Gail Humiston, and Shanna Van Slyke for their assistance in the preparation of this manuscript.

1

Introduction

In this enlarged second edition of *American Penology*, we have expanded our historical materials and extended our contemporary discussion. Through our examination of several centuries, we communicate a story about American penology's past, present, and future. The story begins in the 1600s, in the setting of colonial America. It ends in the year 2009, in what is now routinely termed millennial America. As this story is told through various historical and contemporary settings, America's efforts to understand and control crime unfold. The context, ideas, practices, and consequences of various penal reforms are described and examined. As these reforms evolve, patterns and relationships emerge, culminating in conclusions that may be disquieting to some because of their Orwellian implications, but comforting to others because of their suggestion of greater order, convenience, and public safety.

It is important to acknowledge that, while this book incorporates specific historical conditions and influences in relation to particular penal reform eras, it does not provide histories of these eras. Rather than "doing history," the genre of this book is to use selected historical conditions and influences. The purpose is to frame particular penal reforms, ideas, and practices in relation to the historical period and context from which they emerged and to which they are relevant.

Conceptual Framework

In the first half of the twentieth century, criminological inquiry was focused upon offender behavior and crime causation. The underlying assumption was that the operations of the formal criminal justice system of police, courts, and corrections are not problematic; on the contrary, it was assumed that this system simply operates in accordance with its formally prescribed goals and purposes. As a result, the system did not capture the attention of early twentieth-century criminological researchers.

During the 1960s, however, America witnessed firsthand the patterned inability of police, courts, and corrections to respond effectively to the decade's crime and civil disobedience. As public scrutiny increased, problems emerged that were directly connected to the underlying goals and fundamental purposes of the criminal justice system. Notions of "blind justice" and "disinterested professionalism" as accurate characterizations of criminal justice system practices were quickly discarded as criminal justice agencies were thought to have taken on a self-interested "life of their own" and, in the process, to have displaced their law-and-order, due process, and offender rehabilitation goals.

As these recognitions emerged, unprecedented interest in the critical study of the criminal justice system developed. Research shifted from a fixation with the offender and causes of crime to a preoccupation with the meaning and consequences of past and present crime-control efforts. This book draws upon several themes emerging from this critical literature over the past several decades. One dominant theme is what Cohen (1985) termed the "demystification theme of penology," which resulted from critical examinations of the ideas and consequences of various penal strategies.

Although these various examinations involve different theoretical perspectives, they share a singular curiosity—namely, the interface between penal ideas and consequences—and a singular conclusion—the expansion of control over more of the population (Blomberg and Cohen, 1995). For many, the history of punishment is an unending cycle of good intentions gone bad, with the recurring disparity between ideas and consequences being attributed to a number of factors. For example, some assert that this disparity is due to flawed implementation resulting from misunderstandings in program design, insufficient resources and staff, or other unforeseen developmental impediments (ibid.). Others maintain that the disparity between ideas and consequences is not so accidental; rather, organizational imperatives such as maintenance, survival, and expansion systematically undermine the efforts of well-meaning reformers (Austin and Krisberg, 1981; Blomberg, 1977; Rothman, 1980).

Still others argue that the intentions themselves of penal reformers are suspect from the outset: There are no *unintended* (negative) consequences associated with penal reform, just traditional political and economic imperatives and interests being fulfilled. For example, seemingly benign attempts to decentralize corrections and thereby improve the chances of offender rehabilitation and societal reintegration have been portrayed as efforts to alleviate state fiscal crises while still expanding offender control into the community (Scull, 1977). Other writers depict penal reform initiatives as extensions of economic preservation associated with class conflict and accompanying status panic by the rich and powerful (Platt, 1969; Simon, 1993). According to this theme—depending upon the needs of the labor market—the prison effectively functions as a factory by manufacturing disciplined and reliable workers, or as a warehouse controlling a surplus population of workers who threaten the existing social and economic order (Melossi and Pavarini, 1981; Rusche and Kirchheimer, 1939).

Despite these different interpretations of intent, motive, implementation, and practices, the reported consequences have been consistent: more control over an ever-increasing proportion of the base population. This book acknowledges the utility of each of these interpretations. As a result, they have been incorporated, in part, to help frame and interpret the story of American penology. However, in contrast to some critical arguments, this book also recognizes that motives related to civility, humanitarianism, progress, and what Schlossman (1977) termed "love of the American delinquent" to capture the motives of juvenile court reformers, should not be ignored. Following decades of discussion and debate, many scholars now have come to agree that some combinations of historical contingencies have indeed influenced the course of penal change (Cohen, 1985; Garland, 1990; Lucken, 1997; Rothman, 1971). However, the order and weight of these various historical contingencies remain uncertain, as specific cause-and-effect relationships have seldom been identified. Rather, the combined forces, influences, and relationships are better understood as intermittent, not necessarily linear, and varying in degrees of priority (Lucken, 1998). Certain influences (e.g., religious, economic) are more prominent and meaningful to penal reform than others during different historical and contemporary eras.

In attempting to tell the story of American penology, then, an interrelated framework is employed. First, there are specific historical eras and contexts that are shaped by a number of different contingencies and influences, in which particular ideas emerge to support and inform particular penal reforms. Second, there are the documented ways in which these reforms became implemented and practiced, thereby producing particular consequences. Moreover, it is argued that these various penal reform practices have resulted in cumulative consequences over time. As new penal reforms have been implemented, previous penal practices seldom have been changed or discarded. It is in this regard that the concept of "net widening" is employed. Net widening refers to the tendency of penal reformers to sequentially extend control over more of the base population, rather than to provide alternative control as generally claimed in the promotion of penal reforms. The history of penal reform has been characterized by repeated efforts to modify, differentiate, or change previous penal practices through new and alternative strategies. However, in practice, these reforms became implemented as supplements rather than alternatives to previous practices, thereby extending the overall proportion of the base population subject to some form of penal control or net widening with little relationship to crime's fluctuating trends.

The conceptual framework for this book, therefore, is eclectic. The framework is eclectic because it employs critical, progressive, and bureaucratic perspectives in its efforts to communicate a connection between historical and contemporary contexts, ideas, practices, and consequences of the major penal reforms that have constituted American penology over the past several centuries.

Overview of Book

The challenge this book faces in telling the story of American penology is a difficult one. To accomplish the book's purposes requires selection and imposition upon historical and contemporary eras and related penal ideas and practices. Actual time is not the same as time measured by research, or what is often referred to as social or historical time (Friedman, 1993). Consequently, this book condenses decades and sometimes centuries into a single reform era in the effort to provide clarity and understanding of what otherwise would be an overwhelming mass of details. Moreover, though chapters are devoted to the introduction of new penal reform strategies, the organization of the book should not imply that previously dominant penal strategies were replaced or discarded in response to the latest penal reform. Throughout American history, old and new strategies have coexisted; sometimes the old has gradually declined but, in many instances, old modes of punishment have never declined at all or have even resurfaced later with greater popularity and influence.

Rossiter (1971) considered this historical trend when he noted that history is written, but not made, in chapters. Rather, historical events unfold in an "untidy manner," and those who seek to understand these events must proceed in a way that is neat and ordered. Reflecting Rossiter's observation, this book imposes order upon several centuries of U.S. penal reform experiences in the effort to provide compelling descriptions and interpretations about the story of American penology.

Chapter 2 begins the story of American penology. The chapter briefly describes colonial America's strong English ties, which were expressed in the form of the small closely knit nature of colonial communities, early American crime trends, religiously dictated views on crime's causes and control, and associated colonial criminal codes and punishments. Colonial punishment practices are portrayed in this chapter as functional and responsive to the context, beliefs, and needs of the staunchly religious and closely knit colonial communities. As 1800 drew near, English influences and the pristine colonial context began to wane and America's punishment ideas and practices underwent major transition.

Chapter 3 continues by reviewing what has been termed the Period of Transition. This period refers to the nearly forty years during which America experienced major reforms of its legal codes and introduced incarceration as a form of punishment. Under the combined influences of the Enlightenment, post-revolutionary optimism, early industrialization, and geographic mobility, colonial American ideas about crime's causes and control were no longer consistent with or functional for the rapidly changing needs and sensibilities of Americans and their emerging way of life. Crime and punishment came to be interpreted within the paradigm of free will and the associated "Classical School." The reasoning was that, if the consequences of crime are made more painful than they are pleasurable, specific and general crime deterrence is accomplished and crime is prevented. The focus of the transition period's justice and penal system was upon reforming the laws, apprehending wrongdoers, and then providing swift and sure adjudication and punishment, often through imprisonment.

While Chapter 3 describes the formative origins of American prisons, Chapter 4 chronicles the nationwide proliferation and refinement of the penitentiary. Shaped by a different set of historical conditions and broadly held "urban disenchantment," notions of crime as a product of free will lost some of its influence. In its place, a more deterministic explanation—one that likened crime to a moral disease brought on by the socially disorganized and evil influences of the city—became the theoretical idea that guided Jacksonian penal reformers. Consequently, prisons served the dual purpose of correcting the wayward prisoner through regimen, discipline, and obedience, and of providing the disorganized and depraved city with a model of proper social organization to emulate. The prison walls were not only to keep prisoners in then, but also to prevent the evil city from contaminating the well-ordered prison environment. However, these lofty prison goals were not realized and the prison soon became characterized by organizational survival and managerial concerns, which in turn prompted a new series of penal reforms.

Chapter 5 focuses upon the period in which a major philosophical shift in American penology occurred that involved a broad and unquestioned commitment to individualized treatment and offender rehabilitation. From the 1880s to the 1930s, America experienced an unprecedented call for increased government action to respond to conditions associated with industrialization, urbanization, immigration—namely, a host of social problems including crime. Despite the ever-growing sense of urban disenchantment, there thrived an immutable optimism about the potential of the combined efforts of government and science to resolve crime and other urban problems. This optimism was based upon the belief that, by employing scientific principles, a more informed and effective governmental method of dealing with criminal offenders could be established. This orientation is referred to as progressivism, and its adherents have become known as the progressives. Progressives were driven by the goal of individualized treatment for offenders and concluded that this goal could be realized through a series of penal reform alternatives. These alternatives ranged from the reformatory and juvenile court to indeterminate sentencing, parole, and probation. Ultimately, however, these strategies were implemented in a way that departed from the goals of individualized treatment and offender rehabilitation: Rather than providing alternatives to the previous reliance upon prisons, these reform efforts largely served as supplements, overshadowed by a variety of managerial and offender control matters.

Chapters 6 and 7 continue to trace the progressive reform movement. From the early 1930s to the 1960s, the scientific search for the causes of crime accelerated. This contributed to an expansion of the penal system through program proliferation and offender classifications based upon risk and need and the associated belief that "more is better." Supported by the ideals of individualized treatment and rehabilitation, prisons, parole, probation, and the juvenile court each experienced substantial growth, differentiation, and bureaucratization. But while the penal system experienced unprecedented growth predicated upon the assumed utility of the rehabilitative ideal, actual penal practices remained largely the same—namely, managerially dictated, routinized, and control focused. This pattern of penal growth was largely viewed as a necessary response to the perceived growing crime problem and was unquestioned until the turbulent decades of the 1960s and 1970s.

Chapter 8 shifts the previous chapters' focus on the relationship between historical eras and penal reforms to a more detailed consideration of the research and theory concerning the social organization of the prison. Indeed, it was the research on prisons during this period that first openly challenged the rehabilitative ideal, particularly as it pertains to the competency of the prison to induce offender change. Moreover, such detail of the prison social organization is essential for grasping the full meaning of incarceration from those who know it best—the inmates themselves. Beginning with Clemmer's 1940 contribution and subsequent research by Sykes (1958, 1995), Irwin and Cressey (1962), and Giallombardo (1966), a new and critical appreciation about life behind bars is provided. The arguments presented by these authors are neither pleasant nor optimistic about the potential of prisons to deal humanely or effectively with inmates. Nevertheless, the prison has consistently emerged unscathed from these criticisms and continues to operate as the taken-for-granted sanction of our justice system.

Returning to the book's prior focus on historical eras and penal reforms, Chapter 9 addresses the rise of the prisoner rights movement in the context of the civil rights activism and civil disobedience of the 1960s and 1970s. The progressive agenda that had dominated American penology for the first half of the 1900s fell under direct attack by the 1960s. Faith in the state and its agencies of crime control had dissolved. As opposed to previous reform efforts that expanded the penal system, the new reform movement advocated restraint, with specific checks designed to narrow the power and scope of the penal system. Following numerous lawsuits and legal victories, America's prisoners gained a number of important legal rights and privileges. However, many of the abuses the liberal Warren Court decisions appeared to have remedied quickly reemerged. Further, the increasing conservative makeup of the U.S. Supreme Court over the past several decades has resulted in numerous reversals of the earlier court rulings on behalf of prisoners during the 1960s and 1970s.

Also occurring during the 1960s and 1970s was the decentralization movement, which is examined in Chapter 10. The reforms that featured most prominently at this time are decarceration, diversion, and community corrections—all of which were promoted as being radical alternatives to the formal penal system. The rationale underlying these reforms was that, by providing informal and voluntary forms of community treatment, offenders would avoid the negative labeling, stigmatization, and criminal associations that frequently result from formal system contact and processing. This approach included the promise of reducing the likelihood of future criminal activity by diverting first-time offenders. With legislative authority, theoretical justification, and professional and public support, decentralized penal strategies spread across America. However, the chapter documents that—although the logic behind the various decentralized reforms was radically different from that guiding preceding penal reforms—the decentralization practices and outcomes were not only similar; they were even more far-reaching. In other words, previous penal reforms such as reformatories, parole, probation, and the juvenile court were promoted as alternatives that would *enable the penal system* to provide more individualized offender treatment. In contrast, diversion, deinstitutionalization, and community corrections were promoted as alternatives to what was concluded to be *a very negative penal system* altogether that was doing more harm to offenders than good. But, regardless of these different motivations, efforts at decentralization not only met with more of the same, but also carried more ominous implications and consequences. New levels of control were extended not only to unintended juvenile clients but often to their families as well. When families subject to these new control measures were unable to comply—which was common—a series of repercussions ensued, often beginning with the dissolution of the family unit through the out-of-home placement of youth and sanctioning of parents, and frequently including the creating, perpetuating, and intensifying of subsequent crime.

By the end of the 1970s, declining faith in the rehabilitative ideal and decentralized correctional reforms had peaked. Chapters 11 and 12 move American penology's story forward by assessing the consequences of America's subsequent embrace of a "get tough on crime" ethos. In 1980, with the election of Ronald Reagan as president, there was a pervasive sense of cynicism due to a number of economic downturns and military failures. The response to these conditions was to abandon the liberalism of the past. As Reagan frequently stated in his early speeches following his election, "The problem with our liberal friends is not that they are ignorant, but that they know so much that isn't so!" Penal practices affected by this rejection of liberalism include parole, probation, and other seemingly soft-on-crime strategies. As these practices fell into disfavor, a series of get-tough strategies supporting a new "zero tolerance on crime" orientation were quickly implemented. These chapters consider the historical context of the 1980s and 1990s in relation to this series of get-tough-on-crime ideas and practices, not only for the violent offender, but also for nonviolent offenders, women with children, the mentally ill, the old, and the infirm. Consequences of these get-tough penal efforts include unprecedented numbers of offenders being incarcerated, lengthier prison sentences, prison overcrowding, and associated cost explosions—with the problem of high levels of crime persisting. Other so-called intermediate punishment reforms, which attempted to blur getting tough with community-based efforts, depended much less upon the costly use of imprisonment. But again, like penal reforms before, the cycle remained unbroken: more and more of the base population subject to control, with little if any connection to the occurrence of crime.

Chapter 13 completes our story of American penology by describing the contemporary punishment trends of the new millennium. While much of the get-tough mentality of the previous two decades endures, recent evidence also indicates a diminishing zeal for severe punishment. Accordingly, this chapter examines four trends that exemplify the range of severe and softer punishment developments; namely, supermax prisons, sex offender statutes, death penalty reforms, and offender re-entry. The chapter also considers the common trend of privatization, which—despite representing neither a get-tough nor get-soft approach—continues to gain a foothold in the public penal system because of the previous get-tough strategies and unprecedented expansion of the punishment system.

Chapter 14 concludes by extending the image of the prison as a total institution into mainstream culture and society. As some observers have claimed, we now live in a "minimum" (Blomberg, 1987), "medium," or even "maximum-security" (Marx, 1988) society in which criminal offenders and citizens alike are subject to new technologies and surveillance capacities that record and monitor their everyday lives and daily movements. The chapter considers the past, present, and future of penology in relation to a growing culture of control that has increasingly come to characterize American society. Suggestions of how living in this culture of control may render all citizens as specter in an electronic panopticon (Gordon, 1990), in which their communities, homes, and bodies are becoming increasingly glasslike, or transparent, are provided. Documentation of personal information—our individual histories, where we live, our physiological and psychological states, and our behavior patterns—is not only now possible, but such information is compiled routinely and readily accessible. Further, this type of documentation facilitates the development of predictive profiles regarding our future that are assembled invisibly, automatically, and generally without our consent. In sum, individual behavior is being described, explained, and predicted for frequently trivial and potentially ominous purposes. But, is the future of American penology and its associated growing culture of control merely a new challenge that criminologists and American citizens can effectively confront? Or is the future to be characterized by yet more far-reaching surveillance, visibility, and regulation that is beyond the control of empirically guided criminologists and democratically minded Americans? As these various control mechanisms become more embedded and normalized in society, the implications may be both alarming and reassuring. The chapter closes with discussion of the necessary and increasing public policy role for criminologists as well as individual citizens. It is argued that the role of criminologists in empirically describing and explaining the culture of control can be critical to the development of responsible and tempered penal and related public policies, and may indeed be vital if we are to alter our previous historical pattern in American penology of "reform without change." Moreover, it is asserted that citizens themselves cannot simply sit back passively, but rather must assume responsibility for confronting the control strategies and technologies that pose direct risks to their individual rights and democratic values.

2

Public Punishment in Colonial America (1600–1790)

The American colonial period spanned nearly two hundred years, beginning with the establishment of Virginia in 1607, and concluding after the American Revolution. Because most colonists were of English descent, punishment ideas and practices in the colonies resembled those of England. The policy of transporting convicts from Europe to the various colonies alone ensured that some of the same ideas and practices would take hold in the colonies. However, as Friedman (1993) noted, the physical and social circumstances of colonial life (e.g., starvation, Indian hostility, internal dissent) "bent the English patterns out of shape."

Those coming to the New World were well aware of the natural and man-made dangers that awaited them. One perceived danger was freedom itself, as many wondered whether religious conviction would be enough to ensure fidelity to the laws (Bonomi, 1986). There was a genuine fear that men and women might overindulge in the liberties of the New World and become "worse than brute beasts" (quoted in ibid.). For the Puritans, in particular, the only way to secure their mission as a "light unto the world" was to fix the church and state firmly into a mutually reinforcing relationship (ibid.).

Early colonial settlers brought with them only a basic understanding of English common law. The English common law system established the practices of oral testimony, a jury of peers, and the classification of offenses. However, because of America's geographic separation from England, colonists were only required to "establish laws not contrary to those of England." Consequently, they were free to discard those elements of English law with which they did not agree. For example, criminal codes in colonial America were generally more lenient than in England, particularly with regard to capital punishment. There were differences in the laws between colonies as well. Colonies developed their own ideas about crime and punishment based on their specific religious beliefs and immediate surroundings. For example, Pennsylvania and New England shared a preoccupation with moral offenses, while South Carolina tended to ignore them (Kann, 2005).

Though colonies functioned as "little worlds on their own" (Friedman, 1993), a discernable pattern to the ideas and practices surrounding crime and punishment still could be observed. For instance, in all colonies, public and physical punishments of various types were the norm. Indeed, these two dominant attributes are what set colonial punishment apart from punishments imposed in every other period of American history. This chapter describes these crime and punishment patterns in more detail and the historical contingencies that shape these patterns.

Life in the Colonies

Colonial society was organized around the three primary institutions of community, church, and family. Colonists maintained rigid ideas about the importance of these institutions because they provided the only social safety net and means of social order. Community cohesion and order were made possible by worshipping at the same church, marrying neighbors, and the necessary pooling and sharing of resources (Rothman, 1971). Community cohesion and order were also facilitated by the establishment of small, closely knit communities. Even as late as 1760, there were only seven cities in the colonies with more than three thousand inhabitants (Preyer, 1982). Without question, it was an excessively communal life, which meant that nothing escaped the watchful eye of the collective (Friedman, 1993). Colonial society was "well stocked with moral monitors who did not miss much in the goldfish bowl existence of daily life" (Thompson, 1986).

The importance of community was given its fullest expression in John Winthrop's "City Upon a Hill" speech in 1630. In this famous speech, the founder and governor of Massachusetts repeatedly stressed the primacy of the collective:

> Wee must be knit together in this worke as one man, wee must entertaine each other in brotherly affection, wee must be willing to abridge ourselves of our superfluities, for the supply of others necessities; wee must delight in eache other, make others condicions our owne, rejoyce together, mourne together, labour and suffer together (Winthrop, 1630).

Community order was equally secured through a culturally and spiritually prescribed hierarchy of authority. Obedience—whether to the highest authority of God, or to the lesser authorities of parents, ministers, and masters—was a powerful part of their everyday mindset. Colonists believed that every community member had a particular role to play and that an orderly society rested upon orderly families and orderly gender relationships (Norton, 1991). It was a "paternal society" built on the model of a patriarchal house (Friedman, 1993). In other words, colonial authorities modeled their role after stern fathers, seeking to mend the ways of their wayward children.

Towns, like families, were responsible for their own, and permanent residence was critical in establishing a good reputation. Not surprisingly, outsiders were feared and resisted because they posed a potential threat to the stability of the community. In fact, most colonies enacted settlement laws to exclude outsiders. Settlement laws enabled a kind of moral geography, whereby the ability of indigent strangers to enter and remain in any community was restricted (Vale, 2000). In the words of John Winthrop, "it was lawful to take knowledge of all men before we receive them" (quoted in ibid.). Laws that "warned out" strangers or permitted the rejection of newcomers were based largely on concerns over the visitors' faith and the likelihood of their being unable to support themselves. In 1637, Boston officials were granted the formal right to choose who could be admitted, so as to "keepe out such whose Lives were publickely prophane and scandalous [as well] as those whose judgments were Corrupt" (quoted in ibid). Some colonies required outsiders to furnish a certificate of good standing from the community of previous residence. Though these laws were often unenforceable, the intent of the laws was unambiguous: In order to survive and thrive, communities needed to remain small and be founded on a shared faith and cooperation (ibid.).

The religious screening of outsiders would seem to contradict the very reason for establishing the new world. Though some settlers came to North America for economic reasons, many more came in search of religious freedom. Yet, even as colonists came to the New World under the banner of religious freedom, they did not tolerate religious diversity ("Religion was 'salt,'" 1998). The Puritans of New England and the Anglicans of Virginia, for example, demanded uniformity in religious faith and practice (ibid.). Overall, colonists were not particularly tolerant, liberal, or pluralist in their views. They were, in a word, conformists.

Religion was clearly the salt that flavored colonial life and it permeated every aspect of life (ibid.), if for no other reason than religious institutions had to be rebuilt in the colonies (Bonomi, 1986). Some settlers regarded their communities as "religious experiments" or "plantations of religion" (ibid.). The Puritans, in particular, were looking for a way to serve God and so they built godly cities that were to be ruled by the word of God (Friedman, 1993). The Puritans of the Massachusetts Bay Colony believed they were on an "errand into the wilderness." They envisioned their communities as beacons of light to the entire world. When John Winthrop arrived in Boston Harbor, he proclaimed that "the eyes of the world will be upon us." If the colony and its Christian mandate failed, they would be in Winthrop's words "a by-word [i.e., a laughing stock] among the nations" (Gomes, 1996).

Crime as Sin

In eighteenth-century America, religion entered into all discourse, marked all observations, and gave meaning to every private and public crisis—crime included (Bonomi, 1986). Consequently, in colonial America, there was little if any distinction between crime and sin. An offense against God was a crime against society, and a crime against society was an offense against God. Given this worldview, colonial Americans did not perceive crime to be an entrenched social problem. In other words, they were not consumed with studying the causes and cures of crime because the answer, which could be found within their religious paradigm, was fairly apparent: Crime, like any sin, was a predictable consequence of a fallen world and the active forces of the devil.

In the absence of a crime–sin distinction, colonists judged a number of behaviors to be criminal, ranging from profanity and drunkenness to the more obvious crimes of theft and murder. The blurring of sin and crime is apparent in the speech of officials and offenders. In her final words before being executed for robbery in 1789, Rachel Wall publicly acknowledged that she had been "guilty of a great many crimes, such as Sabbath-breaking, stealing, lying, disobedience to parents, and almost every other sin a person could commit, except murder" (Williams, 1993a). Even sarcasm, swearing, flirting, and gossiping were deserving of punishment. Idleness (being unemployed) also was monitored and subject to prosecution. More serious were crimes of idolatry, blasphemy, witchcraft, and other violations of the faith. For example, until the mid-eighteenth century, the Puritans called for strict punishment for violations of religious laws, such as failing to attend church or failing to pray on the Sabbath. New York and Boston went so far as to forbid traffic through the city on the Sabbath, unless one was traveling to church or to some other urgent lawful occasion (Bonomi, 1986). Drinking and gambling on the Lord's Day were tolerated virtually nowhere. The following charges recorded in historical court documents illustrate the importance of respecting the Sabbath in colonial law.

In 1668 in Salem, the Kitchins were fined for "frequent absenting themselves from the public worship of God on the Lord's days."

In 1682 in Maine, Andrew Searle paid a fine of five shillings for "not frequenting the publique worship of god" and instead "wandering from place to place upon the Lord's days."

Virginia law in 1662 required everyone who had "no lawful excuse" to resort "diligently to their parish church and chappell."

In Plymouth, in 1758 a young boy was brought to court for "irreverently behaving himself by chalking the back of one young girl with Chalk."

In 1656, a Boston man sat in the stocks for two hours because of "lewd and unseemly behavior" on the Sabbath. He kissed his wife having returned from three years at sea (Friedman, 1993: 33).

Colonists were additionally mindful of behaviors that would unduly burden the community. For example, colonists were not preoccupied with sexual offenses solely because of their moral implications; they were concerned with the influence of illicit sexual activity on the well being of the community. It was feared that if a master impregnated a slave/servant, the community would have to bear the responsibility of supporting that child. Out of deference to community, criminal codes were also used to control prices and wages and it was unlawful for merchants to gain unreasonable profits through the sale of goods. For instance, a carpenter was convicted of charging an excessive fee and thus was sent to the very stocks he constructed and overpriced. For the community's sake, criminal codes could further "assist" parents in childrearing: Incorrigible children could be severely punished, even executed, as respect for parental authority was considered a precursor to religious discipline and civic responsibility. A 1648 Massachusetts law prescribed capital punishment for any youth past the age of sixteen who "shall curse or smite their natural father or mother." It should be noted, however, that capital punishment rarely was exercised in this situation.

Although criminal codes clearly existed, what constituted illegal behavior also could be determined on a situational basis (Norton, 1991).
Legislators of the day purposely penned broad statutes, assuming that
specificity was not required because everyone shared the same norms and
values (ibid.). The language of the following Maryland statute illustrates
the preference of flexibility over rigidity: "The Lawes of the Province
and in defect of Lawe, then according to the sound discretion of the said
Governor or other Chiefe Judge and such of the Councill as shall bee
present in Court" (quoted in Norton, 1991: 126).

The loose wording in criminal codes did not mean that colonial authorities
rejected the practice of codification altogether; on the contrary, specific statutes
existed for crimes considered to be troublesome, such as runaway servants and
servant women who gave birth to bastard children (ibid.). However, because
there was a general consensus on what constituted criminal behavior, at least
among those of English descent, establishing a meticulous comprehensive
system of laws was not as crucial to social order. This manner of governance
allowed the community to define [un]acceptable behavior based upon the
circumstances at hand. For example, while a law might declare a certain
behavior to be criminal, it would go unreported and therefore unpunished
if the community viewed it as harmless. Conversely, if no law existed for
behavior the community found reprehensible (e.g., severe child beating),
then members of the community would seek remedy together (ibid.)

A wide range of behaviors was considered criminal in colonial America. For instance, the crimes listed in Tables 2-1 and 2-2 comprise only
2 percent of all offenses committed. This demonstrates the considerable
diversity of behaviors deemed criminal. Yet, the tables also indicate that
the majority of crimes committed were, by today's standards, not very serious. Historical records show that fornication, lewd behavior, drunkenness,
petty theft, assaults, and Lord's Day violations were the most frequently
prosecuted crimes (Powers, 1966). Historical records in New York show
that men overwhelmingly swelled the ranks of the accused and criminal,
accounting for 94 percent of violent crimes and 74 percent of thefts. In
Massachusetts, between 1673 and 1774, women committed only 20 percent
of serious crimes. Women most often were charged with the offenses of
witchcraft, fornication, bastardy, and infanticide (see Table 2-1).

Public and Corporal Punishment

Given the close-knit existence of colonial towns, there was little need
for day-to-day surveillance of possible wrongdoing. In the unyielding

Table 2-1
Crimes Most Frequently Committed by Women

Type	Percentage	Number
Bastardy	37.7	58
Running away	10.4	16
Infanticide	7.1	11
Adultery	6.5	10
Theft	5.8	9
Fornication	5.2	8
Mistreating servants	3.9	6
Assault	3.2	5
Murder	3.2	5
Other	16.9	27
TOTAL	99.9	155

Source: Norton (1991).

Table 2-2
Crimes Most Frequently Committed by Men

Type	Percentage	Number
Contempt of authority, treason	14.5	80
Neglect of duty	12.8	70
Theft	10.0	55
Assault	7.5	41
Running away	7.5	41
Bastardy	5.5	30
Murder	5.3	29
Drunkenness	4.9	27
Killing animals	4.4	24
Aiding runaways	3.3	18
Mistreating servants	2.9	16
Profanity, blasphemy	2.7	15
Other and unknown	18.8	100
TOTAL	100.1	546

Source: Norton (1991).

observance of others' activities, colonists were, in effect, self-policed. Strangers were few, and neighbors protected each other and reported wrongdoing. For the most part, informal social control precluded the need for formal law enforcement, except in times of mass disturbance or an outside enemy threat. What law enforcement did exist tended to be disorganized, understaffed, and comprised of the most elderly members of the community.

When the informal social control mechanisms of family, community, and church failed, colonists employed relatively harsh punishments. In light of the importance of preserving a sense of community, it was not unusual for crimes committed by non-community members to be treated more harshly than those committed by community members. An outsider who committed vagabonding or begging would be banished or shamed before the community, usually by whipping or stoning. However, a member of the community would be treated more leniently for the same offense. This disparity in colonial responses to offenders reflects the classic distinction between welfare-oriented reactions to rule breaking by in-group community members and punishment-oriented reactions to deviating outsiders.

Overall, methods of punishment in colonial America consisted primarily of fines, whippings, mutilation, shaming techniques, banishment, and death. These punishments could be administered individually or in combinations, such as a whipping being followed by time in the stocks, or a fine coupled with a whipping. The acts of 1692 stipulated that a conviction for idleness (being willfully unemployed) was punishable for adults by whippings and hard labor (Vale, 2000). The notion of rehabilitative programming, however, was inconceivable, as colonists had no real expectation of eradicating crime by curing or fixing offenders. It was not that colonists were indifferent or cynical about the ability to prevent or reduce crime. They just were not inclined to fashion sanctions based on individual theories of crime causation. The purpose of punishment was, in the end, primarily retributive: The punishment of crime (i.e., sin) was necessary, regardless of effectiveness, because it was morally right and deserved.

Fines were by far the most frequently imposed sanction and were used nearly three times as often as corporal punishment. The amount of the fine was left to the discretion of the judge, though there was an attempt to tailor the fine amount to the particular offense and class of the offender. For example, a slave master and a slave could both be charged with the same offense, but the master could pay his fine in tobacco leaves, while the slave paid his fine in whippings. As a matter of practice, fines were primarily reserved for the propertied class. Those without property—namely, slaves—had their period of servitude extended or were whipped. However, one ambitious servant who engaged in freelance trading without his master's permission was fined as well as flogged (ibid.). Generally speaking, there were fines for just about any offense, including unauthorized borrowing of horses and peddling quack medicines (O'Toole, 1998).

Whippings were the second most frequently imposed punishment largely because of their ease and convenience. Because everyone has a body, few people escaped some form of corporal punishment in their lifetime. Whippings could be administered for a variety of offenses, such as repeatedly failing to observe the Sabbath; lying; idleness; stealing bread, sheets, or shoes; and sex offenses. In Massachusetts, 46 percent of those sentenced to whippings had been convicted of sex offenses. Whippings also were administered to women found guilty of bastardy and to insubordinate servants and slaves. In the latter case, the whipping could be carried out privately within the home. Servants, slaves, and women were particularly vulnerable to whippings because they lacked the money or property to pay fines. Fining a woman usually meant fining her husband. To ensure that the woman was the one punished, judges resorted to whipping when they deemed it appropriate. Moreover, officials were often reluctant to impose economic penalties on widows or single women, concerned that their estates or dependent children might be harmed as a result (Norton, 1991).

Whipping posts were located near the site of court proceedings and were usually delivered on a day when the colonists had gathered to attend the court session (ibid.). Consequently, whippings not only inflicted physical pain, but humiliation as well because they were administered in public. This ordeal was rendered even more humiliating by the fact that men and women were required to strip to the waist during the whippings (ibid.). As was the case with imposing fines, judicial discretion dictated the number of whippings to be administered. The law typically was vague on this point, relying on generalizations such as "to be whipped" or "to be severely whipped" as a guideline. Some colonies employed biblical scripture as a type of sentencing guideline. In Massachusetts, for instance, the maximum number of whippings was set at forty, as dictated in the Old Testament. In other colonies, the offense of immorality could result in forty lashes but false accusations by servants regarding their masters' chastity could warrant one hundred lashes. In 1742 Delaware, the punishment for stealing less than five shillings in value was fifteen lashes (Newman, 1978). The offense of bearing an illegitimate child was similarly punishable by twelve lashes (Norton, 1991).

Colonists also relied on banishment and various shaming techniques as methods of punishment. Banishment usually was reserved for non-community members, recidivists, and other offenders viewed as permanent dangers. Though banishment may not seem like a harsh sanction, its severity becomes apparent when viewed in the context of community standards. Recall that even outsiders of good standing were questioned and references could be required for admission into a new community. Thus, there were no assurances that a banished offender would be received into another community. It was just as likely that the offender would encounter alienation and rejection and perhaps incidental death, particularly if the punishment was imposed during harsh winter months. If the offender attempted to return to the community from which he was banished, he could be charged with the offense of "defiance of a banishment order," an offense punishable by death.

Shaming techniques assumed a number of forms, including the stocks, pillory, branding, dunking stools, letter wearing, mild mutilation (e.g., burning the hand, ear cropping), carting (i.e., tying an offender to a wagon/wheelbarrow and dragging him or her through the street), the public cage, the "dame's bridle" (an iron head frame with a spiked mouthpiece for gossipers), and heavy irons for runaway servants. "Scarlet letters" or other inscriptions indicating the nature of the crime seem to have been used primarily as a commuted sentence for those claiming benefit of clergy but convicted of serious offenses (Newman, 1978). However, such inscriptions also were used frequently in New York and Massachusetts, particularly for blasphemers and drunkards (Newman, 1978). When imposed, these shaming punishments exposed the offender to verbal and physical abuse (pelting with stones, rotten fruit, or mud) by community passers-by. Rather than subduing the offender and encouraging repentance, shaming often had the opposite effect: The public ridicule often drove the offender to beg, swear, and insult spectators (Kann, 2005).

Colonists employed harsh measures for recidivists, including death and what, for lack of a better term, can be called "shock" death. In the case of shock death, an offender would receive a sentence of death by hanging but later would be granted a reprieve. However, the reprieve was given only after the offender had proceeded through the stages of the execution ritual. The offender would be led from the jail out to the gallows, with the mask placed over his head and the noose placed around his neck, and would then wait for the trap door to open and end his life. The sentenced offender might remain at the gallows for more than three hours, fully expecting to be executed. Finally, the noose and mask would be removed and the offender would then be informed that his or her life had been spared.

The sentence of actual death by hanging could apply to recidivists, murderers, arsonists, horse thieves, and incorrigible youth. In the early criminal codes, only eleven crimes were classified as capital offenses (Newman, 1978). This number varied somewhat over time and between communities, however. For example, in Massachusetts, the 1641 Body of Liberties established twelve offenses as punishable by death. By 1654, twenty-five offenses were identified by this Massachusetts statute as punishable by death. Though the death penalty could apply to a wide range of offenses, it was actually used rather sparingly. Between 1630 and 1692, fifty-six people were executed in Massachusetts, amounting to less than one execution a year. The offenses for which these people were executed include adultery, arson, treason, murder, witchcraft, bestiality, rape, and defiance of banishment. Pennsylvania had the mildest criminal code, permitting only the offense of murder to be punishable by death. Prior to the American Revolution, ninety-four offenders were executed in Pennsylvania, also amounting to fewer than one per year.

Though executions were relatively infrequent events, they were not meaningless or private events. High-profile cases were particularly likely to draw large crowds. Those in attendance might even have traveled long distances to witness the execution. At an 1827 hanging in New York, it was estimated that there were between thirty and forty thousand spectators in attendance. The execution scene was also intended to be a "deeply spiritual experience for all those who witnessed" it (Friedman, 1993). Execution sermons and the anticipation of confession and repentance punctuated the drama and purpose of public hangings. They communicated in stark terms the consequences of disobeying parents and religious instruction. For example, in 1771, the condemned Moses Paul requested that Samsom Occom deliver his execution sermon. In this famous sermon, Occom addressed not only the sins of the condemned man, but warned the "innocent" audience of the perils of their own sin—namely indifference and intemperance—and of the inevitability of death and eternal judgment for all.

The perils of disobedience also were expressed in the written testimonies of the condemned. In a last profession of innocence the night before she was to be executed for murdering her children (December 6, 1785), Elizabeth Wilson wrote: "From sixteen to twenty-one years of age, I had a religious concern, but thro' the subtlety of Satan and corruptions of nature was led away to the soul-destroying sin of fornication, which I believe to be my predominant evil" (Williams, 1993b: 272). In her dying confession in October 1789, Rachel Wall similarly relayed that she had been born to parents of devout faith and religious practice but had left home "without their consent." She hoped her "awful and untimely fate would be a solemn warning and caution to everyone" (Williams, 1993a).

In colonial America, jails were of little significance and were unremarkable in appearance. Architecturally, they resembled any other house or building and were located within the main parameters of the community. Offenders were housed in rooms, not cells, and prison uniforms and lockstep marching were nonexistent. In an attempt to mimic family routines, the keeper (i.e., warden) was expected to be married and his family, along with the offenders, resided under one roof. The conditions of the jail were not as pleasant as the family model would suggest, however. Offenders were required to pay for their keep, and there was little or no attempt to separate offenders by gender, age, or offense severity: Vagrants, prostitutes, runaway servants and slaves, disobedient apprentices, juvenile delinquents, the insane, prisoners of war, and religious offenders all were detained together; women and children were detained with men and others who had committed violent crimes (Kann, 2005). Jails were overcrowded, disorderly, and unsanitary, and there were few or no security measures to prevent escapes.

Importantly, jails were not envisioned as a primary punishment or as a place of rehabilitation. Instead, they were used most commonly as holding places for offenders awaiting trial or punishment. In addition, with debtors, jails were seen primarily a way of "prying open their purses" (Kann, 2005). Table 2-3 illustrates the infrequent use of jail as a punishment in two colonial era Boston counties.

Almshouses and workhouses functioned as alternatives to jail for the relief of the poor and those segments of the population that were not quite criminal. They served as the main repositories for those who were unable to provide for themselves economically due to age or unfortunate circumstances, and as a place of punishment for those classified as the able-bodied poor (i.e., those who chose to remain idle). Overall, this population included widows, orphans, the physically and mentally ill, drunkards, vagabonds, and prostitutes (Vale, 2000).

Church, Community, and Punishment

The structure of colonial America—with its emphasis on family, community cohesion, and neighborly and civic involvement—continues to be glorified even today. In numerous contained or gated housing communities across the country, there are implicit if not explicit attempts to recapture

Table 2-3
Jail Sentences in Colonial America: The Cases of Essex and Middlesex Counties

Date	Punishments	Percentage Involving Jail
Essex County		
1650–1659	471	3.3
1660–1669	742	7.9
1670–1679	719	1.1
1700–1709	244	<1.0
1710–1719	305	0
1720–1727	305	<1.0
1744–1749	127	0
1750–1759	180	1.1
1760–1769	285	<1.0
Middlesex County		
1650–1659	117	5.1
1671–1680	218	3.2
1700–1709	121	1.5
1710–1719	192	0
1720–1729	333	1.2
1730–1739	375	1.6
1740–1749	199	3.0
1750–1759	180	<1.0
1760–1769	188	<1.0

Source: Kuntz (1988).

the conformity, order, and security of this age, such as "neighborhood watches." Though settlement laws are now non-existent, up-front resident fees and housing costs still function to ensure that those who are different are kept out of the community.

While contemporary society has romanticized much of colonial American existence, the cruel realities of this time cannot be overlooked in our current understanding of history. Though colonial communities were no doubt quaint in certain respects, they were also rigid in a way that made life demanding and difficult. In particular, severe punishment awaited anyone who strayed from cultural norms or social and religious authorities.

In a harsh and unfamiliar new world, family, community, economic necessity, and religion contributed to a social context in which specific punishment ideas and practices were viewed as necessary and appropriate. Punishment in colonial America was overwhelmingly public and physical. It emphasized the condemnation of sin and disobedience, and ultimately repentance through shaming and humiliation. Punishment also was considered to be a moral obligation of the community. To neglect this obligation was a sin itself, equally subject to the displeasure of God. This is not to say, however, that the idea of punishing in order to dissuade others was not a part of the colonial mindset. Many of the dying proclamations and execution sermons attest to this fact. Moreover, if authorities feared the offense might spawn imitators or was a serious problem, punishment was even more likely to be made public (Norton, 1991). It was just that their philosophical stance was inclined more toward retribution than the expectation of wide-scale crime prevention. As Dean-Myrda and Cullen (1998: 4) explained, punishment was "harsh not so much because there was confidence that the wicked could be easily transformed into upstanding citizens ... but because it proclaimed the evil of sin and the sanctity of God's laws."

After 1790, the pillars of colonial existence gave way to a new social, cultural, and political order. As the American landscape changed geographically, demographically, and economically, so too did ideas about crime and punishment. The American Revolution heralded the beginning of the Industrial Revolution, westward expansion, and the era of penal modernity. Indeed, reformers were already starting to question capital punishment and the conditions in colonial jails, and began to express mixed views if not outright opposition to physical and public punishments.

3

Penal Code Reform in the Period of Transition (1790–1830)

The close of the eighteenth century was, by all accounts, a period of transition. Between 1790 and 1830, the new republic experienced rapid and marked social changes that culminated in what is now referred to as modernity. The social norms and values consistent with scientific reason, capitalism, free markets, democracy, and egalitarianism were established during this period and are regarded as the hallmarks of the modern age. Nationhood also established a "centralizing presence" that was absent in colonial America. A national government launched the development of federal laws—seventeen crimes against the new federal government were enacted in 1790—as well as the development of postal, roadway, lighthouse, and navigational systems.

In the course of numerous and profound changes that were ushering in a new way of life, the ultimate fate of the nation hung in the balance. Fear, excitement, and internal dissent coexisted with recollections of the perceived security and solidarity of the colonial era. In particular, a growing fear of the consequences of excessive individual liberty began to emerge among civic leaders and citizens alike. Following the Revolution, the frequency and seriousness of crime were seen as increasing, and cries of alarm could be heard in both the burgeoning cities and quieter countryside. Complaints of drinking, gambling, prostitution, robbery, and a general sense of lawlessness were widespread.

In this modern age, post-revolutionary reformers questioned the efficacy and morality of colonial laws. Reformers proposed that penal codes should treat individuals with dignity so as not to transgress "divine justice" (Kann, 2005). Critics also claimed that state-inflicted shaming, physical brutality and public punishments fostered disrespect for the law and were fundamentally unenlightened and unrepublican. It was argued that public hangings and beatings had the effect of desensitizing onlookers on the one hand, and generating sympathy for the offender on the other. Benjamin Rush, a prominent reformer of the day, wrote that "distress of all kinds, when seen, produces sympathy and a disposition to relieve it" (Kann, 2005: 101).

Beginning in the 1790s, reformers, legislators, and penal authorities conceded that public punishments should be abandoned and incarceration adopted. However, the transition from public and corporal punishment was neither immediate nor universal. For example, Pennsylvania's 1786 penal reform law sought to limit hangings and maimings, but continued public punishments particularly in the form of public labor (Kann, 2005). Public hangings and whippings persisted into the nineteenth century in other states, such as Rhode Island and Delaware (ibid.). South Carolina retained its English penal code of 1712 well into the nineteenth century. Amid uneven progress, reformers ultimately were seeking a way to reconcile the promise of liberty with the authority to constrain those who were unable to conform.

Post-Revolutionary America

The Demise of the Colonial Way of Life

In post-revolutionary America, colonial existence was visibly disrupted. Demographic and economic shifts, in particular, upended the order of the small, contained communities of colonial America. Between 1790 and 1830, the nation's population exploded as did the number and density of cities. In 1790, approximately two hundred thousand Americans lived in towns with more than twenty-five thousand residents, and no American city had more than fifty thousand residents. By 1830, the number of individuals living in a city with more than twenty-five thousand exceeded one million, while approximately five hundred thousand lived in cities with more than fifty thousand residents (Rothman, 1971). During this forty-year period, the population of Massachusetts doubled, the population of Pennsylvania tripled, and the population of New York increased fivefold. More specifically, between 1790 and 1830, the population of Boston increased by 84 percent, Philadelphia by 114 percent, Baltimore by 156 percent, and New York by 191 percent. Regions of the country that were once desolate—namely, the Midwest—reached more than three million inhabitants. In short, communities were becoming towns, and towns were becoming cities.

Changes on the economic front had an equally potent effect on society. Specifically, economic shifts reflected a move from field to factory. As factories began to dot the eastern American landscape, self-sufficient farmers increasingly were replaced with wage laborers and salaried employees. Commercial activity accelerated rapidly from a reported $20.2 million in exports in 1790 to $108.3 million in exports by 1807. The number of corporations in colonial America totaled only seven, but there were forty corporations in the first decade following the Revolutionary War. By the turn of the nineteenth century, five hundred corporations existed.

Economic opportunity often translated to social and geographic mobility. Westward expansion and the first wave of eastern seaboard immigration altered customary relationships. Patriarchal authority was eroding, as were colonial notions of the traditional family (Elkins and McKitrick, 1993). Numerous youth left home and at earlier ages, while women claimed more authority within families (Kann, 2005). Further, the communalism that had sustained the colonial lifestyle was giving way to a lifestyle of individualism. The new entrepreneurs made fun of "old fashioned farmers who could not bear to work alone, who always had to call a neighbor"; they charged that "while it may be very pleasant to have our neighbors work with us, it tends to encourage idleness and neglect of business" (Birdsall, 1970). All in all, the end of the eighteenth century witnessed the promotion of a new set of civic values that prized self-interest over self-sacrifice.

Considerable displeasure and concern accompanied these numerous and unfamiliar transitions. While the beginnings of commercialism brought new conveniences and luxuries, the nation was anti-urban at its core. Americans regarded London and other large European cities as cesspools of greed, poverty, and material excess. Still able to recall the pristine colonial setting, citizens feared that American cities would become decaying metropolises. Moreover, the institutions of family, church, and community could no longer absorb the rising numbers of the poor, criminal, insane, and other marginal social types (immigrants, freed blacks) who were seen as threats to the fragile new nation. The informal mechanisms of control that once prevailed were ill-suited for the transformations that were unfolding, particularly in political, social, and moral philosophy.

The Enlightenment

The Enlightenment, also known as the secular rationalist movement, originated in England, quickly spread throughout the European continent, and later found its way to the United States. Humanitarian reform guided by natural scientific laws rather than divine providence was the common interest of this movement. Writers from England (Jeremy Bentham, David Hume, John Locke, Thomas Paine), France (Montesquieu, Voltaire), and Italy (Cesare Beccaria) radically altered beliefs about human nature, society, and the proper role of government. Prominent among these new beliefs were the ideas that men are equal and that human beings are naturally good and can improve or perfect themselves morally. Indeed, the chief concern of the Enlightenment was to procure the ideal relationship between man, society, and the state.

British rationalists and French philosophers lived and traveled in the colonies, particularly Philadelphia. Their ideas directly shaped the content of the U.S. Constitution, the Bill of Rights, and the structure of the new system of government. With memories of England's tyranny still fresh, power in the new republic was viewed as a "thorn in liberty's side" (Elkins and McKitrick, 1993). It was generally accepted that the acquisition and concentration of power were "things" that should not be pursued or desired. The new nation sought virtuous leaders who would abolish any traces of the old parochial laws of English and colonial rule. Americans despised the patronage of British kingship and its "above the law" arrogance, but were equally opposed to the rigid theocracy of colonial America.

Secular rationalists in the United States replaced what had been viewed as savage, arbitrary, and irrational views of the Puritan belief system, and the pre-modern world in general, with the principles of utilitarianism, liberalism, and equality. They held that man is the supreme achievement of God's creativity and ingenuity and that to devalue man's preeminence is an insult to God (Barnes, 1972). In other words, destiny was not divinely predetermined, but was alterable and controllable through scientific achievement and human reasoning. Perceptions of God as an angry judgmental patriarch whose arbitrary demands must be met were replaced with notions of a benevolent God who desired the general welfare and happiness of mankind.

The legal codes of the colonial and British regimes, then, were the common enemies of the new nation. Colonial laws and customs came to be regarded as crude, backward, arbitrary, chaotic, irrational, barbaric, and ultimately ineffective. The rhetoric of the Enlightenment suggested that misguided individuals could be persuaded to exercise moral restraint, good judgment, and self-control. Therefore, severe draconian laws were unnecessary, as free men would voluntarily change their ways (Kann, 2005). However, it was anticipated that the spirit of freedom would have its limits, as freedom carried with it the expectation that all men would be diligent, hard-working, and sober.

Crime as Reasoned Behavior

Following the revolution, civic leaders linked the introduction of extensive liberty to the onset of extensive crime (Kann, 2005). Whether a crime wave truly was underway is unknown, but what is clear are shifts in the types of criminal activity being observed. Between 1790 and 1815, larceny, assault and battery, burglary, horse stealing, and other felonies constituted the majority of crimes for which prisoners were convicted (see Table 3-1).

The Enlightenment ushered in a new paradigm in the study of human nature and, hence, a new approach to explaining deviant and criminal behavior. In stark contrast to colonial America, wherein crime was explained in terms of sin and disobedience to God and earthly authorities, crime in the nineteenth century was attributed to archaic legal codes that were counterintuitive to the theory of free will. Reformers acknowledged that there were limits to the forces of reason and rationality in governing behavior, but they were not willing to subscribe to the old view that people's inherent wickedness and sin were the ultimate and unchangeable sources of crime (Kann, 2005). In other words, the prospect of crime seemed more inevitable than preventable when criminality was attributed to a person's innate sinfulness and Satan's schemes.

As indicated, the leaders of the new republic were greatly influenced by the Enlightenment writings of John Locke, Jeremy Bentham, John Howard, and Cesare Beccaria, among others. Under their influence, first-generation leaders fashioned their ideas after three grand theories; namely social contract, natural law and justice, and utilitarianism (Kann, 2005). Utilitarianism was particularly salient in the reform of the criminal justice system. Indeed, Jeremy Bentham elevated utilitarianism to a moral science in his *An Introduction to the Principles of Morals and Legislation* (1789). His principal claim was that mankind is ruled by the two masters of pleasure and pain. Pleasure and pain dictate the words, thoughts, and actions of individuals, who Bentham held to be fundamentally "hedo-

Table 3-1
Crimes of Conviction and Confinement in the Philadelphia Jail, 1790–1815

Crime	Number
Accessory to a burglary	1
Adultery	1
Arson	31
Assault	14
Assault and battery	191
Assault and battery with intent to murder	4
Assault with intent to commit rape	7
Assault with intent to kill	11
Assault with intent to rob	1
Assist in prisoner's escape	1
Attempt to poison	1
Bastardy	5
Bawdy housekeeping	17
Bigamy	8
Blasphemy	1
Breach of health laws	1
Breaking prison	4
Burglary	161
Burning	8
Cheating	4
Coining	2
Concealing the death of a bastard child	12
Conspiracy	23
Contempt of court	4
Counterfeiting	20
Deceit	3
Defraud	3
Deserting wife	1
Disorderly housekeeping	41
Felony	191
Felony and robbery	3
Forcible abduction	1
Forgery	90
Fornication	3
Harboring convicts	1
Highway robbery	14
Horse stealing	145
House breaking	4
Ill treatment of wife	1
Incest	1
Indenting a check	1
Kidnapping	1

Table 3-1 (cont.)

Larceny	2,897
Maiming	1
Manslaughter	30
Misdemeanor	54
Murder in the 1st degree	2
Murder in the 2nd degree	45
Nuisance	4
Passing counterfeit money	2
Perjury	15
Picking pockets	5
Poisoning	3
Rape	13
Receiving stolen goods	56
Riot	11
Robbery	23
Robbery with intent to kill	2
Robbing U.S. mail	1
Tippling house	3
Uttering counterfeit bank notes	6
Uttering counterfeit dollars	2
Uttering forged check	3
Uttering forged letter of attorney	1
TOTAL	4,264

Source: Historical Corrections Statistics in the United States, 1850–1984.

nistic." A hedonistic nature ultimately is driven by the maximization of pleasure and the minimization of pain. Bentham argued that despite all efforts, man could not free himself of the overriding need to seek that which afforded pleasure and to avoid that which afforded pain. He termed this law of human nature the "principle of utility." Being bound by the principle of utility, humans necessarily engage in behavior that is purposeful. Hence, individuals weigh the anticipated intensity, duration, certainty, remoteness, fecundity, purity, and extent of pleasure and pain derived from their actions. Fecundity refers to the chance that an initial experience of pleasure or pain will be followed by sensations of the same kind (i.e., pleasure will be followed by pleasure, or pain by pain). Purity refers to the chance that the initial pleasurable or painful experience will not be followed by opposite sensations (i.e., pleasure will not be followed by pain, or pain by pleasure). Extent refers to the number of persons affected by a given incident of pleasure or pain. While Bentham did not expect that every decision would involve this comprehensive degree of mental scrutiny, he maintained that the process of making decisions would be approximate because these various considerations will "always be kept in view."

In the nineteenth century, compared with the earlier colonial period, the criminal was no longer perceived to be a sinner who should be punished for offenses against God in accordance with biblical principles. Beccaria maintained that words like vice and virtue had no rightful place in criminal law and that only those behaviors that directly destroy society or injure private security (e.g., life, property) should be classified as crimes (Newman, 1978). In effect, the criminal of the nineteenth century was essentially regarded as a threat to property, life, and social stability and was to be punished for offenses against the state in accordance with legal principles. Consistent with liberal enlightenment philosophy, it was believed that individuals who engaged in criminal activity were offending against "the greater happiness of the community" (Kann, 2005).

Punishment and Deterrence

Colonial penal codes were seen as so severe, inconsistent, and irrational that they actually encouraged deviant behavior. The "old" punishments were also seen as counterproductive in that they instilled in the offender a vengeful spirit against the entire community. Reformers further complained that many of the colonial punishments were of such short duration that they failed to produce a changed subject.

With rational calculation as a significant basis for human choice, reformers held that individuals need to understand the rationale for law and their obligation to comply with it (Kann, 2005). In 1822, Edward Livingston argued that, "When the true principles of legislation are impressed on the minds of the people, when they see the reasons for the laws by which they are governed, they will obey them with cheerfulness, if just, and know how to change them, if oppressive" (quoted in Kann, 2005: 58). Livingston went on to state that "laws to be obeyed and administered, must be known, to be known, they must be read, to be administered they must be stated and compared. To know them is the right of the people" (quoted in Friedman, 1993: 63). The reform message of the new republic was that penal codes needed to be articulated plainly, codified, and uniform. Only then could a rational person truly calculate the costs of crime. This policy position reflects the utilitarian push to classify wrongs and secularize the criminal law further.

In his *Essays on Crimes and Punishment* ([1764] 1963; see also Jacoby, 1979), Cesare Beccaria also described the relationship between free will, criminal behavior, and archaic laws. Beccaria declared, "If we glance at the pages of history, we will find that the laws which surely ought to be the compacts of free men, have been, for the most part, a mere tool of the passions of some" (quoted in Jacoby, 1979: 206). Beccaria asserted that barbarism had no place in punishment, for it was not the intensity of punishment that had the greatest effect on the human spirit, but its duration. He maintained, "Our sensibility is more easily and more permanently affected by slight but repeated impressions than by a powerful but momentary action" (quoted in ibid.: 209). French and other philosophers agreed that to impose suffering upon anyone because they have made another suffer is an act of cruelty, condemned by reason and humanity. It was generally believed that the brutality of legal punishments resulted in the arbitrary administration of punishment; for example, rather than impose death for a minor offense, judges and juries often acquitted the accused or ignored the law.

Beccaria's central thesis was that a certain punishment has a far greater impact than a severe punishment that might never occur. He further reasoned that the more closely the punishment follows the crime, the more just and useful it will be. Put simply, punishment has to be certain and prompt. Beyond the principles of certainty and promptness, Beccaria advocated proportionality in punishment. The notion of proportionality refers to the now-familiar adage that the punishment must fit the crime. Hence, punishment should never be excessive, only severe enough to deter. Bentham echoed this sentiment by maintaining that the pain of punishment was to exceed the pleasure obtained from the offense, but by only the slightest of margins. The French philosopher Montesquieu similarly argued that there should be a proportionate relationship between a crime and its punishment because the deterrent to the commission of a major crime should be more powerful than the deterrent to a less serious crime (Montesquieu, [1748] 1966). In consequence, the effectiveness of punishment depends upon duration, promptness, certainty, and proportionality. Enlightenment thinkers therefore concluded that the key to eliminating criminal behavior is the establishment of a penal code that prohibits unbridled discretion, favoritism, and oppression.

As a matter of principle, Enlightenment thinkers did not oppose or reject the use of punishment. They simply expected that an enlightened system of punishment would be predicated upon moderation, dignity, and decorum rather than retributive instincts. From a utilitarian standpoint, punishment is justified only if the harm it prevents is greater than the harm inflicted upon the offender. Punishment cannot be justified on retributive grounds alone; rather, it can be justified only if it serves a greater social good—namely, crime prevention. It was reasoned that unless punishment can deter crime, it only adds to human suffering. The philosophy of deterrence therefore advocates a forward-looking justification for punishment. Punishment is to prevent future criminal acts committed by apprehended offenders (specific deterrence) or potential offenders (general deterrence) by way of the former serving as an example to the latter. Consistent with the intellectual thinking of the day, punishment was intended to serve functions other than merely vengeance and moral condemnation for past misdeeds.

The combined positions of Bentham and Beccaria formed a school of thought known as "classicism." Adherents of classicism focused on the legal character of the offense, rather than the character of the offender. It was the punishment of the offense that was of paramount interest to these reformers, not the pathologies of the offender. The classical school of justice assumed that rational persons should be subject to one rational system of laws.

To appreciate fully the certain and swift requirements of deterrence, the specific role of police must be acknowledged. Police forces were created during the first half of the nineteenth century. These police forces were full-time agencies whose functions included keeping the peace, crime prevention, and apprehending criminals. Before the establishment of full-time police organizations, in contrast, social order was maintained by watchmen who made rounds at night to deal with disturbances, and constables who provided daytime law enforcement. They arrested vagrants and drunks and delivered offenders before the grand jury. Assisting the watchmen and constables were vigilance committees or yeomen, or volunteer part-time police. However, there were problems and limits to this part-time, haphazard approach to law enforcement, and change was inspired in the new republic with the 1829 establishment of the London Metropolitan Police. While a pattern of increasing law enforcement was already underway in the new republic, it was not until after 1830 that a fully deployed professional police force was formed. The belief was that if crime was to be combated successfully and punishment was to be ultimately effective, a more systematic and reliable method of detecting and apprehending criminals would be necessary. This is not to say, however, that this early version of a modern police force was organized, systematic, or reliable in its crime-fighting efforts.

The Ideal of Penal Code Reform and Incarceration

By the 1820s, most states had amended their penal codes to reflect the various classical school principles. In 1793, William Bradford, Justice of the Supreme Court of Pennsylvania and Attorney General of the United States, expressed the dominant national mood toward the old penal codes:

> We perceive, by this detail, that the severity of our criminal law is an exotic plant, and not the native growth of Pennsylvania. It has been endured, but, I believe, has never been a favorite. The religious opinions of many of our citizens were in opposition to it; and as soon as the principles of Beccaria were disseminated, they found a soil that was prepared to receive them. During our connection with Great Britain no reform was attempted; but as soon as we separated from her, the public sentiment disclosed itself and this benevolent undertaking was enjoined by the constitution. This was one of the first fruits of liberty and confirms the remark of Montesquieu, "That, as freedom advances, the severity of the penal law decreases" (Bradford, [1793] quoted in Barnes, 1972: 104).

One of the first casualties of the new penal codes was the death sentence. For more than a few civic leaders, activists, and legislators, the allure of the hangman lost its luster. For example, Quaker William Penn spoke of "the wickedness of exterminating, where it was possible to reform" (Gorringe, 1996: 154). In 1790, the Pennsylvania legislature abolished the death penalty for robbery, burglary, and sodomy. New York repealed the death penalty except for murder and first-degree arson, and, as of 1796, Virginia reserved the death penalty for murder and certain offenses committed by slaves. All other states followed by sharply curtailing their use of death as a punishment. This trend continued well into the 1850s, as states began debating the utility of capital punishment even for murder. Maine, Vermont, and Michigan were cited as examples of how murders declined in the wake of the complete abolishment of capital punishment ("Capital Punishment," 1846).

However, the widespread attacks on the death penalty were not motivated solely by sheer benevolence. Rather, the abolishment of the death penalty was a utilitarian or pragmatic move aimed at fulfilling the goals of certainty, predictability, and, ultimately, deterrence. Many reformers recognized that those who committed the impassioned offense of murder did not stop to calculate the costs of their actions. Livingston felt that those who were capable of murder were altogether indifferent to the prospect of their own death. He proclaimed that "fear of death will rarely prevent the commission of great crimes" (Kann, 2005). Dr. Francis Lieber, a history professor and contemporary of Livingston, also urged the public that it was "the certainty of an offense not its cruelty that prevents crime" (quoted in Kann, 2005: 115). Other voices of the day argued further that capital punishment would have little effect on those "whose lives were of little account" (Kann, 2005) due to poverty and despair. In fact, it was recognized that the reforms in capital punishment were driven by a desire to increase rather than decrease (the certainty of) the punishment of offenders (Kuntz, 1988). Juries often failed to convict many offenders—property offenders in particular—because death was considered too severe a penalty. Consequently, offenders were escaping penalty, though their guilt was not in question. This problem was articulated in a Philadelphia report entitled, *Considerations on the Penalty of Death*. In that report, Benjamin Rush declared:

> Punishment of murder by death multiplies murder, from the difficulty it creates of convicting persons who are guilty of it. Humanity, revolting at the idea of the severity and certainty of a capital punishment, often steps in, and collects such evidence in favor of a murderer, as screens him from death altogether, or palliates his crime into manslaughter. If the punishment of murder consisted in long confinement, and hard labor, it would be proportioned to the measure of our feelings of justice, and every member of society would be a watchman, or a magistrate to apprehend a destroyer of human life, and to bring him to punishments (quoted in Kuntz, 1988).

William Bradford's *An Enquiry How Far the Punishment of Death is Necessary in Pennsylvania* expressed a similar sentiment. He stated:

> In my opinion the certainty of conviction of a crime punishable by imprisonment by death, and if juries were permitted, by law, to relieve themselves of the terrible responsibility which they now feel in capital cases, growing out of the existence of the death-penalty, convictions would be had where acquittals now take place (quoted in ibid.).

In 1826, Robert Vaux recited what had become conventional wisdom among many penal reformers:

> There is an aversion in Pennsylvania from inflicting death; and the difficulty of convicting when the crime is so great as to defeat in many instances the purpose of justice. The prisoner who has deliberately extinguished the life of a fellow creature may, for want of that clear evidence which our human judges and juries rightfully require, receive, in place of the merited sentence, some very inadequate punishment or escape altogether (quoted in ibid.).

Reductions in the severity of the penal codes also applied to the public and physical aspects of punishment. For example, the Pennsylvania Act of 1791 prohibited branding (Barnes, 1972). That said, penal reformers did not oppose corporal punishments with the same intensity as they did capital or public punishment. Moreover, in an age of rapid growth and social migration, shaming and banishment were no longer appropriate. Provisions for whippings and all other forms of corporal punishment eventually were stricken from the penal codes.

Reformers' newfound insistence on private punishment has been the subject of much debate. For example, it has been suggested that public displays offended the softening sensibilities of the middle and upper classes (Spierenburg, 1984). It also has been proposed that the spectacle of death and public corporal punishments was inconsistent with the political requisites of the new republic (Foucault, 1977). The vulgarity of bodily punishments was seen as a relic of an ancient monarchial regime. A democracy, on the other hand, was premised upon the idea that all men are created equal and are therefore equally deserving of a fair and rational system of punishment. To the extent that egalitarianism was not occurring in the justice process, the removal of punishment from public view at least preserved the legitimacy of the new republic. In other words, it denied Americans the opportunity to judge for themselves the process of punishing. In fact, Kann (2005) writes that reformers were seeking to cleanse the image of punishment and conceal any abuses.

Whatever the reasons may have been for "walling in" punishment (Vale, 2000), it can be reasonably assumed that the deprivation of liberty through incarceration provided an ideal and rational substitute for public shame and bodily torture. It imposed a punishment that conformed to the principle of proportionality, while responding to the various needs and demands of the new republic. The severity of punishment (i.e., the degree of liberty denied) could be calibrated in direct relation to the seriousness of the offense through the duration of imprisonment. In addition to concealing the strong arm of the state, incarceration deprived men of a revolutionary heritage of their most cherished value—liberty. Last, it enabled American reformers to reduce the number of capital offenses while assuring that meaningful punishment would be administered. That is, incarceration provided various substitutions for the death penalty.

According to Pennsylvania law—which served as a model for the nation—those convicted of robbery, burglary, and sodomy should forfeit all property and be sentenced to not more than ten years of hard labor in the jail or house of corrections. Horse stealing was penalized by full restoration to the owner, the forfeiture of an equal amount to the state, and imprisonment and hard labor for not more than seven years. Simple larceny was punishable by full restitution, forfeiture of a like amount to the state, and imprisonment for a term of no more than three years. It also was stipulated in the Pennsylvania statutes that imprisonment and hard labor for two years or less would be punishment for any other non-capital offenses that had been punished by burning in the hand, cutting off ears, nailing the ears to the pillory, or whipping. The number of offenses qualifying as a capital offense, moreover, was reduced. Consequently, second-degree murder was punishable by a sentence of five to eighteen years in prison and manslaughter led to incarceration periods of two to ten years (and six to fourteen years for a second offense). Arson resulted in a sentence of five to twelve years, rape was punished by ten to twenty-one years in prison, and counterfeiting was punished by four to fifteen years in prison and a fine of up to one thousand dollars (Barnes, 1972).

Reality of Penal Code Reform and Incarceration

The nature of penal code reform demanded a comprehensive system of institutional confinement. However, in the rush to abandon old punishment practices, little thought was given to what this substitute for incarceration should look like and how it should operate. Consequently, the earliest American prisons were poorly conceived extensions of the old colonial jails; they were essentially makeshift facilities. For example, in 1773, a Connecticut prison was fashioned out of an existing copper mine (Fried-man, 1993). In 1790, under the new name of Newgate, this prison was deemed little more than a dungeon, overwhelmed by "slippery stinking filth," fleas, lice, and vermin (Kann, 2005). Contemporary observers described the place as "horrid gloom," wherein prisoners were heavily shackled and ate pickled pork thrown on the floor (ibid.). The Walnut Street Jail in Pennsylvania also was converted into a prison. However, the improvised facilities barely could accommodate the influx of prisoners created by the new laws.

Prison overcrowding became a major problem in a number of facilities. In New York, hundreds of offenders were pardoned because there was no place to house them. In 1812, 740 inmates were pardoned. In 1813, 198 offenders were admitted and 134 of them were pardoned. In 1814, 213 of-fenders were admitted and 176 of them were pardoned. Between 1792 and 1822, 5,069 offenders were admitted and 2,819 were pardoned (Barnes, 1972). Prisoners typically completed no more than 50 percent of their sentence and often felt unduly wronged if they were not released early (Kuntz, 1988). Semiannual clemency sessions resulted in the release of forty to fifty convicts simultaneously. Reportedly, lawyers generated a circus-like atmosphere by swarming the prison gates to bargain with inmates. They often circulated petitions with forged signatures and presented faulty evidence of the offender's reformation to governors (ibid.).

Overcrowding was not the only problem that plagued first-generation prisons. In 1826, penal reformer Robert Vaux complained of the lack of classification that kept prisoners of all ages, colors, and sexes in "one common herd" (Kann, 2005: 111). Though few women were incarcerated, those that were could be subjected to a different brand of exploitation: Female convicts could be prostituted in order to obtain valuable information about other inmates. Prison labor amounted to another form of exploitation and was often produced by unsavory means, while inmates were often furnished with liquor as an incentive to increase their productivity (Kann, 2005).

Over a fifty-year period, little evidence was gathered to show that revised penal codes and incarceration reduced crime (Kann, 2005). A statistical report on reconvictions and returns to the penitentiaries of Pennsylvania revealed that 22 percent of those admitted in 1830 had a previous conviction, 11 percent had two prior convictions, and 6 percent had three or more prior convictions (Hood, 1831). Benjamin Rush blamed the failings of the prison experiment on public officials, but reasserted his commitment to the penal philosophy that governed it. As early as 1812, he charged that

> If this original and humane institution, in which science and religion have blended their resources together, has not been attended with uniform success, it must be ascribed wholly to the imperfect manner with which the principles that suggested it have been carried into effect. They have been rendered abortive, chiefly, by the criminals sleeping in the same room, and by the facility and frequency with which pardons are obtained from them (cited in Kann, 2005: 108).

The variety of grim results did not dissuade reformers and public officials from further investing in prisons. Throughout the country, voters and legislatures were convinced of the legitimacy of prison. As a result, they adopted reformers' recommendations to construct even more expensive custodial facilities. For most, incarceration still was considered a vast improvement over the punishments that had gone before. As one warden of the time stated, "When one studies the history of crime and its punishment up to the middle of the eighteenth century, he must be struck with the gruesome fact that the law of crime punishment and penal progress has made its way over dead bodies" (quoted in Rothman, 1980: 29).

Ultimately, penal reformers focused their attention on the architectural defects of the early prison system. In correcting these design defects, they laid the foundation for a new type of prison: the penitentiary.

Enlightenment, Free Will, and Incarceration

The forty-year period immediately following the American Revolution was a time of manifest change—politically, socially, intellectually, and legally. The effects of these changes on the criminal justice system were equally profound, in that colonial ideas about crime and punishment were not merely phased out or outmoded, but often were completely reversed. Most notably, the colonial practice of "warning out" (e.g., banishment) was replaced by walling in and capital punishment was abolished for all but one or two offenses.

The new republic was clearly more optimistic in its expectations about eliminating crime and punishing effectively. Both were problems, but they were problems that could be resolved through human effort and careful reasoning. Specifically, punishments were to be severe enough to deter, but not so severe that the offender would become notorious, martyred, or economically imprudent (Miller, 1980). The penal code reforms were expected to encourage jurors to convict the guilty more consistently, as well as to alter potential offenders' calculi of pleasure and pain (Kann, 2005).

By 1830, it was evident that the promise of a reformed and "enlightened" penal code based on the principles of swift and sure adjudication and incarceration had not been realized. The move toward incarceration was fraught with trial and error and, there being little or no precedent, officials found the task of maintaining orderly and sanitary institutions overwhelming. Prison overcrowding quickly emerged as one of the foremost problems. The earliest institutions also housed a mixture of offenders that included the young, old, men, women, feeble-minded, debtors, witnesses, pretrial felons, and sentenced felons. The perils of such arrangements soon were discovered and acknowledged, leading to eventual alterations in the external and internal design of the prison. Rather than abandon the idea and practice of incarceration altogether, Americans embraced and revised the invention they believed to stand between barbarism and enlightenment. Americans maintained an unbroken confidence in their ability to eliminate crime and to perfect punishment and the prison accordingly. After all, America was a nation of achievers, with a string of economic and political successes behind it that was the envy of the world. Success with criminal punishment certainly was on the horizon.

4

Age of the Penitentiary in Nineteenth-Century America (1830–1870s)

In the decades following 1820, Americans confronted a period of time in which social optimism was blended with a growing sense of fear and disenchantment. This disenchantment stemmed from the rising number of cities that were marked by high population density, vice, and disorder. Though the idea of freedom and liberty for all was cherished and revered, in reality, it proved to be something of a nemesis. For example, it was reported that Bostonians were afraid "lest the sea of ignorance which lies around us, swollen by the wave of misery and vice which is pouring from revolutionized Europe upon our shores, should overflow the dikes of liberty and justice, and sweep away the most precious of our institutions" (Charles Elliott Norton, quoted in Vale, 2000: 60). Racism peaked, communities became stratified, and crime and vice persisted (Pessen, 1969). Popular thought suggested that crime perhaps was not so easily eradicated. Legal reforms based on the notion of free will seemed ineffectual in the face of what came to be viewed as a moral and social disease. In short, crime became viewed as a product of a disorganized and evil city environment.

The impression that all was not right in the new republic prompted what one historian has called a "revolution in social practice" (Vale, 2000). Led by Bostonians, New Yorkers, and Philadelphians, this revolution involved the development of penitentiaries for the criminal, asylums for the insane, almshouses for the poor, and orphan asylums for homeless children. In contrast to previous punishments and social practices, the universal aim of these social reforms was transformation: This new American mindset considered the prospect of curing, whereas seventeenth- and eighteenth-century Americans largely sought to maintain and care for problem populations.

For much of the nineteenth century, American penology focused on reforming the prisons of the previous century. The goal was that the prison would not only reform the criminal through well-organized and monastic regimens but also would serve as a model of proper social organization for inhabitants of the socially disorganized cities. However, the hope of reforming the prison so that men might be reformed was eventually lost in the familiar realities of overcrowding and recidivism. By the outbreak of the Civil War, hopes of eradicating crime through confinement were subsiding both in the progressive-minded North and, most certainly, in the South, where reform expectations scarcely existed. One need only to recall the historical regional variations of this divided nation to understand the North's steadfast commitment to building a better prison, and the South's commitment to inmate leasing and plantations.

Jacksonian America and Beyond

Building a Nation

European observers of the day interpreted the state of the nation well when they characterized Americans as "children of the frontier," "democratic men," "products of equality," and "entrepreneurial seekers" (Pessen, 1969). By the 1830s, Americans were enjoying participation in political life and the seemingly boundless opportunities and freedoms the western frontier offered. Democratic principles (as they knew them) were in full force and American patriotism was running high (Rossiter, 1971). Americans even believed they resided in a providential nation, singled out for the purpose of changing human affairs around the world (ibid.). In the words of one contemporary writer, S.A. Stephens (1820), America defined itself as an "exporter of the spirit," "a redeemer," and, interestingly enough, "an asylum" (quoted in ibid.).

By 1830, the communal rural landscape of pre- and post-revolutionary America remained, but the territories were substantially more populated, mobile, and commercial. Massive westward expansion and burgeoning cityscapes developed along the eastern seaboard. By 1860, 50 percent of the population (i.e., 15.6 million) lived in territories beyond the original thirteen colonies (ibid.). The nation grew from 3.9 million inhabitants in 1790, to 12.9 million in 1830, to 31.5 million in 1860, and to over 50 million by 1880. While an urban revolution had not fully transpired, cities were becoming increasingly important to the vitality of the nation. The urban population increased to twice that of the rural population (Pessen,

1969). In 1790, 5 percent of the population lived in or around urban areas. There were only two cities with populations exceeding 25,000, and not one U.S. city had more than 100,000 residents. By 1860, nearly 30 percent of the population lived in or around urban areas. There were thirty-five cities with populations exceeding 25,000, and ten with population exceeding 100,000. Between 1830 and 1860, New York grew from 197,000 to 806,000 residents. At the same time, Philadelphia's population grew from 80,000 to 566,000 and Boston's population increased from 61,000 to 178,000. The first wave of immigration (between 1820 and 1860) brought 5 million new immigrants to America, and the second wave (between 1860 and 1890) brought an additional 13.5 million. In New York City alone, 3.5 million immigrants arrived between 1830 and 1860 and, by 1855, half of the population was foreign-born German and Irish (Kuntz, 1988).

Booming Economy

The population increases due to immigration were clearly linked to opportunities afforded by a thriving economy. America had just completed its initial phase of industrialization and was poised for economic independence. Though agriculture continued to be the most important economic activity, the push for innovation and diversity in economic affairs was strong, particularly in the North. By 1860, America was ready to challenge England's status as the world's economic leader. The major industries of the day—namely, cotton cultivation, textile and iron manufacturing, and building railroads represented the economies of old and new. New inventions, such as the cotton gin, the telegraph, the sewing machine, and vulcanized rubber, stimulated manufacturing productivity.

The budding economy brought prosperity to many, but it also brought unsettling disruptions to traditional and communal living. Fathers were losing the authority to discipline children, as adolescents focused on their futures in an increasingly competitive market workforce (Rothman, 1995b). Driven by an entrepreneurial spirit, families were uprooted and marriage was delayed (ibid.). Consequently, a smaller nuclear household replaced the extended family household that once had prevailed. Many succumbed to the new temptations of the city, such as gambling, prostitution, taverns, and crime. In fact, social observers of the day acknowledged that the "progress of society necessarily presented new temptations and new facilities for crime" (Lieber and Julius, 1835). With the "progress of wealth and improvement" came crime, particularly in densely populated areas versus the "thinly settled" agricultural districts (ibid.).

Charity, Crusades, and Religion

As the nation became more democratized, so too did religion. Biblical interpretations were no longer the exclusive domain of elite eastern seaboard clerics. Some clerics still were preoccupied with the origins of sin and man's helplessness before God, but many new religious denominations challenged this belief. It was generally held that salvation was for everyone, and that the power to achieve salvation rested within each free-willed individual. Consistent with the optimistic spirit of the times, the new denominations stressed God's humanity and goodness and the perfectibility and responsibilities of man.

The idea that mankind was empowered to improve society and the lives of those within it led to the development of numerous charitable associations. It was this religious and charitable zeal that prompted European observers to label Americans as "neurotic do-gooders" (ibid.). Travelers from abroad noted that America was a land of assorted benevolent associations, the leaders of which were not suffering from the abuses they sought to correct (e.g., alcoholism, gambling) (ibid.). The temperance crusades were a prime manifestation of this reformist and religious zeal. Between 1710 and 1830, hard liquor consumption increased threefold (see Table 4-1). By 1830, annual consumption of hard liquor reached unprecedented levels, with each family consuming approximately 9.5 gallons per year. Americans were drinking more compulsively and in a variety of new settings. Drinking now occurred at funerals, ministerial ordinations, elections, corn huskings, and house raisings. Neighborhood socializing in general seemed to center upon taverns. It was said that every family, even prominent ones, had a resident alcoholic. Not surprisingly, it was assumed that an epidemic of alcoholism had overcome the nation.

The fear that America was becoming a nation of drunkards prompted the development of the American Society for the Promotion of Temperance. This organization held that temperate people should remain so and that all others should kill themselves off. The temperance movement provoked a collective repression so powerful that consumption ultimately fell by 75 percent in the fifteen years following 1830. Temperance crusaders were unceasing in their calculations

Table 4-1
U.S. Alcohol Consumption, 1710–1845[a]

Year	Hard Liquor	Cider	Absolute Alcohol (All Beverages)
1710	3.8	34	5.1
1790	5.1	34	5.8
1830	9.5	27	7.1
1840	5.5	4	3.1
1845	3.7	0	1.8

[a]Consumption in gallons for individuals more than 14 years of age.

of the social costs associated with alcohol, such as pauperism, lost labor, and crime.

Crime as Moral Disease

While alcoholism was one of the most visibly targeted social problems of the day, psychic disorders, opium addictions, and general public and moral disorder offenses were becoming increasingly common. Contemporary reformers viewed the prevalence of "houses of ill-fame" as nearly impossible to suppress. Crimes of violence were increasing, causing concerned citizens to declare that "from nearly all parts of the country accounts of horrible murders were pouring in" (*Prisoners Friend*, 1846). Street gangs, such as the Plug Uglies, Forty Thieves, Swamp Angels, and the Slaughterhouse Boys, further overwhelmed the still loosely structured and understaffed police forces. In the poorer sections of town, officers often left the gangs alone, provided their fighting and associated activities did not spill over into the wealthier sections of town (Friedman, 1993).

The crime problem was most pronounced in the area of property offenses, such as theft and burglary. Historian Friedman (1993) noted that if one asks what the criminal justice system did in the early nineteenth century, the answer would be that it protected property and punished stealing. As reported in Table 4-2, Boston larceny cases were much more likely to receive prison terms than the seemingly more serious cases of assault and battery. In Boston as well as New York, 58 percent of all cases adjudicated were for larceny. In Philadelphia, 71 percent of all adjudicated cases were for larceny. Crimes of theft were also highly specific. For example, the punishment varied depending on whether the stolen object(s) was cattle, mules, or horses. Legal codes also were tailored according to the unique needs of local economies. In 1850s' Mis-

Table 4-2
Sentences for Larceny versus Assault and Battery in Boston, 1830–1840

Year	Fines	Probation	Prison Terms (%)
Larceny			
1830	0	1	9
1835	15	5	80
1840	8	0	92
Assault and Battery			
1830	30	0	70
1835	76	0	24
1840	62	8	30

Source: Kuntz (1988).

sissippi, it was illegal to pack or bale cotton fraudulently. In Minnesota, laws targeted lumbering and logging practices (ibid.).

Overall, the perception was that "safety everywhere was precarious" (Pessen, 1969). A sense of moral panic was even communicated in various newspapers and periodicals. For example, in a column originally appearing in the *New York Tribune*, it was stated that, "It is true, that among the mass of our busy population those things soon fade from their remembrance, but there are those who look on with concern and dismay, anxiously inquiring whether there is any remedy for this state of things" (*Prisoners Friend*, 1846: 174).

Given the increasing complexity of society, a more nuanced understanding of crime was favored by reformers. Crime was increasingly attributed to a number of social factors. For example, Gresham Powers, then a voice of reform, argued that the causes of crime could be found in the rapid growth in wealth, population size, immigration, and commerce and manufacturing. Indeed, criminal activity was more likely to be observed in urban areas with larger concentrations of people, immigrants, and economic activity. Powers subsequently noted that while these various developments brought "blessings," they also brought "consequent evil" (quoted in Kann, 2005).

Edward Livingston, another nineteenth-century reformer, promoted the notion that crime was the product of intemperance, idleness, ignorance, irreligion, and poverty. New York reformer John Griscom situated crime within the context of bad parenting and the absence of "domestic government." He alleged that too many parents allowed their children to "run at large without restraints" (ibid.). Biographical interviews with offenders further revealed that a broken family was noticeably a common denominator among those in prison. In fact, it was widely held that the lower classes were so habituated to bad parenting, alcohol abuse, and ignorance that no amount of informal control could halt their attraction to taverns, gambling, prostitution, and other vices (ibid.).

New York reformer Thomas Eddy believed crime could be traced to excessive passions. Whether appearing in the form of lust, greed, or violence, these passions overwhelmed the virtues of reason and rationality (ibid.). Once more, alcohol frequently was cited as a major problem in provoking these passions. In a letter written to the President of the Pennsylvania Society for Discouraging the Use of Ardent Spirits, a correctional officer working in the Walnut Street Penitentiary contended that intoxication—among offenders and their parents—was the "primary cause of their moral degradation" (Hood, 1831). This officer argued that, upon the offender's release, the temptation to drink was so great that "reason was dethroned, and vice and folly assumed their reign" (ibid.).

These myriad claims about the causes of crime essentially implicated three sources: broken family, intemperance, and a bad environment in general. Taken together, the explanatory account of crime that emerged held that a corrupted community filled with temptation and vice (Rothman, 1971) fostered morally weakened environments (both familial and social) which, in turn, contributed to morally weakened individuals who were unable to resist social vice. For those cognizant of the more stable, cohesive, and harmonious existence of colonial times, America in the mid-1800s was, by comparison, a society in decay.

Statistics on jail and prison inmates informed and reinforced this multi-factored theory of social and moral disease. In 1864, 32 percent of New York jail inmates could not read; 72 percent were without trades, 50 percent were foreigners, and 49 percent admitted frequenting houses of ill-fame and gambling houses (Bittenger, 1870). Statistics of the day also indicate that approximately 60 percent of jail and prison inmates were of foreign parentage and that more than half were orphans or half orphans. The Reverend Dr. Bittenger wrote that there was a "sad uniformity in these figures and a still sadder uniformity in the directness with which they point to ignorance, idleness, orphanage, drunkenness, and licentiousness" (Bittenger, 1870).

Influenced by medical advances of the time, the idea of crime as a moral disease was easily embraced, and the cure (or antidote) for a moral disease was thought to be a moral science. It was assumed that scientific advancements in treating physical ailments could be harnessed to treat vice (Kann, 2005). Though doctors were still ignorant about the sources and treatments of bacterial and viral infections—bloodletting was still practiced, often killing more people than it cured—this did not stop them or others from portraying crime as a curable disease.

The notion of crime as an infectious disease was advanced primarily by then-prominent physician Dr. Benjamin Rush. He and other medical doctors of the day sought to make their mission one of reclaiming mankind from the grip of vice. Medicalizing nearly all behavior, Rush taught that disease is a habit of wrong action and that all habits of injurious tendency are diseases. Under this disease model, crime ultimately can be cured and the "inoculation" against vice, deviance, and crime first required a strong dose of discipline and the closing of establishments of ill repute. As with surgery, the corrupting influences needed to be removed, while the corrupted were nursed back to good moral health in a sanitary environment. Rush claimed that one could be returned to good moral health through constant employment in bodily labor. For the insane and disobedient, he designed what he called an immobilizing tranquilizer chair. He held that two days of solitary confinement would internalize self-control through a guilt-driven conscience. He continued to promote this approach, despite being rumored to have driven his own son to insanity as a result of such experimentation.

Promise of the Penitentiary

Though reformers were motivated to rethink the causes of crime and the purposes of punishment, they were not compelled to abandon the idea of imprisonment. The initial defects of the prison did not dampen the optimism of penal reformers and the irony of retaining imprisonment in a land where liberty was so highly regarded, while difficult, was not considered impossible to reconcile. A prison that could both sequester and employ offenders in labor would cure individuals and society at large by serving as a model of decency and order. The image of prison itself could also be "corrected" by portraying prison authorities as compassionate non-threatening figures (Kann, 2005).

By 1830, penitentiaries were replacing the prisons that emerged in the late eighteenth century. Following the lead of New York, Pennsylvania, and Massachusetts, New Jersey, Ohio, and Michigan each constructed facilities in the 1830s. Other states, such as Indiana, Wisconsin, and Minnesota, followed suit in the 1840s (Barnes, 1972). Importantly, penitentiaries were intended to be different from the earliest prisons in both their form and function. The first American prisons were small and hastily assembled in accordance with deterrence-driven penal codes and served largely as an alternative to death and other corporal punishments. The penitentiaries of the nineteenth century, on the other hand, were architectural testaments to American ingenuity. Awesome in size and elaborate in design—both inside and out—the penitentiaries were intended to resolve newfound social ills and restore order and proper social organization (Rothman, 1971). Architecture and organizational structure were deemed central to reform, such that routine would "recreate fixity and stability to compensate for the irregularities of the society" (ibid.). In fact, one prison chaplain proclaimed that "could we all be put on prison fare for the space of two or three generations, the world ultimately would be the better for it" (Rothman, 1995b).

At the same time the penitentiary was to accomplish the curing of moral disease, it also was envisioned as a place that should be sufficiently terrifying to the public and the offender. Livingston wanted to "wrap penitentiaries in a mantle of mystery" (Kann, 2005) by closing them to visitors. It was reasoned that public ignorance would invite people to ponder "all the horrors by which mystery always aggravates apprehended evils" (ibid.). Rush similarly argued that the public and prisoners should be punished by their own imaginations (ibid.), yet the punishment should always appear worse than it actually was. For Rush, the terrors of the imagination were to be aroused by the internal and external structure of the penitentiary:

> Let a large house ... be erected in a remote part of the state. Let the avenue to this house be rendered difficult and gloomy by mountains or morasses. Let its doors be of iron; and let the gratings, occasioned by opening and shutting them, be increased by an echo from a neighboring mountain that shall extend and continue a sound that shall deeply pierce the soul. Let a guard constantly attend at the gate that shall lead to this place of punishment to prevent strangers from entering it. Let all of the officers of the house be strictly forbidden ever to discover any signs of mirth or even levity, in the presence of criminals (quoted in Kann, 2005: 104).

The moral reform objectives of the penitentiary were to be achieved through the standard features of obedience, routine, silence, labor, separation, surveillance, pure air, healthful labor, seasonable exercise, and adequate food and water. Rules of separation and silence functioned to quarantine the offender from fellow inmates. In the Eastern Penitentiary in Philadelphia, inmates were hooded during any kind of transport, so that they could not recognize or re-infect each other upon release. The doctrine of the Philadelphia Society consistently held that "no two persons charged with or convicted of crime should be in each other's presence, but that from the hour of arrest to the day of discharge, their only association shall be with those who are supposed to be better than themselves" ("What Has Been Done," 1856).

The physical design of the penitentiary was influenced not only by the medical rationales put forth by such physicians as Benjamin Rush, but also by Jeremy Bentham's image of the perfect prison; namely, the "panopticon." In institutions following the "panopticon" blueprint, surveillance and self-discipline were to be assured though the constant and invisible monitoring provided by the central guard tower. The features of separation and surveillance were intended to divide time, space, and bodies in such a way as to purify the pathological, prevent the spread of "disease," and render each man the arbiter of his own monitoring and control (Foucault, 1977).

The details of the internal structure and regimen were considered critical in the reformative process and were thus the subject of intense debate. For example, although solitary confinement was considered a standard feature of prison that many still recommended for the entirety of an offender's sentence, penal reformers contended that the total time in isolation should be partial. Most advocated that only one half to one twelfth of an offender's sentence be spent in solitude, or that the isolation only be at night (Kann, 2005). Though early release through pardons helped mitigate time spent in prison and solitude, isolation for any length of time is predictably unbearable. The average sentence in a U.S. penitentiary between 1844 and 1846 ranged between four and eight years (see Table 4-3).

The controversy over design and regimen is particularly evident in the rivalry between the Auburn and Pennsylvania systems. In the Pennsylvania system, it was decided that offenders should live and work in silence and isolation, or what was known as "uninterrupted solitary confinement at labor" (Lieber, 1838) or "individual separation with labor" ("What Has Been Done," 1856). Advocates of this model believed that complete solitude was the "weightiest moral agent to make the thoughtless thoughtful" (Lieber, 1838); they did not agree with their critics, who warned that isolation led to mental illness and suicide. Rather, advocates of the Pennsylvania system held that the congregation of convicts led only to "contamination," thus jeopardizing the likelihood of reform. It was believed that allowing association not only posed security threats but also facilitated communication, which resulted in frequent and degrading discipline for talkers (ibid.). Pennsylvania model advocates regarded relief from solitude to be a privilege reserved only for the

Table 4-3
Number of Life Terms and Average Length of Imprisonment in
U.S. Penitentiaries, 1844–1846

State	Year	Life Terms	Years	Months	Days
Connecticut	1844	17	6	6	1
	1846	19	6	10	8
Maine	1844	6	4	11	22
	1845	7	4	4	14
	1846	8	4	4	2
Maryland	1845	0	4	0	3
Massachusetts	1844	12	5	1	2
	1845	14	4	11	9
Michigan	1845	1	4	6	11
	1846	0	4	1	13
New Hampshire	1845	11	6	4	20
	1846	10	6	4	11
Ohio	1846	6	5	0	22
Rhode Island	1844	3	5	11	10
Vermont	1844	2	4	2	15
	1845	2	4	0	21
Virginia	1845	12	7	3	2
	1846	13	7	11	3

Source: Kuntz (1988).

well-behaved. Such relief came in the form of visits from chaplains and inspectors, labor within the cell, and exercise in enclosed courtyards (Kann, 2005).

While supporters of the Pennsylvania model claimed that the Auburn system rejected total isolation only because it impeded a more profitable form of labor, supporters of the Auburn model claimed that their opposition was due to the deleterious effects of constant isolation on the offenders' physical and mental health. Thus, the Auburn penitentiary adopted the practice of silent association; that is, prisoners worked together in silence and returned to solitude only at night. Initially, many states followed the Pennsylvania model of total isolation only to later abandon the practice. For example, Maryland introduced solitary confinement in 1809 and abolished it in 1838. Massachusetts authorized it in 1811 and did away with it in 1829. Maine experimented with solitary confinement between 1824 and 1827 and Virginia between 1824 and 1833. Rhode Island introduced it in 1838 and abolished it in 1844. New Jersey retained it the longest, finally abolishing it in 1858 (Barnes, 1972). Most states followed the Auburn system, fearing the reality of too many offenders going insane as a result of continuous isolation.

Despite their differences with respect to time in isolation, each penitentiary system was committed to rules of order, silence, routine, and mandatory labor. This commitment was evident in the assignment of clothing, the scheduling of the day, and the daily diet. During their term of confinement, all "convicts" dressed alike; ate the same food; and slept, moved, and dined in concert. Each convict was allocated a specific number of shoes (two pairs), pants (two pairs), shirts (three), and socks (two pairs). An average summer day at the Auburn penitentiary began at 5:30 a.m. with the ringing of a bell. Cells were then unlocked and men came out and emptied, washed, and placed in a row their "night tubs." The convicts worked until breakfast (7 or 8 a.m.) and, at the ringing of a bell, formed a line and marched across the yard. Upon entering the dining area, convicts faced their plates until everyone arrived. They sat down simultaneously and next to one another in order to prevent across-the-table-glances between offenders (Friedman, 1993).

At Auburn, food portions were equally specific and uniform. Convicts were given no more than 2 ounces of pepper for every 100 rations. At Sing Sing Prison, the daily ration consisted of 6 pounds 9 ounces of food a day; this food included beef, pork, flour, mush, molasses, and potatoes (ibid.). In the Pennsylvania system, the following dietary schedule was mandated:

Sunday	1 lb of bread, 1 lb of coarse meal made into broth
Monday	1 lb of bread, 1 qt of potatoes
Tuesday	1 qt of Indian meal made into mush
Wednesday	1 lb of bread, 1 qt of potatoes
Thursday	1 qt of Indian meal made into mush
Friday	1 lb of bread, 1 qt of potatoes
Saturday	1 qt of Indian meal made into mush (Barnes, 1972: 138).

A half-quart of molasses to every four prisoners was permitted on Tuesday, Thursday, and Saturday (Barnes, 1972).

In 1826, Louis Dwight—the Auburn silent system's most ardent advocate—described the type of discipline enforced as a testimony to its transforming powers in, *A Brief Account of the Construction, Management and Discipline of the New York State Prison at Auburn*:

> At Auburn we have a more beautiful example still of what may be done by proper discipline, in a prison well constructed. It is not possible to describe the pleasure which we feel in contemplating this noble institution, after wading through the fraud, and the material and moral filth of many prisons. We regard it as a

model worthy of the world's imitation. We do not mean that there is nothing in this institution which admits of improvement; for there have been a few cases of unjustifiable severity in punishments; but, upon the whole, the institution is immensely elevated above the old prisons. The whole establishment, from the gate to the sewer, is a specimen of neatness. The unremitted industry, the entire subordination and subdued feeling of the convicts, has probably no parallel among an equal number of criminals. In their solitary cells they spend the night, with no other book but the Bible, and at sunrise they proceed, in military order, under the eye of the turnkeys, in solid columns, with the lock march, to their workshops; thence, in the same order, at the hour of breakfast, to the common hall, where they partake of their wholesome and frugal meal in silence. Not even a whisper is heard; though the silence is such that a whisper might be heard through the whole apartment. The convicts are seated in single file, at narrow tables, with their backs towards the center, so that there can be no interchange of signs. If one has more food than he wants, he raises his left hand; and if another has less, he raises his right hand, and the waiter changes it. From one end of the shops to the other, it is the testimony of many witnesses, that they have passed more than 300 convicts, without seeing one leave his work, or turn his head to gaze at them. This is the most perfect attention to business from morning till night, interrupted only by the time necessary Iodine, and never by the fact that the whole body of prisoners have done their tasks, and the time is now their own to do as they please. After supper, they can, if they choose, read Scripture undisturbed and then reflect in silence on the errors of their lives. They must not disturb their fellow prisoner by even a whisper (quoted in Barnes, 1972: 136).

One might assume from this account of penitentiary life that the institutional environment was the paragon of order and obedience. However, as Rothman (1995b) pointed out, these "scenes of order and routine masked a much harsher reality." The penitentiary, though heralded as a structure that would reform, failed by most estimations.

The Penitentiary in Practice

Ironically, it was a Massachusetts prisoner who wrote that the reformers' goals were "lovely but visionary" (Kann, 2005). If nothing else, the penitentiary was promoted as more humane than the corporal punishments of earlier generations. However, institution officials did not hesitate to employ harsh measures in the face of even the slightest acts of disobedience. Breaches of codes of silence and other rules were met with severe punishments, and inmates often were threatened with hunger or beatings. New York, Massachusetts, and Ohio, in particular relied on whippings, considering them to be a morally and financially effective way of disciplining wayward inmates.

Other corporal punishments also were employed in these states and elsewhere. In Pennsylvania, the iron gag was used against "talkers";

Maine preferred the ball and chain (Rothman, 1995b). In other institutions, offenders frequently were suspended in the air by their toes or thumbs for disciplinary purposes. The stretcher, similar in principle to the medieval rack, was also used as a way of inflicting discipline and inducing obedience. Sweat boxes, which consisted of unventilated cells located on either side of a fireplace, frequently were used. A Pennsylvania prison investigation conducted during 1834 and 1835 revealed that inmates were frequently tied up in the winter, while buckets of cold water were thrown upon them from extreme heights, freezing on their head and body (Barnes, 1972). In 1878, a New Jersey investigating committee found that authorities had habitually poured alcohol on epileptics and then set fire to the alcohol in order to detect possible faking of a seizure.

In the absence of corporal disciplinary action, the inhumanity of normal living conditions was still apparent. Upon their visit to the United States, Frenchmen Gustave de Beaumont and Alexis de Tocqueville described total silence as the silence of death, as if someone had just entered catacombs. In Cincinnati, they found that half of the inmates were imprisoned with irons and the rest were thrown into disease-infested dungeons (de Beaumont and de Tocqueville, [1833] 1997). Numerous other observers and charitable prisoner associations also commented on the atrocities that accompanied this "advanced" form of punishment. Charles Dickens, who visited the Philadelphia prison in the 1840s, abhorred what he termed the "depth of terrible endurance, which no man has a right to inflict upon his fellow creature" and declared:

> Those who devised this system ... and those benevolent gentlemen who carry it into execution, do not know what they are doing. I hold this slow and daily tampering with the mysteries of the brain to be immeasurably worse than any torture of the body. The wounds it inflicts are not upon the surface, and it exhorts few cries that human ears can hear. They are nothing more than men buried alive, to be dug out in the slow round of years, and in the meantime dead to everything but torturing anxieties and horrible despair. Those who have undergone this punishment must pass into society again morally unhealthy and diseased (Dickens, [1842] quoted in Barnes, 1972: 203).

By 1852, numerous legislative reports and commissions conceded that penitentiaries did little more than incapacitate and that conditions actually were worsening. It was concluded that the likelihood of recidivism was far greater than were the odds of reform. The ineffectiveness noted by critics is illustrated in part by the recommitment rates for Sing Sing Prison (see Table 4-4). No clear pattern emerges from these figures, however, as to whether longer or shorter sentences were more likely to increase recidivism.

Table 4-4
Recommitment Rates for Sing Sing Prison, 1817–1842

Term of Incarceration (in years)	Ratio Recommitted	Number Recommitted
1	1/3	3
2	1/17	109
3	1/13	145
4	1/10	68
5	1/6	218
6	1/6	19
7	1/5	96
8	1/11	6
9	1/15	2
10	1/9	49
11	1/7	1
12	1/10	4
13	0	0
14	1/10	13
15	1/9	3
16	0	0
17	1/1	2
18	1/3	1
19	1/0	0
20	1/3	3
21–30	1/4	2
More than 30	0	0
Life Imprisonment	1/8	34

Source: Kuntz (1988).

In 1857, an article appearing in the *Journal of Prison Discipline and Philanthropy* roundly criticized the penitentiary for its mechanistic processing of offenders and counterproductive effects: The article's author declared, "Those whose business it is to restrain or punish him, do it in such a bungling way, that the attempt is quite as likely to fail, as to succeed; and in either event, the last state of the offender will probably be worse than the first" (p. 143). Rumblings of reform gone bad were further fueled by evidence of more serious offenders being admitted to the penitentiary. In Connecticut between 1828 and 1840, of the state's total of 839 inmates, 343 were convicted of burglary and robbery, 78 for attempted murder, 42 for rape, and 45 for arson and escape. The increasing gravity of offenses made it easier to justify various corporal punishments within the institution. The fact that the majority of inmates also were immigrants made indifference to inhumane treatment easier as well. Between 1830 and 1835, 20 percent of the inmates at the Auburn prison had been born outside the United States. By the 1850s, the percentage of foreign-born inmates increased to 32 percent. By 1860, 44 percent of the inmate population at Auburn was foreign-born, immigrants comprised 40 percent of the Massachusetts prison populations, and 46 percent of the Illinois prison population was foreign born. Included in these groups were not just European immigrants, but also African Americans, Asians, and Native Americans.

By 1860, the rules of separation and isolation had long been abandoned as a result of overcrowding. For example, in Philadelphia during 1861, 801 inmates occupied 489 cells, with total admissions numbering 20,801. Those inmates given early releases due to overcrowding totaled 7,674, with another 6,578 being released outright by the sentencing judge because of overcrowded prison conditions (Kuntz, 1988). An 1867 report by the New York legislature estimated that approximately one third of all prisoners were double celled. In 1867 New Jersey, prisoners lived as many as four to a cell that measured 7 feet by 12 feet or less (Friedman, 1993). Everywhere, overcrowding was so problematic that pardons (i.e., sentence commutations) had become an integral part of securing the safety and order of prisons. An 1856 report indicated that the "indiscriminate exercise of the pardoning power had deprived penal inflictions of half their terror" ("What Has Been Done," 1856). Yet, without the growing likelihood of pardons, it was feared that rule infractions would become too frequent and that the minds of convicts would become "soured and intractable" (quoted in Kuntz, 1988). A contemporary observer noted that in the absence of early release via pardons, inmates were "less sensible to the influences of kindly treatment," which in turn encouraged the need for harsher disciplinary measures (ibid.).

With penal reform theory all but vanquished, managerial and fiscal concerns ultimately determined the operations of the penitentiary. Indeed, monetary considerations effectively shaped the rules of separation at both the Pennsylvania and Auburn systems (Miller, 1980). While cruel punishments were being routinely administered within overcrowded prisons, administrative corruption was becoming widespread. Bribery of guards by inmates was not uncommon (Rothman, 1995b). One inmate author of the day wrote that it was an "absolute impossibility to find men of decency and integrity to administer penal reform plans" (quoted in Kann, 2005). Boston's Prison Discipline Society was equally critical of the rampant corruption of the nation's prison guards (Kann, 2005).

The society characterized them as "men destitute of humanity, men of violent and virulent passions, men of obscene and profane conversation … men who would accept a bribe … and defraud the state (quoted in Kann, 2005: 185).

Southern Justice

The expectations of the northern reformers had collapsed under the weight of fiscal crises, corruption, disobedience, and overcrowding. In the South, however, the expectations of offender reform were somewhat meager, if not absent altogether. For example, in New Orleans, men were housed with hogs and often chained up (de Beaumont and de Tocqueville, [1833] 1997). Few efforts to emulate either the Auburn or Pennsylvania systems were underway before the Civil War and, following the Civil War, penal conditions only deteriorated into further chaos and corruption. The South adopted a punishment philosophy based on impending economic needs. Their system was based not on philanthropic ideas, but on the idea that the "possession of a convict's person is an opportunity for the state to make money; that the amount to be made is whatever can be wrung from him" (Cable, 1884: 586). This philosophy took the form of the convict lease system, which served as a slavery model for rebuilding a war-ravaged economy and infrastructure (e.g., railroads).

By the late nineteenth century, the lease system was fully operational in Tennessee, North and South Carolina, Kentucky, Georgia, Texas, Alabama, Arkansas, Mississippi, Florida, and Louisiana. Under this system, offenders—90 percent of whom were newly freed blacks—were leased to private companies. These companies, in turn, paid the state a sum of money for the cheap labor. For example, eleven hundred prisoners in Georgia were leased to three companies on twenty-year contracts for the sum of twenty-five thousand dollars (McKelvey, 1936). In 1867, Mississippi operated its penal system under a similar arrangement, as did Louisiana, Arkansas, Tennessee, and Florida.

What distinguished the type of labor found in the lease system from the prison labor of northern institutions is that inmates in the South could be leased out anywhere in the United States. These "branch prisons" often were in areas remote from the original prison (Cable, 1884) and many and sometimes all aspects of the offender's punishment (custody, supervision, labor materials, health care, housing) were under the immediate authority of private contractors.

Predictably, the lack of oversight in the leasing system led to many illegalities and forms of corruption. For example, companies often lagged behind in their payments to states and neglected to provide information and reports requested by authorities. On the other side, states sought to maximize their gain through the best possible bargains. Consequently, inmates were shuffled from one company to the next without permanent quarters. They lived in camp-like facilities, and there was little in the way of order, rules, or surveillance. Given these conditions, it was not uncommon for states to lose track of how many offenders were under supervision. Moreover, the prevalence of escapes was markedly higher under the lease system (in which 49 out of 639 inmates escaped) than in the five largest U.S. prisons (wherein 63 out of 18,400 inmates escaped) (Cable, 1884). Shackles were used to prevent escapes, as was the ball and chain (ibid.).

This manner of operation led one commentator to declare that the scheme of leasing was an "insult to the intelligence and humanity of any enlightened community" (Cable, 1884). Offenders resided in quarters in which there was barely running water and no heat during the winter. Their clothes were typically tattered, while shoes were considered a privilege. Friedman (1993) wrote that inmates labored in sweltering conditions under which they often "died like flies." Indeed, mortality rates under the lease system were far higher than they were under the penitentiary system. Mortality reports given to state authorities by contractors often indicated that inmates were "shot," "killed," "found dead," "drowned," or died from such diseases as dropsy, scrofula, and consumption. Twentieth-century historian McKelvey noted, "While the prisoner of the North may have grown pale and anemic gazing through the bars in a tower, the southern counterpart dragged his chains through long years of hard labor, driven by brutal torture, often times to his grave" (1936: 172).

The convict lease system gradually was replaced with the plantation/farm model and the "good road and chain gangs project," which existed well into the twentieth century. While each of these approaches was touted as "quintessential southern progressive reform" and as an example of penal humanitarianism, the reality was far from humane (Lichtenstein, 1993). So gruesome was the treatment of "negro convicts" that one scholar was compelled to issue the following warning in advance of an exposé on southern prison camps: "Please reader, do not read this chapter unless you can steel your heart against pain" (Tannenbaum, 1924: 74; quoted in Lichtenstein, 1993).

Urban Disenchantment, Moral Reform, and the Penitentiary

In the 1830s, America certainly was optimistic about its prospects as a new nation, but the drawbacks of democracy and commercialism could not be overlooked. New freedoms threatened established norms and values, and society—as many Americans once knew it—was essentially crumbling even as it was advancing politically and economically. Criminal activity was on the rise and was attributed to a morally depraved environment wrought by unchecked growth, drinking, immigration, poverty, and irreligion. Nevertheless, having conquered England on more than one occasion—and now surpassing England as the economic leader of the world—Americans had little reason to believe they could not conquer a much weaker foe in crime.

Much like their reform predecessors, enthusiastic penitentiary advocates did not foresee the shortcomings and flawed implementation of their ideas. The silent system had little staying power because it was virtually unenforceable. Solitary confinement was also too expensive, not to mention deleterious to inmates' mental health. Despite laws and policies to the contrary, inmates were not always treated with kindness and uniformity. With the exception of overt mutilation, nearly every form of corporal punishment known to colonial America was transferred into the prison system as a way of enforcing prison regimen and rules. In the South, different and even more corrupt and brutal conditions prevailed under the convict lease system.

That said, the rise of the Pennsylvania and Auburn systems did mark a step in the way of progress, at least in terms of some prison conditions, classification, and differentiation. Unlike the previous prison practice of herding offenders of all kinds into one place, mid-nineteenth century systems separated felons according to the seriousness of their crimes and assigned separate living quarters to males and females. Perhaps these minor advancements provide sufficient evidence of progress, despite glaring missteps along the way. In any event, Americans were unwilling to part with the idea of incarceration. If nothing else, penal institutions were convenient because they housed the "strange alien hordes" (i.e., immigrants and undesirables), and their very failure (i.e., recidivism) contributed to the persistence and expansion of the American penal system (Rothman, 1971). Rather than abolish the penitentiary, a new kind of institution (the reformatory) would appear, along with community-based alternatives to incarceration.

5

Progressivism and Reformatory, Parole, and Probation (1880s–1920s)

The Progressive Era was distinguished by sweeping policy changes that are still a part of twenty-first-century social welfare and criminal justice systems. A major thrust of this movement was defining a new role for government in public and private affairs. The call for government engagement in the lives of citizens and corporate matters was based on the idea that government should be responsive to and responsible for the national quality of life. The need to expand the role of government was especially prompted by the new challenges of unchecked industrialization, urbanization, and immigration. American cities were increasingly afflicted with poverty, disease, overcrowded slums, and crime—the magnitude of which demanded government intervention. Family, friends, and small charitable organizations were ill equipped to handle these problems that were occurring on such a massive scale.

Given the harsh reality of inner-city conditions, environmental determinism became the predominant school of thought on the cause of crime. Social-structural explanations of crime guided much of the discourse on penal reform; however, biological and psychological theories of crime were put forward as well. In the end, whether the causes of crime were located in societal or in individual anomalies, the less fortunate and criminally wayward were not to be punished or reformed for presumed *moral* failings; they were to be rehabilitated for failings brought on by psychological, biological, and/or social irregularities.

Progressivism embraced the notion that government would be the outstretched hand that made rehabilitation possible. The rehabilitation of criminals in particular would come about through theoretically informed strategies that facilitated differentiated treatment. This progressive re-structuring would expand the existing prison system already consisting of 2200 prisons of different grades throughout the United States and collectively housing an average of 60,000 prisoners at any given time ("Prison Reform," 1872). New penal strategies would include adult reformatories, indeterminate sentencing, parole, probation, and the juvenile court (discussed in the following chapter).

These reforms increased the number and type of penal strategies available to the state, but the goal of individualized treatment went largely unrealized. Like the prison and the penitentiary before, the promise and the reality of progressive penology were far apart. Rather than providing more individualized treatment alternatives to the penitentiary, these reforms instead were implemented as supplements to existing practice. Moreover, corporal discipline and managerial concerns continued to thwart what was to be a more "progressive" and scientifically informed justice system.

Progressive America

Progressivism can be understood as a collection of movements aimed at the improvement of social, political, and economic life. Diverse ethnic groups and classes mobilized these movements, for diverse ethnic groups and classes. In more complex terms, progressivism was the response to pervasive anxiety and vulnerability related to the rapid escalation of industrialization, immigration, and urbanization. In seeking to address these threats to order, progressivism sought to Americanize immigrants and turn the nation into a "melting pot," as well as curtail the abuses and dangers of unregulated private power and corporate capitalism (Diner, 1998; Unger and Unger, 1977).

Progressive reform efforts began at the local and state levels in the 1890s and reached the national level by 1900. Several unresolved political questions shaped the agenda of progressives. To what extent should the government intervene in the affairs of the economy? How much should it tax its citizens? How far should government go to ensure the extension of full democracy to all citizens and groups? (Cashman, 1988). Woodrow Wilson answered these questions in part by declaring that industry, science, and government should be used to place "our businessmen and producers under the stimulation of a constant necessity to be efficient, economic, and enterprising" (Luke, 1986). Herbert Croly proposed a more interventionist role for government when stating, "The American state will make itself responsible for a morally and socially desirable distribution of wealth" (quoted in ibid.). These statements reflect the dire conditions wrought by the combined ills of industrialization, immigration, and urbanization.

Industrialization

The Industrial Revolution reached its peak at the turn of the twentieth century. The United States outperformed the world in both agricultural and industrial output, even as its agricultural economy was on the decline. The United States was the leading producer of coal and was rich in natural resources, including iron, gold, silver, copper, lead, and petroleum. By 1919, the United States supplied two-thirds of the world's oil. This period witnessed the beginning of monopoly capitalism, wherein just a few companies owned the bulk of the nation's industry. The Rockefellers owned Standard Oil, James B. Duke owned American Tobacco Company, the Carnegies owned U.S. Steel, and J.P. Morgan owned the House of Morgan. Coca-Cola, Levi Strauss, Eastman Kodak, Sears Roebuck, and R.J. Reynolds were equally powerful corporate players (Cashman, 1988).

The material progress of the United States was unparalleled and could be attributed to the growth of industrial production. Productivity was continually improved through mechanization, and mechanization was continually improved through a number of inventions. In 1900, a columnist for the *Washington Post* remarked that, "in every department of science and intellectual activity, we have gone beyond the wildest dreams of 1800" (Parshall, 1998). An Englishman writing about his visit to America in 1900 proclaimed, "life in the states is one perpetual whirl of telephones, telegrams, phonographs, electric bells, motors, lifts, and automatic instruments" (quoted in Diner, 1998). By 1910, Americans could buy any number of automatic and electrical devices, such as sewing machines, fans, irons, washing machines, vacuum cleaners, stoves, heaters, and automobiles. In 1900, eight thousand Americans owned cars. By 1920, eight million owned cars: Americans were no longer just producers; they were mass consumers (ibid.).

The inventions of Thomas Edison and Alexander Graham Bell, in particular, revolutionized the nation's consumption and production capacities. The following excerpt from a 1929 AT&T report (quoted in Cashman, 1988: 23) illustrates the importance of efficient production levels:

In 1781, one man working one day produced:	*In 1925*, one man working one day produced:
500 lbs. of iron	5,000 lbs. of iron
100 ft. of lumber	750 ft. of lumber
5 lbs. of nails	500 lbs. of nails
1/4 pair of shoes	10 pairs of shoes
1/2 ton of coal	4 tons of coal
20 square feet of paper	200,000 square feet of paper

The Industrial Revolution could not have taken place through invention, ingenuity, and raw materials alone. It also depended on a plentiful supply of labor. Six million people were employed in manufacturing in 1900, increasing to 8.25 million in 1910. In construction, 1.64 million were employed in 1900, increasing to 2.31 million in 1910. Two million were employed in transportation in 1900, which increased to 3.2 million by 1910. The number employed in trade increased from 2.87 million in 1900 to 3.62 million in 1910 (Cashman, 1988). Indeed, a well-known Boston civic association proclaimed that each human being should be regarded as "a matter of profit and value," and that each child born was a "machine begun" (quoted in Vale, 2000). Adult and child immigrants performed much of this labor. Overall, immigrants accounted for 14 percent of the population between 1900 and 1910, but comprised 25 percent of the labor force.

Immigration

In 1789, Jedidiah Morse coined the term "immigrant" to describe the foreigners that were settling in New York (Cashman, 1988). The period most associated with the "huddled masses," however, would come much later: Between 1890 and 1917, a total of 17,991,486 immigrants came to the United States. Upon arriving, these immigrants generally moved to the industrial Northeast—New York, Massachusetts, Pennsylvania, and Illinois in particular (ibid.; see Table 5-1). More than one million immigrants arrived successively in 1905, 1906, 1907, 1910, 1913, and 1914. They came from Norway, Italy, Germany, Russia, the Mediterranean, Poland, Hungary, Ireland, Ukraine, and Canada, among a few. In 1910, almost 80 percent of New York's population consisted of the foreign-born and their children.

Their reasons for coming to America were no different from those of earlier immigrants. They sought religious and political asylum as well as economic opportunity. The hysteria over coming to the United States

Table 5-1
Immigration to the United States, 1890–1917

Origins	Number	Percentage
Central Europe	4,879,000	27.1
Southern Europe	4,369,000	24.3
Northwest Europe	3,637,000	20.2
Eastern Europe	3,328,000	18.5
Canada and Newfoundland	744,000	4.14
Central and South America	473,000	2.63
Asia	468,000	0.13
Australia and New Zealand	23,500	0.08
Pacific Islands	3,500	0.02

Source: Cashman (1988).

was best captured by Russian immigrant Mary Antin in her memoirs entitled, *From Plotzk to Boston:*

> America was in everybody's mouth. Businessmen talked of it over their accounts; the market women made up their quarrels that they might discuss it from stall to stall; people who had relatives in the famous land went around reading their letters for the enlightenment of less fortunate folk. . . . Children played at emigrating; old folks shook their sage heads over the evening fire and prophesied no good for those who braved the terrors of the sea and the foreign goal beyond it; all talked of it, but scarcely anyone knew one true fact about this magic land (quoted in Cashman, 1988: 153).

From the perspective of Americans descended from British colonists, the new immigrants came speaking "strange" languages, wearing "strange costumes," and engaging in "strange" customs (ibid.). The city was a showcase of intermingling and diverse cultures, but also became a growing overcrowded slum and public health nightmare. The established elite feared this burgeoning immigrant class that "lived stooped in tiny attics" (Vale, 2000). It was at this time that Andrew Carnegie began his project of building more than 1650 public libraries across the country in a campaign to ensure the "education and improvement of the poorer classes" (Marcus, 1999) In his estimation, the immigrants thought little of moral and intellectual culture (ibid.).

Urbanization

The combination of industrialization and immigration produced a city life and degree of urbanization that was both imposing and menacing. Cities were the most dynamic part of the nation by the turn of the twentieth century (Unger and Unger, 1977). The tremendous growth in city life already begun in the mid-nineteenth century accelerated and became far more concentrated at the turn of the twentieth century. For example, between 1890 and 1920, Brooklyn grew from 2.5 million to 5.6 million residents. At the same time, Chicago's population expanded from 1 million to 2.7 million, and Philadelphia's population increased from 1 million to 1.8 million. Los Angeles and Detroit experienced even greater increases, as their populations swelled from 205,000 to 994,000 and 50,000 to 577,000, respectively.

The city was a powerful magnet for all Americans (ibid.). It offered a variety of jobs, including typists, school teachers, accountants, lawyers, unskilled factory workers, and journalists. Yet, cities were also alienating and intimidating places. Despite the swirling activity and masses of people, their vastness bred a sense of loneliness. Sociologist Emile Durkheim described the sense of isolation and detachment experienced by so many as anomie. Crime, high suicide rates, broken homes, prostitution, and alcoholism were some of the manifestations of this anomie (or normlessness) and were increasingly familiar features of city life. In 1893, one journalist described the slums (or tenement districts) within the city as "reservoirs of physical and moral death" (quoted in Vale, 2000). For many, the city seemed almost inhumane and unlivable. The numerous charitable associations and volunteer organizations alone could not effectively combat these social ills, especially unemployment. Coping with unemployment in the late nineteenth and early twentieth century was primarily a private burden that was shared with family, friends, and neighbors (Vale, 2000).

The perilous conditions of the city prompted two developments that were at the heart of the progressive movement's insistence at and success in mobilizing government intervention: exposé journalism and settlement houses. The journalists of the day were determined to do more than simply record the events of the big city. They also researched controversial, disturbing, and sensational topics that would attract and captivate readers. Soon, a group of editors, novelists, and essayists—known as muckrakers—spotlighted the many wrongdoings and dark corners of social, economic, and political life. For example, in his book *Civilization's Inferno* (1893), journal editor Benjamin Flower traced the vast polarization of wealth to landlords and tax policies that favored the rich and overlooked the poor. He wrote of the poor that, "Over their heads perpetually rests the dread of eviction, of sickness, and of failure to obtain employment, making existence a perpetual nightmare, from which death alone brings release" (quoted in Vale, 2000: 68).

Journalistic attacks on the corporate community began to escalate in 1903 under publishing mogul William Randolph Hearst. He promoted the practice of exposé (or muckraking) journalism, which documented the dealings of those in power. Exposé journalists paraded before the public the social injustices, economic dangers, and political corruption that affected everyone but the most powerful (Unger and Unger, 1977). Article after article was devoted to the shady and harmful misdeeds of the medicine patent business, the stock market, Standard Oil, local government, and the beef industry (Cashman, 1988). Upton Sinclair's novel, *The Jungle* (1906), represents one of the better-known examples of this critical journalistic writing. Sinclair described in detail the exploitation of workers and the deplorable conditions of the meatpacking industry.

Journalistic commentaries advocated strong government and "radical economic changes" to improve the quality of national life in general and the lives of the poor in particular (Flower, 1893). A collaboration of universities, churches, and philanthropists sought to enact this change by forming what was known as the settlement house (or settlement idea). Led by Jane Addams and others in Chicago and Robert A. Woods in Boston, settlement houses took on the "enemies" of the modern city. These enemies included "unsanitary housing, poisonous sewage, contaminated water, infant mortality, the spread of contagion, adulterated food, impure milk, smoke-laden air, ill-ventilated factories, dangerous occupations, juvenile crime, unwholesome crowding, prostitution, and drunkenness" (quoted in Vale, 200: 72). Settlement houses were located in the slum districts of thirty-six states and were occupied by those who functioned as both anthropologists and civic activists. In these service-center social laboratories, advocates sought to serve the urban poor and immigrants, while instilling in them middle-class norms and values. Settlement house advocates documented the ill effects of industrialization and urbanization and used this data to influence public policy. They fought for workers' compensation, consumer protection, child labor laws, clean water, honest government, tenement regulation, equal opportunity for blacks and immigrants, and improved recreational and educational opportunities (ibid.). In seeking to study the conditions of neighborhoods, districts, and cities, the settlement mission inevitably overlapped with the emerging ideas about criminal behavior and penal policy.

Crime and Positivism

It has been said that how we govern ourselves is related to how we govern crime (Garland, 1998). Perhaps nowhere is this axiom more evident than in the era of progressivism. One of the basic tenets of progressivism is that scientific knowledge enables the government to master seemingly untamable social forces (Diner, 1998). This belief extends not just to the hard sciences and industry, but also to the social sciences and human behavior. Progressive scientific knowledge produced several theories that were expected to quell the force of crime in society. Psychological, biological, and sociological perspectives coexisted with varying degrees of popularity and policy impact.

As the ideas of Sigmund Freud gained notoriety, psychological explanations of criminal behavior were entertained as well. The common thread among various psychological explanations of behavior is that criminality or deviant behavior in general can be attributed to various mental and subconscious conflicts (Healy, 1915). William Healy argued that "all conduct is directly an expression of mental life" and that behind every action is "the idea, the wish, or the impulse existing as mental content." In effect, humankind was not driven entirely by rational and purposeful calculation; irrational and hidden desires were equally—if not more—powerful determinants of human behavior. Though sometimes nebulous and vague in their assertions, psychological interpretations won many enthusiastic supporters. The language of psychiatry merged well with the increasingly fashionable and respected language of science. It was perhaps also believed that the habits of mind were easier to fix than hardened slums or predetermined biological defects (Rothman, 1980).

Under the direct influence of Italian criminologist Cesare Lombroso and indirect influence of naturalist Charles Darwin, the notion of inferior or degenerative criminal classes was popularized in certain academic and policy circles. Biological explanations held that criminals are born, thus constituting a less evolved class of human species. Drawing upon such evidence as physical appearance (e.g., jawbone shape, head size) and the prevalence of criminal behavior across generations of families (Dugdale, [1877] 1979; Goddard, 1912, 1914, 1915), it was concluded that criminality is an inherited or congenital condition (for a modern discussion of anthropological and biological perspectives see Baron, 1977; Ellis and Hoffman, 1990; Fishbein, 1990; Mednick, 1987; Rowe and Osgood, 1984.) In fact, the topic of the 1888 meeting of the New York Academy of Anthropology was the "Relation of the Physical to the

Mental Constitution in Criminals." With full confidence and assurance in scientific achievement, one meeting participant declared that future study "will demonstrate that it is possible to classify by well-defined physical and mental characteristics those persons who commit crimes against the person and those whose offences relate to property" (Butts, 1888).

Since biological theories espouse that criminal genes are inherited, they also hold that an expedient and humane way of eliminating the "idiotic and feeble-minded" (Barnes, 1972) is to sterilize its members. This belief provided the foundation for the Eugenics Movement, also known as Social Darwinism. Eugenicists advocated policies that deny procreation rights to certain individuals and groups. By declaring nine hereditary diseases to be illegal, hereditary health courts staffed by physicians aided in the screening process. The Vermont Eugenics Survey had a similar purpose. This twelve-year project was designed by social scientists of the day to identify and study "good" and "bad" families and then eliminate those listed as bad ("Vermont," 1999). The final report was circulated among policy makers, leading to the passage of Vermont's sterilization law in 1931, which resulted in the sterilization of several hundred poor rural Vermonters, Abenaki Indians, and others deemed unfit to procreate.

Not surprisingly, sterilization practices were applied to offenders, especially those of immigrant background. Following the precedent of Indiana in 1907, twenty-three states legalized the sterilization of the "hopelessly defective and the habitually criminal groups" (Barnes, 1972). By 1930, thirteen of those states—California, Delaware, Idaho, Maine, Minnesota, Montana, Nebraska, New Hampshire, North Dakota, Oregon, Utah, Virginia, and Wisconsin—had formally active sterilization laws. Having sterilized more than five thousand offenders, California was by far the most active in its use of such laws; no other state approached even five hundred. Although sterilization laws were challenged as unconstitutional, they were ultimately upheld by the U.S. Supreme Court in the case of *Carrie Buck v. Virginia* (Barnes, 1972). The radical policies of eugenicists were not embraced by all experts and reformers, however. For example, in an article touting the El Mira Reformatory, Ausburn Tower (1886) argued that eminent physicians were in agreement about the fact that a "tendency to crime is like insanity, and deserves treatment like any other disease." It is "inherited and inheritable like any other family idiosyncracy [*sic*]."

Mainstream approaches to crime, such as the reformatory and other upward-mobility policies that addressed social-structural inequities, were supported by a number of reformers as well. These policies were fueled largely by sociological explanations of crime that had their formative beginnings in the documentation of the conditions under which new immigrants lived and worked. A description of these conditions read that

> When, in certain parts of Boston and New York, 1,200 people are crowded on an acre, it is difficult to individualize one's immediate neighbors sufficiently to be on human terms with any considerable portion of them. These non-individuated neighbors comprised a mass public of "nomadic factory hands who form no neighborhood ties, join no neighborhood associations, and involve themselves in no effort for community betterment" (quoted in Vale, 2000: 73).

Against this backdrop of what would later be termed "social disorganization," it was quite conceivable that poverty, low wages, disease, overcrowded living arrangements, and unemployment could drive anyone to crime. In 1900, 5 percent of the population owned nearly half of the property, while more than one third of the nation's 76 million residents existed below the poverty level (Bok, 1992). Robert Hunter's observations of the inner city in the book *Poverty: Social Conscience in the Progressive Era* ([1904] 1965) brought this line of reasoning into focus. He argued that the poor largely are not immoral individuals who rebuked the virtues of work and thrift; rather, they are simply the overworked and underpaid victims of capitalism's robber barons, and their plight is due to a "poverty of opportunity"—an explanation developed later by sociologist Robert Merton.

When investigating the causes of crime, these men of social and behavioral science and progressive ideology sought to intervene rather than to assign moral blame. Though quite dissimilar in their assumptions, psychological, biological, and sociological perspectives comfortably coexisted because a penal system dedicated to rehabilitating each offender according to their unique and aberrant circumstances demands flexibility of thought. Each perspective was therefore consistent with the fundamental premise of progressive penology: "Disease is controllable, remediable; so is crime. Disease may be prevented; so may crime. Disease must be wisely, humanely, untiringly managed; so must crime" ("Prison Reform," 1872: 379).

Promise of Progressive Penology

The tenets of progressive penology were articulated formally during the 1870 National Congress on Penitentiary and Reformatory Discipline in Cincinnati. At this conference, penal reform advocates Enoch

Wines, Franklin Sanborn, and Zebulon Brockway were committed to revising the penal system that they alleged was outright ineffective. In their view, the use of isolation, lockstep marching, and striped uniforms debilitated one's manhood. Brockway further argued that the existing system of pure punishment and retribution failed to reform, not only because of its reliance on the fixed sentence, but also because it was founded upon a "mystic morality." One could neither see nor measure motives and morals, and yet the philosophy of deterrence assumes that free will is based on (rational) motives that can be affected through certain, swift, and harsh punishment (Brockway, 1997). Brockway argued that criminals do not make the essential cause-and-effect link between crime and punishment, largely because most offenders do not believe themselves to be guilty of any crime. He further dismissed Classical assumptions on the grounds of the brutalizing effects of increased penal severity, as well as for the incapacity of society to calibrate correctly its cost–benefit calculus to differing penal severities.

With these criticisms in mind, the conference leaders crafted what has become known as the Declaration of Principles (Barnes, 1972). It is reported that these thirty-seven principles were so highly regarded that they took on the aura of a sacred creed for decades to come. The sum of these principles was the promotion of individualized care and the scientific treatment of offenders based upon a medical model (ibid.). Whereas deterrence strategies focus on the nature of the offense, progressive strategies would focus on the nature of the offender. Consequently, variously motivated offenders were to be individually treated. In the same way that medical doctors obtained the medical histories of their patients, "behavioral" doctors were to obtain the *life* histories of their "patients." It was believed that "more comprehension of the case leads to more comprehensive modes of managing it" ("Prison Reform," 1872: 380). Zebulon Brockway, then superintendent of the Detroit House of Correction, championed this approach, stating that "to treat a prisoner as a patient, to study his symptoms and make the applications they require, to punish him for what demands punishment, to teach him, to reform him, to raise him, and to cure him—these are all parts of a system which has any promise of success" (ibid.). These component parts came together through the gradual establishment of the reformatory, indeterminate sentence, parole, and probation.

Reformatories

One of the specific recommendations of the 1870 conference was the establishment of adult reformatories. These reformatories—in conjunction with the indeterminate sentence, a mark/classification system, intensive academic and vocational instruction, constructive labor, humane disciplinary methods, gain time, and parole—were to give the institution an altogether "different prison procedure."

The model for this new institution was the Elmira Reformatory, which opened in 1876 in New York. New York was the first of many states to implement the concept of an adult reformatory, and was subsequently followed by Michigan in 1877, Massachusetts in 1884, Pennsylvania and Minnesota in 1889, Colorado in 1890, Illinois in 1891, and Kansas in 1895; Ohio, Indiana, and Wisconsin implemented their systems in 1895, 1896, and 1899, respectively (Pisciotta, 1994). These reformatories were to be patterned after Elmira, but not all states followed New York's example precisely. For instance, there were state-by-state variations in eligibility criteria (e.g., age, offense) and in daily offender routines. Michigan proved to be the exception on all counts by adhering to an expressly punitive philosophy and a lease-for-profit labor system.

Reformatories were envisioned as laboratories for a new scientific method of dealing with offenders. In these proposed "prison science" laboratories, offenders were not to be referred to as "prisoners" or "convicts," but instead as "inmates," known by their name and not a number (Towner, 1886). This change of status, so to speak, was intended to "build up the individuality and responsibility of the new character being formed" (Towner, 1886). Generally, these inmates were expected to be between the ages of 16 and 30, convicted of a felony, and to have never before spent time in a prison. The prison science that was to govern the process of changing offenders was to depend upon knowledge acquired through scientific methods—not the charity of philanthropists and ministers. At Elmira, in particular, staff systematically "compiled all the information that it was possible to gather" in "great books as large as the ledgers of a counting-house" ("The Elmira Reformatory," 1885: 486). Staff at Elmira also employed a vocabulary that was part medical and part educational. Consequently, inmates were referred to as students or patients. Indeed, Elmira often was dubbed the "college on the hill" or the "reformatory hospital."

Because the reformatory was tied to the new biological, social, and psychological sciences, the regimen of the reformatory was to be organized around principles that were measurable. For example, if the sentence was for a fixed term, the system would rely on the potential for early release and, if not, an indeterminate sentence structure. Either system would instill in offenders a self-regulated discipline because release dates were to be based on visible proof of reformation. Once satisfactory progress had been demonstrated, the offender would be released to enter into a period of community supervision known as parole. Meanwhile, daily life and activities in the reformatory were to consist of paid work, job training, schooling, physical exercise, and a well-planned diet. This schedule reflected the adage that good habits of mind were best developed through good habits of the body.

The most celebrated feature of the reformatory was its classification/grading system. This system served the purpose of gauging whether an offender was on the road to reform. "Students" were to be evaluated according to three factors; namely, participation and performance in work (vocational) and in school (educational), as well as compliance with rules. Three grades or levels existed, with all offenders beginning their term of confinement in the second grade. In the second grade, the inmate bore no distinguishing marks, such as a uniform, and was required to work eight hours every day and dine in his or her cell (Towner, 1886). However, inmates at Elmira were not permitted to stay in the intermediate or second grade under any circumstances. The purpose of this rule was to instill a sense of upward mobility and to teach that "rising or falling depends upon oneself" ("The Elmira Reformatory," 1885). Movement between the three grades depended on one's performance in each of these areas. At Elmira for example, if the offender conformed to the rules for at least six months, he could move up to the first grade. This afforded such privileges as comfortable light blue uniforms, larger cells, spring mattresses, daily writing allowances, extended library and bedtime hours, and better dining room conditions and food. Demotion to the third grade, however, brought all the "rigors and hardships of a penitentiary" (Towner, 1886); inmates were clothed in coarse red uniforms, engaged in lockstep marching, and denied mail, library, and visitation privileges (ibid.).

Though work had always been a salient aspect of the incarceration experience, the value and meaning of work in the reformatory was different than in the penitentiary system. Although no talking was to be permitted, the men in the reformatory were allowed to "use their eyes as they choose" (Towner, 1886). The work regimen in the reformatory also included payment that was intended primarily to instill a morality of industriousness, or the formation of a new social habit. As Simon (1993:

29) noted, "Work was no longer aimed at facilitating an independent process of moral reformation, but an opportunity to subject offenders to the discipline of industrial labor." The following statement issued by Brockway illustrates this point. He argued that the "purpose of imprisonment and of treatment is to prepare such for industry, to train and transfer them from economic worthlessness to worthfulness" (Brockway, 1997). A quotation from the Report of the Special Committee to the Prison Association of New York on Convict Labor by the California Penological Commission in 1887 further emphasizes the purpose of work in prison and, more broadly, in society:

> Industrial labor is not only the most powerful agency of reformation; it is the indispensable instrument, without aid of which reformatory results are wholly unattainable, industry is the essential prerequisite of healthy life and progress in all human society; and to such a degree that any community deprived of productive labor must quickly lapse into moral corruption and decay (quoted in Simon, 1993: 28).

Indeterminate Sentencing and Parole

In addition to the establishment of reformatories, a second outgrowth of the 1870 Cincinnati conference was the indeterminate sentence. The indeterminate sentence was introduced at the Elmira Reformatory where it was believed that the "entire discipline of the institution rested upon the indeterminate character of the sentence" ("The Elmira Reformatory," 1885). The indeterminate sentence was replicated throughout the United States in the last quarter of the nineteenth century such that, by 1910, nearly every adult reformatory used an indeterminate sentencing structure (Pisciotta, 1994; Barnes, 1972). By 1915, twenty-six states had indeterminate sentencing laws and, by 1923, almost half of all offenders admitted to U.S. prisons were sentenced under the indeterminate sentencing structure (Rothman, 1980).

Whereas the determinate sentence is tied to the nature of the offense and thus treats offenders with more of a one-size-fits-all approach, the indeterminate sentence allows for adjustments based on the evolving progress of the individual offender. Courts were not to fix or limit the duration of the sentence as offenders (theoretically) held the keys to their own release. Brockway aptly noted that "captivity is always irksome," but "the indeterminateness of the sentence breeds discontent, purposefulness, and prompts to new exertion" (Brockway, 1997). It was in the offender's own best interest to improve his behavior, giving rise to the then-popular maxim "be cured or be kept" (Miller, 1980).

The typical sentence was a minimum of one year without a specified maximum. At the conclusion of the minimum sentence, a prison board would determine an offender's release date. Readiness for release was to be determined by the number of credits gained or lost within the reformatory institution, but it did not depend on institutional conduct alone. The factors that could affect release also included the social influences relevant to the offender's "constitutional and acquired defects and tendencies" (quoted in Friedman, 1993). Thus, the parole board was to be furnished with information about the offender's habits, activities, associations, and reputation. Altogether, they considered the offense of conviction, offense history, institutional conduct, work record, academic progress, attitude, and future plans. These items of information were considered essential for determining the perceived risk of recidivism. It should be noted, however, that the notions of indeterminateness and demonstration of reform as requisites for release never were taken to their absolute extreme: Few, if any, offenders remained in prison until their natural death solely because reform had not yet been demonstrated.

Parole made the indeterminate sentence a more attractive feature to public officials. However, the concept of release for good behavior was not entirely new. Different versions of early release such as "gain time" or "good time," already had been in place since 1850 when they were used as alternatives to corporal punishment to motivate offenders who were not willing to work as expected. By 1890, thirty-eight states had enacted gain time laws, increasing to forty-six states by 1910. If no disciplinary infractions were accumulated, an inmate could expect to serve approximately one half to one third of his or her sentence (Miller, 1980).

What distinguished parole from gain time laws, however, was the expressed intent of extending the reformative process into the community through a period of close supervision. The promise of offender supervision upon release provided officials with a measure of comfort in the face of potential public outcry over crime rates and early release in general. Specifically, the idea of improving the reformation process via the community helped to cement the appeal of parole (Simon, 1993). Offender supervision would be exercised by parole officers who were expected to be policeman, detectives, social workers, psychiatrists, work supervisors, and judges all at once. Parole officers, not unlike probation officers, were to be the students of the new social sciences and specially trained for the task of reforming offenders. Officers were to be model citizens, capable of continuing the reform process that presumably had begun in the institution.

Though the complementary strategies of parole and the indeterminate sentencing were first introduced together in the Elmira Reformatory, parole soon developed independently across the United States. By 1900, every reformatory had parole, and twenty states had parole laws for institutions other than the reformatory—namely prisons and penitentiaries. By 1910, forty-one states had parole laws in place. By 1922, parole was used in forty-four states and the indeterminate sentence was used in thirty-seven states (U.S. Department of Justice, 2003). By 1923, half of all prison releasees in the United States were under a system of parole (Rothman, 1980).

Probation

Though probation emerged during the Progressive Era, its implementation and operation were not linked to the reformatory, as was the case initially with the indeterminate sentence and parole. The rationale for probation, however, was still consistent with overall desire to differentiate and treat offenders. The practice of probation was inspired, in part, by the efforts of a Boston shoemaker named John Augustus. Augustus voluntarily posted bail and served as a guardian to approximately two thousand offenders. The courts charged Augustus thirty dollars' bail for thirty days' suspension of sentence, and then reduced the charge to one cent and court costs if the probationer did not reoffend. At the time of Augustus's death in 1859, he had bailed (though not necessarily served as guardian for) 1152 men, 794 women, and about 3000 girls (Duffee, 1989).

Boston institutionalized the practice in 1878 by implementing a paid probation officer system. In 1891, a second Massachusetts statute authorized a statewide probation system (Friedman, 1993). Several states (such as New York, New Jersey, Michigan, Illinois, Pennsylvania, Maryland, Vermont, Rhode Island, and California) followed the lead of Massachusetts by implementing their own probationary systems (Barnes, 1972). By 1930, the federal government and approximately thirty-six states and Washington, D.C., had legislation that enabled the practice of probation (Rothman, 1980). However, only nineteen states actually used probation on a routine basis (Barnes, 1972). At the outset, probation was primarily an urban phenomenon, as all major industrialized states and every major industrialized city used probation regularly. In more rural states, such as Texas, Kentucky, Tennessee, the Dakotas, Nevada, and Wyoming (Rothman, 1980), probation rarely was employed as a sanction option.

Unlike parole, probation was designed as a dispositional sentencing alternative to incarceration. It was intended to be a suspended sentence for those who did not need confinement to be reformed. To determine suitability for probation, probation officers were given the task of conducting pre-sentence investigations. Ultimately, these investigations were to assist judges in sentencing decisions. Pre-sentence investigations, much like the investigations of the parole board, were to uncover every significant detail of the offender's life. They were to examine the personal history (vital statistics, place of birth, residence, education, immigrant status), childhood experiences (truancy record, injuries, early associates, habits of indulgence, grudges, ambitions, parental control), family, (grandparents and sibling information, including education and causes of death), neighborhood and home situation (economic status, number of boarders, moral condition) and personality of the offender (ibid.). Equipped with this extensive knowledge of the offender, probation officers were expected to identify the cause or source of the offender's problem and recommend an appropriate sentence and treatment.

In their supervisory capacity, probation officers—like parole officers—were to be all things at once, ranging from policeman, friend, and social worker to human behavior expert. Presumably having been educated and trained in the social sciences, probation officers were to be gatherers of facts and capable of converting those facts into an individually tailored treatment plan. This plan was to include not only contacts with the offender, but contacts with the offender's family, community, and employer. The officers were to become immersed in the life of their probationers so that they could mold offenders into "normal" and productive citizens. Consequently, it was anticipated that officers would maintain small caseloads of approximately fifty offenders (ibid.). Mary Richmond's book, *Social Diagnosis* (1917), provided this new group of criminal justice professionals with an occupational handbook of sorts to guide them in their supervision efforts.

Progressive Penology in Practice

Reformatories

Although the intentions behind the reformatory were admirable, they were not always met in practice for a variety of reasons—administrative, political, financial, and human. An article appearing in an 1881 issue of the *National Police Gazette* harshly condemned the states, managers, and correctional officers that were privy, yet indifferent, to the "numerous complaints regarding the management of prisons, reformatories and other place of detention and punishment" ("Prison Abuses," 1881). The article alleged that "those who have been placed in charge of these institutions would seem to be of that class who lack the faculty of discriminating between punishment and abuse" (ibid.). The article further reported:

> In the light of recent revelations regarding the management of reformatory institutions, the conclusion is logical that those in charge of them entertain contrary views and practice them in a manner which is a disgrace to civilization, to say nothing of the different states which tolerate the continuance of such a system (p. 2).

The article even assailed those charged with investigating abuse: "Appointing committees of investigation will not avail. This plan of reform has been tried so often, and has proven so farcical in every case that the people are disgusted with it. Politics and politicians should have no hand in the appointment of managers of reformatory institutions" (p. 2).

The various abuses that took place in the reformatory institutions were perhaps best documented by contemporary criminologist Alexander Pisciotta. In his book, *Benevolent Repression: Social Control and the American Reformatory Prison Movement* (1994), he detailed the findings from external investigations conducted of Elmira in 1893, Colorado in 1895, and Pennsylvania in 1892. He concluded that the reformatory offered little more than scientific jargon and justification for practices that were neither new nor humane.

Pisciotta found that at Elmira and various other "sister" reformatories, overcrowding, understaffing, and gross mismanagement were the rule rather than the exception. The offender population that was housed in reformatories was not as intended either. Designed for youthful offenders just beginning their criminal careers, reformatories actually housed the same seasoned criminals found in regular prisons and penitentiaries. In effect, they housed the classified poor, "illiterate," or ethnically "inferior degenerates" feared by middle-class reformers, sociologists, eugenicists, and bio-statisticians (Miller, 1980). Enoch Wines himself reported that blacks went to prison more often than whites for similar offenses and for longer terms (Wines, 1888). The highly regarded classification and treatment scheme, moreover, was marred by violence, revolts, smuggling, arson, and homosexuality. Inmate disobedience was indeed a severe problem that incurred severe penalties. The nickname given to the leader of the reformatory movement, "Paddler Brockway," clearly is suggestive of the tactics employed within the walls of the reformatories.

Brockway's command of public relations masked the corporal punishments he administered on a routine basis. In short, brutality was carried out and justified in the name of "prison science" and rehabilitation (Pisciotta, 1994). Euphemisms, such as "spanking of patients," "positive extraneous assistance," or "harmless parental discipline," essentially gave scientific credibility to beatings and cruelty (ibid.). Beatings were administered in "interview" rooms, using a twenty-two by three-inch-wide leather strap that weighed more than one pound when wet. The strap beatings were applied to the bare buttocks; however, no part of the body—not kidneys, eyes, nor face—were spared from hands-on beatings. Inmates and chaplains alike testified that offenders would reemerge with missing teeth and purple bodies (ibid.). T.B. Patton, superintendent of the Pennsylvania Reformatory, employed similar disciplinary measures. However, in his public characterizations of these beatings as "punishment rituals" he was perhaps not as clever or discreet as Brockway.

Corporal punishments were not the only methods of disciplining inmates in the Elmira Reformatory. Solitary confinement was utilized for those who were not reformed by "spankings." Solitary confinement, or what Brockway termed "rest cure," could be as physically impairing as the direct beatings. For days and sometimes months at a time, inmates would survive on nothing more than bread and water. While in confinement, inmates could be shackled to a sliding ring on a bar or to the floor for hours at a time. Depending upon which device they were shackled to, inmates either were prevented from standing upright or were forced to keep their hands above their heads. With no window openings or illumination and little ventilation, offenders were surrounded by the stench of their urination and defecation (ibid.).

More subtle forms of intimidation also were exercised in the reformatory. Brockway was known to have regularly engaged in verbal attacks, either personally or through threatening notes. For example, in one note, Brockway wrote: "Ide, are you either a lunatic or a jackass? If the former, you should be sent to an asylum, if the latter, you should be knocked on the head; and if you don't improve your record, whatever you may be, I will knock you on the other end" (quoted in ibid.: 40). On many occasions, Brockway warned inmates who could not endure the military drills or solitary confinement that he would either kill them or send them out in a box. Altogether, it was discovered that Brockway administered 19,497 blows to 2,578 inmates between October 1888 and September 1893. In 1889, the number of inmates paddled was 261, increasing incrementally to 681 by 1893. During this same period, inmates spent 7,609 days in "rest cure" cells and 18,681 notices and warnings were issued (Pisciotta, 1994).

The inability of the reformatory system to dispense with inhumane treatment regardless of the prospect of parole was not the only example of ineffectiveness. For the most part, the plan to treat offenders based on classifications informed by offender histories fell short. In the Colorado reformatory, inmates were neither classified nor separated. The sick were housed with the healthy and the young with the old. School programs were without essential supplies (e.g., books) and the economic incentive work program was undermined as well. For example, inmates may have earned forty cents a day, but they paid thirty-two cents for room and board in addition to paying to see the doctor and dentist. They also could be fined approximately sixty cents for rule infractions. Consequently, with no money to spare because of payment allocated to basic necessities, offenders would accrue written reprimands for failure to pay fines. This resulted in the offender being demoted to the third grade which, in turn, jeopardized their prospects of early release.

Indeterminate Sentencing and Parole

The rationale for indeterminate sentencing and parole may have been rooted in the laudable goals of reform, training, and second chances. However, in the day-to-day application of these reforms, the original vision was often distorted or lost. For instance, the use of fixed sentences without guidelines, which was the general practice, allowed for sentencing disparities. It was hoped that parole boards would release offenders in a consistent way through the use of indeterminate sentences, thus reducing the likelihood of disparities. Predictably, however, indeterminate sentences without guidelines fueled sentencing disparities, with offenders of identical legal status still serving sentences of different lengths. Wardens, furthermore, used such disparities and resultant uncertainty as methods for gaining control over potentially unruly inmates. In this regard, the threat of denied early release or parole served the needs of institutional control. In addition, indeterminate sentencing and parole also combined to serve the administrative functions of relieving prison overcrowding and inmate idleness (Miller, 1980; Simon, 1993). Yet private sector contracts and the inmate leasing system drew considerable opposition from civilian labor groups, occupying inmates with meaningful work became extremely difficult.

The process of early release to parole was flawed in a number of other important respects. The decision to release was not determined by a panel of behavioral experts as had been anticipated by reform visionaries. Rather, parole board members consisted primarily of other state officials, friends of politicians, and/or individuals with no relevant qualifications (Rothman, 1980). Moreover, those charged with the task of making such decisions had little or no time to conduct proper inquiries into the offender's achievements or failures while incarcerated. The boards met a few times a year, during which time they were to determine the fates of several hundred offenders. In fact, as Rothman (1980) and Pisciotta (1994) noted, the process of determining release typically lasted no more than three to five minutes. During those few minutes, there were no formal parole guidelines to follow. Legal factors associated with the case typically were recounted, along with questions seeking to elicit verbal assurances of good behavior from the offender. Questions of this nature included: "What would you do if released?" and "Are you through with drinking?" (Rothman, 1980). The physical appearance of the offender could also be taken into consideration. Was the offender well built, neat, or unkempt? Readiness for release was particularly influenced by whether the potential parolee had secured a job or a job sponsor (Simon, 1993) and a place of residence (Pisciotta, 1994). However, the requirement of retaining a job or job sponsor was greatly relaxed, given the need to expedite releases due to overcrowding.

While such release practices resolved the managerial and fiscal demands of institutions, they were rather unresponsive to public demands and the promise of continued reformation upon release. Parole supervision had little to offer the offender in the way of rehabilitation and little to offer the public in the way of safety. Speaking to the issue of parole in 1930, Barnes contended that the only good to come from parole was that it got men out of prison sooner (Barnes, 1972). Barnes claimed that parole was nothing but a "palpable paper parole, which neither provided supervision nor encouragement to reform." Work was the primary element of the supervision process, and it undoubtedly was the most important one. This did not mean that other aspects of reintegration were unimportant; they were just secondary to the focus on work. For example, parolees were to adhere to four basic rules or conditions: (1) remain employed; (2) submit monthly reports signed by their employer; (3) not quit or change jobs; and (4) in all respects, conduct oneself with honesty, sobriety, and decency, avoiding low or evil associations, and abstain from intoxicating drinks (Pisciotta, 1994). Hans von Hentig observed the irony in this latter condition by noting that, "In complying strictly with every one of these conditions, the parolee would at once draw the attention of his neighbors to his being either a crank or a convict who has been released on parole" (von Hentig, 1942: 364; also quoted in Simon, 1993: 57). In other words, how did one who came from a lower-class community—where the criminal element was most likely to reside—stay aloof from those who were of low associations? Consequently, parole violations and revocations were frequent and easy to justify. Offenders had little or no recourse for contesting these violations and revocations, as lawyers were not permitted at parole hearings; the offender could submit only documents in his defense.

Probation

The practice of probation fared no better in meeting the ambitious objectives of the progressive agenda. Relative to its intentions, probation failed from the outset. Probation officer positions, like parole officer positions, were not occupied by those trained in the social sciences. Probation officers were to be selected from the ranks of the new college graduates, but instead were selected from volunteers, political supporters of judges, state attorney and police personnel, and various other individuals lacking the credentials for changing the lives and habits of offenders. Nor were the working conditions of probation officers likely to attract college graduates. Salaries, which ranged between $900 and $2,500 dollars per year, were low compared to the average $1,200 per year salary for the unskilled factory worker (Rothman, 1980). The work environment served as an added disincentive, as officers were thrown together in one room where noise and crowding served as constant distractions. Overwhelming caseloads only contributed to the likely frustration. Historical documents show that in Newark, New Jersey, thirty-seven probation officers were responsible for 5,800 cases, amounting to approximately 150 cases per officer. In Milwaukee, three officers were charged with the supervision of 839 offenders, yielding a caseload of nearly 280 offenders (ibid.).

The ability of probation officers to provide informed decisions to judges and supervision to offenders was predictably impeded by these working conditions. Consequently, pre-sentence investigations were comprised of a few facts and much speculation and were described as "dossiers of gossip" (ibid.) rather than scientifically based reports. In "watching over the offender" (ibid.), probation officers fared no better than their parole counterparts. Personal contact with offenders was rare and, in some jurisdictions, amounted to no more than ten minutes a year (ibid.). Probation officers had little opportunity to "know" their probationers by becoming familiar with their life, family, work, and community environment. Supervision regimens ultimately dissolved into the nominal ritual of collecting monthly reports.

Probation also defaulted on its most basic function as an alternative to prison. Though probation was conceived as an alternative to state imprisonment, this locally funded program generally was implemented as an alternative to local jail sentences, or nothing. This outcome is not surprising when one considers that states required local jurisdictions to absorb the costs of supervising state-remanded offenders. In response, local jurisdictions simply complied with the state mandate to use probation, but did so in a way that served their fiscal needs (ibid.). Very importantly, it was with this misapplication of probation that the pattern of implementing alternatives to incarceration as supplements began.

Progressivism and Individual Treatment

Progressivism sought to address the disturbances associated with massive immigration, industrialization, and urbanization. As a social movement, progressivism enlisted citizens from all walks of life for the purpose of safeguarding the quality of American culture and society. It attracted maverick journalists, college student idealists, opportunists, men, women, and the middle class, in an all-out effort to expose the deceit and corruption of politicians and corporate capitalism (Unger and Unger, 1977). As a result of these collective efforts, it was proposed that government and science were best equipped to improve and correct society.

It was out of this context of social, economic, and government engineering that an ambitious penal reform agenda was conceived. Prompted by the failures of the existing system—and shaped by a progressive social context and theories of the scientific community—the reformatory, indeterminate sentencing, parole, and probation emerged. What these reforms share in common is the formal intent to investigate, classify, and then treat each offender according to his or her individual biological, psychological, and sociological circumstances. However, the promise and the reality of these monumental reforms diverged considerably. The simple premise of the reformatory, indeterminate sentencing, and parole was that confinement ought to continue until reformation was demonstrated and that, for young salvageable offenders, a second chance should be afforded. However, the reformatory fell short of providing humane and effective methods of social re-education. Meanwhile, parole was rendered a mere mechanism to ease prison overcrowding and to extend the control of the institution into the community, while probation was conceived as an alternative to incarceration but acted as a supplement in practice, thereby expanding control over populations previously not subject to incarceration.

Overall, progressive penology failed in the eyes of its designers, even though it could be viewed as a success in the eyes of the reforms' users. Prison wardens treated parole and the indeterminate sentence like control tools. Judges used probation to enhance their sanctioning options and, in effect, their discretion. Prosecutors improved their conviction rates as the prospect of parole and probation facilitated plea bargaining. Finally, through parole, legislators won favor with their constituents: Legislators claimed that they contained prison costs through parole releases and that they were able to deflect blame for the release of dangerous offenders to parole boards (ibid.). This pattern of reform failure and expanded control is evident in yet another of the progressive movement strategies; namely, the juvenile court.

6

Progressivism and the Juvenile Court (1900–1960s)

Before juvenile courts, children in trouble with the law could be handled according to the Common Law Principle of Responsibility. The common law principle specified three categories of youth that were differentiated by age and an associated presumption of criminal intent. Specifically, children under the age of seven were presumed incapable of harboring criminal intent and were not to be subject to criminal sanctions. Children between the ages of seven and fourteen were presumed possibly capable of harboring criminal intent and could be subject to criminal sanctions. Youth aged fourteen and older were presumed definitely capable of harboring criminal intent and were to be subject to criminal sanctions. As a result of the possibility that children aged seven or older could be subject to adult-like criminal sanctions, including the death penalty, the development of the juvenile court was commonly hailed as a major benevolent reform that spared children from the harsh punishments meted out to adult criminals (Mennel, 1973). However, historical evidence suggests children were largely spared from adult-like punishments before the creation of the juvenile courts.

To illustrate, a review of fourteen leading cases involving determinations of criminal responsibility of children in America between 1801 and 1882 demonstrates that children generally were treated more leniently than were adults. In these particular cases, seven youths were charged with homicide, one with manslaughter, five with larceny, and one with trespass. Of the fourteen cases, the jury verdict was not guilty in ten of the cases; the child charged with malicious trespass was found guilty with the sentence not reported; two slave children aged eleven and twelve were executed; and the remaining child was sentenced to three years in prison for grand larceny. Moreover, given this period's prevalent racism and discriminatory practices, it is unlikely that the two executed children would have received the death penalty had they been white (Platt, 1977). Nonetheless—and despite the fact that children in trouble with the law were generally handled differently from adult offenders—the popular belief was that countless troubled children were treated like adult offenders before juvenile courts.

In light of this view, the development of juvenile courts at the turn of the twentieth century is considered one of the most ambitious and influential reforms of the Progressive Era. Juvenile courts were envisioned as means to save children from criminal prosecution through individualized treatment with exclusive attention provided on a case-by-case basis. Such a policy necessarily required expansive court discretion and control. In fact, late nineteenth- and early twentieth-century child labor laws and mandatory school attendance, coupled with the newly emerging juvenile court, embodied a growing treatment and rehabilitative ideology that came to be known as the "twentieth-century rehabilitative ideal" (Allen, 1964). This general rehabilitative ideology would later be applied not only to children, but also to adult criminal offenders as well as the mentally ill. Consistent with the experiences of earlier penal reforms, however, the juvenile court's formally prescribed goal of individual treatment was not realized in its everyday practices. As characterized by Bortner (1984), the juvenile court's espoused mission of individualized treatment has been little more than a tarnished ideal.

Juvenile Court as Progressive Ideology

Progressive ideology and its associated penal reforms emerged in the context of the late nineteenth century anxiety over America's fast-developing corporate capitalism. The juvenile court, reformatories, indeterminate sentencing, parole, and probation were all part of a continuing stream of progressive experimentation aimed at responding to various social problems wrought by rapid industrialization, immigration, and urbanization (Schlossman, 1977).

Beginning with the Haymarket Riot of 1886, America's industrial centers were experiencing repetitive strikes, worker-related violence, and numerous business failures. Organizations like the Socialist Party and Industrial Workers of the World were increasing their demands for major changes in the social and economic conditions of workers. Emerging from this conflict was a corporate-sponsored plan to save capitalism. A strategy was needed that could simultaneously regulate and stabilize production, while mollifying popular protest and militancy among workers (Platt, 1977). The ultimate choice, according to Williams (1966), was between a reformed capitalist system and a revolutionary movement. Given these high stakes, the pressures for effective and far-reaching reform were intense.

If America's newly emerging capitalist system was to prosper, not only were changes in business and industry necessary, but so too were changes in the education and preparation of the young. Scientific management arose as a means to increase efficiency and effectiveness in business and industry. Intelligence testing, compulsory school attendance, and child labor laws ensured that children would receive proper education and skills for the industrial economy's changing employment needs. The prevalent thinking was that whatever is best for the newly emerging economy is best for the public interest as well (Center for Research on Criminal Justice, 1975).

Progressive reformers considered previously held values and institutional strategies to be ineffective in successfully overcoming the turmoil associated with mass immigration, industrialization, and urbanization. Integral to the overall progressive reform agenda is what Platt (1977) termed "the child-saving movement." Like reformatories, indeterminate sentencing, and parole and probation reforms, the child-saving movement developed in response to rapid social change and to a growing acceptance of positivistic explanations of delinquency and the benefits of scientific social casework for rehabilitating offenders (Mennel, 1973; Ryerson, 1978; Schlossman, 1977). The progressives believed that by conducting individualized inquiries into the lives of troubled youth, the antecedent causes of their misbehavior could be identified. Once the antecedent causes were identified, an individual treatment plan could be implemented that would overcome these antecedent causes, thereby correcting the youth's subsequent behavior. This was the goal and promise of scientific social casework.

While the child-saving movement attracted individuals from a variety of political and social class backgrounds, its most ardent supporters were the daughters and wives of the old landed gentry and the industrial nouveau riche. Platt (1977) contended that the general tone of the child-saving movement was both forward-looking and conservative in that it combined concern for the needy in the new industrial order with traditional class biases. While the rank and file members of the child-saving movement were aligned with corporate America, they also were concerned with alleviating the misery and suffering of the immigrant poor. In particular, they sought to educate and socialize immigrant children in accordance with the needs of corporate capitalism.

Immigrant children were to be molded into citizens committed to the American way of life. Various reform efforts would ensure not only the status quo but also the realization of the American dream for immigrants and other children in distress. The task, as stated by Henderson in 1899, was one that combined the welfare of the defective with the good of the community:

> The supreme test of philanthropy is not found in the blind and instinctive satisfaction of a kind impulse, nor in the apparent comfort of dependent persons, but rather in the welfare of the community and of the future race. Deliberately, rationally, and with widest possible knowledge, we must try our success by this standard. Not that we admit any real conflict between the welfare of the defective and the good of the community. We follow the logic of the doctrine of solidarity to its extreme limits, and admit that every human being, even criminals and idiots, are members of the social body. To wound them is to hurt all, and the loss of the least of them would be a loss of the whole human race (Henderson, 1899: 25).

Ultimately, one of the reform strategies that emerged to accomplish these interrelated goals was the juvenile court.

Promise of Juvenile Courts

Officially prescribed juvenile court goals and practices were grounded in the notion of individualized treatment within a non-adversarial system. Juvenile courts were not to operate according to due process, adversarial proceedings, presumption of innocence, and rights to a jury trial and defense counsel, but rather upon the presumption that troubled children were in need of treatment and care. The juvenile court was to serve as a "surrogate parent" for these troubled youth by providing them the approximate care that would be provided by responsible and caring parents.

Given the purpose of individualized treatment, punishment was not included among the juvenile court's functions. In fact, juvenile court judges' robes, terminology, and the physical design of court facilities reflected the "new" treatment or "medicalized" approach. Juvenile court judges routinely employed medical metaphors such as disease, treatment, cure, and pathology during their handling of cases. Juvenile court facilities were designed like medical clinics rather than traditional courtrooms.

Juvenile court judges wore white robes rather than black robes, consistent with the role of doctor or clinician rather than jurist. Such practices are consistent with the juvenile courts' underlying concept of *parens patriae a*nd the goal of individualized treatment through scientific social casework (Rothman, 1980; Schlossman, 1977).

The concept of parens patriae provided juvenile courts with broad discretion in dealing with troubled youth. Since the court's purpose was to save and treat youth instead of determining guilt or innocence and administering punishment, progressives reasoned that broad and largely unfettered discretion was necessary if juvenile courts were to be successful in fulfilling their goals. As Schlossman wrote, juvenile court judge Ben Lindsey—who presided in Denver, Colorado, during the early 1900s—was by far one of the court's earliest and famous boosters.

> Lindsey's engaging tales of delinquents who responded positively to his counsel, who confided intimate secrets to him, who after appearing in court obeyed parents they had previously scorned, and who attended school, worked steadily, and reported regularly to probation officers provided a glowing commentary on the achievements of one early juvenile court. If one is to believe Lindsey (and there is little solid evidence to challenge his view) neglected, dependent, and delinquent children in Denver received more solicitous treatment than would have been possible in a city where stricter rules of evidence and procedure applied. Lindsey appears to have wielded his enormous power with discretion, humanity, and shrewdness. By taking familial, social, and economic factors into account, and adding a dose of his remarkable intuition, Lindsey mediated constructively between an impersonal criminal code and the distinctive problems of children. Despite the seeming contradiction, he ruled as a benevolent judicial despot (Schlossman, 1977: 56).

Judge Lindsey became an early role model for juvenile court judges and a major spokesman for the juvenile court movement throughout the country. Lindsey authored numerous books and articles that were largely drawn from his Denver court experiences and made numerous speeches across the nation. In the opinion of Schlossman, while other judges, probation officers, and child welfare workers wrote and spoke about their juvenile court experiences, it was Lindsey who "came close to dictating the form and content of contemporary opinion on the subject for at least two decades, especially through his artful renditions or didactic sentimental stories" (ibid.).

Since the role of the juvenile court was that of surrogate for the child's parents, the handling by the court of numerous childhood-related difficulties and problems that extended beyond lawbreaking was assumed appropriate and necessary. Consequently, four categories of troubled children were established and subsumed under the jurisdiction of the juvenile court:

1.   *Delinquent children*. Children who had committed an act that if committed by an adult would be a crime;

2.   *Status offenders*. Children who could not be handled by their parents or guardians, or were engaged in behavior felt harmful but not considered criminal if engaged in by an adult;

3.   *Neglected children*. Children whose parents or guardians were failing to provide them necessary care and guidance; and

4.   *Dependent children*. Children whose parents or guardians, for what ever reasons, are unable to provide and care for them (Paulsen and White-Bread, 1974: 32).

Such broad juvenile court authority over children can be understood as part of a larger effort to enforce what Empey (1982) termed "the modern concept of childhood." To summarize, the modern concept of childhood assumed (1) that children go through several developmental stages; (2) that throughout these stages children are fundamentally different from adults; and (3) until children develop full emotional capacities, they should be quarantined from adult habits, vices, and responsibilities (ibid.).

Thus, the juvenile court emerged as a benevolent surrogate not only for nonfunctioning parents but also for ineffective schools. The first juvenile court act passed in Illinois in 1899 specified, "The care, custody, and discipline of a child shall approximate . . . that which should be given by its parents" (ibid.: 334). Additionally, the Educational Commission of Chicago voiced concern that its Compulsory School Attendance Act was not sufficient to counteract the culture conflict experienced by marginal children. The juvenile court was to be the solution to parental and school failures. As Harpur emphatically explained in 1899, "We should rightfully have the power to arrest all the little beggars, loafers, and vagabonds that infest our city, take them from the streets, and place them in schools where they are compelled to receive education and learn moral principles" (pp. 163–164).

To accomplish individual treatment, juvenile courts were to implement a series of interrelated procedures. The first procedure was intake, during which children were referred to the juvenile court. Parents, school authorities, and the police could make these referrals. At the point of intake, juvenile courts were to have a number of decision options. These options included releasing the child with a warning, placing the child in detention while the case progressed, filing a petition for formal juvenile court disposition, or referring the child to another agency or criminal court for more serious offenses. Ideally, the procedures and decision alternatives were to enable juvenile courts to provide each troubled child with individualized and therapeutic treatment that was responsive to the particular needs and characteristics of the child in question.

The use of probation officers was (and continues to be) fundamental to juvenile court practice. Probation officers conducted the social casework histories and screening of children, made recommendations to the judge before court dispositions, and provided case supervision following court dispositions. The probation officer's social casework histories of youth were intended to capture the child's past, thereby enabling identification and description of specific antecedent events, problems, circumstances, experiences, associations, or family characteristics that contributed to or caused the child's behavior problems. Based upon the probation officer's determination of the contributors to or causes of the child's behavior problems, the probation officer could recommend dismissing the case, handling the case informally through counsel and release, or referring the case to court for formal disposition. Further, probation officers determined whether the youth should be held in detention until court proceedings and case disposition. For children judged by investigating probation officers to be in need of formal juvenile court adjudication, a hearing was held in which the probation officer provided assistance to the judge. The primary function of juvenile court judges at the adjudication stage was to determine if the child was delinquent, pre-delinquent, or dependent and neglected. In theory, judges and probation officers in the adjudication process attempted to do for the child what caring parents would do when confronted with a troubled child.

Ultimately, the juvenile court judge decided what was to be done with the child and this decision was referred to as a disposition. There were two general categories of juvenile court dispositions: (1) children were judged suitable for return to their home under the care of parents or guardians, and (2) children were judged suitable for some form of out-of-home placement. If the child was returned to his or her home, he or she was normally supervised by a probation officer who met regularly with the child and family and used other appropriate community resources for assistance. Children judged suitable for out-of-home placements could be placed in a variety of public or private correctional or treatment facilities. Both a return-to-home or out-of-home disposition by the juvenile court involved the use of indeterminate sentencing. This meant that juvenile courts could maintain control over children until the age of majority (eighteen or twenty-one, depending upon state law) or until the child was deemed no longer in need of court jurisdiction.

Overall, juvenile court intake, adjudication, and disposition were conceived as analogous to medical diagnosis and treatment. The stated intention of juvenile courts was to provide individualized diagnosis and treatment for each child, thereby ensuring ultimate rehabilitation and full societal integration by these children.

Juvenile Court in Practice

During the past several decades, a number of researchers have examined the implementation and characteristic practices of juvenile courts. Then and now, a major focus of this research has been termed the "goals versus practices" of juvenile courts. What has emerged consistently throughout these studies has been a finding of disparity between the juvenile court's official goal of individual treatment and the court's routine practices of youth control (Bortner, 1984; Platt, 1977; Rothman, 1980).

Between 1899 and 1925, juvenile courts proliferated across the United States. While the philosophy and goals of the courts reflected the progressive ideal of individualized treatment, the actual design, organization, and jurisdiction of the courts differed widely within and between states. Many of these permutations were substantial and resulted in very different organizational structures, procedures, and practices. For example, Rothman (1980) specified that some states designated juvenile courts as chancery courts, thereby empowering them to implement their individual rules and procedures to handle different youth problems. Other jurisdictions, including Massachusetts, New York, and Washington, D.C., viewed juvenile courts essentially as criminal courts and mandated very specific rules and procedures to govern their operations. Additionally, considerable local variation in court practices occurred, with some juvenile courts handling all crimes committed by youth and others dealing only with less serious offenses. Most juvenile courts handled neglect cases as well as adoption, truancy, adults contributing to the delinquency of minors, and commitments of youth to mental institutions (ibid.).

The juvenile court's ad hoc design and jurisdictional differences were the results of a tendency by early juvenile court supporters to view the court in very ideal and vague terms; consequently, there was little guidance or specificity in statutes establishing the courts. Lemert (1970) attributed the failure of juvenile courts to implement a common set of legal and operational procedures to five factors:

1. The line of continuity between traditional courts of law and the juvenile court proved to be very tenuous, owing to the use of lay judges and the low level of commitment and interest among legally trained judges assigned to it.

2. Relatively few appeals were taken from juvenile court decisions and when they were, higher court decisions sustained wide limits of discretion for the lower court; hence, an important source of clarification necessary for the creative growth of law was absent.

3. Early probation officers and welfare workers connected with the court were nonprofessional and had little conception of procedure or its importance.

4. Clients of the court tended to be powerless people, often ethnic minorities, who were poorly equipped to make articulate demands on the court.

5. Legal counsel was seldom present to initiate adversary or other action that might have generated continuity with criminal or other legal procedure (ibid.: 25–26).

While juvenile courts as a whole did not implement a common set of operational procedures, individual courts developed their own procedures. According to Lindsey and Burrough (1931) and Hart (1910), juvenile courts implemented unique operational features based upon their day-to-day interactions with a variety of individuals and groups, including parents, police, probation officers, judges, welfare workers, and church representatives, who primarily reflected the interests and values of the local communities in which the courts operated. The associated organizational resources available to judges also dictated the structure and activities of the court.

As a result of ambiguous legislation and diverse community interests, values, and functional needs, juvenile court organization and procedures developed in an uneven and fragmented fashion. By 1925, a majority of states had passed juvenile court legislation and the courts varied considerably in their respective levels of probation services, use of social case histories in dispositions, availability of detention facilities other than county jails, and the education and experience levels of judges (Belden, 1920). During the 1930s, with the advance of social work, psychiatry, and psychology, and the increasing professionalization of probation officers, an accelerated treatment focus was embraced by a number of juvenile courts, particularly the larger urban courts.

Following World War II, many juvenile courts experienced major increases in the volume of cases, which resulted in increased court bureaucratization. For example, California's population increased by 50 percent during the 1940s. During this decade, the state's juvenile courts responded to this rapid population growth with increased commitments to state reformatories. Specifically, the state's youth reformatory population increased from 1,300 in 1941 to 2,526 in 1953 (Blomberg, 1978).

Before World War II, California's response to increased juvenile court commitments to the state's reformatories was to build more reformatories. However, during World War II and into the early 1950s, there were lags in the construction of new state facilities. These construction lags resulted in excessively long local detention stays for those juveniles awaiting state reformatory placement. Consequently, many local jurisdictions were forced either to rely upon jails to hold these youth or to construct new and larger detention facilities.

However, confusion remained as to the explicit role and function of local juvenile courts and the associated role and function of the state. In 1941, California's response to this general confusion was the establishment of the California Youth Authority to treat state-committed youth. In 1943, the California legislature expanded the Youth Authority's duties to include the development of uniform juvenile court and probation standards and practices throughout the state. The Youth Authority's specific juvenile court and probation duties included inspecting local detention facilities and camps that received state funds and requiring each county to submit annual probation reports. Penalties for noncompliance were never specified and the Youth Authority never exerted formal authority over any county for noncompliance. Consequently, and despite the Youth Authority's efforts, California juvenile courts continued to develop in an uneven and fragmented manner.

What primarily characterized California's juvenile court experiences from the 1930s to the 1960s—as well as other juvenile courts across the country—were locally determined court functions and associated services and practices. That is, local juvenile court functions, services, and practices reflected particular community values, group interests, and functional necessities. In rural counties throughout the country, children tended to be grouped into one of two dispositional categories: (1) those good enough to remain in their homes subject to probation supervision or (2) those who had committed serious enough crimes to be held in a state reformatory. In larger urban counties, local juvenile court services were more numerous and differentiated. They included detention facilities that separated delinquent from dependent and neglected youth; local institutions, camps, ranches, group and residential homes; and specialized probation services with varying caseload sizes and treatment modalities resulting in multiple types of court dispositions.

Ultimately, the philosophical preferences held by individual juvenile court judges for handling troubled youth were blurred with the dispositional alternatives available to the judges. As a result, juvenile court decisions within any given jurisdiction perhaps should be understood not so much as individualistic but rather as typical and routine. Youth coming before judges were categorized as appropriate for an available juvenile court disposition and were routinely processed into that dispositional alternative. Generally, as the numbers and types of youth problems changed, so too did the number and types of dispositional alternatives. In effect, the type of justice received by an individual youth was determined substantially by when and where the justice was administered.

Pezman (1963: 1–2) described several cases in Depression-Era Los Angeles that demonstrate the time-and-place association of juvenile court decision practices:

> In 1932, depression-ridden, transient boys were coming to Los Angeles in great numbers. Available detention facilities were filled to maximum capacities. Continuing arrivals necessitated the returning of the boys to their "point of origin" at county expense. Transients throughout the nation learned: "If you ride the rods out to California, they will send you home on the cushions." Several amusing incidents illustrate the not-so-amusing problem: One small boy, it is recalled, promised the judge to return and stay home in Indiana if he would be allowed to see his favorite motion-picture star in person. The judge, in an indulgent mood, made arrangements and the boy not only met his favorite "cowboy" but also was allowed to ride the actor's famous horse. A month later the boy returned to California and appeared again before the judge, this time with three other transient companions. The boy explained to the judge: "You see, judge, my friends didn't believe I met him (the cowboy). They want to ride on his horse, too." Another boy, from the Deep South, listened to the judge remark: "This is the third and last time I am going to see you in this court." "What's the matter, judge," the boy responded questionably, "you going to quit?" To discourage the arrival of these transient children, the Los Angeles Board of Supervisors met in special session and approved a plan to establish temporary work camps to help them earn passage home. The plan carried the endorsement of the judge of the juvenile court, the probation officer, and the county forester and fire warden.

Friedman (1993) concluded that the evidence on early juvenile courts demonstrates that they were viewed as popular courts among immigrant and working-class parents. He argued that these parents employed the courts as a means of controlling their troublesome children. Essentially, the courts were used as a weapon in the clash of cultures between Old World parents and children in a new American world and culture. Most delinquent cases handled by the courts involved boys. However, when girls were brought before the courts, a different standard often prevailed: Specifically, girls were regularly brought before the courts by their parents for sexual misbehavior, which did not trouble the parents of boys.

The following case summaries taken from Schlossman (1977) illustrate the often minor nature of cases referred to juvenile court probation officers and the haphazard types of resolutions reached:

In July, 1914, a probation officer received word that sixteen-year-old Gerald Muldower refused to work, stayed out late at night, and smoked cigarettes. Upon investigation it was learned that Gerald's parents were dead, and he was living with his grandparents who had filed the complaint. Further inquiry revealed that Gerald had been unemployed for nearly two years, refusing to work ever since he lost a finger on his last factory job. Confronted with these "charges," Gerald promised the probation officer that he would seek employment and pay board to his grandparents. Whether Gerald was threatened with a court appearance is impossible to determine. But he quickly corrected his errant ways and obtained a job in a hardware store, after which the officer closed the case as a successful settlement.

Three weeks earlier a similar case had required more affirmative action. Mr. Pildowski complained about his two teen-age boys who refused to work or attend school and who spent their days "bumming around" railroad tracks or frolicking in outlying woods. The probation officer advised the boys to find work, but to no avail. After two unsuccessful visits to their home, he called them into his office and employed scare tactics, threatening to bring formal charges (probably for truancy or incorrigibility) against them. The ultimate fate of these boys remains unclear; presumably they found the officer's threat frightening enough to find employment. At any rate, this case was also listed as a successful settlement.

The complaints parents brought against their own children were often extreme, leaving the court with few dispositional options. It was a pleasurable, if rare, achievement to resolve one of these cases out of court. An example was the case of Mrs. Sherman, who accused her son Israel of staying out late at night and stealing. At first Mrs. Sherman insisted that Israel be locked up for at least a year, but a probation officer convinced her to see whether the three of them might be able to talk out their problems. Israel, perhaps realizing that unless he agreed to the talk he would be taken into court and possibly committed, volunteered to place himself on probation. The officer approved and also forced Israel to plead for forgiveness while on his knees. Were it not for the probation officer's early intervention, Israel would surely have been brought into court on a charge of incorrigibility and would have been subject to the vagaries and uncertainties of the judicial decision making process.

Other cases similarly highlighted ambiguity in probation officers' attempts to "prevent" delinquency. Overt criminal acts rarely entered into complaints. Consider the accusation of Mrs. Elvehrer, who alleged that a neighbor's child was molesting her children. Upon investigation, the probation officer realized the complaint had no basis in fact; the children were being used as pawns in a quarrel between two adults. The officer sternly warned both parents to stop their fighting; once they agreed he closed the case as a successful resolution. Similar to the Elvehrer case was a neighbor's complaint charging a young girl with truancy. Investigation revealed the girl had a valid work permit and that the neighbor was simply trying to upset the girl's mother.

This type of complaint frequently backfired. For instance, Mrs. Wolenski charged in April 1915, that Peter Czerzak, who lived in a nearby rear basement apartment, was neglecting his four-year-old daughter. Unable to locate Czerzak, the probation officer decided to investigate Mrs. Wolenski's house. Finding it in a "very filthy condition," she warned Mrs. Wolenski to clean up or she would bring her family into court and charge her with neglect. Similarly, Mr. Padrewski complained that three neighborhood youths had attacked his son Lewis. The investigating officer learned, however, that Lewis had actually instigated the quarrel and moreover, that the boy surreptitiously smoked cigarettes. The officer concluded that Lewis was "to all appearances a bad boy and will need watching." From accusers, Mr. Padrewski and his son had become the accused.

However ambiguous the relation of out-of-court settlements to delinquency "prevention," such settlements were often accompanied with extrajudicial punishments. Two cases in August 1916 demonstrated this practice. In the first case, Mr. and Mrs. Esk complained that their thirteen-year-old daughter, Denise, was incorrigible. When they brought her to the probation office, she was "very saucy" to her mother, accusing her of immorality, among other things. Thereupon the probation officer, on her own initiative and against the parents' remonstrations, placed Denise in detention for four days. Realizing that they had no control over the proceedings, the Esks dropped the charges against Denise after her release. In the second case Mrs. Debrink complained about her daughter Ellen's "sauciness" and brought her to the probation office to discuss their problems. Ellen, however, refused to pay any attention to the probation officer, whereupon he placed her in detention for several days and then put her on probation (Schlossman, 1977: 149–153).

The cases described thus far all originated with parents or neighbors. While charitable agencies and school authorities initiated fewer cases, the cases they did initiate required more immediate and affirmative action:

For example, in November 1916, a public school teacher alleged that every day all the Mordinski children arrived at school hungry. Upon investigation the probation officer uncovered a rather bizarre situation. Mr. and Mrs. Mordinski had been having a bitter dispute over the latter's refusal to transfer half of her property rights to her husband. In the interim Mr. Mordinski had refused to provide money for food and had not eaten at home in six months. When the probation officer arrived at the house the cupboards were indeed empty. Somehow the probation officer was able to effect a quick reconciliation between husband and wife; Mrs. Mordinski agreed to her husband's demands and Mr. Mordinski promised to give her money for food. The officer's early intervention may not have prevented delinquency, but it certainly prevented malnutrition.

Compared to their representation in cases brought to court, girls appeared disproportionately in out-of-court settlements. About half of the cases in the logbook involved girls of varying ages. Moreover, in stark contrast to their response in cases brought to court, the probation officers generally responded pragmatically to female moral improprieties. Seemingly comparable offenses could be found before the court as well as in out-of-court settlements, thus highlighting the centrality of discretion in the court's modus operandi. One never knew quite what to expect from the probation officers.

Consider the investigation of a complaint (origin uncertain) that sixteen-year-old Eloise was pregnant and was bragging about her condition to young girls in her neighborhood. Eloise's mother had died seven years earlier, her father worked half days, and three of her five siblings still lived at home. Eloise cooked and kept house for them and her father, thus helping to keep the family intact. Although she admitted to being pregnant, Eloise denied having told anyone but relatives. Furthermore, she was to be married to the child's father in less than a month. The reaction of the probation officer—nearly always a woman in cases like this—was temperate. After due consideration of alternatives, the officer decided to wait out the month and let the marriage take place. Thus the probation officer, who was clearly shocked at Eloise's condition, held her moralism in check. One may conjecture, based on other cases involving young unwed mothers, that had Eloise not been engaged she would have been allowed to have the baby and then would have been sent to the House of Good Shepherd. But in this instance, quite reasonable, the officer left well enough alone.

Another sex-related case further demonstrated the use of noninstitutional remedies for female sexual promiscuity. This time a group of boys and girls—schoolmates—were involved equally, but the boys, as usual, escaped with little more than a stern warning. The boys had formed a club devoted to group masturbation and the enticement of young girls into intercourse. The probation officer was content to break up the club and did not insist that its members be tried in court. For the boys' indiscretions she urged an educational solution. "I advised the parents that, as each of these boys had now arrived at the age of understanding, that it would be well if, instead of administering corporal punishment, they would take their boy and advise and educate him along the lines of sex hygiene and point out the danger they were putting themselves in by their acts."

Though the girls received harsher treatment, none was institutionalized. Jamie, age ten, whose immorality was confined to necking in nickel shows with the most amorous of the boys, was confined indefinitely to home under parental supervision. Nancy, age eleven, who had played kissing games regularly with boys and masturbated with female partners was, similarly, confined. Even Irma, age fourteen, who admitted to frequent casual intercourse with numerous paramours, was merely forced to transfer schools (ibid.: 149–153).

These case summaries demonstrate several juvenile court trends. Much of the intervention by juvenile court probation officers involved individual youth and family problem-solving rather than delinquency prevention. In their problem-solving efforts, juvenile court probation officers operated with substantial power over the youth and their families. Further, while these cases document the practice of handling cases unofficially and without formal court involvement, what is remarkable is that some of these cases received court attention in the first place. Whatever the court's treatment or rehabilitative impact, these types of cases and informal handling practices enabled the court to exert new mechanisms of moral authority and control in the form of a surrogate parent. Further, these expansive court powers went unquestioned.

During the 1960s, however, a series of legal changes were ushered in by the Warren Court in the landmark *In re Gault* case of 1967. Specifically, the Warren Court directly challenged the notion of juvenile courts as caring, supportive, substitute parents by confronting the fact that the courts actually acted as legal entities meting out punishment. Juvenile courts came to be viewed as more like adult criminal courts, in which due process and various legal safeguards were necessary and fundamental. The Warren Court's reasoning was that, because the courts could commit youth to reformatories wherein they could be deprived of liberty for years at a time, it was necessary to recognize the rights of youth to due process procedures and safeguards.

Since the inception of juvenile courts, criticism has been centered upon the lack of services available to the courts to accomplish their individualized treatment goals. Underlying this criticism has been the assumption that expansion of court services through various reform efforts would result in more individualized and effective youth treatment, thereby reducing delinquency. While studies have documented the movement of numerous juvenile courts from limited youth supervision agencies to local-level correctional establishments complete with diagnostic, institutional, probation, and various community-based youth and family services, the reported results of these various court service reforms have been quite opposite to expectations. Specifically, it has been shown that the court's expansion of services has stemmed less from the explicit treatment needs of youth than from the perceived maintenance and growth requirements of the court's organizational bureaucracy (Blomberg, 1978; Platt, 1977; Schlossman, 1977).

For example, Schlossman (1995) illustrated the juvenile court's pattern of organizational and clientele growth through consideration of the court's reliance upon state reform schools. Between 1950 and 1970, the total youth population placed in the country's reform schools by juvenile courts increased 75 percent from thirty-five thousand to sixty-two thousand. The number of public reform schools increased to almost two hundred, excluding several hundred additional local ranches, camps, group homes, and private institutions for the court's placement of less serious youth receiving out-of-home dispositions.

Juvenile Court: Advancing Individual Treatment

The juvenile court emerged at the turn of the twentieth century as part of the progressive strategy to confront societal turmoil. Juvenile courts were to serve the twofold purpose of individually treating, educating, and morally developing problem youth, and providing for the continued welfare of the larger society. Between 1900 and the 1960s, juvenile courts proliferated throughout the country and substantially expanded their scope, services, and youth population subject to their control.

Different historical models have been applied to explain the origins of penal reforms, leading to different explanations. As applied to the juvenile court, was the rise primarily the result of a conspiracy by the "haves" over the children of the "have nots," rendering this movement a planned system of control over the indigent, powerless, and dangerous classes, and juvenile court reformers merely tools acting on behalf of the entrenched powerful class (Austin and Krisberg, 1981; Platt, 1977)? Or were juvenile court reformers selfless humanitarians whose only purpose was to rescue helpless children from brutal and seedy jails as well as the gallows (Henderson, 1899; Mack, 1909; Mennel, 1973)? As argued throughout this book in relation to the sources of past penal reforms, the juvenile court's origins were at once determined by a combination of economic interests, fears, optimism, and, to invoke Schlossman (1977), "love of the American delinquent."

Efforts to explain the patterned disparity between juvenile court goals and practices have been centered increasingly upon the juvenile court's organizational and bureaucratic character (for a review of this literature, see Blomberg, 1978). These juvenile court organizational studies focus upon actual working conditions, available dispositional alternatives, and the larger environmental effects on the court organization. The juvenile court's formally prescribed goals of individual treatment are considered in conjunction with other operational, organizational, and bureaucratic factors in ultimately shaping and determining the court's everyday youth handling practices. These factors include the ambiguity and multiplicity of goals, relationships with other juvenile justice agencies, conflict between quality of individual youth treatment and routine production requirements, and everyday operations within an environment characterized by ever-present conditions of uncertainty and resource scarcity.

No matter how the origins and operations of the juvenile court are understood or interpreted, it is necessary to recognize the important role of the juvenile court's medicalized philosophy and associated methods of individual treatment and rehabilitation in stimulating a broadly embraced ideological ethos in early twentieth-century America. The court's individual treatment and rehabilitation functions were accelerated by the criminal justice system's handling of adult criminal offenders and by the mental health system in its handling of the mentally ill. This ideological ethos became known as the twentieth-century rehabilitative ideal. The next chapter considers the emergence of the twentieth-century rehabilitative ideal and its influence on the search for the causes of crime and on the development of American penology from 1900 to the 1960s.

7

Twentieth-Century Rehabilitative Ideal and "Correctional" System (1900–1960s)

The juvenile court, probation, indeterminate sentencing, parole, and the reformatory all stemmed from the broad social mission of the progressive agenda. The premise behind the progressive-based penology was that scientific casework would reveal the causes of crime and appropriate rehabilitation strategies. This premise was termed by Francis Allen (1964) as the "twentieth-century rehabilitative ideal."

The twentieth-century rehabilitative ideal fueled a search for the causes of crime that was undertaken in large part by the newly created University of Chicago. The university's sociology department, known as the Chicago school, shaped the prevailing wisdom on crime until the late 1930s. In fact, theoretical developments between the late 1930s and 1960s were often little more than attempts to refine, modify, or integrate existing Chicago school research and theories. While numerous theories emerged during this latter period, the common explanatory factors involved the characteristics of individual criminal offenders, their group associations, and their immediate area of residence.

Not immune to the proliferation of criminological theory, federal, state, and local justice systems underwent substantial organizational expansion and program differentiation. The ideological force driving this expansion was that more knowledge about the offender enables better individualized treatment which, in turn, necessitates more program options. Foucault (1977) referred to this escalating spiral of life history, theory, and programming as a knowledge–power dyad, wherein knowledge of the offender generates more power over the offender.

While conclusive evidence on the causes of crime remains illusive, the penal system—which would ultimately be designated the "correctional" system—continued to expand on all levels. This sixty-year period of growth, however, was concerned with refining existing strategies rather than creating new ones. Reforms launched during the Progressive Era continued over several years, extending to both youth and adults, and rural as well as urban jurisdictions. This gradual but persistent process of expanding the penal system was reflected in several domains. Among them were rehabilitation, classification, professionalization, and bureaucratization.

Rehabilitative Ideal and Crime Causation

While attempts to explain and correct criminal behavior occurred early in the nineteenth century, the broad optimism, scope, and development of scientific disciplines associated with the twentieth-century rehabilitative ideal were unique and unprecedented. Underlying the twentieth-century rehabilitative ideal are four assumptions:

1. Human behavior is a product of antecedent causes. This assumption established the fundamental principle of the rehabilitative ideal. The reasoning is that all individuals are products of a particular past. Individual personal histories shape who and what people are and how they think and act. For example, individuals who grow up in poverty or in affluence, individuals who drop out of school or excel in school, children of divorced or two-parent families, children with many siblings or no siblings, children raised in abusive homes or nurturing and supportive homes—these are the kinds of antecedent causes that are believed to shape and determine individual behavior, whether criminal or law abiding.

2. The antecedent causes of human behavior can be identified and it is the obligation of behavioral scientists to discover and describe the antecedent causes with all possible exactness. Individual case histories can be developed in which particular antecedent event(s) will emerge as more significant than others in causing an individual's behavior patterns. For example, through the construction of individual case histories, such events or circumstances as group associations, childhood sexual or physical abuse, chronic school truancy or failure, and living in dilapidated slum areas where crime is rampant and a way of life, emerged as particularly salient in causing particular problem behavior.

3. Knowledge of the antecedent causes of problem behavior enables scientific treatment of human behavior problems. Once the contributing

causes of an individual's problem behavior are identified, individual treatment plans can be designed and implemented that target the contributing causes of behavior problems, thereby neutralizing these causes and altering the individual's subsequent behavior. For example, if an offender's behavior is judged to be caused by previous physical or sexual abuse, specific counseling and other related therapy can be designed and administered to counteract or overcome the identified negative antecedent causes of the offender's previous criminal behavior patterns.

4. Measures employed to treat criminal behavior serve a therapeutic function: They are thought to be in the best interest of the offender and of society by making those treated contributing members of society. For example, once an offender receives successful treatment, it was believed that there would be not only a reduction in recidivism, but also an actual contribution to society as the offender successfully reintegrates into society by holding a job, paying taxes, and raising a family.

Beginning in the late 1890s, Rockefeller grants amounting to several million dollars transformed a small Baptist College in Chicago into one of America's foremost universities—the University of Chicago. In 1900, the president of the University of Chicago, William Rainey Harper, searched the nation for prominent professors so that he could establish the university's academic foundation (Schwendinger and Schwendinger, 1974). In awarding grants to the university, Rockefeller was particularly interested in establishing an urban social work purpose. Rockefeller, like other Chicago industrialists, was concerned about what he perceived to be instability among the workforce. Most of the industrial workforce in Chicago lived in the slums, which were believed to be a breeding ground for unrest and related social problems among the workers and their children (ibid.).

The university's sociology department (or the Chicago school) began with the singular goal of improving the slums. In fact, much of its initial academic work involved charitable social services for Chicago's ethnic slums. Often, the university scholar's role was to speak out publicly in defense of ethnic groups and to call for various corrective actions aimed at improving the inferior living, working, and educational conditions in the slums. The early research was focused upon describing the difficult living conditions and associated feelings of slum residents through journalistic accounts framed within a social work orientation. Burgess and Bogue (1967: 5) described the community activist role of early Chicago school researchers:

Quite often they defended the foreign groups publicly and spoke out for tolerance, sympathy and understanding. Much of the earliest "social research" was little more than the discovery and reporting to the public that the feeling and sentiments of those living in the ethnic slums were, in reality, quite different from those imputed to them by the public.

Social Disorganization and Culture Conflict

Beginning in the 1920s, the journalistic and social work orientation gave way to the ambition of explaining the social and economic forces at work in the slums and their role in shaping the way slum residents thought and behaved. The early theme that arose from these efforts was referred to as "social pathology" or "social disorganization." The social disorganization approach became one of the Chicago school's fundamental contributions to the explanation of crime. The theoretical imagery underlying the social disorganization theme is that there are characteristic processes and interactions whereby individuals are socialized and social control and community social organization are maintained. When these characteristic processes and interactions are disrupted, social control is weakened and social problems emerge in the form of violations of morals, customs, and the law.

Yet, as theorized by early Chicago school spokesmen Robert Park and Ernest Burgess (1924), while there are breakdowns in socialization and social control processes that result in problems such as crime, there is an inherent capacity within American society to confront and overcome these breakdowns. Specifically, Park and Burgess theorized that American society is characterized by ever-present conditions of competition, which generate conflict that is manifested in such social problems as crime. But American society possesses the inherent capacity to accommodate and/or correct both the conditions leading to conflict and other social problems like crime, thereby enabling the assimilation of all of society's members into American common culture. Together, these assumptions reflect the image of American society as an ongoing social system that becomes disrupted by social change. Social change results in social disorganization and conflict, which precipitates social problems like crime. But as social reorganization progresses through accommodations and corrections resulting in assimilation, social problems disappear. The analogy is one of a non-terminal disease that, with treatment, can be cured.

The trend in Chicago school studies of crime, then, was to identify and describe various social correlates of crime that, taken together, could provide a grounded explanation of crime to guide various accommodation or correction efforts. For example, Shaw (1930, 1931, 1938) and Shaw and McKay (1972) contributed to a series of comprehensive ethnographic studies reflecting the conditions and circumstances of life in Chicago's slums. These researchers depicted crime and delinquency as inevitable reactions to the overwhelming environmental forces at work in the slum neighborhoods of Chicago. Shaw and McKay (1972) documented that high-crime and delinquency neighborhoods suffered from a number of pathological conditions, such as large numbers of foreigners, bad housing, poor sanitation, rapid population increases, and residential turnover. Moreover, the researchers found that, despite rapid population increases and turnover, crime and delinquency rates in particular geographic neighborhoods remained constant. As a result of this observation, crime and delinquency became viewed as a function of geographic locality rather than individual psychology. Shaw and McKay explained:

> It appears to be established, then, that each racial, nativity, and nationality group in Chicago displays widely varying rates of delinquents; that rates for immigrant groups in particular show a wide historical fluctuation; that diverse racial, nativity, and national groups possess relatively similar rates of delinquents in similar social area; and that each of these groups displays the effect of disproportionate concentration in its respective areas at a given time. In the face of these facts it is difficult to sustain the contention that, by themselves, the factors of race, nativity, and nationality are vitally related to the problem of juvenile delinquency. It seems necessary to conclude, rather, that the significantly higher rates of delinquents found among the children of Negroes, the foreign born, and more recent immigrants are closely related to existing differences in their respective patterns of geographical distribution within the city (p. 162).

The general theory of crime and delinquency that evolved from the social pathology or social disorganization research of the University of Chicago became known as culture conflict. The thinking was that the culture of slum neighborhoods is in conflict with the larger and more dominant culture of middle-class America. As these slum neighborhoods become subject to ameliorative reform efforts such as improved housing, better sanitation, improved schools, and health care, the communities and residents will become reorganized around middle-class norms and values and social problems such as crime and delinquency should decline.

Differential Association

A refinement of the theoretical reasoning of culture conflict occurred in 1938. In attempting to account for his contribution to the theoretical refinement, Sutherland (1947) identified several incidents that played pivotal roles in his efforts to move criminological theory beyond culture conflict. First, Michael and Adler's (1933) critical appraisal of American criminology as essentially atheoretical antagonized Sutherland and turned his attention to the need for theoretical abstraction. Second, Professor Dean Ruml of the University of Chicago once asked a group (of which Sutherland was a part), "What do you know about criminal behavior?" (*The Sutherland Papers*, edited by Cohen, Lindesmith, and Schuessler, 1956: 16). Sutherland indicated that he could only summarize certain research findings on high-incidence crimes and refer to certain propositions that had been proven to be false. Sutherland recalled that he was unable to state any verified propositions and therefore recognized the need for such. Third, in the examination of a doctoral candidate, Sutherland recounted that Professor Louis Wirth asked, "What is the closest approach to a general theory of criminal behavior?" (ibid.: 17). The only possible answer was culture conflict, which Sutherland indicated he found to be quite lacking. A final influence that pushed Sutherland toward an alternative theory of crime is his 1930s' research with Thorsten Sellin: In their organization of national crime data, they encountered problems when attempting to apply the culture conflict framework to explain their data (ibid.: 16–17).

Indeed, Sutherland concluded that the Chicago school's research findings on the city's slums actually demonstrated differential social organization rather than social disorganization. He argued that the slum neighborhoods were characterized by specific community sentiments and ongoing activities that were directly connected to the creation, transmission, and, most importantly, indoctrination of delinquent and criminal behavior (ibid.: 13–18). Sutherland's "differential association theory" contended that people become delinquent or criminal through a form of learning that is structured by the individual being exposed to an excess of definitions favorable to the violation of law relative to definitions unfavorable to the violation of law. According to differential association theory, delinquency and crime are learned through the same processes that law-abiding behaviors are learned. Sutherland's theory of differential association consists of the following nine propositions:

1.   Criminal behavior is learned.

2.   Criminal behavior is learned with other persons in a process of communication.

3.   The principal part of the learning of criminal behavior occurs within intimate personal groups.

4.   When criminal behavior is learned, the learning includes (a) techniques of committing the crime, which are sometimes very complicated, sometimes very simple; (b) the specific direction of motives, drives, rationalizations, and attitudes.

5.   The specific direction of motives and drives is learned from definitions of legal codes as favorable and unfavorable.

6.   A person becomes delinquent because of an excess of definitions favorable to violation of law over definitions unfavorable to violation of law.

7.   Differential associations may vary in frequency, duration, priority, and intensity.

8.   The process of learning criminal behavior by association with criminal and anti-criminal patterns involves all of the mechanisms that are involved in any other learning.

9.   Though criminal behavior is an expression of general needs and values, it is not explained by those general needs and values since non-criminal behavior is an expression of the same needs and values (ibid.: 8–10).

Sutherland was very familiar with numerous crime and delinquency statistics and related research findings in criminology and believed that differential association theory could usefully be applied to explain the patterns emerging from various statistics and studies. Sutherland recounted that, upon returning from a seminar with professors Lindesmith and Sweetser, Sweetser questioned why "the explanation of juvenile delinquency in the slum area [doesn't] apply, in principle, to murders in the South" (ibid.: 18). Sweetser's question was the specific occasion for the formulation of differential association theory. Sutherland explained:

> The hypothesis of differential association seemed to me to be consistent with the principal gross findings in criminology. It explained why the Molocean children became progressively delinquent with the length of residence in the deteriorated area of Los Angeles, why the city crime rate is higher than the rural crime rate, why males are more delinquent than females, why the crime rate remains consistently high in deteriorated areas of cities, why the juvenile delinquency rate in a foreign nativity is high while the group lives in a deteriorated area and drops when the group moves out of that area, why second generation Italians do not have the high murder rate that their fathers had, why Japanese children in a deteriorated area of Seattle had a low delinquency rate even though in poverty, why crimes do not increase greatly in a period of depression. All of the general statistical facts seem to fit this hypothesis (ibid.: 19–20).

Anomie and the American Dream

During this same year that Sutherland proposed differential association theory, Robert K. Merton (1938) published an article entitled, "Social

Structure and Anomie." In this article, Merton presented another general theory of criminal behavior that came to epitomize structural functional explanations of crime. Merton was particularly interested in explaining why the incidence of crime in America was considerably higher than in other Western industrial nations such as England, France, and Germany. While Sutherland was interested in explaining specific distributions of crime within American society, Merton was interested in explaining the overall high incidence of crime throughout America.

Merton argued that all Americans, regardless of social status, are subject to a common socialization process that stresses high aspirations and open access to the means for achieving these high aspirations. Merton claimed that everyone raised in American society is taught to believe that, through hard work and postponed gratification, they can achieve anything for which they are willing to work and sacrifice. This belief is known as the American Dream. However, as Merton elaborated, the American Dream is more myth than reality. Because Americans do not have equal access to the means for achieving high aspirations, many ultimately suffer relative deprivation (i.e., deprivation relative to their high aspirations), which can result in anomie. Those suffering from anomie (or normlessness), in turn, experience disappointment and frustration that facilitates drift into various nonconformist behaviors, including crime. Merton further proposed that such drift into crime is particularly understandable because—in America—emphasis is not on how one succeeds but rather on the amount of material possessions that are automatically assumed to be indicative of success.

Merton concluded that American society has a much higher incidence of crime than other Western industrial countries because of its uniformly high aspirations and its failure to provide equal access to the means necessary to achieve these commonly held high aspirations. In other Western industrial countries, a highly stratified and well-defined socialization system existed. In effect, in these countries, people are born into a particular place or social status and their social status determines their socialization and levels of aspirations; consequently, there is much less likelihood of major disparities in aspirations and achievement and, as a result, there is less relative deprivation, anomie, and crime (Merton, 1938, 1949).

Theoretical Extensions and Integrations

Sutherland and Merton's theories of crime dominated criminological thought for the next several decades and were not subject to serious challenge until the 1960s. Moreover, in the 1950s, Sutherland and Merton's theories influenced various theoretical accounts of crime and delinquency. For example, Cohen (1955) contended that lower-class boys are driven into delinquent gangs through a process he termed "reaction formation." Employing Merton's theory of relative deprivation and anomie, Cohen argued that lower-class boys are largely unable to succeed in middle-class structured public schools. These lower-class boys react to their public school failure by forming an alternative delinquent subculture. This subculture takes the middle-class norms and behaviors of the larger society and turns them upside-down. Cohen argued that the delinquent boy's subcultural norms and behavior patterns, when measured against middle-class norms and behaviors, emerge as malicious, hedonistic, non-utilitarian, and generally free of adult-like restraint (ibid.).

Another delinquent subculture theory was offered in 1958 by Miller, who argued for a culturally centered theory of crime that was distinct and disconnected from middle-class culture and associated behaviors. Miller contended that while middle-class culture focused upon achievement, hard work, and postponed gratification, lower-class culture's "focal concerns" were centered upon toughness, masculinity, and skills at such things as imaginative profanity. Borrowing from Sutherland's emphasis on learning and differential association, Miller concluded that these lower-class focal concerns were learned and resulted in culturally institutionalized delinquent behavior and associated lifestyles (Miller, 1958).

In 1960, Cloward and Ohlin provided an integration of elements from the delinquency and opportunity theories of the Chicago School, Merton, and Sutherland. Cloward and Ohlin contended that delinquents could pursue different and independent delinquent lifestyles. They argued that lower-class youth who experience relative deprivation and turn to delinquency will learn and pursue those delinquent opportunities that are readily available to them—be they drugs, alcohol, violence, prostitution, or gambling (Cloward and Ohlin, 1960).

Overall, then, what emerged from the development of theories of criminality and delinquency was a continuing focus upon the individual offender and associated correlates of criminal behavior. From the early 1900s to the 1960s, various offender-based theories assessed the role of the offender's residence, group associations, socialization, and/or learning. Guided by the rehabilitative ideal, the concern was to identify the various causes and correlates of crime, thereby enabling the development of correctional strategies that could treat those causes successfully.

Growth and Refinement of the Correctional System

During the early decades of the twentieth century, American penology experienced major organizational growth and bureaucratization. The prevailing rehabilitative thinking guiding this growth was that successful criminal and delinquent rehabilitation could be accomplished only through individualized treatment. Moreover, individualized treatment requires a range of prison, parole, probation, and juvenile court programs that can be matched to the particular needs of various offenders. As a result, the template for twentieth-century penology was "more is better."

As of 1940, the penal system was comprised of prisons, reformatories, parole, probation, juvenile courts, local jails, and a declining number of workhouses (see Table 7-1) However, the main focus of the system was on expanding and differentiating prisons, parole and probation. What occurred over the subsequent decades was a series of efforts to rationalize, professionalize, differentiate, bureaucratize, and generally perfect these major components of the American penal system.

Prison Expansion, Differentiation, and Treatment

Until the late nineteenth century, the federal government relied upon state prisons to house federal prisoners and to provide leasing arrangements for private employers. However, Congress banned the leasing of federal prisoners in 1887, and, between 1885 and 1895, the number of federal prisoners increased from 1,027 to 2,516. As a consequence, Congress developed federal prisons, the first of which was in Leavenworth, Kansas, in 1897. Atlanta, Georgia, became the second site for a federal prison in 1902, while Alderson, West Virginia, was chosen as the site for the first federal prison for women in 1928 (Rotman, 1995).

These first federal prisons were operated separately and without centralized administration. As Rotman summarized:

Federal prisons erected in early 1900s were generally run as separate entities without any central organization. The problems caused by prison congestion and the need for a more efficient record-keeping system to facilitate the goal of proper classification and segregation of prisoners, led to the creation of the Federal Bureau of Prisons in 1929. The first Director of the Bureau was Sanford Bates, who was responsible for a number of important improvements. Bates altered the method of selecting wardens, substituting a merit system for political patronage. Wardens were trained at a special Bureau Facility and were promoted up the ranks within the Bureau. In 1937, the Bureau of Prisons placed all prison employees under the Federal Civil Service, throwing off the last vestiges of political patronage. Also, the Bureau began a system of staff

Table 7-1
Defendants Sentenced by State and Type of Sentence, 1940

State	Defendants Sentenced	State Prisons and Reformatories		Probation and Suspended Sentences		Local Jails and Workhouses		All Other Sentences	
		Number	Percent	Number	Percent	Number	Percent	Number	Percent
California	4,987	1,524	30.6	1,689	33.9	1607	32.2	167	3.3
Colorado	1,054	628	59.6	371	35.2	39	3.7	16	1.5
Connecticut	780	230	29.5	250	32.1	265	34.0	35	4.5
D.C.	1,088	680	62.5	297	27.3	108	9.9	3	0.3
Idaho	473	246	52.0	132	27.9	83	17.5	12	2.5
Indiana	2,233	1,180	52.8	689	30.9	220	9.9	144	6.4
Iowa	1,697	698	41.1	303	17.9	585	34.5	111	6.5
Kansas	1,130	805	71.2	211	18.7	105	9.3	9	0.8
Massachusetts	2,647	1,429	54.0	735	27.8	–	–	483	18.2
Michigan	2,186	933	42.7	1,098	50.2	105	4.8	50	2.3
Minnesota	1,807	788	43.6	719	39.8	240	13.3	60	3.3
Montana	453	351	77.5	62	13.7	24	5.3	16	3.5
New Hampshire	381	104	27.3	202	53.0	66	17.3	9	2.4
New Jersey	5,519	1,960	35.5	2,098	38.0	1,053	19.1	408	7.4
New Mexico	685	360	52.6	237	34.6	47	6.9	41	6.0
New York	7,834	3,227	41.2	2,845	36.3	1,719	21.9	43	0.5
North Dakota	426	262	61.5	50	11.7	77	18.1	37	8.7
Ohio	4,453	2,090	46.9	1,880	42.2	295	6.6	188	4.2
Oregon	976	504	51.6	326	33.4	132	13.5	14	1.4
Pennsylvania	12,328	1,619	13.1	3,411	27.7	5,442	44.1	1,856	15.1
Rhode Island	571	116	20.3	423	74.1	27	4.7	5	0.9
South Dakota	416	246	59.1	95	22.8	60	14.4	15	3.6
Utah	320	153	47.8	122	38.1	33	10.3	12	3.8
Vermont	325	117	63.0	91	28.0	66	20.3	51	15.7
Washington	1,343	770	57.3	381	28.4	182	13.6	10	0.7
Wisconsin	2,664	917	34.4	1,052	39.5	364	13.7	331	12.4
Wyoming	250	147	58.8	78	31.2	8	3.2	17	6.8
TOTAL (27 states)	59,026	22,084	37.4	19,847	33.6	12,952	21.9	4143	7.0

Source: Historical Corrections Statistics in the United States, 1850–1984.

rotation whereby any promotion was accompanied by a transfer to another facility. Prior to these changes, prison employees had moved up within the same prison and became entrenched in that prison, which had led to inflexibility and idiosyncrasies within the separate facilities (Rotman, 1995: 187).

The classification of offenders in the federal system was based upon the Bureau's criminological study of prisoners. Specifically, low-risk offenders were sent to non-custodial camps, while more serious offenders were sent to Leavenworth and Atlanta. Offenders judged likely to benefit from agricultural training were sent to McNeil Island, while the physically and mentally impaired were sent to the hospital prison in Springfield, Illinois. Following its opening in 1934, the most serious and hardcore federal prisoners were sent to Alcatraz. While the bureau's classification system was far more comprehensive than the classification efforts of most states, some states were implementing similar prison classification methods and were expanding their range of prisons (ibid.). During this time, an increasingly complex array of minimum-, medium-, and maximum-security facilities were developed at the state and federal levels.

From the outset in 1929, the Federal Bureau of Prisons declared rehabilitation to be its fundamental goal and continued to develop an institutional network to facilitate offender classification and individualized decisions regarding custody and treatment needs. This commitment to rehabilitation was so broadly shared that, in 1954, the American Prison Association changed its name to the American Correctional Association. This was the major professional organization for federal as well as state and local correctional professionals throughout the country. Like the bureau, the association proclaimed offender treatment to be its mandate and counseled its membership to rename their "prisons" "correctional institutions" and to refer to the punishment blocks within these institutions as "adjustment centers" (ibid.). It was even agreed upon that the "antiquated bastilles" and "huge factory like institutions" were barriers to individualized treatment (Bell, 1956). As a result of this philosophical shift, several states turned away from heavy reliance on maximum-security institutions and implemented smaller, more open, and minimum-security facilities.

The California prison system exemplified this new "correctional" approach. Soledad Prison was constructed just after World War II with a number of atypical facility characteristics, including fences as substitutes for granite walls, cell blocks with day rooms and outreach windows, interior walls painted with pastel colors, well-equipped libraries, gyms, and educational facilities, and better food, relaxed discipline, and a selection of counseling and education programs. Rotman (1995: 191) pointed out that California's Chino Prison, in particular, was an exemplary therapeutic prison community:

> Commissioner Richard McCee was the innovative administrator of the California Department of Corrections. According to the evaluative research units set up by McGee, the Chino experiment demonstrated the effectiveness of the therapeutic community method to change the antisocial behavior of offenders. The institution was decentralized into small units, with counselors housed in each of them. Convicts were used as

therapists. The prison became a community center for special training, work release, and family contacts. Therapeutic communities focused on the transformation of the institutional environment, creating a network of compensatory social interactions, a network that was intended to replace the hierarchical structure of the institution with a horizontal association of mutually responsible human beings who would resolve their common problems through a process of intensive social interaction. The vehicles of this process were the frequent meetings and group discussions in which decisions were reached through the participation of both inmates and staff. The demand for active participation was intended to counteract such notorious negative effects of institutions as depersonalization, dependency, and loss of initiative.

The treatment process within these various prisons was to involve a team of professionals—comprised of psychologists, caseworkers, sociologists, vocational counselors, and psychiatrists—that would test, interview, and develop life history information for each entering inmate (Irwin, 1980). The classification team would then evaluate the tests and life history and plan the inmate's therapeutic regimen. In the final classification stage, a team would periodically review the inmate's rehabilitation progress and recommend any necessary changes in treatment (ibid.).

Three fundamental types of treatment programs generally were available in the prison, including therapeutic, academic, and vocational (ibid.). The most heavily relied upon treatment approach was group counseling. Counseling modalities stressed mostly theories of social learning and attempted to combat the negative influences of institutional living. The majority of prison systems also established elementary and high school curricula by the 1950s and a number of states had arrangements with colleges and universities that would allow inmates to complete college-level correspondence courses while incarcerated. Vocational programming during the 1950s took the form of training in cooking, baking, butchering, dry cleaning, shoe repairing, sewing machine repairing, sheet metal machining, printing, plumbing, painting, welding, and nursing (Irwin, 1980).

Expansion of Parole and Probation

Parole began as a component of the nineteenth-century reformatory and indeterminate sentencing movements but soon developed independently with its use becoming more widespread across the United States. Beginning in 1900, many prison managers sought to expand parole as a means to avoid new prison construction. For example, as of 1910, there were three federal penitentiaries and parole was granted at each of these institutions. By 1936, parole release was authorized in 46 states (see Table 7-2), with fifteen states (including California) employing parole in more than 80 percent of their prison releases (Cahalan, 1986). By 1939, Virginia, Florida, and Mississippi were the only states without parole systems (ibid.).

During the early implementation of parole, primary attention was given to the release rather than the supervision process. Preparation for parole was the responsibility of institutional parole officers, who as staff members, participated in classification procedures, the development of social histories, and in social case work involving the prisoner and his or her family in the community (Department of Justice, 2003). Upon release, the offender was to be under the supervision of a parole officer, as well as an advisor of the inmate's own choosing. The frequency of contact between the offender and the officer could range from every few days to once a month, depending upon the risk posed by the offender.

Table 7-2
Extent to Which Parole Was Used for Released Offenders
in the United States, 1936

Jurisdiction	Percent Paroled	Jurisdiction	Percent Paroled
Colorado	94	Arkansas	47
Indiana	94	Arizona	46
New Hampshire	94	Oregon	45
Vermont	94	Iowa	41
New York	93	Tennessee	38
Washington	91	South Dakota	36
Ohio	87	Texas	29
Illinois	87	West Virginia	29
Michigan	86	Rhode Island	25
New Jersey	86	Nebraska	23
Nevada	85	North Carolina	23
Pennsylvania	85	North Dakota	23
Maine	83	Louisiana	20
Kansas	82	Oklahoma	14
Massachusetts	81	Florida	12
Utah	78	Delaware	10
Connecticut	77	Missouri	8
New Mexico	67	Wyoming	8
Montana	62	Maryland	5
Minnesota	58	South Carolina	1
Kentucky	53	Idaho	0
Wisconsin	51	Virginia	0
California	49	Mississippi	0

Source: Historical Corrections Statistics in the United States, 1850–1984.

As Simon (1993) pointed out, however, more than ten years passed between the adoption of parole in 1893 in California and the actual implementation of a community supervision apparatus. In this interim phase, "Parole was used, much as the pardon power had been, to select for relief a few worthy cases, or to mitigate apparently excessive sentences. Parolees were released with little more than a bona fide and approved job, a private sponsor, a list of rules, and a sheaf of monthly reports to be completed" (ibid.: 45). California implemented a more complete parole system in 1910, with a parole officer, an assistant parole officer, and a clerical worker. The state's early operations centered upon reviewing monthly reports and processing revocation orders for parole violations discovered by the police, while the state parole officer was located in San Francisco and therefore made few personal contacts with parolees across the state (Berecochia, 1982).

Initially, then, community supervision was not seen as a necessity because parole was to be used only for a select few low-risk offenders with impeccable community ties. At the end of World War I, many states revised their parole laws to authorize the use of parole for a much broader array of offenders, including recidivists and murders. Rather than being used for only a select few low-risk offenders, parole became the preferred method of releasing inmates. Other states also adopted various indeterminate sentencing laws that made parole the presumptive release mechanism and provided parole authorities with substantial discretion in release decisions.

According to 1931 figures, the average length of time on parole supervision, was between twelve and fourteen months (U.S. Department of Justice, 2003). Although the majority of inmates were released to parole supervision, only about 64 percent of parolees were actually under the supervision of a full-time salaried parole officer (ibid.). Consequently, parole conditions were somewhat cursory, requiring that one be employed and be a "good citizen." Simon noted

Parole agents were given much discretion in enforcing parole's conditions, and the idea of supervision training seemed to hold little value. There was a shared understanding of what constituted normal behavior and the community itself provided much of the day-to-day monitoring. If the parolee refused to work, or was a troublemaker at home, the parole agent could respond to the complaints of the employer or family by threatening to re-imprison the parolee. Parole agents could lean on the community, as the community imposed its own informal behavioral requirements. Therefore, control and normalization did not flow from the agent but through him. Parole was a three-sided structure—offender, community, and agent—with the most important factor being the community (Simon, 1993: 68).

Beginning in the 1950s, a purportedly new parole model was in place. This new "clinical model" emerged in response to declining demand for unskilled workers and an increasing proportion of minorities in the prison population. Actually, the new clinical parole model reflected many of the original progressive beliefs regarding offender classification, training, and treatment. As Rothman (1980) noted, while the progressive penal agenda subsided in the 1920s and 1930s, renewed interest developed following World War II. In effect, a new optimism in government fueled the rebirth of the progressive-like approach of the 1940s and 1950s.

The clinical model stresses the professional capacity of parole agents to craft treatment programs that are responsive to the individual needs of the parolee and that can operate independently of the community. The clinical model was conceptualized as a sequential process that begins with an initial interview between the newly released parolee and the parole officer. The purpose of this initial interview is twofold: first, to gather objective information about the parolee; and second, to begin the important process of influencing, guiding, treating, and motivating the parolee. Once established, the treatment and guidance relationship between the parolee and officer was to evolve over time.

Simon (1993) argued that the development of the clinical model in parole represented an institutional acknowledgement of a potential "underclass." He contended that policy makers of the 1950s and 1960s believed there was a class of people who could not be absorbed into the labor force until they had been altered and fully prepared for the labor force. "Where once parole could satisfy its aim by reinforcing the disciplinary capacity of the community, parole in the 1950s and 1960s attempted to develop a model of supervision that could operate independently of the community" (ibid.: 100). Perhaps in response to this more difficult class of offender, the average length of parole supervision increased from fourteen months in 1931 to twenty-nine months by 1965 (U.S. Department of Justice, 2003).

The adoption of probation did not occur with the same speed and continuity as did the adoption of parole (see Table 7-3). During the early implementation of probation, its differential and fragmented use was apparent. Some states used probation, while others used a suspended sentence that did not necessarily involve a period of direct supervision. State differences in court organization also contributed to diverse uses and structures of probation. In 1935, approximately 30 percent of convicted offenders in states that participated in the use of probation were placed on probation (ibid.).

Table 7-3
Adoption of Adult Probation Statutes, 1878–1938

Jurisdiction	Year First Statute Was Passed	Jurisdiction	Year First Statute Was Passed
Massachusetts	1878	Wisconsin	1909
Missouri	1897	D.C.	1910
Vermont	1898	Delaware	1911
Rhode Island	1899	Illinois	1911
New Jersey	1900	Arizona	1913
New York	1901	Georgia	1913
California	1903	Montana	1913
Connecticut	1903	Idaho	1915
Michigan	1903	Virginia	1918
Maine	1905	Washington	1921
Kansas	1907	Utah	1923
Indiana	1907	Federal Government	1925
Ohio	1908	West Virginia	1927
Colorado	1909	Oregon	1931
Iowa	1909	Tennessee	1931
Minnesota	1909	Maryland	1931
Nebraska	1909	Kentucky	1934
North Dakota	1909	Arkansas	1937
Pennsylvania	1909	North Carolina	1937

Source: Historical Corrections Statistics in the United States, 1850–1984.

The probation supervision process was not altogether different from the parole supervision process. Both relied heavily on law enforcement to be their eyes and ears in the offender's community. In fact, the use of law enforcement officers as probation officers nearly destined the practice to be an exercise in control rather than treatment. This tension between treatment and control existed in the prison as well, but it took on a new character in probation and parole. Because probation and parole officers had treatment and sentence enforcement responsibilities, conflict was inherent in the officer's role. Moreover, given that probation and parole caseloads routinely exceeded one hundred, unwieldy caseload management necessarily shaped probation and parole practices. The caseload dilemma for probation and parole has been described in detail by Morris and Hawkins (1976). The authors reported that the best estimates

available from current research indicates that an average of 35 cases per officer is about the highest ratio likely to permit effective supervision and assistance in either service. Of course, no caseload standard can be applied to all types of offenders. The optimum overall caseload of 35 is based on a determination of what an average caseload would be when different types of offenders were given the appropriate types and degrees of supervision. Up to 20 persons in a caseload of 35 could receive close intensive supervision; if none required such supervision, the caseload could be larger (ibid.: 35).

Overall, by 1965, 67 percent of people under correctional supervision at any given time were in the community. Fifty-four percent of these were on probation, while 13 percent were on parole or some other form of aftercare (U.S. Department of Justice, 2003).

Uneven Progress and Correctional System Failure

Overall System Expansion and Control

Throughout the twentieth century, the correctional system took on new and unplanned dimensions. A number of studies have argued that during this period of refinement, the actual practices associated with prisons, parole, and probation were largely characterized by offender punishment, control, misuse, and management. The intentions-versus-reality disparity perhaps was most poignantly pointed out by a prison architect who joked that the following phrase should be etched into the stonework of a main prison gateway: "Abandon Hope All Ye Who Enter Here" (Bell, 1956). This is of course a far cry from the intention expressed in the slogan proposed by the then-director of the U.S. Bureau of Prisons: "Enter Prisoner—Exit Citizen" (ibid.). In the case of prison, parole, and probation decisions, it also has been documented that—instead of decisions based upon offender treatment needs—such decisions were determined largely by such legal variables as seriousness of offense and prior record: Legal variables (rather than offender characteristics and associated treatment needs) were reported to be the best predictors of prison sentence length, when an offender would be paroled from prison, and whether or not an offender would receive probation, prison, or reformatory placement (Wellford, 1975).

Regarding prison classification decisions and inmate receipt of counseling, education, and vocational training, a number of goal-versus-practice disparities existed. To begin, multidisciplinary classification teams seldom were employed in prisons (Irwin, 1980). In 1956, the director of the Federal Bureau of Prisons noted that "in the area of diagnostic, training and treatment personnel," the system suffered from both "austerity and scarcity" (Bell, 1956). Statistics from the 1950s indicate that roughly thirty-five or forty full-time psychiatrists, sixty psychologists, four hundred social workers, sociologists, and institutional parole officers, and a mere handful of employment-placement officers were unevenly distributed across roughly two hundred state and federal penitentiaries, reformatories, and camps (ibid.). Consequently, as Irwin (1980) later pointed out, counseling centered upon groups and was generally employed to maintain control over offenders. The group counseling leaders tended to be correctional workers with little if any clinical background, while psychiatrists or psychologists rarely were used (ibid.). Teachers with meager educational backgrounds and without teacher certification credentials typically staffed prison educational programs. Moreover, prison teachers were generally required to teach general education subjects rather than within an area of specialty. Teaching materials such as textbooks were typically outdated, and educational technology and teacher training designed to deal with the largely under-educated and illiterate offenders were nonexistent (Glaser, 1966). Although numerous vocational training programs were available in prisons, Irwin (1980) pointed out that these programs were largely oriented toward meeting specific maintenance-related needs within the prison rather than toward providing offenders with marketable employment skills.

At the same time that probation and parole were becoming more popular, they fell short of meeting their stated goals. For example, at the first National Conference on Parole in 1939, the then Attorney General declared parole to be a "source of scandal" (Bell, 1956). Since the inception of probation and parole, it was apparent that officers had little time to provide individualized counseling and treatment to their respective clients. Given the size of the caseloads and the additional responsibilities of having to conduct pre- and post-sentence investigations, supervision often amounted to little more than random checks (Carter and Wilkins, 1976). It was widely acknowledged that the ideal caseload for each probation or parole officer should be fifty to sixty-five offenders; yet, for decades, caseloads had averaged approximately one hundred and fifteen offenders per officer (Bell, 1956). In the 1950s and 1960s, average probation and parole caseloads greatly exceeded optimum levels. More than 76 percent of all misdemeanants and 67 percent of all felons on probation comprised caseloads exceeding one hundred. Further, fewer than 4 percent of probation officers across the country operated with caseloads of less than forty probationers. Consequently, in some states, maximum parole supervision required only monthly visits to the parolee's home and place of employment. Minimum supervision required a visit every three months (ibid.).

Lemert (1993) explained that, through a practice he termed "bank loading," only those probation and parole cases that are particularly difficult or problematic receive any level of individual care or control. In effect, probation and parole officers must attempt to "manage" and "control" their respective caseloads with little or no time for such lofty concerns as individualized treatment. Rather, their focus is on the difficult or exceptional cases. As Lemert argued, the most common caseload management technique for probation and parole officers is therefore bank loading. This is what parole and probation officers have always done—concentrate on serious cases and ignore the rest (ibid.).

The increasing size and scope of the system is also worth noting, particularly given the implementation of alternatives to incarceration. Between 1880 and 1960, the incarceration rate (per 100,000 population) in state and federal prisons nearly doubled (see Figure 7-1). However, the actual extent of penal control expanded beyond this figure due to increasing reliance on probation and parole. In fact, as acceptance of probation grew, it was not uncommon for many serious second- and third-time felons to receive sentences of probation. Even some violent felony offenders served their sentences in the community, though they were subject to special probation conditions (Clear and Cole, 2000).

Figure 7-1
Federal and State Prison Incarceration Rates, 1880–1960

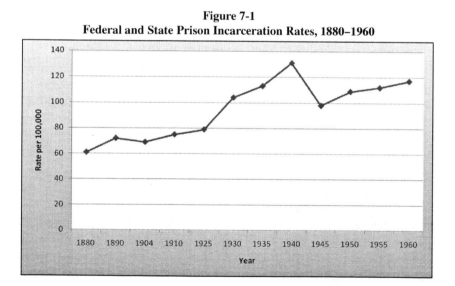

Unfortunately, other than at the federal level, no attempt was made to collect yearly state probation and parole data until the mid-1960s. Nevertheless, it is likely that the addition of state probation and parole data would demonstrate that the extent of penal growth during this period was actually much more substantial. Penal system expansion is also illustrated in the escalating correctional expenditures during this time period. For example, between 1902 and 1970, expenditures on state-run penal systems increased from $14 million to more than $1 billion. Moreover, from 1942 to 1970, states' penal system costs doubled every decade (U.S. Bureau of Census, 1975). By 1965, the annual operating costs for institutional and juvenile corrections totaled slightly more than $320 million; adult felony corrections—institutional and community based—totaled roughly $509 million, while misdemeanant corrections (institutional and otherwise) reached nearly $177 million. Thus, in 1965 alone, annual operating correctional expenses in the United States amounted to roughly $1.5 billion.

Rehabilitative Ideal: Explain, Treat, and Eliminate

At the turn of the twentieth century, America faced numerous and profound social challenges. Nevertheless, it was believed that these challenges could be overcome through government interventions that were scientifically guided. The strategy for combating social ills was fairly straightforward: Determine the cause of the problem and develop policies and practices to correct it. The twentieth-century rehabilitative ideal reflects the Progressive-Era approach to confronting social problems through the combined efforts of government and science. Hence, progressive ideology set in motion an explicit mission for the criminal justice system: Explain, treat, and eliminate criminal behavior.

The twentieth-century rehabilitative ideal gave rise to what is now known as the "correctional" system. The overall goal of rehabilitation necessitated the search for the causes of criminality, which in turn led to more complicated and individualized explanations of crime. These explanations resulted in further differentiation and classification of offenders and correspondingly diverse penal strategies. The need to differentiate and classify offenders spawned the development of various professional groups capable of making these distinctions and of administering treatment. As domains of professional expertise and other organizational demands increased, correctional agencies expanded and became more bureaucratized in order to accommodate the various and often-competing demands.

Given this set of developments, it is not surprising that a words-versus-deeds disparity emerged in all sectors of the penal system. For example, it was held that probation, parole, and institutional distinctions would result in more individualized offender treatment, thereby yielding greater assimilation into and the perfection of American society. However, the actual everyday practice of this burgeoning "correctional" system involved struggles with caseload management, routinized control, and treatment competency. Offenders tended not to be treated as individuals, but rather as categories or groups for the more convenient purposes of management and control. And while the anticipated discovery of the cause of crime was enthusiastically pursued, answers remained inconclusive. Was it culture conflict, learning, anomie, reaction formation, or differential opportunity? How could a fast-developing penal bureaucracy respond to inconclusive theories in fulfilling its offender treatment and rehabilitation goals? Were the goals of treatment and rehabilitation mere disguises for governmental efforts to control and punish? Or was this instead yet another case of good intentions gone awry during implementation?

Parole and especially probation were promoted as substitutes to the dominant practice of incarceration. However, instead of providing alternatives, these programs served as supplements. The salient consequences of these supplemental functions were increasing numbers of penal clients and escalating costs throughout the twentieth century. Until the turbulent decades of the 1960s and 1970s, this pattern of growth resulting from the rehabilitative ideal largely went unquestioned.

8

Prison Subcultures (1950s–1960s)

The targets of the penal reforms discussed thus far have been somewhat silenced. While much has been said about the subjection of offenders to brutal conditions of punishment and confinement in the course of reform, inmate responses to these conditions have not been explored. More specifically, the psychological impact of confinement and the social organization of life behind bars have not been examined from the perspective of the inmate.

At this historical juncture, discussion of prison life is fitting for several reasons. First, the body of research that enabled an understanding of prison life evolved from the theoretical developments of the twentieth-century rehabilitative ideal. Sociology was developing as a scientific discipline, with the objectives of describing and explaining the origins and inner workings of deviant subcultures. The prison—a mini-society in its own right—provides an excellent opportunity for investigating the requirements of social order and the transmission of deviant norms and values. Social-psychological, cultural transmission, and functionalist theories provide frameworks for describing and explaining the origins, structure, and function of the inmate social system.

Second, the problem of order in prisons had become particularly strained by the 1950s, with more than fifty riots breaking out between 1950 and 1953. Beginning in 1952, approximately forty prison riots transpired in a span of only eighteen months. In light of this unrest, prison research sought to explore the socialization patterns of inmates, as well as the power relations involved in the administration of prisons. It was generally assumed that prisons operated under conditions of absolute power, but the presence of inmate social systems and riots cast doubt over that assumption. Were prisons really "total systems of power" (Sykes, 1958)?

Social-psychological research on the prison environment illuminated the relatively hidden world of institutional operations and the effects of imprisonment on the rehabilitative chances of offenders. Prior to this research, much of the literature and recorded history of prisons was composed of exposés of wrongdoing and corruption by prison officials (Sykes, 1995). This new body of research unearthed a deeper comprehension of prison life that called into question the very notion of prison as a place of rehabilitation. The architects of this new research—Clemmer, Sykes, Irwin, and Giallombardo—forged what has become the conventional wisdom on inmate subcultures and adaptations to prison life that continues today.

Prison Community

Sociological interest in the prison began with *The Prison Community* (Clemmer, 1940). In this pioneering research, Clemmer studied the ways in which the prison community influences and shapes the attitudes and behavior of prisoners. Writing in the aftermath of the immigration waves and in the Chicago school tradition of the culture conflict perspective, Clemmer employed the concept of assimilation as an analytical framework. He defined assimilation as a person learning "enough of the culture of a social unit into which he is placed to make him characteristic of it" (ibid.). Borrowing from this general definition, Clemmer then coined the term "prisonization" to describe the process of "taking on in greater or lesser degree the folkways, mores, customs and general culture of the prison."

Clemmer proposed that all inmates undergo certain experiences that make them a part of the prison community. One such universal experience is that, upon entering the prison community, the inmate is compelled to accept an inferior role. This inferior role is reinforced by one's anonymous status, conferred by a prison number that replaces his or her name. The standard-issue uniforms that prevent individual expression further accentuate the imposed anonymity and inferiority. In the eyes of the warden and prison staff, the inmate is to be without distinction and power. Goffman (1961) would later refer to this intake procedure as part of a symbolic "stripping and mortification process." Goffman saw this ceremonial process as a practical and necessary feature of any "total institution" responsible for the care and management of large numbers of individuals.

A second universal experience at prison entry is learning the ways and means of the institution. Clemmer posited that inmates learn the rules that govern the organization and operation of the prison, such as the appropriate "ranks, titles and authorities of the various prison officials." Learning the new habits for daily existence constitutes a third universal prison experience. New habits include not only altered patterns of sleeping, eating, and working, but an eventual reinterpretation of these activities. In explaining the altered meanings given to these activities, Clemmer noted that upon entering the prison, inmates are generally thankful and eager to begin work in any job. However, after some time passes, inmates move from being satisfied with anything to desiring a "good job." He noted that the same process affects inmate preferences for food and shelter. This transition from being easily satisfied to articulating preferences reflects the fact that after a few months of incarceration, all activities and amenities assume new meaning and importance. For example, even throat lozenges can become a valued commodity in a state of deprivation, as they move from being an insubstantial form of medicine to a cherished piece of candy.

Clemmer's analysis of prison life extends beyond the universal features of prisonization. Having concluded that not all inmates are indoctrinated to the same degree by these experiences, he aimed to identify the factors that "bred or deepened criminality and antisociality and made the inmate characteristic of the criminalistic ideology in the prison community" (ibid.). In short, he sought to identify the factors that accelerate or delay the prisonization process. Clemmer found that five factors exert the most pronounced effect on this process. Included among these factors are the inmate's pre-prison personality, the type and extent of relationships maintained with persons outside and inside the prison, and the inmate associations that were not of the inmate's choosing, such as their cellmates and workmates. A final factor affecting the degree and pace of prisonization is whether the inmate truly accepts the creeds and codes of the prison subculture or merely follows them in order to survive. Clemmer acknowledged that these five factors are not the only determinants of prisonization, but they are the most impressionistic. Though not as significant as these other determinants, he added that age, race, and criminal record should not be discounted in the prisonization process (ibid.).

Clemmer's work highlights the fact that the prison experience necessarily disrupts the inmate's personality and that prospects for successful community reintegration depend on how "prisonized" the inmate becomes. In testing Clemmer's hypothesis that the longer the prison sentence, the greater the likelihood for extreme forms of prisonization, Wheeler (1971) affirmed that an inmate's conformity to socially prescribed norms varies with length of stay and the number of close associations within the prison. He found this relationship to be consistent with an inverted U-shape: Prisonization effects are least evident at the beginning and end of a sentence and are greatest midway into a sentence. Wheeler concluded that the inmate's apparent re-acceptance of conventional norms toward the conclusion of the sentence occurs in anticipation of release and preparatory adjustment to life on the outside. He also found that, within the broader inverted U-shape pattern, the degree of prisonization varies by role types. For example, prisonization effects are greatest for "right guys" and "square Johns" midway into the sentence, while effects are greatest toward the end of the sentence for "outlaws." Sykes and Messinger (1960) and others (e.g., Irwin and Cressey, 1962) similarly expanded Clemmer's thesis to include the effects of institutional structure on the prisonization process. That is, prisonization is presumably less severe in treatment-oriented institutions than in custody/disciplinarian-oriented institutions.

Though Clemmer's contributions to the understanding of prison communities and socialization are many, he did not address the impact of prisonization upon release. How long does it take before conforming attitudes resume? How does prisonization affect adjustment on the outside as measured by recidivism? Clemmer also did not address questions surrounding the origins of the prison subculture. He described the process of prisonization or assimilation into an existing culture, but took the prior existence of the prison subculture as a given. This omission paved the way for the seminal works of Gresham Sykes (1958) and John Irwin and Donald Cressey (1962).

Deprivation Model

In *The Society of Captives* (1958), Sykes employed a social-psychological perspective to study the inmate social system of the New Jersey State Maximum Security Prison. Specifically, he examined the impact of the prison environment (i.e., the social) on the mentality and self-concept (i.e., the psychological) of the inmate. In adopting this perspective, Sykes called attention to the often forgotten or ignored truth that physical pains, such as corporal punishments, are not the only pains endured while confined. Sykes further suggested that psychological pains can be just as damaging as physical ones. These psychological pains—or what he termed the "pains of imprisonment"—have their roots in the extremely "depriving or frustrating" nature of the inmate's captivity.

These pains contribute to a new set of functional but deviant norms and values that are later deported to the outside upon release. This thesis has been referred to as the deprivation model.

Pains of Imprisonment

Relying on participant observation and inmate interviews over a period of three years, Sykes (1958) concluded that five deprivations constituted the greatest pains of imprisonment. One such pain was the deprivation of liberty, which went beyond the obvious dimension of being confined to a secure institution. Inmates experienced the loss of liberty most acutely in their inability to freely relate with outsiders, primarily family and friends. Visitation and correspondence were regulated and monitored in ways that "frustrated" the ability to maintain close ties. Sykes found that 41 percent of inmates in the New Jersey Prison had no outside visits, which exacerbated their sense of isolation. Inmates came to define themselves through the lens of society, which meant seeing oneself as a social leper not fit for decent society. Sykes proposed that inmates ultimately adapted to this psychological pain by rejecting their rejecters.

Closely aligned with the deprivation of liberty was what inmates described as the deprivation of autonomy, or the loss of self-determination. This deprivation refers to the all-encompassing regulations that preclude individual decision making about the most basic and mundane of daily functions (e.g., eating, sleeping, showering, interacting). Sykes (1958) reported that inmates view these regulations as little more than "gestures of authoritarianism." Inmates do not perceive these regulations in the same way as do their captors, who contend that managing large numbers of people in a small space with limited resources demands a vast system of rules. According to Goffman (1961), inmate antagonism toward rules likely is aggravated by the fact that officials feel no obligation to explain the rationale for their system of rules. Though prison rules and regulations may be reasonable on their face, Sykes warned that prolonged exposure to such an environment leads to helplessness and dependency. The diminished capacity to do for oneself is perhaps best illustrated by a former inmate's account of his struggle with opening doors after being released from prison: He stated that even after several months of freedom, he automatically stood at every door he encountered, waiting for someone else to open it.

The third pain identified by inmates in Sykes's (1958) study was the deprivation of goods and services. While inmates have their basic necessities met (i.e., food, shelter, health care, recreation, and clothing), Sykes argued that a greater underlying material loss was being overlooked. To clarify the implications of this loss, Sykes considered the psychological value of ownership and possession of necessities and amenities in a society that determines self-worth by the quantity and quality of individual possessions. Sykes contended that inmates have difficulty rationalizing their material loss because it cannot be justified in gratifying terms. In other words, the deprivation of goods and services is not the result of "self-sacrifice in the interests of the community," nor the result of "present pleasures foregone for pleasures in the future." Rather, the impoverishment is self-created; consequently, the inmate's self-worth devolves into personal inadequacy.

In Sykes's (1958) estimation, the deprivation of heterosexual relationships has a particularly detrimental effect on the male psyche. He claimed that, with few exceptions, a man's self-concept is linked foremost to his feelings of masculinity. And, in the all-male prison environment, this masculinity is constantly and openly challenged. Borrowing from Charles Cooley's (1902) concept of the "looking glass self," Sykes noted that the portion of the inmate's self-image that is developed through simple interaction with women is missing. Added to this is the sexual frustration that results from the lack of heterosexual relationships, while surrendering to that frustration through homosexual encounters only further degrades the self-concept.

The final deprivation identified by inmates is the loss of security. One inmate in Sykes's (1958) study indicated that the "worst thing about prison is you have to live with other prisoners." That was not to say that inmate solidarity is non-existent, it is just that numerous "outlaws within this group of outlaws" make solidarity fragile and uncertain. Inmates went so far as to describe one another as "vicious" and "dangerous." It was further communicated that one does not need to be routinely robbed, beaten, or raped to experience the loss of security, as the fear of eventually being "tested" is sufficiently overwhelming. Sykes concluded that the inmate's manhood and self-concept—not to mention physical well-being—hinges upon his reaction and his ability to cope with this pervasive sense of insecurity.

Adaptations

Sykes (1958) found that adaptations to the pains of imprisonment were numerous and could include escaping physically or psychologically, mounting a violent insurrection, or seeking peaceful change though legal means. Sykes maintained that these are unlikely and risky recourses for the average inmate, though, and that the more realistic mode of surviving the pains of imprisonment is through the patterns of social interaction established by the inmates themselves. Such patterns of interaction were termed "adaptive endurance" and formed the basis of Sykes's deprivation thesis on the origins of prison subcultures.

The patterned social interaction that constituted the inmate social system, or "society of captives," was not characterized by pure inmate solidarity, nor was it characterized by constant predatory behavior between inmates. Instead, adaptive endurance, or patterned social interaction, fluctuated between the two extremes of "collectivistic" and "individualistic" orientations. As one moves closer to the collectivist orientation, the greater is the inmate solidarity and the less severe are the pains of imprisonment (Sykes and Messinger, 1960). Moreover, the greater the inmate solidarity, the greater will be the adherence to the inmate code that governs daily life. According to this code, inmates are not to (1) interfere with other inmates' interests (i.e., "don't be nosey," "don't have a loose lip," "keep off a man's back," "don't put a guy on the spot"); (2) lose their head (i.e., "play it cool," "do your own time," and try to keep feuds and grudges to a minimum); (3) exploit fellow inmates (i.e., "don't break your word," "don't welsh on debts"); (4) weaken (i.e., "don't whine or cop out"); or (5) be a sucker (i.e., guards are not to be trusted, and the inmate is always to side with other inmates). The inmate who basically follows this code is known by other inmates as a "real man" who "pulls his own time" and consequently is viewed by other inmates as a man of integrity and autonomy.

As the term "individualistic orientation" implies, most inmates give verbal rather than actual allegiance to the code. Despite verbal allegiance to the code, several inmates adopt "alienative" responses to the pains of imprisonment. The "rat" or "squealer" violates the code of communication with guards on occasion, whereas the "center man" always sides with officials (Sykes, 1958). A "gorilla" violates the inmate code by forcefully taking from other weaker inmates, whereas the "merchant" uses economic exploitation to manipulate other inmates. Sykes found that the merchant is among the most alienated because he is too willing to pursue his own well-being at the expense of others. Other inmates violate the code through their sexual conduct. "Wolves," "punks," and "fags" are so labeled because of their homosexual activity: Wolves are the aggressors, punks are sexually submissive, and fags are simply homosexual by nature.

"Ball busters" are inmates who give guards a hard time through constant and blatant disobedience. Because their behavior results in the potential punishment of all inmates, they are regarded by their fellow inmates as fools. Inmate roles also include "toughs" and "hipsters." Toughs are considered touchy and a threat because of their unpredictable outbursts. A hipster is a "wanna-be" who pretends to be tough by targeting inmates who are more passive or submissive.

It is not accurate to say that these various characterizations serve merely as nicknames or as forms of inmate jargon. They are, as Sykes (1958) termed them, "argot roles." These roles reflect the principles of the inmate code and serve as cues for interaction with other inmates and correctional officials. These general labels given to inmates by other inmates effectively function as a kind of classification system. This "inside" classification system helps inmates navigate their prison experience by identifying other inmates in terms of their needs, roles, and threats.

Sykes's (1958) perspective on the origins and features of the inmate social system is not without its critics. For all its insights, his thesis does not allow for the possibility that the origins of prison subcultures or inmate behavior lay outside the prison environment. A counter theoretical perspective—known as the importation thesis—offers a different interpretation of the origins, features, and consequences of inmate subcultures. This perspective was developed most thoroughly by John Irwin and Donald Cressey.

Importation Model

Irwin and Cressey (1962) alleged that Sykes's deprivation model overlooks the values and social capital that offenders bring into prisons. They asserted that inmates are not simply "blank slates" upon entering the prison community and that the normative systems and antisocial behaviors developed on the outside inevitably are imported into the prison. Many of the behaviors and attitudes that govern group interaction outside the prison govern inmate interaction inside the prison. Irwin and Cressey illuminated their importation thesis through a typology of subcultures that identified the pre-prison characteristics of offenders. This typology explains not only the origins of prison subcultures, but also the influence of these subcultures on rehabilitative efforts in the prison and, ultimately, on the likelihood of recidivism.

Thief–Criminal Subculture

Irwin and Cressey (1962) maintained that a thief–criminal subculture has a discernable presence in the prison. It is comprised of inmates known as "right guys" or "real men" and inmates who generally are regarded as trustworthy, cool-headed, and reliable. However, consistent with their thesis, Irwin and Cressey argued that the attributes of trustworthiness and dependability are not exclusive to the thief–criminal subculture found in the prison. Rather, these attributes [pre]exist in the thief–criminal subculture outside the prison, as illustrated by the familiar adage "honor among thieves."

According to Irwin and Cressey (1962), inmates who are aligned with the thief–criminal subculture view it as their primary "reference group." Consequently, their self-image is derived from their connections to criminal subcultures inside and outside the prison, and they do their time as if committed to a thief–criminal life but not necessarily a prison life. Those belonging to this subculture genuinely want to be released from prison and, until that time arrives, they want a minimum of conflict. This means that members of this subculture do not seek status and prestige within the institution, but instead seek things that make incarceration more bearable. This can include radios, contraband books, food, socks, and gadgets that enhance leisure time.

Convict–Prison Subculture

Acknowledging the contribution of Sykes (1958), Irwin and Cressey (1962) conceded that a convict–prison subculture does emerge in response to the deprivations of freedom, wealth, and goods and services. However, they also argued that the distinguishing features of this particular subculture are not directly determined by these deprivations. For example, inmates associated with the convict–prison subculture consist of gorillas, merchants, and toughs, whose core values revolve around utilitarianism and manipulation. Citing Miller's (1958) study of lower-class delinquent subcultures in free society, Irwin and Cressey argued that autonomy, cunning, toughness, fatalism, and defiance of authority are the focal concerns of inmates as well as delinquent youth. In contrast to the thief–criminal subculture, members of the convict–prison subculture desire acceptance only from those within the prison. They acquire positions of status by means available only in the prison and have a vested interest in sustaining the existing order of the prison.

Legitimate Subculture

Finally, Irwin and Cressey (1962) also identified a legitimate prison subculture that seems to reject both the values of the thief and those of the convict subculture. This subculture consists of "accidental" criminals, such as the drunk driver who hit a pedestrian, the manslaughter murderer, or middle-class embezzler. These particular criminals subscribe to pro-social attitudes and behaviors on the outside and on the inside. Moreover, they come to the prison with anti-criminal and anti-prison ties and look to do their time in the most legitimate way possible. They are among those that participate in inmate councils, work on the inmate newsletter, and spend time in religious study. This subculture is composed of inmates that prison officials refer to as "good prisoners."

Indications of the nature and strength of inmate ties to inside and outside communities are an implicit part of the Irwin and Cressey typology. These ties were identified by Clemmer (1940) as important in determining prisonization and, subsequently, reintegration success. Irwin and Cressey used this subculture typology to understand the impact of rehabilitative efforts and the likelihood of recidivism upon release. For example, if deviant norms and values are indeed imported, and if thieves maintain their ties to the criminal subculture inside and outside while convicts maintain their ties to the prison subculture exclusively, then instilling new norms and values (or breaking old bad ones) will be extremely difficult. Predictably, Irwin and Cressey (1962) found that rehabilitative potential is highest for those aligned with the legitimate subculture and lowest for those in the convict–prison subculture. Hence, recidivism is most likely to occur in the convict–prison subculture because convicts remain the primary reference group. For these inmates, release is merely a short vacation from prison life. For those in the thief–criminal subculture, the prison is a "pitfall" or disruption to outside life. Their likelihood of recidivating is not as low as for those in the legitimate subculture, but neither is it as high as for those in the convict–prison subculture.

Irwin's contribution to the study of prison subcultures extends beyond the importation thesis. In *The Felon* (1970), Irwin addressed the more universal question of how convicts resolve to do their time. Irwin concluded as Sykes had that some inmates fail to cope entirely and instead slip into suicidal or psychotic behavior. Those who do cope, do so either by "doing time," "jailing," or "gleaning." These three modes of coping correspond closely with the subculture typology just presented in that "jailers" make the prison their world, while "gleaners" make the best of the situation through participation in education and other self-improvement programs. An important point to emerge from *The Felon,* however, is that no matter how inmates choose to do their time, they all acquire what Irwin termed the "convict identity." The convict identity, like prisonization, is acquired in degrees, but it hinders the future of all felons, no matter how much time passes since release. Irwin argued that the "convict identity" affects one's ability to make it on the outside, despite significant positive lifestyle changes. For the "old cons" who served especially long sentences, the convict identity is particularly entrenched; these inmates succumb to the identity completely and, in Irwin's words, are "suited for nothing more than dereliction on the outside or death in prison" (ibid.).

Female Inmate Subcultures

It has been argued that both deprivation and importation theories can be seen as compatible because life before prison can help to shape how inmates adapt and react to institutional deprivations. This blended approach can be seen partially in Giallombardo's (1966) study of female subcultures. Based on her observations at the Federal Reformatory for Women in West Virginia, she concluded that the pains of imprisonment do stimulate the formation of a subculture, but that the characteristics of female subcultures are best explained by factors external to the prison.

Giallombardo (1966) found that, in large part, the pains of imprisonment are just as intense for women as they are for men. Women, too, find the deprivations of liberty, autonomy, material goods, and heterosexual relationships "frustrating to the extreme." Unlike their male counterparts, however, women cite companionship and separation from their children and families as major pains of imprisonment (see also Kassebaum, 1972). A major exception to this otherwise shared prison experience is the loss of security. Unlike men, women generally do not fear sexual and violent exploitation. Instead, their insecurity stems from the untrustworthy character of female inmates. Giallombardo claimed that, in the female inmate social system, distrust is so pervasive that inmate solidarity is little more than "calculated solidarity." Females determine their loyalties and actions on a situation-by-situation basis, in accordance with self-interest and preservation rather than moral obligation. Thus, while men fear being literally stabbed in the back, women fear a metaphorical stab in the back. To explain the phenomenon of calculated solidarity, she claimed that the conventional rivalry to secure a male partner is brought into the prison and manifests itself in the socialization patterns of female inmates.

Giallombardo and others held that the importation of culturally determined roles into the prison also is exhibited in attempts to replicate family structures. It is in the context of creating pseudo or "make believe" families that homosexual roles and relationships are played out in the female subculture. In other words, these pseudo families evolve naturally from psychological and physiological needs such as feeling wanted or needed, being appreciated, economic fears, and peer acceptance and intimacy (Hensley et al., 2002; Ward and Kassebaum, 1965). As is the case with male inmates, there are female inmates who engage in homosexual behavior regardless of their incarcerated status (i.e., lesbians), and those who do so only by virtue of their confinement (i.e., turnouts). Overall, Giallombardo (1966) noted that the pseudo-family roles are intricately structured. They include the "femme" or "mommy," which is the most highly coveted role and parallels the role of the wife in free society. They also include the "stud broad," which is patterned after the "daddy" or father role. This role also affords considerable prestige in the female inmate subculture as it constitutes the only semblance of a male within the institution. However, polygamy is an accepted and common feature of the pseudo family. While finding and sustaining stable relationships are of paramount importance, there are often multiple wives present in one pseudo-family. Additional wives generally fulfill a specific and individualized function. Some serve an economic purpose by helping to secure material gains. Other wives refrain from homosexual activity and serve only in an emotional capacity. However, the wives or family members who engage in homosexual relationships attain the greatest status. These various membership roles within the pseudo-families have been interpreted as enabling women in prison to function in the same capacity as they had on the outside, or as a way to recover what was lacking in their natural families (Hensley et al., 2002).

Alienative roles, such as the "chippie," "jive bitch," and the "snitcher," are common in female as well male prison subcultures. The label of chippie is given to prison prostitutes who engage in sexual relations for material gain or sexual gratification. This label distinguishes between those who are involved in promiscuous sex versus love/relational sex. The snitcher in the female subculture parallels the rat or squealer in the male subculture. Similar to the members of the legitimate subculture identified by Irwin and Cressey, the "accidental criminals" of the female prison are known as "squares." They, too, possess anti-criminal loyalties and generally refrain from homosexual activity. They are viewed by their fellow inmates as naïve, suckers, and even unwitting in their betrayals because they are so easily manipulated by prison officials. Consequently, squares are viewed as the pariahs of the female prison community. The jive bitch, on the other hand, is highly purposeful in her betrayals; her sole intent is to create conflict and break up relationships between inmates. Her weapon is not violence, but lies, distortions, and the previously mentioned metaphorical backstab.

Though many of the argot roles identified in the female subculture involve self-interest and untrustworthy behavior, there are some loyalties that are maintained in female institutions. "Rap buddies" and "homeys" are inmates who foster a reasonable assumption of mutual trust. "Connects" work in the prison economy and are respected for supplying needed goods and information. "Boosters" are the partial female equivalent of the merchant, except that they win respect rather than scorn from other inmates.

Giallombardo's (1966) study revealed obvious similarities between the female and male subcultures, but important differences as well. Absent are the argot roles of wolf, tough, gorilla, ball buster, hipster, and the right guy. The absence of the right guy role, in particular, reflects the diminished importance of the inmate code and the attendant notions of fair play and loyalty. A second important distinction is that male conflicts typically result from power struggles, whereas female conflicts center upon the struggle for maintaining marriages; kinship ties constitute the principal factor of social integration. In light of these findings, Giallombardo concluded that the female inmate social system is not merely a functional response to the pains of imprisonment, as Sykes had proposed for the male inmate social system. While these pains provide the necessary conditions for the emergence of a social system, the pains alone do not explain the characteristics of the female subculture. Rather, the characteristics of the female inmate subculture are shaped by the same conditions that shape female existence in free society.

Total Power and Institutional Control

What is evident from these various depictions of prison life—whether based on the male or female experience—is the apparent lack of total power by prison authorities. How else could one explain incidents of disobedience, fraud, rape, violence, murder, and the other illegal exploits of the ball busters, gorillas, chippies or merchants? To answer this question, one can again consult the work of Sykes, who was able to explain the generally orderly conditions of the prison despite the absence of total power.

In *The Society of Captives* (1958), Sykes challenged the conventional belief that prisons are institutions of total power. He suggested that the exercise of total power within the institutional setting is more theoretical than real and that maintaining order is a delicate balancing act that involves exchange and reciprocity. In effect, officials are engaged in a continuous struggle with their captives and enlist the assistance of inmates to ease this struggle and facilitate order (see also Cloward and Ohlin, 1960; Sykes and Messinger, 1960). Such arrangements are necessary at times to compensate for what Sykes termed "the defects of total power."

Sykes (1958) attributed the defects of power to a number of sources. First, he argued that the power of prison officials is not based on freely given authority. He reasoned that, in order for power to be exercised effectively in any realm, the authority must be viewed as legitimate. If it is not, those who are subjected to it will feel no moral obligation to comply with rules and regulations. Because many inmates claim to be innocent and view their convictions and incarcerations as unfounded, there apparently is no "just" cause to respect these agents of "unjust" authority.

The reality of a limited use of force also contributes to the defects of power. Although use of force was not outlawed by any means during the 1950s or the 1960s, Sykes proposed that repeated acts of force are eventually limited in their effects. Physical force might temporarily subdue the inmate but, on a repeated basis, will have little impact both in the long term and in more complicated situations. For example, neither the mass movement of inmates in an orderly fashion nor the securing of good work habits on a daily basis can be ensured through repeated acts of physical force on the part of prison officials (Sykes, 1958).

In an environment wherein authority is not viewed legitimately and force is limited, a system of rewards and punishments could serve as a viable alternative for securing order and compliance. Yet, Sykes (1958) claimed that even this strategy was destined for defeat. Many of the punishments administered in prison lose their "potency" because they do not constitute a discernible departure from the pains and deprivations already experienced: Inmates already are subjected to a steady diet of violence and threats of violence from other inmates in addition to strict rules from officials. What form of punishment remains? Moreover, punishment often serves as a status symbol to an offender, having the unintended effect of becoming a reward.

From Sykes's (1958) perspective, the system of rewards is equally flawed because rewards are provided immediately upon admission to prison. Mail, visitation, recreation, and "gain time" privileges are given at the outset of one's time in prison. Consequently, inmates often view these privileges as rights or obligations, rather than as rewards to be earned on a separate and gradual basis. For inmates, rewards and punishments can therefore become blurred, in that the only punishments available are rights that can be denied.

Lastly, Sykes (1958) claimed that defects of power can be attributed to correctional officers who fail to exercise their control and authority properly. Officers frequently ignore certain infractions and basic security requirements, or even join inmates in criticizing higher-ranking prison officials. For a number of reasons, officers often take the path of least resistance when it comes to the enforcement of rules. Sykes proposed that correctional officers, like most anyone, want to be liked by those with whom they have constant contact. The need to be liked has a greater urgency in the prison setting, however, for if one is not liked, he or she risks exposure to violent retaliation in the event of a riot.

The need for correctional officers to be liked has implications for day-to-day management as well. Inmates can act out in a number of ways, which does not bode well for the officers in the eyes of their superiors. The officers' job performance is judged by how well they are able to "handle" those in their charge; thus, a system of give and take serves the purpose of "handling" inmates in a way that gives the appearance of order and good job performance. The officer–inmate relationship, then, is not one of complete dominance by the former over the latter; it is a relationship characterized by cooperation and exchange via bargaining, "deals," and "trades." In exchange for inmate cooperation and certain levels of order, prison staff members overlook certain infractions and permit an underground economy in which inmates barter for various and often illegal goods.

Sykes (1958) concluded that the power defects are structurally induced. That is, the defects cannot be eliminated simply by hiring more qualified, better paid, or better trained staff. Rather, the cooperative relationship between staff and inmates is a functional feature of a social system beset with unavoidable pains and deprivations. Indeed, it is this unofficial feature of cooperation and exchange that prevents the prison from descending into total and perpetual chaos. For this reason, Sykes advised that any prison reform aimed at gaining more control that does not heed the culture of inmates is destined for failure.

Living in Prison

Recent research grounded in the tradition of Clemmer, Sykes, Irwin and Cressey, and Giallombardo has produced new and different findings, but the essential arguments of these early scholars have not been overturned. Clemmer's prisonization hypothesis, for example, has been subject to much empirical testing over the years, with mixed results (Ramirez, 1984; Rhodes, 1979; Thomas, 1975; Walters, 2003). Much of the inconclusiveness of this theory, however, stems not from the question of whether prisonization occurs, but from the question of what factors—institutional or otherwise—most affect the trajectory and intensity of this process.

The deprivation perspective developed by Sykes also has been advanced, again revealing new and sometimes more inconclusive findings. Flanagan (1980), for instance, found that prisoners ranked missing somebody as the most severe pain, followed by missing social life, and then feeling that life is wasted. Wright (1989; as reported in Dhami et al., 2007) observed that prisoners identify support as their greatest need, followed by activity, structure, privacy, and social stimulation. In an extension of Irwin and Cressey's importation approach, Dhami and colleagues (2007) examined the effect of education and employment on various prison adaptations and found support for importation. Further, Hochstetler and DeLisi (2005) perhaps have set the stage for future research on importation by framing some questions that linger still: "If something is imported into the prison, what is it?" What are the most likely imported characteristics?" and "What are the mechanisms of transference?"

More generally, it is apparent that profound increases in African-American and Hispanic inmate populations and the growth of prison gangs have altered, but not negated, the strength and structure of the inmate social system in male prisons. Though prisoner identities still are an integral part of adaptive endurance, they have also become divided along the lines of ethnicity and race rather than criminal history, home affiliation, or shared prison experiences. For example, Chicanos view blacks and whites as more likely to "snitch," and so they place extreme importance on friendship and loyalty only to their own ethnic group. Modified patterns of inmate interaction and socialization also stem from the rise of inmate gangs and a younger "state-raised" generation of offenders. Violence, rather than "doing your own time," has become the more respected mode of adapting. Inmate gangs—such as the Texas Syndicate, the Mexican Mafia, and the Aryan Brotherhood—are highly militant and organized, and are quite willing to impose death on those inmates who violate their codes.

According to Ralph (1997), this increased propensity for violence renders the sanctions available to prison officials virtually meaningless.

The more gangs rule themselves and other inmates, the more the system of reciprocity and exchange between staff and inmates weakens. Certain hostilities and divisions always have existed between the staff and inmates, but the power balance was kept in check. Ralph contended that such a balance may be teetering in a dangerous direction, as gangs are at constant war with each other and are seeking to control not only the inmate subculture, but the institution itself.

In *Well-Governed Prisons* (1993), DiIulio offered an alternative to Sykes's model of governance that he claimed is better suited for the new and highly volatile prison climate of the twenty-first century. He argued that effective, well-ordered prisons are possible and that the belief that cons necessarily will "run the joint" is mistaken. At one time, administrators did permit some degree of inmate control through inmate councils and the "building tender" system, which used inmates to discipline other inmates. Following the prisoner rights movement, however, such practices have been declared illegal on the grounds that they contribute to an unsafe, insecure, and more violent environment.

Employing a public management approach, DiIulio assumed that the effectiveness of any prison organization depends upon a stable team of like-minded executives structured in a paramilitary, security-driven, bureaucratic setting. The quality of management and prison life also depends on cooperative relationships with outside actors (i.e., legislators, judges, and community activists), and not inside actors (i.e., inmates). The presence of order (i.e., low rates of violence and other misconduct), good amenities (i.e., availability of clean cells, decent food), and good service (i.e., availability of various rehabilitative programs) is not contingent upon a "better class" of inmates, but rather upon effective prison administration (ibid.). DiIulio rejected the conclusions of most sociologists and penologists; namely, that the "ineffective prisons" of the 1950s and 1960s are unavoidable. Instead, he reasoned that the responsibility for ineffective prisons ultimately rests with the failures of administration and he argued that the failures of the past can be corrected.

9

Prisoner Rights in the Age of Discontent (1960s–1970s)

Never has there been a time when the prison was not subject to outside inspection. From the outset, penological commissions, charitable associations, and various social critics noted the promise of the prison, but they also acknowledged the brutality of institutional conditions and the failure of different confinement strategies (e.g., rules of silence, separation) to reform or deter offenders. In the twentieth century, external scrutiny gained momentum, with academics lending a critical new voice through empirical and theoretical analyses. These scholarly investigations documented the capacity of the prison to foster deviant norms and values, inflict psychological damage upon its inmates, and ultimately undermine rehabilitation efforts.

Despite more than a century of critical reflection and analyses, however, the legitimacy of the prison never has been seriously challenged. That is, while investigations and research might have raised awareness and sparked reform, the essence of the prison—and the nation's commitment to the prison—has largely remained unchanged. This is due not only to the perceived necessity and convenience of the prison, but also to an inherent belief in the benevolent intentions of the state and its "disinterested" professional agents. Prior to the 1960s, therefore, it was widely believed that an effective correctional system was within reach and that the problem of crime could be overcome eventually. All that was needed in this "march of progress" was increased knowledge, resources, and time.

However, during the 1960s, faith in the capacity of the government to control crime took a decidedly downward course. Various formal and informal institutions that had been considered the guardians of social order became regarded as suspect. Many academics charged that correctional practices were doing more harm than good and that the traditional response of "more [state control and intervention] is better" had become the problem rather than the solution to crime control. As the behavior of the criminal justice system came under increased scrutiny, reforms aided by the academic and legal communities sought to restrict the powers of the state.

This chapter reviews the development and outgrowths of these reform efforts in the context of the prisoner rights movement and the moratorium on capital punishment. Both movements expanded constitutional protections afforded to convicted offenders, which was no simple feat. Neither prisoners nor prisons have a popular political constituency advocating on their behalf. As Jacobs (2004) noted, prisoners are not typically perceived to be among the "deserving poor," and being on the side of allocating resources and rights to improve prison conditions wins few if any votes. Yet, the 1960s fostered a social context in which even prisoners were seen as citizens who deserved constitutional protection.

Radicalism and Social Reform

By all accounts, the mechanisms of informal and formal social control were well at work between 1950 and 1960. Few groups seriously disputed existing social arrangements and crime rates were at their lowest level since 1900. In fact, social life was deemed to be so conformist and lacking in diversity and individual expression that the student population of this period was dubbed the "silent generation" (Skolnick, 1969). Art, science, learning, entertainment, and information all were mass-produced, creating a narrow and singular vision of the "norm." On the surface, American society was characterized by consensus and prosperity. Beneath the surface, however, was a fragmented culture—marred by racism, sexism, and many other forms of social discrimination.

The Hippie Generation

The beat poets of the late 1950s were among the first of many activists in this age of discontent. Unlike many of their successors, though, they voiced their opposition through fairly tepid means. They retreated into the silent protests of intellectualism and poetry, or what was often referred to as "dropping out" (Gross, 1986). It was the more raucous methods of the "hippie" subculture that sparked the revolution for which the 1960s are best remembered. Hippies were more strident in their disdain of social conventions, and their need to separate from the hypocrisy of the old culture is what drove their opposition. Consequently, hippies displayed their rejection of the establishment through drug use, rock music, language, dress, and communal living. Rather than organize and infiltrate the system they sought to overthrow, hippies argued that authenticity of lifestyle alone would alter politics and economics. In effect, antisocial behavior and civil disobedience would tear down the "pig-power structure" (Gross, 1986).

This protest philosophy led to demonstrations that often were festivals for radical and unconventional behavior. As one participant of these demonstrations stated: "I support everything that puts people in motion, which creates disruption and controversy, which creates chaos and rebirth" (Rubin, 1971, quoted in Gross, 1986: 111). Another proclaimed:

> What's needed is a new generation of nuisances. A new generation of people who are freaky, crazy, irrational, sexy, angry, irreligious, childish, and mad. People who burn draft cards, and dollar bills . . . who burn M.A. and doctoral degrees . . . who lure the youth with music, pot, and LSD . . . who redefine reality . . . who wear funny costumes (ibid.).

Counterculturalist Gridley Wright wrote in 1969: "I don't believe that there is anything like rights and justice and to the degree I would see myself as hung up with concepts like that, I would be in a circular bag, because there never have been rights and justice" (ibid.: 110).

The nihilism expressed in these statements stemmed from a deep and growing disillusionment with American society. Poverty was not randomly distributed, but instead was disproportionately concentrated among blacks and women (Bok, 1992). Politicians lied unabashedly and mislead the American public. Activism rooted in authenticity and defiance, however, had little political influence: Many social justice enthusiasts of the day realized that reform could not be achieved by simply dropping out or adopting a hippie lifestyle.

Government Protest and Civil Rights

The rumblings of social and political dissent may have been featured in the writings of beat poets and the dress and music of counterculturalists, but it was a series of more momentous events that ignited reform on a broader and more permanent scale. *Brown v. Board of Education* in 1954, the 1955 murder of a black child, Rosa Parks' personal protest in 1955, and Martin Luther King's entry into the civil rights struggle were among the signature moments in the democratization of World War II society. Reflecting King's efforts "to awaken a sense of moral shame in the opponent" (Skolnick, 1969), the civil rights movement gained momentum with the Mississippi freedom rides to register black voters in 1961 and the 1963 March on Washington for Jobs and Freedom. The civil rights cause further strengthened with Freedom Summer of 1964, and the 1965 King-led march from Selma to Montgomery, Alabama.

Despite seeking peaceful means to racial integration, organizers in the South met with legal and violent forms of retaliation. Southern judges, prosecutors, and local bar associations routinely suppressed civil rights and worked to maintain terrorist racism instead of prosecuting and punishing it (Skolnick, 1969). When nine hundred college students volunteered to register black voters and teach the concepts of freedom in Mississippi schools in the summer of 1964, the result was three student deaths; one thousand arrests; thirty-five shooting incidents; thirty bombings of homes, churches, and meeting houses; and eighty beatings (Graham, 1992). During marches in Alabama the following year, a young black boy and a Unitarian minister died at the hands of state troopers. More bloodshed followed on 7 March 1965—later dubbed Bloody Sunday.

The violently repressed peaceful tactics of civil rights activists in the South were not embraced by all. Other groups had grown impatient and frustrated as government promises to deal with urban decay, racial tensions, and poverty had gone unfulfilled for far too long. The civil rights movement on the West Coast and in the North assumed a more aggressive and isolationist stance, believing the government to be wholly untrustworthy as a protector of rights and promoter of general welfare. In response to inadequate progress in achieving justice, more militant leaders emerged (e.g., Malcolm X, Huey Newton, Eldridge Cleaver), who preached a message of separation as opposed to integration, often with violence.

Malcolm X and other leaders portrayed black racism as a global third world issue linked to the history of "white" colonialism. Lending credence to this perspective is the fact that many black Americans were expected to fight and die in wars for free market capitalism abroad, even though they could not achieve full economic independence and political freedom at home. Against this backdrop, Malcolm X described his objectives for civil rights as "complete freedom, complete justice, complete equality, by any means necessary." He went on to say, "You show me a black man who isn't an extremist, and I'll show you one who needs psychiatric attention" (quoted in Skolnick, 1969: 99).

The creation of the Black Panther Party in 1966 reflects this call to action "by any means necessary." The Black Panther Party for Self-Defense was established in Oakland, California, to move black power into the electoral arena and to defend against the actions of the police. For example, having abandoned faith in the criminal justice system to carry out impartial enforcement of the law, the Black Panthers pledged to police the actions of the Oakland Police Department. Their guiding philosophy is that "the Panther never attacks first, but when he is backed into a corner, he will strike back viciously" (Skolnick, 1969). The result of these and numerous other impassioned calls to action in the fight against police brutality was the outbreak of ghetto violence in Los Angeles, Chicago, Cleveland, Dayton, San Francisco, Atlanta, Omaha, and numerous other communities throughout the country. The Watts riots of August 1965 resulted in 4,000 arrests, while the Chicago riots resulted in 3,000 arrests in three days. The Detroit riot of 1967 produced 43 deaths, 7200 arrests in nine days, hundreds of injuries, 1,300 destroyed buildings, 5,000 newly homeless, and approximately $50 million in damages (Graham, 1992). Less destructive riots erupted in the ghettos of Boston, Cincinnati, Milwaukee, and Newark. In Newark, 1,500 were arrested after five days of rioting in April 1968. In the week immediately following the death of Martin Luther King, protests in D.C. and Baltimore resulted in 7,444 and 5,500 arrests, respectively (Skolnick, 1969).

Residents of poor black communities—rural and urban alike—were not the only participants in acts of civil disobedience. Teachers, doctors, nurses, ministers, and priests from white America decried the hypocrisy behind the government's foreign policy and its timid response to racial and economic inequality at home. Students at Berkeley, Chicago, Columbia, and the University of Wisconsin led hundreds of anti-war and civil rights demonstrations. In 1965, 25,000 students protested the Vietnam War and, by 1968, the protests involved 300,000 students (ibid.). In the 1967–1968 academic year, 71 separate demonstrations occurred on 62 campuses. Between January and June 1968, a total of 38,911 students produced 221 demonstrations at 101 colleges (Skolnick, 1969). Far from being the silent generation, the students of the 1960s sought to affect social change and invigorate the democratic process.

The women's rights movement advanced alongside the anti-war and black civil rights movements, albeit at a slower pace. While the black and women's civil rights movements remained separated in their struggle, both shared a history of oppression by a white male power structure. Blatant sexual discrimination was officially incorporated into a number of existing criminal and civil laws. For example, under Texas law, women were charged with murder for killing their husband's mistress, yet men were charged with justifiable homicide for killing their wife's boyfriend. Civil laws in seven southern states made fathers the presumptive guardians of their minor children, while Washington law prevented married women from filing suit in a state court unless their husbands joined in the suit, and union laws in Ohio prevented women from holding nineteen different jobs (Graham, 1992).

Corrective action in the form of civil rights legislation was far from immediate. Segregated classified ads were still prevalent in 1966. The Equal Employment Opportunities Commission found persistent violations by race, origin, and religion in twenty-one newspapers and 18,000 advertisements. Employers placed ads calling for "white attendants," "Anglo carhops," "executive sales positions for men," "lady in charge in shop," and "insurance trainees, men age 22–25." In 1969, women accounted for only 7 percent of all physicians, 1 percent of all engineers, 3 percent of all lawyers, and 8 percent of all scientists. Law and medical schools typically held female admissions to a 7 percent quota, despite higher scores by women than men on entrance exams (Graham, 1992). Sandra Day O'Connor, though a top graduate of Stanford Law School, was refused employment in law firms for any position other than legal secretary. College-student female activists were even excluded from leadership positions and were ridiculed by male activists who rallied against discrimination of Native Americans, African Americans, and other ethnic groups (Rhode, 1989).

The demand for civil rights initiated by blacks and women soon expanded into a mass group rights movement including Hispanics, American Indians, college students, welfare recipients, soldiers, gays, lesbians, consumer advocates, and a variety of environmental groups (Feenberg, 1986). One disenfranchised group after another—the poor, welfare mothers, mentally ill, handicapped—stepped forward to take their rightful place in mainstream America. All considered themselves oppressed by the contradictions of American society, in both the public and the private arena. Each group had its own history of exclusion, leaders, and methods, but all were seeking inclusion and the full promise of citizenship rights by way of group grievance (Jacobs, 1997).

It is from this context that prisoners launched their fight against inhumane and unfair treatment. In fact, the prisoner rights and civil rights movement have much in common. Both met with violent resistance and were about integrating or—in the case of prisoners—reintegrating alienated groups (Pallas and Barber, 1980). At times, the movements also involved the same people and the same tactics. Those who were politically active on the outside often found themselves arrested and confined on the inside (Wald, 1980). Moreover, inmates engaged in the prisoner rights struggle relied on riots, strikes, and class action lawsuits equally to improve the conditions in which they lived.

Prisoner Rights

Riots and Revolution

Pallas and Barber (1980) characterized the prisoner rights movement as unfolding in three stages. The first of these stages is reflected in the riots of the 1950s, which were motivated mainly by demands for decent food, shelter, health care, early parole, and good treatment in general. These early riots tended to erupt in a spontaneous and disorganized fashion and thus had little success in bettering prison conditions. In fact, they often proved counterproductive, as once the rioting had concluded, prison officials not only tended to ignore inmate demands but, to secure order in the future, officials also resorted to more restrictive conditions and corporal disciplinary measures.

The second stage of the movement coincided with the increased organization of Muslim inmates (ibid.). Incarcerated black Muslim leaders spent their time instructing other black inmates in the tenets of the faith. Though peaceful means of education and self-discipline were preached, the spread of Islam was viewed as a threat to institutional order. Prison administrators responded to this threat through a number of repressive measures: Religious meetings were disbanded, outside communication was cut off, Muslim ministers were transferred, and inmates were thrown into isolation. Only by appealing to the courts were Muslim inmates able to reverse these measures and hold religious meetings, purchase the Koran, and receive Muslim visitors (Vogelman, 1971).

In response to years of mounting dissent and disorder, officials continued to employ tactics that only aggravated an already volatile prison atmosphere. Privileges (e.g., out-of-cell work, study activities), along with the basic amenities of daily living (e.g., showers, canteen, mail, television), became rewards for passivity and obedience. Activism, on the other hand, was punished through isolation; denial of rewards and denied parole; and unofficial beatings, gassings, destruction of personal property during cell searches, and murder (Wald, 1980). Activist inmates were frequently targeted for death by officials through such covert means as intentional neglect of medical care, staged suicides, the bribing of other inmates to kill other inmates, and outright shootings under the pretext of escape attempts (ibid.).

The third, or revolutionary, stage of the prisoner rights movement—which lasted from about 1968 to 1975—was the culmination of these worsening conditions (Pallas and Barber, 1980). This final stage can be distinguished from the earlier stages by the manner in which inmates organized and the public support given to inmates in their quest for justice. For example, this highly politicized stage of the prisoner rights movement owes much to the Black Panthers, whose influence was most pronounced in the California prison system. In California as well as in New York, a high degree of inmate solidarity developed. Prisoners of all races, faiths, and ethnicities became a unified "class," vowing to avenge the injustice committed even against a single inmate (ibid.). The San Quentin race riot of 1967, moreover, involved almost half of the prison's four thousand inmates (ibid.); and in 1968, prisoners united again in a strike that shut down the prison's industries. In October 1970, inmate strikes overpowered the Long Island branch of the Queens House of Detention, sparking mini-revolts throughout a number of New York City jails. Inmate revolts continued at Soledad, Folsom, and San Luis Obispo prisons in California. The work stoppage at Folsom in November 1971 has been recorded as the longest, most nonviolent prison strike in history: Nearly all of the 2,400 inmates remained in their cells for nineteen days without food while enduring constant physical and emotional intimidation. Their demands—articulated in a 31-point manifesto—called for a stop to injustice and discrimination, the denial of political and legal rights to prisoners, and exploitation in work programs (ibid.). In May 1971, at New York's Attica Prison, inmates organized under the name of the Attica Liberation Front. Employing the popularized language of political amnesty, they communicated twenty-nine demands, including the right to organize economically and politically, to participate in choosing the officials who ruled them, and to protest without repercussions. They further demanded better working and living conditions, that the current warden be fired, and that transportation to a non-imperialist country be provided for those who wished to the leave the United States (ibid.). In Massachusetts in 1973, numerous outside leftist groups, journalists, and liberal legislators helped inmates organize; the end result of this act of defiance, as with the other inmate revolts, generally was dismal. More repressive measures were instituted and, in some instances, state police were called in to govern prisons. In other cases, the killings, gassings, and beatings of prisoners accelerated (Martin, 1980).

Much of the inmate activism undoubtedly was fueled by awareness of a sympathetic audience. Outside support for prisoner rights transcended the traditional divides of social, economic, and racial status. White college students were aligned with their cause, as some of them too had been incarcerated for drug busts, war protests, and free speech rallies. Similarly, Vietnam veterans understood the plight of the prisoner, as many veterans were incarcerated in federal prisons. Feminists arrested for their acts of civil disobedience took their message to the female prisons. By way of a shared anti-establishment rhetoric, each of these groups directly or indirectly contributed to the groundswell of support for prisoner rights. These various activists went so far as to compare American prisoners to the "political prisoners" of the third world (Wald, 1980).

In 1970, The American Bar Association (ABA) gave much-needed teeth to the prisoner rights movement by founding the Commission on Correctional Facilities and Services. As an advocate of correctional reform, the ABA operated the Resource Center for Correctional Law and Legal Services. By 1974, twenty-four state bar associations established special committees devoted to prison reform (Jacobs, 1997), and a number of inmates won their court cases (Jacobs, 2004).

Petitioning the Courts

It is widely assumed that, prior to the 1960s, never was a prisoner given his or her day in court (Wallace, 1992). The literature generally has suggested that this hands-off posture of the government was a function of a "slaves of the state" interpretation of inmate rights (*Ruffin v. Commonwealth,* 1871). Throughout the nineteenth and early twentieth centuries, however, the court frequently heard prisoner grievances and found conditions of institutions and actions of custodians to be in violation of legal norms (see, e.g., *Neat v. Ute,* 1881; *Avery v. Everett,* 1888; *McElvaine v. Brush,* 1891; *Westbrook v. Georgia,* 1909; *Anderson v. Salant,* 1916; *Kusah v. McCorkle,* 1918).

Wallace (1992) argued that statutory remedies available to courts in those cases may have been quite limited, but that courts were not entirely inactive or indifferent. Rather, Wallace contended that the hands-off approach more accurately describes the court's philosophy and behavior in the decades prior to the 1960s. The inactivity of the courts in the affairs of prisons in the 1940s and 1950s is a reflection of the judicial philosophy that courts lack the expertise to intervene in the business of correctional administration and that intervention by the courts will only undermine prison discipline and generate litigation overload (Wallace, 1994). In 1954, the position that courts should not interfere or encroach on the rights of states in the matters of prison rules and regulations was officially expressed in *Banning v. Looney* (DiIulio, 1990). Specifically, this deferential position by the courts was invoked not because inmates were truly considered "slaves of the state," but because courts were upholding what they believed to be an appropriate separation of powers between the executive and judicial branches.

Wallace's interpretation of the history of court involvement in corrections may be unique, but his point is well taken. It is reasonable to assume that judicial involvement goes through periods of activism and retrenchment. The period commonly understood as the heyday of the prisoner rights movement (1960–1980) was a period of intense judicial activism. Most of this activism occurred at the district court level and was grounded primarily in the conditions and operations of particular prisons and jails (Jacobs, 2004). Though the U.S. Supreme Court did not play a powerful role in this movement, it did issue some early decisions that were influential with regard to religion and access to the courts.

The Warren Supreme Court (1953–1969) set the tone for judicial activism. Prone to broad interpretations of the Constitution, the Warren Court was committed to extending constitutional protections to minorities, many of which were confined in institutions (Branham and Krantz, 1994). During this period of high judicial activism, the extent of involvement by the federal judiciary in jails and prisons was second only to the Court's commitment to dismantling segregation in public schools (Feeley and Hanson, 1990). Litigation brought by black Muslims was among the most successful in mobilizing the prisoner rights movement. Between 1961 and 1978, an estimated sixty-six federal court decisions were issued relating to Muslim prisoners alone (Jacobs, 1997).

Jacobs argued that religious persecution may have brought the courts into the prison, but it was the deplorable conditions that kept them there. The number of lawsuits filed provides an indication of the courts' increased receptivity to inmate claims. In 1960, 1,305 federal and 872 state prisoner lawsuits were filed. By 1969, 3,612 federal and 9,312 state lawsuits were filed. This constitutes a 177 percent increase in federal filings and a 968 percent increase in state filings—despite the fact that prison populations were slightly declining in both systems (Thomas, 1988). By 1974, federal and state lawsuits reached a high of 18,410.

Freedom of Religion

The right of inmates to exercise their religion freely was fought on two constitutional grounds; namely, violation of the First and of the Fourteenth amendments. For example, following the ruling in *Fullwood v. Clemmer* (1962), the Washington, D.C. Department of Corrections was forced to permit Muslim religious activities within the prison. In denying Muslims the opportunity to practice their religious beliefs, it was ruled that correctional administrators had been denying inmates their First Amendment right of freedom of expression. The legal question at hand, in this case, was whether the Muslim faith constituted a religion or merely a personal philosophy. The grounds for the ruling were that the Muslim faith qualifies as a religion because of its belief in a supreme being (Allah) who controls the destiny of man (Cripe, 1990; Vogelman, 1971).

This ruling paved the way for the decision in *Cooper v. Pate* (1964), in which inmates successfully sued for the right to use the Koran and for a place and opportunities to worship. In *Cruz v. Beto* (1972), the meaning of religious freedom was further examined as a due process issue, as inmates contested a state policy of paying for only Catholic, Jewish, and Protestant clergy and for Jewish and Christian bibles. The Court ruled that inmates must be afforded "reasonable opportunities" to exercise their faith of choice in a way comparable to others, as required by the Fourteenth Amendment's equal protection clause. Yet, it was also decided that the state does not need to provide everyone with the resources (e.g., staff, space) for this to occur.

Communication Rights, Legal Resources, and Access to the Courts

The First and Fourteenth amendments also were employed in the struggle against the censorship of inmate mail. The broad question to be addressed by the First Amendment was whether it provides protection against censorship of inmate mail (Branham and Krantz, 1994). This question, in turn, relates to the Fourteenth Amendment guarantee of due process; namely, the implications of censorship of mail for communication with lawyers. In short, does mail censorship violate due process rights by impeding access to the courts? In *Palmigiano v. Travisono* (1970), the federal court established restrictions on the censorship of mail (Wallace, 1992), but the matter was given further clarification by the Supreme Court in *Procunier v. Martinez* (1974) and *Wolff v. McDonnell* (1974). In the former case, inmates charged that existing state regulations governing the censorship of mail were overly restrictive. Existing regulations prohibited letters wherein inmates "unduly complained," "magnified grievances," or engaged in writings that expressed inflammatory political, racial, religious, or other views (Branham and Krantz, 1994). Institutional regulations also prevented the mailing of "otherwise inappropriate letters."

Ultimately, the Supreme Court ruled in favor of the inmates by declaring the (aforementioned) regulations unconstitutional. In *Procunier,* the Court ruled that restrictions on mail have to serve an "important" or "substantial" government interest not related to the suppression of expression. To safeguard against unreasonable censorship, states were to provide the following: (1) a notice to an inmate when a letter written to or by an inmate is going to be censored; (2) an opportunity for the author to protest the censor decision; and (3) a review of censorship by another official other than the one who makes the initial decision to censor. However, in demonstrating these interests, the state does not have to provide "certain" evidence that these interests would be threatened.

Further clarification by the U.S. Supreme Court was given in *Wolff,* in which a Nebraska inmate challenged a prison rule that allowed correctional officers to open and inspect mail in the presence of prisoners. Justice Byron White wrote that it was permissible to open the contents of an envelope and put it on the table, as long as the readable portions were not read (Smith, 2000). Beyond mail censorship, several conditions made access to the courts unduly difficult. These conditions included access to legal books and papers, delays, lack of assistance in preparing documents, and being restrained in efforts to obtain counsel even when the inmate can afford one personally.

The problem of access to legal resources was partially remedied in *Bailleaux v. Holmes* (1961). The court ruled that prison authorities could not stifle the study of law when it can be shown that this impedes one's right of access to courts (Vogelman, 1971). A major decision regarding access to legal resources was issued by the U.S. Supreme Court in *Johnson v. Avery* (1969). This case centered on the matter of inmate lawyering and, incidentally, inmate protection against staff mistreatment. Historically, prison rules had forbidden jailhouse lawyering (JHL). The reason given for the prohibition was that it provides too much power for legally skilled inmates, which, in turn, challenges the prison staff's authority and facilitates the abuse of other inmates through extortion and sexual favors. To restore the balance of power, so to speak, JHLs often were subjected to harassment and abuse by institutional staff. This maltreatment eventually pushed JHL underground (Jacobs, 1997).

In *Johnson v. Avery,* the court ruled that the absence of JHLs put an unreasonable burden on other inmates' right of access to the courts. The court ruled that prisoners are entitled to obtain legal assistance from other prisoners, unless the prison provides alternative means by which they can file the necessary legal documents (Smith, 2000). The court did put restrictions on when and where JHLs could render assistance, and it forbade formal compensation of any kind. Right of access to the courts was addressed again in *Gilmore v. Lynch* (1970), *Haines v. Kerner* (1972), and *Bounds v. Smith* (1977). In *Gilmore,* the federal court ruled that limiting law books in prison libraries also impedes prisoner access to the courts (Wallace, 1992). In *Haines,* the court affirmed that special attention should be given to inmate petitions and, in *Bounds,* the court affirmed that adequate law libraries and trained personnel must be provided.

Disciplinary Measures and Due Process

The Fourteenth Amendment essentially asks the question, "What process is actually due citizens" so that they might be protected against the arbitrary action of government (Branham and Krantz, 1994)? One of the specific implications of the right to due process is that procedural steps must be followed when life or liberty is threatened. A critical step in the prisoner rights movement was demonstrating the relevance of due process, even though guilt had already been established. In effect, does due process apply when someone is being punished?

In *Wolff v. McDonnell* (1974), the Supreme Court addressed the question of whether prisoners deserve due process protections under the conditions of disciplinary cell confinement (Rhine, 1990). The Court ruled that due process rights do apply (i.e., fair procedures), because the state does give some valued things to prisoners that can later be taken away. While it is not necessary that the same standards of due process be applied as in the trying of the original charge of conviction, the Court conceded that a "mutual accommodation between institutional needs and objectives and the provisions of the Constitution" must be met. Translated into practice, advance-written notice of institutional charges against a prisoner is to be given at least twenty-four hours prior to appearance before the disciplinary board. The Court ruling also requires a written statement by the fact finders as to the evidence relied upon and reasons for disciplinary action, which is to be provided to the inmate. An inmate also is permitted to call witnesses and present documentation in his or her defense as long as it does not pose a threat to institutional safety. Finally, *Wolff* established that the prison disciplinary board must be impartial and, if an inmate is illiterate, that substitute counsel be provided (ibid.).

In a later but related case, *Hewitt v. Helms* (1983), the meaning of due process was clarified. In this decision, the Supreme Court outlined the process "due" inmates upon transfer to administrative segregation (i.e., segregation for the protection of the inmate). In these circumstances, the inmate is to be given "some notice" of the reason for the transfer, though it does not have to be in writing. The inmate also is to be given the opportunity to express his or her views about the transfer, though it does not need to be in person (i.e., written notice suffices). The Court further ruled that the inmate be given the opportunity to have the transfer decision reviewed by a prison official after the transfer, though the review again does not have to be a formal hearing. Finally, the Court ruled that periodic reviews by prison officials are required for the duration of the inmates' segregated confinement (Branham and Krantz, 1994).

Overall, the courts seem to have agreed that due process rights do apply in a number of inmate situations, particularly disciplinary hearings that might result in a sanction or grievous loss such as gain time. Due process requirements, in the form of orderly procedures, also apply to classification assessments, intra-prison transfers, and transfers to administrative/segregated confinement. In effect, procedural safeguards are to be applied to all actions taken by officials, but the quality and quantity of the safeguards vary to the extent that life, liberty, or property potentially is denied.

Conditions of Confinement and Use of Force

The cases having the strongest influence on the conditions of imprisonment are the class action suits that challenged the constitutionality of the prison conditions in general, including cell size, quality of lighting, ventilation, sanitation, nutrition, and medical care (Jacobs, 2004). Conditions of confinement in southern states drew the greatest attention of the courts. Lack of resources and institutional disrepair contributed to not only poor sanitary conditions and medical care, but also to the abuse of inmates by other inmates who had been selected by prison authorities to govern the institution (Smith, 2000). But the South was not alone in having prison conditions challenged or in having judges issue remedial orders. Throughout the country, the Eighth Amendment was applied to a number of confinement situations, including deficiencies in medical care; failure to provide inmates with protection from other inmates; and use of unreasonable force by correctional officers in situations of self-defense, protection of other inmates, and enforcement of rules.

Pugh v. Locke (1976) provides one of the most infamous examples of judicial decisions affecting general conditions of confinement. In his opinion, the presiding judge gave a scathing critique of the Alabama penal system. Among the litany of charges leveled, the judge noted the following: broken and unscreened windows that created a serious problem with flies and mosquitoes; old and filthy cotton mattresses that led to the spread of contagious diseases and body lice; exposed wiring; facilities overrun with roaches in all stages of development; one functioning toilet for more than two hundred inmates; toilets that did not flush and were overflowing; no working classification system; food stored in infested units; and the practice of packing six inmates into four-by-eight-foot cells with no beds, no lights, no running water, and a hole in the floor for a toilet that could be flushed only from the outside (Judge Johnson, 1976; opinion quoted in Smith, 2000).

Lawsuits concerning conditions in isolated confinement, specifically, illustrate the complexities and inconsistencies surrounding Eighth Amendment rulings. The points of contention in these cases generally revolved around the maintenance of personal hygiene, the physical conditions of the cell, exercise allowed, diet, and duration of isolation. For example, in *Wright v. McMann* (1967), the Supreme Court ruled that when inmates are deprived of soap, water, towel, toilet paper, toothbrush, and clothing, the conditions have become constitutionally intolerable (Palmer, 1991). However, another court decided that it is constitutionally acceptable to allow water and a shower only on every fifth day (*Ford v. Board of Managers of New Jersey State Prison,* 1969), while a different court found it constitutionally acceptable to deprive an inmate of all hygiene materials for seven to ten days, with no reading material, in a cell inhabited by mice and roaches (*Bauer v. Sielaff,* 1974). Though consensus ultimately was lacking regarding what qualifies as unconstitutional conditions, the factors judged to be relevant on a consistent basis are the physical condition of the inmate, the condition of the cell, and the personal hygiene of the inmate (ibid.).

Along these lines, *Estelle v. Gamble* (1976) set the standard for many Eighth Amendment claims, particularly those relating to inmate medical care. The critical factor emerging from this ruling is the standard of "not inadvertence or error committed" in good faith, but the presence of "obduracy and wantonness" (ibid.). In other words, the court ruled that to constitute cruel and unusual punishment, officials must act with deliberate indifference to an inmate's (medical) needs; if the officials' actions reach only the level of negligence (i.e., the failure to act reasonably), the inmate is to be directed to seek remedy in civil state courts.

It was not until much later in *Farmer v. Brennan* (1994) that the requirements of deliberate indifference received adequate clarification regarding to the following criteria: (1) officials must be aware of facts revealing that an inmate faces a substantial risk of serious harm, (2) officials actually must deduce from these facts that the inmate is at significant risk of being seriously harmed, and (3) officials must take reasonable steps to prevent harm from occurring. Inappropriate action is generally defined as preventing an inmate from receiving care or delaying the administration of care, and taking superficial or no steps in responding to inmate complaints. What qualifies as a medical deficiency transcends isolated instances and includes systemic and institutional policies: For example, insufficient staffing, equipment, or record keeping—or the employment of non-English-speaking physicians—qualify as unconstitutional (Branham and Krantz, 1994).

A particularly salient issue driving the prison riots, strikes, and peaceful demonstrations that occurred between the 1950s and 1970s was the constitutionality of the use of force. The standard rule at the time was that prison officials could use force, but the reasonableness of the force was to be decided on a case-by-case basis (*Jackson v. Allen,* 1974; Palmer, 1991). Reasonableness of force hinged on such criteria as the degree of force being used by the inmate, the staff's reasonable perception of injury, and the means used to resist the assault. Following the bloody Attica riots, inmates alleged that officials had engaged in unreasonable and unprovoked brutality. The court agreed:

Injured prisoners, some on stretchers, were struck, prodded, or beaten with sticks, belts, bats, or other weapons. Others were forced to strip and run naked through gauntlets of guards armed with clubs, which they used to strike the bodies of the inmates as they passed. Some were dragged on the ground, some marked with an "X" on their backs, some spat upon or burned with matches, and others poked in the genitals or arms with sticks. According to the testimony of the inmates, bloody or wounded inmates were apparently not spared in this orgy of brutality (Palmer, 1991: 15).

Equal Protection, Equal Treatment

The Fourteenth Amendment not only requires that due process be extended to citizen and inmate alike, but also that it is applied equally—regardless of race, gender, or religion. Inmates also are guaranteed equal protection (i.e., treatment) under the law. For example, mounting racial tensions in prisons during the early 1960s prompted correctional administrators to resort to racially segregated units. In *Washington v. Lee* (1966), a federal district court struck down segregation schemes citing that such schemes violate the Fourteenth Amendment's equal protection clause. The court acknowledged that, in certain "isolated instances," segregation may be justified, but for only a "limited period" of time. The Supreme Court affirmed the ruling of the lower court, by concluding that legitimate institutional safety needs sometimes could override concerns about racial discrimination. Nevertheless, subsequent rulings on racially segregated units generally required that institutions find some alternative means of securing order and safety, such as increasing the supervision of inmates, disciplining and isolating problem inmates, and decreasing the prison population (Branham and Krantz, 1994).

The Fourteenth Amendment also applies to gender discrimination claims and provided the basis for much of the women's prisoner rights movement. The "parity movement," as it was termed (Rafter, 1990), is distinctive from the male prisoner rights movement. In the words of Aylward and Thomas (1984), there were no "sisters in litigation." Female inmates were far less litigious and far less politicized than their male counterparts. In fact, it has been suggested that their interest in litigation bordered on apathetic. When litigation did come to pass, it had a unique focus: Their lawsuits dealt primarily with the issue of disparate treatment in the area of housing and programming, rather than abuse or maltreatment by staff (Wheeler et al., 1989).

Because so few women were incarcerated, with even fewer incarcerated for extended periods of time, female facilities were scarce. Women offenders were often housed in converted hospitals, youth facilities, hotels, or in portions of male facilities (Chesney-Lind, 1991). Consequently, if the sentence was lengthy in duration, women often were transferred across state lines to facilities equipped for long-term incarceration. Feminist activists viewed this as unfair and unequal treatment because women, unlike men, were being housed thousands of miles away from their families. In *Park v. Thompson* (1976), the high court of Hawaii agreed, ruling that the prohibition on visitation constitutes a "grievous loss." This ruling, however, had a profound but unanticipated national impact: Counter to the feminists' decarceration objectives, the ruling led to a national campaign to build more female facilities.

The parity movement also focused on women's access to law libraries, vocational and educational programming, specialized treatment programs, and medical services. Inadequate prison services and programs were justified by system officials on the same grounds as the earlier transfer policies. The "demand" was simply not there and the number of female inmates was too small for concern. Outdated and substandard vocational programming was further justified by system officials on the grounds that women are not the major breadwinners of the family (Smart, 1976). In reviewing such claims, the courts required that females receive a "parity of treatment" (Branham and Krantz, 1994). Programs for females do not have to be identical to those for males, but they do need to be "substantially equivalent . . . in substance if not form" (*Glover v. Johnson,* 1979). For example, simply because a male prison has an auto mechanics course, such a course does not have to be provided in a female facility—but a program that makes female inmates equally economically viable upon release does have to be provided.

Probation and Parole

The prisoner rights movement did not deal exclusively with inmate issues. Offenders serving time in the community were still in custody of sorts, as their liberty could be quickly denied at the discretion of the probation or parole officer. The U.S. Supreme Court first addressed the issue of parole revocation in *Morrisey v. Brewer* (1972). The ruling in this case established that parolees have the right of due process and that the revocation process must unfold in two separate stages. In the first stage, the offender must be notified of the nature of the violation and the impending preliminary hearing. During this preliminary hearing, probable cause for the violation will be determined, and the offender is to be present, able to speak on his or her own behalf, and permitted to submit documents and cross examine witnesses (Branham and Krantz, 1994). At the second stage—the revocation hearing—the same rules and protections apply as in the preliminary hearing, but the due process standards do not need to reach the level of those afforded at a full criminal trial. *Mempa v. Rhay* (1967) established that probationers have a right to counsel during revocation hearings (Palmer, 1991) and, in *Gagnon v. Scarpelli* (1973), the Supreme Court asserted that the procedural protections articulated in *Morrisey* apply to probation revocation proceedings as well.

This period of remarkable judicial activism in the area of offender rights extended to the administration of capital punishment as well. Just as discrimination, injustice, and unfair practices were at the heart of the civil rights and the prisoner rights movement, these same issues framed the controversy surrounding the death penalty.

Abolishing Capital Punishment

Prior to 1965, the death penalty had not been challenged on constitutional grounds. In post-revolutionary America, for instance, the death penalty was abolished for the majority of offenses on humanitarian and utilitarian grounds. In the 160 years that followed, it was the method of execution that was subject to debate and reform (Bedau, 1997a). It was not until the Warren Court that the constitutional validity of capital punishment was questioned (Nakell and Hardy, 1987). The question of constitutional validity includes procedural (Fourteenth Amendment) and substantive (Eighth Amendment) concerns.

The Supreme Court's review of *Rudolph v. Alabama* (1963) provides the first indication of the court's willingness to consider the constitutionality of the death penalty. This case directly addressed whether death is an appropriate sanction for the crime of rape, but is also germane to the broader cause of civil rights: Those who had been sentenced to death in rape cases consistently were black men whose victims were white women (Bedau, 1997a). In *Rudolph*, the Court failed to declare the statute in question unconstitutional, but the constitutionality of capital punishment was revisited in *Maxwell v. Bishop* (1965), in which the courts again ruled that death in the case of rape is constitutional on procedural grounds because the intent of the said statute is not discriminatory. However, before *Maxwell* was settled, efforts to end the death penalty in rape and other cases had spread to Florida, California, and all other death penalty jurisdictions. For example, in *Akens v. California* (1972), the state struck down the death penalty as unconstitutional in its application. Several states followed California's lead, believing the country's death penalty was under constitutional review.

Finally, in a 5–4 ruling in *Furman v. Georgia* (1972), the Supreme Court ruled that the death penalty, as administered, violated the Eighth and Fourteenth Amendments in all the cases before the court. Of the five Supreme Court justices, only Brennan and Marshall considered the death penalty unconstitutional under any circumstances. Justice Brennan maintained that the death penalty is unconstitutional for any crime, any person, using any method. All five justices concurred that the death penalty is unconstitutional on the grounds that it is arbitrary, unfairly applied, and racist. Justice Stewart likened the randomness of death penalty decisions to "being struck by lightning" (Bedau, 1997a). Further, it was obvious that the death penalty disproportionately affected the poor and minorities, leading the Court to conclude that one could readily observe the difference between those who received death and those who did not (Branham and Krantz, 1994). The Court perceived a gross lack of procedure in all decisions relating to the administration of the death penalty and that, given its irreversible nature, "super due process" is warranted in all cases (Bedau, 1997a).

The *Furman* decision invalidated the existing death penalty statutes and spared the lives of 589 death row inmates throughout the country. Immediately following this ruling, thirty-five states used the *Furman* decision as a guideline for developing a constitutionally acceptable statute (Nakell and Hardy, 1987). During this moratorium, hundreds of sentences were commuted to life imprisonment.

Gregg v. Georgia (1976) served as the test case for states that had revised their death penalty statutes. The Georgia statute stipulated several criteria that made the death penalty acceptable to the Supreme Court. First, Georgia provided limits on discretion by requiring that the sentencer find beyond a reasonable doubt that at least one of ten aggravating factors be present. A second feature is a provision of automatic review by the Georgia Supreme Court in all death penalty cases. The statute also features a two-phase trial system, whereby guilt or innocence was decided in one phase and sentencing in the second (Bedau, 1997a). All in all, the Georgia statute provided a point of comparison for the statutes that did not pass constitutional muster. For example, in *Woodson v. North Carolina* (1978) the Supreme Court cited three reasons why a mandatory death penalty statute was unacceptable even though it addressed the problem of arbitrariness: (1) when the law conflicts with standards of decency such that juries will acquit defendants in order to avoid the imposition of sanctions, (2) when the law merely shifts discretion to juries, and (3) when the law removes the right of a defendant to an individualized sentencing hearing in which mitigating circumstances could be presented (Branham and Krantz, 1994).

The validity of mandatory death penalty statutes was repeatedly challenged in *Roberts v. Louisiana* (1976), *Coker v. Georgia* (1977), and *Eberheart v. Georgia* (1977). In all of these cases, the defendant was black and the victim was white. *Roberts* abolished mandatory death for the offense of killing a police officer, while *Coker* abolished it for the offense of rape and *Eberheart* abolished it for kidnapping. The Supreme Court did not strike down all mandatory death statutes, however: The decision to uphold the legality of such statutes rests upon whether the statute, in any way, prohibits the presentation of mitigating circumstances (Branham and Krantz, 1994). Ultimately, the Court held that legislatures are prohibited from defining certain crimes for which death must be imposed, but they are not prohibited from identifying when death cannot be imposed (ibid.).

Discovery of Prisoner Rights

In 1968, *Life* magazine journalist John Lindsay wrote that it is "a matter of concern when Americans find the ordinary channels of discussion and decision so unresponsive that they feel forced to take their grievances to the street" (quoted in Skolnick, 1969). While the social activism noted by Lindsay was not entirely unprecedented in American history, the activism of the 1960s and 1970s is distinctive. It lasted longer, involved more people, and was more militant and hostile to established authority and institutions (ibid.). The prisoner rights movement is similarly distinctive in that it lasted several years, involved scores of inmates and lawsuits, and relatively radical means of redress. Nevertheless, as social activism in general diminished, so too did activism on behalf of offenders and inmates. The romanticism of the movement eventually gave way to divisions within the movement. Many attorneys were not paid for their efforts, nor did they always get along with those they represented. Activists also learned the hard lesson that most prisoners were not political leaders in the making; more often, they were simply individuals with a criminal past who typically were unskilled and uneducated (Wald, 1980).

The results of the prisoner rights movement have since drawn both praise and criticism. Prison reform advocates have argued that activism of any kind has rightfully expanded access to the courts and given voice to traditionally powerless groups (Feeley and Hanson, 1990). Advocates of judicial intervention further applaud court rulings that address past harms and prevent future harms by restructuring the bureaucracies responsible (Bradley, 1990). According to this perspective, then, the prisoner rights movement produced much-needed reforms, such as improved jail conditions and the abolishment of the southern prison plantation (slave) model of confinement; and increased professionalism of correctional staff, increases in correctional accountability, and more uniform policies via accreditation standards (Feeley and Hanson, 1990).

Critics, on the other hand, have argued that the power of the executive and legislative branches is undermined by judicial activism. Advocates of judicial restraint believe that the courts overstep their authority when they alter social policy and the rules that govern social institutions. These legal traditionalists maintain that the rightful role of the courts is the interpretation of the law—not the governance of malfunctioning bureaucracies (ibid.). Consequently, advocates of judicial restraint asserted that the prisoner rights movement resulted in greater loss of control by institutional authorities, which contributed to greater inmate-on-inmate and inmate-on-staff violence. They also claimed that it led to increases in staff turnover, lower staff morale, and a breakdown in effective management—not to mention the prohibitive costs associated with court compliance.

The latter perspective on prisoner rights has prevailed of late, leading to reversals and curtailments of many of the rights previously gained. The most profound disruption in prisoner rights came from the passage of the Prison Litigation Reform Act of 1995. The intent of this federal law was to restrict the judiciary from recognizing and enforcing prisoner rights (Jacobs, 2004). For example, the law limits the remedies federal judges can impose in prisoner rights cases (ibid.). Provisions in the law also make it more expensive and difficult for prisoners to obtain legal representation in institutional litigation. Conservative courts have also reinterpreted the parameters of prisoner rights. For example, in *Lewis v. Casey* (1996), Supreme Court Justice Thomas held that prisoners have no constitutional right to legal resources and assistance, and that the right of access to the courts should be limited to solely protection against interference in filing legal papers. Courts have also rejected arguments that parole boards should be prohibited from considering illegally obtained evidence during revocation hearings and that prisoners should be given adequate notice and a hearing before disciplinary action is taken. In *Hudson v. McMillian* (1992), justices Thomas and Scalia questioned whether the Eighth Amendment even does provide protection to prisoners against abusive actions by correctional officers (Smith, 2000).

This retrenchment in prisoner rights is of course troubling, given that inmates still suffer from negligent medical care, beatings (and killings) by guards and other inmates, and visitation and communication policies that impede rather than promote pro-social ties. Moreover, prisons do not age gracefully and the running of safe, clean, hygienic, operational, and humane institutions is an ongoing challenge. As Jacobs (2004) noted, prisons and jails need continuous reform because the risks and realities of staff corruption, capitulation to inmates, and brutality constantly threaten the goal of a humane and well-ordered institution.

10

Decentralizing Corrections (1960s–1970s)

The decentralization movement was an outgrowth of the same social context that spawned the prisoner rights movement. Specifically, the crisis of legitimacy in American institutions that led to increased recognition and rights for incarcerated offenders also fueled the decentralization of corrections movement. The rhetoric of the decentralization movement was broader than prisoner rights, however, in that "total institutions" for the "dangerous, the defective, and the dependant" all were seen as problematic (Lowman and Menzies, 1987). A chorus of critics believed that prisons, mental hospitals, and orphanages were uniformly impervious to reform and improvement. Rather than reform and refine them yet again, it was widely concluded that society "ought to get on with the work of emptying them" (Scull, 1977). In place of the traditional emphasis on institutionalization, what developed was a broad-scale effort to convince policy makers and the public of the value of community care and community corrections.

The prison research of Clemmer, Sykes, Irwin, Cressey, and Giallombardo supplied a ready foundation for decentralization efforts. However, a growing criminological perspective known as labeling theory functioned to expand and solidify this rationale. By concentrating on the damaging behavior of the justice system rather than on the illicit behavior of the offender, labeling theory upended the field of criminology. In stark contrast to previous theories of crime and delinquency, labeling theory argues that interaction with the criminal justice system actually can create, intensify, and perpetuate criminal behavior (Cicourel, 1968; Emerson, 1969; Schur, 1971). The theoretical logic can be summarized as follows: The state labels and stigmatizes offenders, thus subjecting them to criminal associations that, in turn, make criminal careers more likely.

Under this framework, the previously unquestioned rehabilitative agenda of "more is better" became viewed as dubious, if not detrimental. The call for less state intervention and more community-based strategies became the new panacea in criminal justice. Some, like scholar Edwin Schur (1973), even called for "radical non-intervention." For reasons that were part theoretical (i.e., labeling) but also fiscal, appeals to community meant that other (less stigmatizing) organizations would now pick up the slack. To decentralize corrections was to replace the formal processing of offenders with various informal and preferably voluntary forms of community treatment. Community was broadly understood to mean private non-profit and for-profit agencies, volunteer organizations, and various partnerships between local government and other non-governmental entities.

Labeling Theory: Justifying Decentralization

Though labeling theory was popularized during the 1960s and 1970s, the general idea had appeared much earlier, with key elements reflecting the symbolic interactionist tradition (Mead, 1934; Blumer, 1969). Frank Tannenbaum (1938) commonly is credited for providing the first statement of labeling theory through the notion of the "dramatization of evil." According to Tannenbaum, the dramatization of evil is initiated in response to acts of normal, youthful misbehavior (e.g., playing baseball in the street and hitting a ball through a neighbor's window). He argued, "The process of making the criminal, therefore, is a process of tagging, defining, identifying, segregating, describing, emphasizing, making conscious and self-conscious; it becomes a way of stimulating, suggesting, emphasizing, and evoking the very traits that are complained of" (ibid.: 20).

Tannenbaum (1938) identified several justice system consequences that later provided a basis for diversion, deinstitutionalization, and other community-based efforts. He contended that youth entering the criminal justice system are subjected to a forced "companionship" with other similarly defined children, which results in "a new set of experiences that led directly to a criminal career." Tannenbaum concluded that the best policy is "a refusal to dramatize the evils." Thus, diversion, deinstitutionalization, and other community-based programs officially were intended as means of eliminating the potential for the dramatization of evil. Such alternative responses to deviance would reduce the number of offenders exposed to criminal justice system processing and the damaging labels and associations wrought by that exposure.

In *Social Pathology* (1951), Edwin Lemert introduced two fundamental concepts that refined labeling theory. These concepts are primary and secondary deviance. Primary deviance refers to the range of deviant or criminal acts committed for a variety of situational or personal reasons. Those who commit primary deviant acts do not consider their deviance to be fundamental to their identity. Rather, their deviant acts are spontaneous or situational forms of behavior. In contrast, secondary deviance occurs when the actor no longer detaches his or her deviant behavior from his or her self-identity. Of particular importance to Lemert is the explanation for the shift from primary to secondary deviance. Lemert argued that this shift involves a sequential process of primary deviant acts followed by gradually amplified negative social audience reactions. As a result, the deviant actor assumes a deviant self-identity over time that is followed by secondary deviance, which reaffirms the individual's deviant identity.

Neither Tannenbaum nor Lemert's labeling theory contributions received major attention when they were first published. However, as the decade of the 1960s unfolded, such writings proliferated. Key contributors to the ongoing development of labeling theory include Howard Becker (1963), John Kitsuse (1964), and Kai Erikson (1966). According to Cullen and Agnew (1999), this group of scholars argued in their respective extensions of the earlier work of Tannenbaum and Lemert, that societal reaction—not the offender—should be the focus of criminology's quest to determine the causes of crime.

During the course of the 1960s, the popularity of labeling theory reached the point of challenging the dominant functional perspective. John Hagan (1973) proposed that labeling theory's rise to prominence in the 1960s can be attributed to its interesting argument; he argued that criminologists are drawn to ideas that challenge the conventional wisdom on causal sequence. Cullen and Agnew (1999: 272) later agreed, noting

> Common sense would dictate that arresting, trying, imprisoning, and rehabilitating offenders would make crime less likely; after all, the manifest function of processing offenders through the criminal justice system is to reduce their recidivism and to make society safer. However, the unique twist to labeling theory was the claim that these very efforts to prevent crime actually cause crime.

But labeling theory's "interesting argument" had been articulated decades earlier without gaining even a moderate foothold in criminology. In the 1960s, however, the times were ripe and, and as result, labeling theory had a captive and receptive audience. Labeling theory was, indeed, "the" theory for the times. Given the developing crisis in American institutions, a theory that directly and forcefully critiques one of these major institutions—namely, the criminal justice system—was broadly embraced. In effect, "a theory that blamed the government for causing more harm than good struck a chord of truth that resonated with the times. Labeling theory, of course, did precisely this in arguing that the criminal justice system stigmatized offenders and ultimately trapped them in a criminal career" (ibid.). The policy directive emerging from labeling theory is clear: Reduce the criminal justice system's intervention into the lives of offenders. Young offenders are to be diverted from the system whenever possible, and all offenders (adult and juvenile) are to be dealt with in ways that keep them out of reformatories and prisons.

Development of the Decentralization Movement

Feeley and Sarat (1980) argued that the issue of crime and what to do about it became a signature political issue with the presidential campaign of 1964. The national government was caught up in a "war mentality" against domestic social ills and foreign enemies, and the preferred weapon was the massive mobilization of national resources. The federal government's response to the problem of crime therefore was found in the application of the war metaphor and culminated in the passage of the Omnibus Crime Control and Safe Streets Act of 1968 (ibid.). This act established the Law Enforcement Assistance Administration (LEAA) to implement a national strategy for waging America's war on crime.

Before the safe streets act, a small grant-in-aid program created in 1965 was charged with assisting state and local law enforcement. Following the 1965 passage of the act, the attorney general created the Office of Law Enforcement Assistance (OLEA), and over the three-year operation of OLEA, twenty million dollars in grants was awarded. While OLEA did not have a specific congressional mandate to guide its funding decisions, it did demonstrate the federal government's commitment to doing something about the problem of crime—without increasing federal control over state and local government (Feeley and Sarat, 1980).

Subsequently, President Lyndon B. Johnson established the President's Commission on Law Enforcement and the Administration of Justice in 1965. The commission was organized into a series of task forces that dealt with such crime problems as organized crime, drugs and crime, and components of the criminal justice system including police, courts, penology, and juvenile justice. By 1967, the commission had completed its assignments, which resulted in nine different reports on specific crime problems and aspects of the administration of criminal justice. These reports are the result of two years of work by more than five hundred professionals working as staff or in consultant capacities (Feeley and Sarat, 1980).

Ultimately, the various task force results were integrated into a series of two hundred conclusions and recommendations, which was published as *The Challenge of Crime in a Free Society* (U.S. President's Commission on Law Enforcement and Administration of Justice, 1967a). Unlike previous justice reform thinking, this report espoused the view that crime in America will not be remedied by merely expanding the capacity of the criminal justice system. In fact, a number of the task-force reports concluded that, because of the negative effects associated with labeling by the criminal and juvenile justice systems, reform efforts should be directed toward the development and implementation of various alternative, "prejudicial dispositions." Prejudicial dispositions meant handling cases "unofficially" through the use of various non-institutional responses to law breaking, such as diversion, deinstitutionalization, and various other community-based programs.

For example, the U.S. President's Commission Task Force on Juvenile Delinquency and Youth Crime concluded that formal juvenile justice system action

> may actually help to fix and perpetuate delinquency in the child through a process in which the individual begins to think of himself as delinquent and organizes his behavior accordingly. That process itself is further reinforced by the effect of the labeling upon the child's family, neighbors, teachers, and peers, whose reactions communicate to the child in subtle ways a kind of expectation of delinquent conduct. The undesirable consequences of official treatment are heightened in programs that rely on institutionalizing the child. The most informed and benign institutional treatment of the child, even in well-designed and staffed reformatories and training schools, may contain within it the seeds of its own frustration, and itself may often feed the very disorder it is designed to cure (U.S. President's Commission on Law Enforcement and Administration of Justice, 1967b: 8).

The 1968 Safe Streets Act was passed in order to launch the nationwide implementation of decentralization reforms and other presidential task-force recommendations. The Johnson administration wanted quick action that would demonstrate its dedication to effective crime policies. The Safe Streets Act, under the purview of the Justice Department, provided a major grant-in-aid program to assist states and local government in their efforts to effectively confront crime. The first step was to develop a comprehensive procedure for dealing with state and local crime problems that incorporated the numerous recommendations of the President's Commission task forces. Ultimately, the procedures involved a state and local fund-matching requirement under the administration of LEAA. The average annual funding for LEAA from its inception through 1980 was approximately $850 million a year.

Beginning in the late 1960s and continuing through the 1970s, the decentralization strategies of diversion, deinstitutionalization, and community corrections were the centerpieces of the federal funding of penal reform initiatives. In direct contrast to the assumption guiding penal reform from 1900 to the 1960s, the President's Commission concluded in 1967 that the infusion of more resources for the purpose of expanding correctional services would not result in more effective individualized treatment or offender rehabilitation. Rather, the commission argued that such individual treatment and rehabilitation goals were unrealistic expectations. Such expectations were seen as reflective of a grossly optimistic view of what was known about the phenomenon of crime and what a fully equipped correctional system could do about it. The commission maintained that experts in the field of correctional treatment agreed that it was difficult to develop effective offender treatment programs mostly because of the continuing lack of understanding of the causes of crime and delinquency. The commission concluded that, until the field of human behavior develops well beyond its current stage, sufficient understanding is not likely to be provided (U.S. President's Commission on Law Enforcement and Administration of Justice, 1967b).

The commission found that criminological research supports the view that crime and delinquency are not merely acts of individual deviance but are patterned behaviors resulting from a variety of societal influences well beyond the reach of probation officers, correctional counselors, and psychiatrists. Moreover, because it was believed that the justice system does more harm than good by labeling and perpetuating subsequent crime and delinquency, programs aimed at avoiding the system altogether became the mainstream of LEAA correctional funding. Within and outside of the LEAA, reformers proposed that federal funds be used to divert offenders from the criminal justice system. The implementation sequence of LEAA's correctional reforms began with juvenile diversion programs in the late 1960s. During the mid-to-late 1970s, deinstitutionalization of status offenders and various community treatment programs for juvenile and adult offenders experienced major growth as well. Overall, between 1968 and 1978, LEAA funded more than 1,200 community programs at an estimated cost of $112 million (Beckett, 1997).

Goals and Practices of Decentralization Reforms

Diversion

Juvenile diversion programs were the early mainstream of the decentralization movement. As envisioned by the President's Commission, diversion is to result in a narrowing of official juvenile justice jurisdiction to only those cases of "manifest danger." The bulk of troubled youth are to be diverted and accepted into neighborhood agencies designated as Youth Service Bureaus. Referrals to the bureaus can originate with parents, schools, or other sources, with the majority of referrals originating with the police and juvenile court. The commission specified that the bureaus' services can include individual, group, and whole-family (parents and siblings) counseling; placement in group or foster homes; and work, recreational, special remedial education, and vocational training services. It was maintained that "the key to the Bureaus' success would be voluntary participation by the juvenile and family in working out and following a plan of service or rehabilitation" (U.S. President's Commission on Law Enforcement and Administration of Justice, 1967a).

The major model of operation followed by diversion programs was that of system modification (Obrien and Marcus, 1976). System modification specifies that diversion programs are intended to provide police and juvenile court intake staff with alternatives to traditional juvenile justice system processing, thereby minimizing youth contact with the formal juvenile justice system. Actual referrals to diversion programs are by police, probation, juvenile court, parents, schools, and—surprisingly—many youth through self-referrals. In their study of diversion intake practices, Cressey and McDermott (1973) found that juvenile court intake officers occupy the central role in the diversion referral process. The authors concluded that the nature of the informal relationships between diversion programs and court intake units is ultimately crucial in the rate of diversion.

While the treatment modalities of most diversion programs included a range of individual, group, and family services, the distinction between individual youth and their families was not sharply maintained in the implementation of treatment. Typically, counseling and social casework approaches were employed with individuals, groups, and families, and this was supplemented with the use of various community treatment sources for referral including mental health, marital counseling, and welfare.

Rutherford and McDermott (1976) conducted a national assessment of diversion programs with the goal of developing a program typology. The typology includes legal, paralegal, and non-legal diversion program types. Police, juvenile court, and probation-provided diversion programs fall under the legal or paralegal program types, while private-agency-provided diversion programs fall into the non-legal or paralegal program types. The authors identified the following characteristics for each program type:

- *Type I: Legal.* Legal diversion programs, whether formal or informal, were administered by official justice agency personnel (i.e., police, probation, court); formal legal sanctions could be imposed; explicit or implicit coercion was present; programs were staffed by official agency personnel; and the programs were located on or within official agency premises.

- *Type II: Paralegal.* The paralegal diversion programs operated outside official agencies but were funded and administered by the official justice system and were staffed by official justice personnel (in kind, sabbatical, etc.). These programs were physically housed within official justice agency premises, had access to official justice agency records, received their clients from the official justice system, and maintained a formal or informal method of reporting on client progress in cooperation with official justice system.

- *Type III: Nonlegal.* The nonlegal diversion programs were client focused; client participation was voluntary; any form of program coercion was discouraged; no sanctions were imposed for nonparticipation or termination of program services; a client advocacy role was emphasized, and clients perceived the program as non-legal; the program determined staff appointments and maintained its goals without pressure from funding sources (Rutherford and McDermott, 1976: 12–15).

Legal diversion programs are the dominant models operating throughout the country. Early studies portray diversion as an important alternative to the formal justice system primarily because of the anticipated reduction in negative labeling and subsequent crime on the part of those offenders subject to diversion (Lemert, 1971; Polk, 1971; Rosenheim, 1969). Several later studies by Mahoney (1974) and Morris (1974), however, speculated critically about the potential of diversion to produce unintended consequences. Mahoney, for example, argued that the prevailing liberal reformist belief that juvenile and adult offenders get a bad deal from the official justice system can result in blindness to some of the less desirable aspects and potential of diversion programs. In consideration of the negative potential of diversion, Morris speculated that these alternative programs would ultimately result in more pervasive but less severe control over a larger proportion of the base population. Morris elaborated that if police are provided broader latitude to decide whether to arrest or divert, there will be fewer arrests, but overall, more individuals will be subject to arrest and/or diversion.

Toward the late 1970s, a series of empirical studies on diversion programs appeared. The most consistent finding of this research was a patterned outcome of net-widening by diversion programs (Austin and Krisberg, 1981; Blomberg, 1977; Hylton, 1982; Klein, 1979; Lemert, 1981). The concept of net-widening refers to the previously documented outcome of penal reform alternatives being implemented as supplements, thereby increasing the overall proportion of the base population subject to some form of correctional control. Specifically, these studies documented that diversion practices were largely applied to youth and families who—prior to diversion—would not have been subject to contact with the official justice system. Diversion programs not only drew the bulk of their clients from groups previously not subject to imminent official justice agency processing, but also placed many of these clients into family intervention services that involved not only the diverted youth but their siblings and parents as well. As a result, diversion's net-widening was far more expansive than that of previous penal reforms.

In a review of studies reporting on client behavior changes resulting from diversion programs, Klein (1979) reported that three studies cited positive findings of less delinquency (Baron et al., 1973; Klein, 1974; Ku and Blew, 1977), two studies cited findings of negative effects of more delinquency (Elliott, 1978; Lincoln, 1976), and eight studies cited equivocal findings (Berger et al., 1977; Binder, 1976; Carter and Gilbert, 1973; Elliott, 1978; Forward et al., 1974; Klein, 1974; Lincoln et al., 1977; Stratton, 1975). The only study employing random assignment to diversion and non-diversion alternatives was that of Lincoln et al. (1977), which reported substantially lower rates of recidivism for diverted youth as compared to youth who received official juvenile court processing. However, those youth released outright (i.e., without any form of program services) were found to have the lowest recidivism rates.

In assessing the specific client effects of diversion caused by net-widening, several studies reported upon diversion's capacity to increase client jeopardy, official system penetration, and subsequent behavior difficulties. For example, in a comparative study of adult offender diversion programs, Mullen (1975) found that offenders referred to diversion programs but who were unable to meet the program's requirements were subjected to a form of double jeopardy: They were returned for prosecution on their original charge, prosecuted vigorously, convicted, and placed on probation supervision. Mullen further pointed out that most of the offenders handled in this manner would not have been subject to formal court processing if not for the practice of diversion.

Similar findings in juvenile diversion programs were reported, particularly in relation to youth whose families were unable or unwilling to comply with the various requirements of diversion programs' whole-family intervention efforts. Specifically, Blomberg (1977) found that, when families were unable to comply with diversion's family-intervention requirements, the children in those families routinely were referred to the juvenile court for suitable out-of-home placement. He cited the following case to illustrate this potential:

> A fourteen-year-old boy with no prior record was referred to family intervention from probation intake on a runaway charge. His father and stepmother subsequently agreed to participate in the family intervention counseling program. During the counseling sessions the fourteen year old, his sixteen and ten year old brothers, the stepmother, and father were all required to be present. The case worker indicated that the father felt that by working and earning the living he was carrying out his family responsibility and that his wife should be able to handle the boys. The stepmother did not feel she could control the boys, especially the two older ones. The case worker felt there was a general sibling rivalry for the stepmother with sexual overtones in the case of the sixteen year old. Following the mandatory five counseling sessions, the case worker recommended continued family therapy which the father refused. The case worker made several follow-up visits to the home and subsequently recommended that all three boys be removed from the home because of continued difficulties between the boys and stepmother. Ultimately the two older boys were placed in the home of a relative. The ten year old was placed in a group home from which he ran away twice attempting to return home. Following the second runaway, he was referred back to the juvenile court and because of the runaway record and what was determined to be general behavior deterioration, he was found to be incorrigible and subsequently placed in a custodial institution (ibid.: 280).

Further, Polk (1981) reported that, in many instances, when families encountered difficulties in complying with diversion's program requirements, the parents were referred to criminal court on charges of contributing to the delinquency of minors or of moral neglect.

The potential to create or intensify subsequent behavior difficulties associated with diversion was supported by Klein's (1975) study on the relationship between rates of rearrest and alternative dispositions. Klein found that providing diversion services to youth who otherwise would have been released outright may well have increased their subsequent rearrest rates. This is because of their increased visibility to their diversion authorities and police, rather than because of increased rates of misconduct.

Deinstitutionalization

Diversion reforms opened the window to a sweeping trend of decentralization that included deinstitutionalization and various other forms of community programming. The Juvenile Justice and Delinquency Prevention Act of 1974 initiated a second wave in the decentralization movement that demonstrated federal resolve in delinquency control and juvenile justice reform. The 1974 act is based upon the recognized need for a comprehensive, continual, and well-funded approach. To accomplish this goal, Congress established the Office of Juvenile Justice and Delinquency Prevention (OJJDP) as a semiautonomous agency within the LEAA.

Underlying the 1974 act was the belief that a major shortcoming of the juvenile justice system was excessive use of secure confinement in detention facilities and juvenile justice institutions. The excessive use of secure confinement was further complicated by the indiscriminate mixing of minor and serious offenders often with adult offenders (Sarri, 1983). The major reform initiative emerging from the 1974 act called for termination in the use of juvenile detention and correctional institutions for juveniles who commit acts that would not be criminal if committed by adults; namely, status offenses.

OJJDP's twofold goal in the deinstitutionalization of status offenders was (1) to reduce the use of secure confinement, and (2) to encourage the development of community treatment alternatives for status offenders. The first goal was derived directly from labeling theory's contention that, when minor offenders are formally processed by police, courts, and corrections, these offenders take on a delinquent identity and organize their subsequent behavior accordingly. The second goal reflects legal concerns for equity and justice. The belief was that it is not appropriate to hold those who have not committed criminal acts in secure confinement. These two program goals (as summarized by Kobrin and Klein [1983]) involved a strategy that connected a primary concern "with deinstitutionalizing status offenders, that is, with diverting them from detention and correctional institutions and, having done so, with bringing about a reduction in their subsequent offense behavior by providing the backup of community-based remedial services" (p. H).

Several deinstitutionalization efforts preceded the 1974 act: the 1972 Massachusetts program, the 1960s California community treatment program, and a number of other program efforts (for further discussion, see Empey, 1982: 487–489). The most cited and controversial effort was that by Massachusetts. In 1972, Jerome Miller, director of Massachusetts youth services, responded to a series of crises in the state's training schools by simply shutting them down. All functions previously performed by the closed training schools were transferred to the community. However, it was the 1974 act that led to nationwide recognition and implementation of deinstitutionalization of status offenders.

Helium (1983) reported that Wisconsin and Alaska prohibited the post-adjudication commitment of status offenders in 1971, and New Mexico followed in 1972. In 1973, three states—South Dakota, Texas, and Nevada—prohibited post-adjudication commitments of status offenders, as did five additional states by 1974 (New Jersey, Massachusetts, Iowa, Maryland, and Illinois). New Jersey and Maryland prohibited post-adjudication detention as well. While three states prohibited detention and three others prohibited commitment in 1975, seventeen additional states prohibited or reduced the use of detention and twenty-five states prohibited or reduced the use of post-adjudication commitment for status offenders by 1978 (Helium, 1983). By establishing eligibility for federal delinquency funds contingent upon deinstitutionalization progress, the 1974 act effectively provided a major incentive that led to nationwide legislative and policy implementation of the deinstitutionalization of status offenders.

The 1974 act also mandated the development of various community treatment alternatives to incarceration. As envisioned, these community treatment alternatives would include youth advocacy programs as well as various other education, family intervention, counseling, and employment assistance programs. Corry (1983) identified the deinstitutionalization programs in Pima County, Arizona; Alameda County, California; and Spokane County, Washington, as exemplary program sites. The Pima County effort—while opposed by local politically powerful groups—had the power of a crusade. A charismatic juvenile court judge who was determined to end the excessive use of detention and institutionalization in the jurisdiction led the so-called crusade. The program was focused upon the development of youth advocacy and delinquency prevention in the county's high-delinquency areas. There existed in Alameda County a long-held support for avoiding detention and institutionalization whenever possible. As a result, the probation department was successful in developing a family crisis intervention program with a high level of professional competency. The program's community focus was on the county youth service centers, which were located in high-delinquency areas. In Spokane County, there was a substantial degree of community receptivity to the deinstitutionalization of status offenders program. A constituency of community leaders assisted in the development of Youth Alternatives, which provided round-the-clock program services for status offenders. These services were focused upon family crisis intervention and case diagnosis with the use of some private sector youth service agencies.

During the late 1970s, a series of evaluation studies appeared that reported on the results of the deinstitutionalization program reform movement for status offenders. Like diversion and numerous other penal reforms before it, the deinstitutionalization movement's deeds did not match its words or goals. Post-program recidivism rates showed little difference between deinstitutionalized and institutionalized youth (Coates et al., 1978). However, in a systematic review of the literature reporting on the shortcomings of this movement, Klein (1979) persuasively argued that deinstitutionalization (as well as diversion) was not implemented as intended and, as a result, what has been reported as program failure actually has been a general failure to implement the programs properly.

In assessing national trends in the use of detention during the 1970s, Sarri (1983) concluded that, while there has been substantial federal and state effort to reduce reliance on detention, detention and jailing are used much more extensively than is necessary. More specifically, regarding the 1974 act's call for the deinstitutionalization of status offenders, Sarri concluded that—despite leading many states to legislate and develop deinstitutionalization programs—"It is still the case that the act too had far less impact than was desired. If we are to comprehend why so many policies and programs have failed to achieve their objectives, we must investigate more thoroughly societal views about social control of youth development" (ibid.: 318). Consequently, whether we accept Klein's interpretation of an implementation failure or we prefer Sarri's societal views on youth control, the end result is the same for the deinstitutionalization reform movement: The goals cannot be readily seen in the practices.

Decentralizing Adult Corrections

The earliest and most visible decentralization reforms were juvenile diversion and deinstitutionalization. These programs set the stage and provided specific rationales and program models that adult programs came to embody during the 1970s. In fact, diversion and deinstitutionalization rationales and program components were fundamental to community-based reform efforts for adults.

In 1973, the LEAA initiated the Exemplary Projects Program, which identified programs of proven merit, verified their achievements, and widely disseminated information about these programs. The Des Moines community-based corrections program was both the first exemplary project and the first to be replicated in five jurisdictions across the county. The Des Moines program was not a crime-fighting program as such, or a program that targeted habitual or violent offenders. Rather, the program addressed some of the problems for which it was counter-productive to employ traditional criminal justice sanctions. Specifically, the Des Moines program provided several graduated community-based service alternatives to traditional criminal justice sanctions for minor and nonviolent offenders. Even though many prosecutors and judges were inclined to be lenient with such offenders, they often were im-peded by the limited alternatives available to them. Like diversion and deinstitutionalization programs, the Des Moines program provided alternatives to confinement before and after trial, as well as various helping services for defendants and convicted offenders who desired these services. The Des Moines program was designed to make the man-agement of criminal justice more efficient and to increase rehabilitation potential by enabling more individualized and proportionate sanctions and services for offenders.

The Des Moines program's four graduated components were release on recognizance, supervised release (i.e., pretrial release), intensive probation, and residential facility services (e.g., work release centers). Offenders' eligibility for a particular graduated component was based upon a numerical score reflecting the seriousness of offense, prior record, employment record, and several other community integration variables. The LEAA selected five sites to replicate the Des Moines program: Salt Lake City, Utah; Duluth, Minnesota; Orange County, Florida; San Mateo County, California; and Baton Rouge, Louisiana. The evaluation of the five replication efforts documented that not all of the Des Moines program components were amenable to replication. The local residential facility was replicated successfully in all five sites, but probation services proved unsuccessful in replication attempts due to the different laws governing probation at the national, state, and local levels.

Overall, the evaluation of the five-site replication determined that each site implemented the Des Moines program as a means to address some of their respective criminal justice needs rather than as a commitment to the Des Moines program concept. As concluded by the LEAA,

The communities that received a replication grant originally sought the grant in order to meet immediate needs of its own criminal justice agencies. And as each replication addressed those special needs, it tended to assume its own distinctive character. It is safe to say that the manner in which, and the extent to which, each replication varied from the Des Moines model pretty accurately reflected the special local problems the replication was expected to resolve (U.S. Department of Justice, 1979: 43).

What the LEAA concluded from the Des Moines program replication results was that communities that do not share some of the characteristics of the Des Moines community and criminal justice system provide an unfavorable environment for replication. Specifically, some of the characteristics in Des Moines that shaped the character of the program include an overcrowded jail, substantial geographic distance from urban centers, slow rate of geographic and demographic change, strong sense of community and receptivity to reform, and allowing local officials to administer corrections in their own way. Stated specifically, the more the replication site varies from the prototype, the less the likelihood of successful replication.

Decentralization: Not Less—More

Officially, decentralization reforms were intended as alternatives to a potentially damaging and counterproductive correctional system. This shift in the perception of the value of traditional punishment is reflective of the larger crisis in American society and its major institutions. Rather than continue with the prevailing tradition of "more is better," the new approach was to avoid contact with the formal correctional system through community-based alternatives. Only the most serious offenders—those who posed a "manifest danger" to the community—were to receive traditional correctional processing. Ultimately, all of these reform efforts were to reduce negative labeling and criminal associations as well as to increase justice and equity in the handling of less serious offender groups.

This new era in penal reform produced not only more of the same outcomes, but results that were laden with ominous overtones and dismal implications. At the juvenile and adult level, the decentralization of corrections into the community was not slowed by the negative or mixed results of various programs. In fact, rather than differentiating the handling of offenders, diversion, deinstitutionalization, and community programs substantially expanded corrections populations, which of course contradicts the very logic of labeling theory. The net-widening pattern associated with the decentralization of the correctional movement is exemplified by a comparison of correctional caseloads in 1965 and in 1976. The total caseload for both incarcerated and community-supervised adults and juveniles in 1965 was 1,281,801, or 661.3 per 100,000 population. However—after more than a decade of diversion, deinstitutionalization, and community corrections experiences—the 1976 total correctional caseload had increased to 1,981,229, or 921.4 per 100,000 population. This 1965–1976 comparison demonstrates an increase in numbers of 54.6 percent and a rate increase of 39.3 percent. During this eleven-year period, the increase in the numbers incarcerated was 83,782, while the number on probation and parole increased by 190,557. These figures underestimate the total population subject to some form of correctional control, moreover, because they do not include many minor offenders, their families, and others subject to diversion, deinstitutionalization, and various community correction services. Furthermore, this major burst in correctional clientele occurred during a period of stable crime rates (Austin and Krisberg, 1981).

Though community corrections programs proliferated despite frequently diverging from their intended goals, rehabilitative efforts eventually halted with the publication of a major study by Robert Martinson (1974). Martinson's study was focused upon determining the most effective means for rehabilitating offenders. After reviewing the findings of numerous treatment program evaluations and taking into account the program setting (i.e., institutional versus non-institutional), clientele (i.e., juvenile versus adult, male versus female) and treatment modalities (i.e., individual versus group), Martinson's over-arching conclusion was that, with few exceptions, rehabilitation programs have had little effect on recidivism. From this conclusion emerged the phrase "nothing works." In fact, such claims combined with the questionable record of LEAA-sponsored correctional reforms (e.g., deinstitutionalization, diversion, and community corrections) led Congress to abolish the LEAA in 1980. The common perception at the end of the 1970s was that, despite pouring millions of dollars into reforms aimed at diversion and rehabilitation, crime continued to pose a major social problem. This perception of reform failure was a driving force behind the law-and-order approach that began in the 1980s (Dean-Myrda and Cullen, 1998).

11

Conservatism and Law-and-Order Punishment (1980s–1990s)

The 1970s ended on the dismal notes of crisis and failure. In the wake of the Vietnam War, the Iran hostage affair, Three Mile Island, high unemployment, and crippling inflation, there was little reason left for optimism. For some, the belief that the 1960s had left the nation morally bankrupt only deepened the sense that radical change was needed. To overcome these national problems, nothing less than a political, cultural, and economic reversal seemed appropriate. Ronald Reagan orchestrated such a reversal in 1980, the main theme of which was to quash liberalism in all its forms. Reagan ushered in a "new day" marked by smaller and more conservative government, an ethos of individual responsibility, and a strong national defense. The moral excesses of the countercultural movement also were publicly denounced through campaigns advocating sexual restraint and drug abstinence. Signs and slogans touting "just say no" and "zero tolerance" became a regular part of the conservative landscape.

Although the wars on drugs and crime are perhaps the most notable examples of the "zero tolerance" posture, entering the decade of the eighties, pollsters reported that Americans were mostly concerned with the economy, the Vietnam War, the cold war, and civil rights (Dyer, 2000). The nation's overall crime rate between 1973 and 1982 was relatively stable, as was the murder rate between 1976 and 1993. With the exception of those living in urban poverty, the majority of the nation was, in statistical terms at least, safer. According to Dyer (2000), it was not until political officials publicly compared their investment in the war on crime with World War II expenses that fear of crime among the public escalated.

Though anxiety over crime had not been a part of the national conscience before, crime quickly became the centerpiece of nearly every political speech, campaign, and policy. Whether this fear of crime was manufactured and exploited for political gain or was truly justifiable has been a matter of ongoing debate (see Beckett, 1997), but what has not been disputed are the magnitude and consequences of governmental action in response to this "crime problem." The final decades of the twentieth century witnessed a strategic shift in crime policy that has universally been dubbed the "get-tough movement." Whereas the past one hundred years of penal policy had been shaped almost exclusively by the assumptions and expectations of the rehabilitative ideal, notions of retribution, deterrence, and incapacitation molded the get-tough movement. Liberals accepted the demise of rehabilitation on the grounds that, if punishment could not be effective, at least it could be fair. Conservatives, meanwhile, worked to ensure that criminals would not be coddled and that victims would be protected through lengthy prison terms. The effects of this overhaul—not surprisingly—have been neither magnanimous nor particularly effective, especially in terms of the war-like costs that have been expended.

Reversing Course

On the domestic front, the 1960s and 1970s are perhaps best known for their social activism, civil rights, and welfarist policies. Conversely, the 1980s are commonly remembered for supply-side and trickle-down economics and what has since been characterized as a "culture of greed." Although it cannot be said that the economic policies of the 1980s unilaterally shaped the direction of the prevailing culture, the two were indeed intertwined and linked directly to the Reagan presidency. The 1981 presidential inauguration of Ronald Reagan and the debut of the flamboyant nighttime soap opera *Dynasty* (Feuer, 1995) may have been purely coincidental, but the shared timing of these events was telling nevertheless. Together, they affirmed a new economic order and cultural ethos that Harrison and Bluestone described as the "great U-turn" (1988).

Political Economy

Reagan's vision for the nation was to reverse the liberalist policies of the previous two decades. He marked this policy shift in decisive terms by seeking to reduce the size of government, the amount of taxes, the number of business regulations, and the inflation problem (Ashford,

1990). He further advocated the privatization of certain government operations, the reduction or elimination of welfare and job programs, and the rebuilding of warfare programs. Monetary assistance to the poor was no longer seen as helping the downtrodden or the alienated, but rather it came to be viewed as subsidizing the undeserving. Reagan conservatives celebrated notions of the self-made man who had "pulled himself up by his own bootstraps."

These various economic policies benefited certain segments of the population, but devastated others. During Reagan and Bush's tenures, economic polarization increased dramatically, with the richest fifth of families earning nearly 43 percent of the nation's total income. This is nine times more than what the poorest fifth took in (Steinberg, 1997). By 1990, the term "millionaire" was rendered meaningless: There were more than 100,000 deca-millionaires and the number of billionaires increased from a handful in 1981, to 26 in 1986, 49 in 1987, and 52 by 1988 (Phillips, 1991). Altogether, the number of millionaires and billionaires increased by more than 250 percent and average annual CEO compensation increased from $373,000 to $773,000 (ibid.).

Unfortunately, much of this wealth was generated from "paper entrepreneurialism." As corporations profited from mergers, hostile takeovers, downsizing, multi-nationalizing, and de-industrializing, product output and reinvestment suffered. Between 1973 and 1985, junk bonds and stock trading increased 900 percent, while the nation's total output only increased by 300 percent (Harrison and Bluestone, 1988). The end result was that the rich got richer, the poor got poorer, the middle-class got squeezed, and foreign competitors—particularly Japan—dulled the competitive edge of American industry. Between 1978 and 1992, plant closings eliminated four million high-paying blue-collar manufacturing jobs (Steinberg, 1997). In 1982, one in ten Americans was unemployed (Harrison and Bluestone, 1988) and "corporate downsizing" forced the white-collar sector into unemployment or part-time work. By 1985, every one of the forty-two different categories of U.S. industry had introduced wage freezes, wage cuts, or other concessions such as part-time work. Quality jobs and the nation's manufacturing base were vanishing and being replaced with low-paying service sector jobs, or what the *Washington Post* termed "McJobs" (ibid.). Between 1979 and 1984, three in five jobs (58 percent) paid $7,400 a year or less, compared to only one in five jobs between 1963 and 1979 (ibid.).

From 1980 to 1993, the number of persons living in poverty increased from 29 million to 39 million. Of those living in poverty, one in five was a child (Irwin and Austin, 1997). From 1977 to 1988, the average after-tax family income for the bottom 10 percent fell by 10 percent, yet it increased 74 percent for the top 10 percent (ibid.). Wages for Middle America stagnated, with the average family income falling to levels found in the 1970s (Phillips, 1991). Worsening economic conditions had even more ravaging effects on the poorest sectors of society. The loss of unskilled manufacturing jobs, the flight of the black middle class from urban America, and the federal government's check on the growth of safety-net programs contributed to a class that was permanently stuck in ghetto living, or what Wilson (1987) termed the "underclass." The underclass, as described in a *New York Times* article, was "the miserable human residue, mired in hard-core unemployment, violent crime, drug use, teen-age pregnancy, and one of the world's worst human environments, [which] seems to be a partial perverse result of the very success of other blacks" (quoted in Lilly, Cullen, and Ball, 1995).

The age of conservatism was not without successes, but the downside was noticeably steep. The accumulation of individual wealth came at the expense of the majority of the population, and the more universal gains were largely deceptive. Though Reagan halted the recessionary cycle by fortifying national defense, the recovery was orchestrated under the precarious condition of deficit spending. During Reagan's presidency, the government spent $1.3 trillion more than it collected in taxes and other government receipts (Harrison and Bluestone, 1988). The total cumulative national debt later soared to $7 trillion (Malabre, 1987). In four years, the United States went from being the leading world creditor to being the leading world debtor (ibid.). Interestingly, this pattern of deficit spending was not limited to the government. Deficit spending was a broader cultural phenomenon in a society that valued material excess.

Valuing Decadence

In 1985, Ivan Boesky assured the graduates of Berkeley that "you can be greedy and still feel good about yourself" (quoted in Sewall, 1997: xi). In 1988, a California stockbroker declared, "only a sucker would work for less than $200,000 a year" (cited in ibid.). In the movie, *Wall Street*, Michael Douglas's character proclaimed, "Greed is good," and a pending graduate of Harvard confided to his minister, "I'm not greedy, I just want all I can get, legally, of course" (quoted in Gomes, 1996). These statements sum up the philosophy of life for many Americans in the 1980s, a decade often termed the "decade of narcissism" or "the society of the spectacle."

As the young idealists of the 1960s aged into mainstream America, the ethic of parsimony was pushed aside by the goal of "getting mine" (Sewall, 1997). The hippies and "yippies" (i.e., Youth International Party) of the 1960s had become the "yuppies" (i.e., young urban professionals) of the 1980s. Pursuing a very different version of the good life, yuppies donned Rolex and Cartier watches, Izod casual wear, and Ralph Lauren suits. They revered physical fitness, upward mobility, a busy lifestyle, and BMWs. These values were repeatedly exalted in the popular television programs of the day, including *L.A. Law, Dallas, Dynasty, Miami Vice,* and the *Family Ties* character, Alex Keaton. In real life, these values were on display in Donald Trump's real estate pyramids, Michael Milken's junk bond profiteering, and what Harvard theologian Peter Gomes described as the cityscape's "glass temples to the gods of commerce banks, insurance companies, and brokerage houses" (Gomes, 1996).

Material excess was fashionable and moderation was for those who could not afford otherwise. In the "he who dies with the most toys wins" culture, those who could not afford it simply charged it. Not unlike the bloated deficits of the federal government, by 1986 the average American family had accumulated personal debts of more than $11,500, home mortgages not included (Harrison and Bluestone, 1988). The total amount borrowed by consumers between 1981 and 1986 increased from $394 billion to $739 billion. Credit card debt alone increased from $55 billion in 1980 to $128 billion in 1986 (ibid.).

By the time George Bush assumed the presidency, the "casino society" (coined by Strange and quoted in ibid.) that produced the stock market crash of 1987, the savings and loan scandal, and the incarceration of high-profile entrepreneurs was on the decline. Expressing his own disdain for the flagrancy of the nouveau riche, Bush promised a "kinder, gentler" America. Americans, too, were beginning to raise their eyebrows at the displays of conspicuous consumption. Bruce Babbitt declared that the arrests of Rhodes scholars for insider trading contribute to the populist sentiment that a privileged class is getting rich at the expense of the rest of the economy (Phillips, 1991). Nevertheless, Bush largely retained Reagan's policies, advocating no new money for education, the elderly, transportation, or children in poverty (ibid.). The Bush presidency tempered cowboy capitalism and the vanity of the privileged, but a "kinder, gentler" posture toward crime and criminals was not forthcoming.

Neo-Conservative Criminology

The Reagan–Bush years gave new legitimacy to individual theories of crime. Both presidents were proactive in dispelling the idea that street crime and other social problems had socioeconomic causes (Beckett, 1997). Reagan maintained that "here in the richest nation in the world, where more crime is committed than in any other nation, we are told that the answer to the problem is to reduce our poverty. This isn't the answer." He went on to declare that the American people had "lost patience with liberal leniency and pseudo-intellectual apologies for crime" (quoted in ibid.: 48). George Bush similarly announced, "we must raise our voices to correct an insidious tendency—the tendency to blame crime on society, rather than the criminal" (quoted in ibid.).

These assertions set the stage for a new approach to crime, one that invoked the old ideas of classicism and moralism. Though distinct, each framework located the source of crime within the individual, which fit well with the "rugged-individualist" theme of republicans. For example, rational choice theory (Cornish and Clarke, 1986), which is largely a restatement of the classicist doctrine of free will, assumes that criminals are opportunistic actors, capable of calculating the consequences of their behavior. Based on the "expected utility" principle of economic theory, rational choice holds that human decisions are determined by the maximization of profit and the minimalization of loss. The theory further posits that the decision to engage in criminal activity also includes the selection of specific crimes at specific times and places. However, in contrast to the free will of the enlightenment age, rational choice theory allows for certain intrusions on the thought process, such as fear, inaccurate information, and a morality that can disrupt the hedonistic calculus (Lilly et al., 1995). The equally popular routine activities theory also has its roots in free will. Cohen and Felson (1979) maintained that crime is an event precipitated by three factors: freely motivated offenders, suitable targets, and the absence of capable guardians of persons or property. To the extent that these factors increase and converge, victimization rates will increase. Hence, decreases in victimization rates will only occur when there is a consistent reduction in at least one of these criminogenic factors.

Amid talk of free will and rational actors, the crime debate acquired a distinctly moral edge. Some social observers posited that crime is the result of a declining morality, due largely to the breakdown of traditional values, and especially the traditional family. Even though the "social breakdown" thesis (Sassoon, 1995) explains crime in societal terms, the presence of a "willing self" is still assumed. In effect, criminal behavior is attributed to a deficient personal character that is outwardly reflected in the sum total of one's deeds (Lamb, 1996). Under the social breakdown thesis, explanations of criminal behavior or deficient moral character are often reduced to claims of immoral behavior brought about by poor child rearing.

In *Crime and Human Nature* (1985), Wilson and Herrnstein promoted an integration of moral and biological perspectives. They argued that certain individuals are more disposed toward criminality than others, as evidenced by their repeated involvement in crime. They reasoned that criminal dispositions begin prior to infancy and are only later nurtured by (negative) family, school, labor market, and/or criminal justice experiences. In their estimation, what ultimately separates the predisposed offender population from the law-abiding—or generally law-abiding—population are the influences of genetics, class, and morality.

The influence of social determinism on penal policy was nearly eradicated by these and other conservative views. Offenders had been successfully recast as rational, menacing, and morally defective actors. Without doubt, theories attributing crime to individual will and portrayals of criminals as domestic enemies made the war on crime more palatable, if not wholly justifiable. The reigning image of the offender as a dangerous and ubiquitous threat—à la Willie Horton—validated the law-and-order agenda that came to dominate public policy.

Law-and-Order Punishment

The notion of a war on crime was not unique to the Reagan and Bush administrations. Lyndon Johnson in 1965 and Richard Nixon in 1969 also waged wars on crime. The Reagan–Bush war on crime was, however, unique in terms of its scope and character: it was far more extensive, expensive, and punitive. It was premised on the uncomplicated logic that with enough punishment and enough incarceration, crime could be reduced (Clear, 1994). Moreover, even if the goal of reducing crime is not realized through deterrence or incapacitation, get-tough punishment still can be supported on the grounds of justice (i.e., retribution) alone. From the federal to the local level, any politician who did not subscribe to the get-tough mentality was immediately attacked as "being soft on crime."

Justifying Punishment

Martinson's (1974) "nothing works" conclusion on offender treatment dealt a severe blow to the rehabilitative ideal. Yet still another blow was delivered in a report entitled *Doing Justice* (von Hirsch, 1995). Issued by the Committee for the Study of Incarceration, this report established retribution as the dominant philosophy for sentencing and punishment. Rather than the state attempting to "do good" through tenuous works of rehabilitation, the report maintained that the rightful aim of punishment is to "do justice."

In one respect, "doing justice" means that a person's claim to fair and just treatment should always supersede the achievement of societal aims. Therefore, punishment can only be justified as censure for deeds already committed—not for offenses that might be prevented in the future. The notion of doing justice is further tied to the concept of "just deserts," which can be understood as proportionality and consistent sentencing for similar offenders. Proportionalism rests upon the idea that penal sanctions and the imposition of suffering should be limited and calibrated according to the seriousness of the offense. Hence, offenders never should receive a sanction that exceeds or diminishes the harmfulness of the act committed. (Proportionalism, however, does not require an exact exchange of harm, as required in the ancient doctrine of *lex talionis*.)

The notion of retributive justice as proportionality and fairness appealed to both the liberals and conservatives of the time. Its appeal was based largely on the fact that it resolves the moral and practical problems associated with rehabilitation. These problems primarily include unwarranted disparities and discretion in the sentencing and paroling of offenders as well as treatment program ineffectiveness. Under the doing-justice model, retribution also repaired its historical reputation as the unenlightened vengeance-based philosophy. The notion of proportionality helped to moderate the more extreme perspective by placing notions of fairness in a central role in retributive penal theory (von Hirsch, 1995).

At the same time that retribution was being embraced by liberals and conservatives, those with even more conservative leanings reclaimed the merits of deterrence. A product of eighteenth-century utilitarianism, the philosophy of deterrence remained relatively unchanged in its contemporary conceptualization. It was still premised on the notions that all humans possess free will and that criminal behavior can be prevented through certain and swift punishment. Contemporary applications of deterrence did change, however, on the dimension of severity. The rhetoric of twentieth-century deterrence discards limits on severity and permits the escalation of penalties until the desired prevention effects are achieved.

Given the failure of the rehabilitative ideal, the philosophy of incapacitation also found favor as an overriding justification for punishment. Under this philosophy, punishment is justified on the grounds of social self-defense and crime reduction. However, in the context of this philosophy, crime reduction will occur not because the offender has been transformed successfully or because the law accurately anticipates the offender's cost–benefit calculus. It will occur by way of sheer physical restraint, lost opportunity, and the overall interruption of the criminal career of the offender. Crime reduction effects are presumably guaranteed for as long as the offender is incarcerated or otherwise sufficiently constrained.

The interruption strategy of incapacitation is conceived on two different levels. General incapacitation approached crime control through policies that increase incarceration for all categories of offenders. Selective incapacitation proposed that only certain offender groups—either the most habitual or the more dangerous—be targeted, given the cost and other counterproductive effects of incarceration. Integral to the success of selective incapacitation, then, is the use of risk assessment instruments that can accurately predict which offenders will persist in their criminal careers.

Though at odds conceptually and in terms of policy implications, the philosophies of retribution, deterrence, and incapacitation coexisted in the "new penology" age (Feeley and Simon, 1992), if for no other reason than they were not "rehabilitation." Of course, this does not mean that these philosophies were given their purest or ideal expression in the penal reforms and practices of this era. Certainly, many penal reforms have been justified in their name and their advocates have attempted to remain true to the principles of their respective philosophies. Yet, in the end, philosophy is not responsible for empirical reality. Down through the ages, penal reforms have been consistently dogged by political expediency, implementation problems, and unintended consequences. The get-tough era, which was characterized by an unusually high degree of penal reform activity, proved no exception to this historical pattern. The most notable reforms and practices of this time, or what Dyer (2000) has termed the "weapons of war," include the war on drugs, abolition of parole and the indeterminate sentence, mandatory minimums, habitual offender statutes, intermediate punishment, truth-in-sentencing and three-strikes legislation, and the expanded use of capital punishment.

The War on Drugs

Drug use, as measured by the percentage of Americans who report using illicit drugs in the past thirty days, dropped from 14 percent in 1979 to 6.2 percent in 1991. Marijuana usage, in particular, dropped from 13 percent in 1979 to 5 percent in 1991. During this time, cocaine usage also dropped from 2.4 to 0.9 percent (Bennett, 1994). The percentage of high school students using cocaine was up from 1975, but stayed relatively constant between 1981 and 1984, dropping substantially after 1987 (ibid.). Crack cocaine use, however, had increased among the urban underclass. Consequently, claims of a new crack epidemic were not entirely unfounded (Walker, 1985). Between 1985 and 1989, cocaine-related emergency room incidents increased from 10,248 to 42,145 and cocaine-related deaths increased from 717 to 2,496 (ibid.). What was regarded as a crack cocaine epidemic provided much of the rationale for the war on drugs.

In an attempt to reduce the lawlessness thought to be associated with drug use, the war on drugs was waged in nearly every corner of society. The workplace, amateur and professional athletics, the educational system, and the criminal justice system all were impacted by the grip of a "drug-induced" panic, despite the fact that overall drug use was on the decline. An attack on soft drugs was renewed, coupled with the expansion of anti-drug education programs. Search and seizure protections also were eroded so as not to "handcuff" police. Drug testing for the criminal and non-criminal, furthermore, became more common.

Various efforts to control the supply of and demand for drugs were federalized. Federal anti-drug expenditures increased from $873 million in 1979 to $12.7 billion in 1995 (U.S. Office of National Drug Control Policy, 1995). Under the Bush administration, the commitment to the war on drugs was formalized through the passage of the Anti-Drug Abuse Act of 1988 and the appointment of a "drug czar" in 1989. The drug czar presided over the newly formed U.S. Office of National Drug Control Policy, which was charged with the execution of the following objectives: Street-level drug enforcement was to be intensified; and federal, state, and local law-enforcement efforts were to be integrated. Cooperative arrangements with foreign countries to halt the flow of drugs into the country also were forged under the succeeding administrations of Bill Clinton and George W. Bush. For example, the war on drugs was waged abroad with the passage of Clinton's $1.3 billion "Plan Colombia" (Driver, 2001), later renamed the "Andean Regional Initiative" under George W.

Bush. Both initiatives provided military and financial aid to Colombia to combat the growth of illicit heroin and cocaine crops.

Determinate Sentencing, Parole, Habitual Offender Statutes, and Mandatory Minimums

Reform was tied not only to the war on drugs, but also to charges of system leniency, ineffectiveness, and sentencing disparities. Slowly but steadily, states dismantled key strategies based upon the philosophy of rehabilitation by eliminating or restricting parole use and indeterminate sentencing. The federal government helped certify this movement with the 1984 Sentencing Reform Act. This act abolished parole in the federal system and authorized the U.S. Sentencing Commission to replace the existing indeterminate sentencing structure with a guidelines-prescribed determinate sentencing structure requiring harsher and longer sentences. Under this act, the discretion once afforded to federal judges in the sentencing process was severely curtailed, as few or no departures from the prescribed sentencing guidelines were permitted.

Between 1976 and 1979, seven states abolished all or most of their paroling authority's discretion (Ringel, Cowles, and Castellano, 1993). By 1979, eighteen states had restricted their use of parole and six additional states had abolished it altogether. Between 1979 and 1982, sixteen more states restricted parole use and three more states abolished parole (Clear, 1994). By 1990, this national trend of eliminating or restricting parole use extended to six more states, including Illinois, California, and Minnesota. In the end, fourteen states abolished discretionary parole board release for all offenders (Ditton et al., 1999).[1]

Other states, such as New Jersey and Pennsylvania, abolished indeterminate sentencing, but retained parole. Most states retained some form of post-prison supervision, though it was often carried out under a different name (e.g., control release) or as a split sentence (i.e., incarceration followed by a term of probation). For example, 72 percent of all state and federal prisoners in 1977 were released under the parole system. That figured dropped to 48 percent by 1983, to 40 percent by 1988, and to 39 percent in 1993. Nevertheless, the proportion of releases to some form of post-supervision was 82 percent during this period of declining parole use (Holt, 1998). By 2000, parolees represented only 11 percent of the nearly 6.5 million persons under correctional control (i.e., jail, prison, probation, post-prison supervision) and more than half of these parolees were being supervised in the four states of California, New York, Texas, and Pennsylvania (Petersilia, 2003).

The sentencing guideline, determinate sentencing, and parole reforms did not, in and of themselves, lead to more punitive sanctioning. In fact, federal and state sentencing reforms were intended to do more than just impose tougher punishment. A doing-justice philosophy was to guide their development, for the purpose of bringing fairness and uniformity to sentencing practices. Sentencing guidelines sought to ensure that "like" offenders would receive "like" sanctions and that prison release dates would be determined objectively at the outset of the sentence. Specifically, release dates and sentence reductions were to be established by mathematical calculation, rather than by parole board interpretations of rehabilitative progress. This is not to say that the more altruistic objectives of proportionality and fairness did not get lost or entangled in the more fashionable goals of getting tough and reducing crime. For example, the simultaneous spread of habitual offender and mandatory minimum laws was consistent with getting tough and crime reduction and reflected the influence of incapacitation and deterrence philosophies.

Habitual offender statutes were designed to punish repeat offenders of any kind beyond what sentencing guidelines might normally prescribe for a particular offense. These statutes are not a form of structured sentencing, but they do permit sentencing enhancements for offenders classified as habitual or career criminals. In contrast, mandatory minimum statutes designate a required period of incarceration for select offenses, even a first offense. Mandatory minimums overwhelmingly target drug and firearm offenses, but often extend to burglary, rape, murder, and some combinations of offenses. The New York Rockefeller Drug Laws of 1973 authorized the first and most severe mandatory sentences in the nation. They called for a fifteen-year mandatory prison term for anyone convicted of selling more than two ounces of a controlled substance or of possessing more than four ounces of a controlled substance (Hansen, 1999). Delaware also enacted its mandatory minimums in 1973, but added new provisions in 1981. Ultimately, more than 222 mandatory sentencing provisions were enacted in Delaware, though just eighteen of these provisions were responsible for 94 percent of the prison admissions (O'Connell, 1995).

By 1983, forty-three states had mandatory prison terms for one or more violent crimes, and twenty-nine states and the District of Columbia had mandatory terms for narcotics offenses (Gordon, 1990). As of 1990, Florida had ten separate mandatory laws, three of which related to drug crimes, two that related to habitual offenders, and three dealt with the use of firearms. Six of the Florida laws were passed in 1988–1989 alone

(Walker, 1985). For example, selling drugs within one thousand feet of a school draws a mandatory minimum sentence of three years. The operation of a drug enterprise yields a mandatory sentence of life or no less than twenty-five years. Use or possession of an automatic firearm or machine gun results in an eight-year sentence (Bales and Dees, 1992).

The Federal Sentencing Reform Act of 1984 also authorized mandatory minimums for federal drug offenses and offenses involving the use of a firearm (Schulhofer, 1993). The formal objectives of the federal code parallel those of their state counterparts: They were to assure "just" (i.e., appropriately severe) punishment, effective deterrence and incapacitation, elimination of sentencing disparities, incentives for offenders to turn others in, and courtroom efficiency resulting from pressure to plead guilty (ibid.). This first round of federal legislation took effect in 1987, but through 1990, new mandatory minimums were added and existing ones were enhanced (ibid.). The results of this congressional activity are one hundred separate mandatory minimum sentence provisions, located in sixty different statutes. The majority of the provisions never have been used, as 94 percent of the cases processed were attributed to controlled substances and firearm possession (ibid.). Commenting on the rigidity of mandatory sentences, particularly as they relate to drug enforcement, U.S. District Court Judge Spencer Letts stated:

> Congress decided to hit the problem of drugs, as they saw it, with a sledgehammer, making no allowance for the circumstances of any particular case.... Under the statutory minimum, it can make no difference whether he is a lifetime criminal or a first-time offender. Indeed, under this sledgehammer approach, it could make no difference if the day before making this one slip in an otherwise unblemished life, the defendant had rescued fifteen children from a burning building, or had won the Congressional Medal of Honor while defending his country (quoted in Dyer, 2000: 166).

Intermediate Punishment

Because Americans found an almost equally despised enemy in government taxation, the enormous costs incurred by the get-tough strategies were partially defrayed by reduced spending on education, welfare, and various other social programs. However, the relief provided by such budgetary maneuvering was both minimal and temporary. Ultimately, the simultaneous public demand for protection from crime and from higher taxes prompted the development of an alternative reform strategy known as intermediate punishment.

Intermediate punishment supplied a major line of defense in the overcrowding crisis created by these reforms. In fact, it was argued that, in the absence of fiscal crisis and prison overcrowding, there would have been little incentive to develop intermediate punishments (Lurigio and Petersilia, 1992). States obviously lack the resources to lock up every offender and numerous lawsuits required that states immediately reduce their prison populations. The same trend occurred in local jails, wherein overcrowded conditions had similarly reached the threshold of cruel and unusual punishment.

As correctional expenditures reached unprecedented levels, policy makers were faced with the difficult task of complying with court orders and remaining tough on crime without bankrupting the public coffers. Intermediate punishments helped reconcile these competing interests by providing community-based sanctions that were certainly tougher than nominal probation, but less costly than incarceration. In effect, intermediate punishments filled the void in sentencing options that was created by the dual system of probation and prison. Home confinement, electronic monitoring, boot camps, and intensive supervision probation were among the many intermediate punishment programs implemented to reduce reliance on incarceration, save money, be punitive, reduce crime, and—incidentally—to provide more proportionate sanctions.

Given the potential of intermediate punishments to satisfy these wide-ranging objectives, their adoption proceeded with little opposition. With intensified manual and technological monitoring (which much later would include global positioning satellite capabilities), the option of home detention, multiple conditions (e.g., daily logs, community service, treatment, restitution, drug tests), smaller caseloads, and more frequent contact, intermediate punishments offered a punishment package that fit varying levels of offender risk. All at once, intermediate punishment could incapacitate offenders in the community by controlling their movements in time and space. It also held out the prospect of deterrence by being more punitive than nominal probation and thus more effective at reducing recidivism. It was assumed that rational offenders would refrain from criminal behavior, knowing that increased surveillance will lead to rapid detection of wrongdoing and rapid response by the criminal justice system.

By 1989, forty states and the District of Columbia operated intensive supervision programs, and twenty-six states and the District of Columbia operated separate house arrest programs. Of these twenty-six states, twenty-three states and the District of Columbia coupled house arrest with electronic monitoring. Shock incarceration (i.e., boot camps) or split sentencing was being practiced in sixteen states, while other intermediate punishment programs were used in ten additional states (Byrne and Pattavina, 1992). Intermediate punishments have since become a regular feature of correctional systems in every state, though different jurisdictions often employ different terminology to those programs (e.g., community control, house arrest, home confinement, intensive supervision probation).

Truth-in-Sentencing and Three-Strikes Legislation

No sooner had intermediate punishment been implemented to ease the burdens posed by drug, habitual offender, and mandatory minimum laws that elected officials pursued yet another round of get-tough measures. Truth-in-sentencing and three-strikes laws emerged in the 1990s to curb the early release of violent offenders who had been displaced from prison by typically non-violent drug offenders. In 1987, the federal government enacted the first truth-in-sentencing law, with the aims of restoring public confidence in the sentencing process and increasing time spent in custody in relation to the actual sentence meted out in court. Specifically, the idea behind truth-in-sentencing legislation is that an inmate should have to serve at least 85 percent of the maximum sentence that is originally imposed. Consequently, inmates sentenced under a parole and indeterminate system could no longer be released after the prescribed minimum time had been served, regardless of good behavior.

The federal government encouraged states to adopt their own truth-in-sentencing laws in return for federal aid in the construction of state prisons. The 1994 federal crime bill created a $10 billion pool of money to be allotted only to those states willing to implement truth-in-sentencing laws (Dyer, 2000). By 1995, twenty-nine states had implemented 85-percent requirement truth-in-sentencing laws; other states opted for less stringent requirements such as 50-percent requirements or 100 percent of the minimum requirement (Ditton et al., 1999). Sixteen states refused the federal financial incentive, however, realizing that the amount given could not fully compensate for the effects of truth-in-sentencing legislation on top of the outstanding costs already incurred from the previous reforms. For example, in contemplating the federal incentive for truth-in-sentencing laws, Virginia estimated that, if it abolished parole and adopted truth-in-sentencing, it would have to build twenty-five new prisons at the cost of $2 billion. Moreover, it would cost an additional $500 million annually to operate a correctional system subjected to truth-in-sentencing mandates (Mauer, 1996).

Three-strikes laws emerged around the same time as truth-in-sentencing legislation with the goal of imposing the ultimate prison sentence: life without the possibility of parole for a third felony conviction. These laws were promoted specifically as a way of keeping habitual offenders off the streets. In 1993, Washington was one of the first states to put a three-strikes provision on the ballot. This provision required life in prison without the possibility of parole for people convicted of three or more serious or violent felonies. A national push for three-strikes laws followed the 1993 Polly Klaas murder in California. Twelve-year-old Polly Klaas was murdered by Richard Allen Davis, a California prison parolee who had been released after serving eight years of a sixteen-year sentence, despite having numerous prior convictions for kidnapping, assault, and other crimes (Benekos and Merlo, 1994). Public outrage over Davis's early release led to California's three-strikes law. The first two strikes extend to "serious" felonies, while any felony qualifies as a third strike. Further, juvenile offenders convicted of, for example, two residential burglaries can be convicted years later and be sent to prison for life for a nonviolent crime such as passing a bad check.

By 1997, twenty-four states and the federal government had some form of three-strikes legislation (Walker, 1998). The majority of these states included violent felonies, such as murder, rape, robbery, arson, and assaults on their list of "strikeable" offenses. Some states, however, included nonviolent offenses such as the sale of drugs. State laws also exhibited variation in the number of strikes that were needed for an offender to be considered "out." In eight states, only two strikes were required to bring about a sentence enhancement (Austin et al., 1999). State laws further differed in terms of the length of imprisonment for offenders who had "struck out." For example, mandatory life sentences were to be imposed when offenders are out in Georgia, Montana, Tennessee, Louisiana, South Carolina, Indiana, New Jersey, North Carolina, Virginia, Washington, and Wisconsin (ibid.). In three other states, parole was still possible after an offender was out. In New Mexico, offenders that struck out were not to be eligible for parole until after thirty years, while Colorado offenders could become eligible for release after forty years.

Since the implementation of these laws, California appears to be the only state to have extensively applied the three-strikes provision. However, it is not clear exactly how many truly serious or violent offenders have been incarcerated as a result. Six months following California's enactment of the three-strikes law, more than half of the three-strikes cases filed involved such nonviolent felonies as shoplifting, auto burglary, theft of cigarettes, and, in one Los Angeles case, theft of a pizza. The effect of this law on the California criminal justice system was substantial. Six months after enactment of the California three-strikes law, the Los Angeles County Jail, which was already under court order for overcrowding, was housing an additional 1,700 inmates (Skolnick, 1995). More cases were also brought to trial instead of being plea bargained, thus contributing to court backlogs and higher financial costs related to increased processing of criminal cases. According to the California Legislative Analyst's Office, jury trials in the state increased from 150 to 300 percent in most counties (Dyer, 2000). The California Department of Corrections further estimated that three-strikes would require an additional twenty state prisons to be added to the present twenty-eight and the twelve prisons already on the drawing board. The cost of fully implementing the three-strikes law to the California Correctional System was estimated at $6.7 billion a year (ibid.).

Should other states follow California's enforcement approach to three-strikes laws, the financial impact would certainly be devastating. However, to date, the application of these laws in other states seems to have been more symbolic than substantive (Austin et al., 1999). Austin and colleagues noted that, in all twenty-four three-strikes states, provisions for penalty enhancements already had been in place. Therefore, the authors argued that three-strikes legislation was not truly designed to have an significant impact on the system. For example, in Washington, only 115 offenders have been admitted to prison under the three-strikes law since 1993. In Georgia—a two-strike state—fewer than 10 percent of annual prosecutions in Atlanta are based on this law. The Federal Bureau of Prisons, meanwhile, has not admitted any inmates under three-strikes since 1998.

Death Penalty

Within four years of the *Gregg v. Georgia* (1976) decision, thirty-five states opted to modify— rather than abolish—capital punishment. Several states (e.g., Colorado, Illinois, Maryland, and Montana) made further revisions that increased the number of aggravating circumstances that could be considered in capital cases. At the federal level, new capital offenses also were designated. For example, the Omnibus Anti-Drug Abuse Act of 1988 extended the sanction of death to homicides occurring in the course of drug activity.

Throughout the 1980s and 1990s, federal and state governments were unwavering in their support of the death penalty, despite the persisting problem of racial bias in the sanction's application. In recognition of this bias, the anti-drug abuse act required that the role of race in capital punishment be examined. Responding to this legislative mandate, the Federal General Accounting Office (GAO) reported that 82 percent of capital punishment studies showed that race is indeed a relevant biasing factor, particularly when the victim is white and the defendant is black (Vito, 1995). The GAO analysis further concluded that race is a biasing factor at all stages of the criminal justice system and that offense variables cannot fully account for the racial disparity in the use of the sentence of death (ibid.).

Despite the showing of racial bias, the Supreme Court ruled that a legislative body would be best to provide a remedy to this problem. The House of Representatives responded to this ruling by drafting the 1991 Fairness in Death Sentencing Act. The draft of this act required that defendants provide evidence of racial bias and, if bias could be demonstrated, the sentence would be reduced to life in prison (ibid.). However, with little public debate, the act was summarily defeated (ibid.).

Enabling legislation and a willing public combined to send more and more offenders to death row. In 1987, 299 offenders were admitted to death row, bringing the total number under sentence of death to more than 2,000 by 1988. By 1993, that figure had increased to 2,802 (Gordon, 1990; Vito, 1995). Though the execution rate did not initially keep pace with death row admissions, the pace of executions did hasten noticeably, as shown in Figure 11-1. The pace of executions would likely accelerate further with Clinton's Counter-Terrorism and Effective Death Penalty Act of 1996. This act essentially eliminates the right to appeal by shortening the process of filing habeas corpus to one year (Dyer, 2000). States such as Florida and Texas replicated the federal precedent, claiming that the current process of administering capital punishment was too expensive.

Though monetary issues tended to dominate discussions of the post-conviction death penalty process, the shortening of the appeals process is a decidedly moral issue. It usually takes at least six to ten years to prove one's innocence, even with the advent of DNA testing (Dyer, 2000). For example, since 1976, Illinois has executed the same number of people as it has released due to a post-conviction finding of innocence. In Louisiana, it took one inmate thirty years to prove his innocence and twelve years for an Oklahoma inmate to be released due to DNA evidence (Dyer, 2000).

An equally troubling pattern in death penalty practice has been considerable variability in the use of capital punishment by region. Of the ninety-three executions carried out between 1977 and 1987, eighty-seven

Figure 11-1
U.S. Execution Rates, 1977–2000

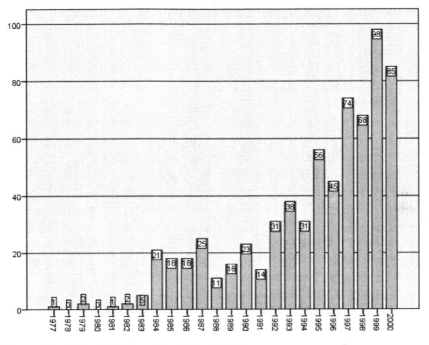

Source: Death Penalty Information Center (2009).

occurred in the South. Seventy-five percent of them took place in Texas (26), Florida (17), Louisiana (15), and Georgia (12) (Gordon, 1990). The remaining six executions were in Utah, Nevada, and Indiana. As with the many other get-tough measures, the realization of deterrent effects from capital punishment has been inconsistent at best, if not absent altogether. Evidence of deterrent effects was reported in select older studies (e.g., Sellin); however, more recent research indicates that there are no deterrent effects or, worse, there may actually be "brutalization" effects (i.e., increases in violent crime and murder attributed to exposure to executions) (Forst, 1983; Cochran and Chamlin, 2000).

Consequences of Law-and-Order Punishment

The collective impact of these various policy shifts—whether the war on drugs, the abolishment of parole, the introduction of mandatory sentences, or the adoption of intermediate punishment—was not as tidy and effective as the rhetoric and legislation that enabled them would suggest. Texas Republican Senator Kay Bailey Hutchinson (1999) perhaps said it best when she stated that the "first casualty of war is the truth."

War on Drugs

The incarceration of unprecedented numbers of drug offenders is one of the most consistent and profound consequences of law-and-order reform activity. In 1979, only 6 percent of the entire U.S. prison population was comprised of drug offenders (Blumstein, 1995). By 1994, 25 percent of the state inmate population was serving time for either drug possession or the sale or manufacturing of drugs. The effects of the war on drugs have been particularly acute in the federal system, in which 60 percent of the inmate population was serving time on drug charges (Blumstein, 1995; von Hirsch, 1995). In the first ten years after Congress toughened federal drug laws, the number of people incarcerated for drug offenses increased by more than 400 percent, nearly twice the growth rate for violent criminals. For example, between 1980 and 1994, the number of drug offenders incarcerated in federal prisons rose from 4,749 to 46,499. By 1990, 89 percent of first-time drug offenders with no prior record were being sentenced to an average of 68.4 months by the federal courts. Overall, more people were in prison in the United States for drug offenses than for all offenses in England, France, Germany and Japan combined (*New York Times*, 1999).

While these astounding figures might suggest that the war on drugs proceeded according to plan, high incarceration rates did not equate to unmitigated success. Government reports consistently indicated that the war on drugs had little appreciable effect on drug use and crime. For example, in Delaware, despite a 45 percent increase in the number of felony drug offenders incarcerated, reductions in drug activity were not realized (O'Connell, 1995). The National Drug Control Strategy also reported that

> Since 1992, there has been a substantial increase in the use of most drugs, particularly marijuana, among American youth. Meanwhile, record levels of illegal drugs are entering the U.S. from Mexico; more than $10 billion in drugs crossed our Southwest border in 1997, and the Border Patrol in Texas, alone, seized $765 million worth (Hutchinson, 1999: A-15).

The questionable impact of the war on drugs extends to policies abroad as well. Critics have charged that the aerial crop spraying in Colombia has damaged the environment and the health of indigenous communities. U.S. financial and military intervention in Colombia also has been condemned for contributing to regional destabilization and increased violence by paramilitary groups (Amatangelo, 2001; Driver, 2001). Senator Hutchinson has further remarked that many members of Congress take their frustration out on Mexico because they feel powerless to stem the tide of demand at home. She went on to say: "We'll win this war on drugs only by telling the plain truth—and that is that too many countries, including Colombia, produce drugs. Too many countries, including Mexico, traffic in drugs. And too many countries, including the United States, use drugs" (Hutchinson, 1999: A-15).

Habitual Offender Statutes, Mandatory Minimums, and Incapacitation

The likelihood of incarceration and length of actual time served increased for offenses other than drugs as well. Between 1981 and 1987, the probability that a conviction would lead to a prison sentence increased by 41 percent for burglary and by 166 percent for rape. Actual time served also increased by 54 percent for burglary and by 129 percent for rape (Clear, 1994). In 1985, the average sentence for a first-time admission to prison nearly doubled to sixty-seven months (Clear and Cole, 1993). Prior to federal penal code reform, 52 percent of federal convictions resulted in prison, compared with 74 percent following reform (Walker, 1985). Average time served in federal prisons also increased from twenty-four months in 1984 to forty-six months in 1990 (von Hirsch, 1995). In the four years immediately following the implementation of the new federal laws, the proportion of sentences to prison increased from 52 to 60 percent, sentences to probation decreased from 63 to 44 percent, time served for violent crimes increased by an estimated 37 percent, and time served for drug crimes increased by 123 percent (McDonald and Carlson, 1992). Nationally, as of 1992, 13,937 inmates were serving "natural life" sentences, with another 52,054 serving sentences of life without the possibility of parole. An added 125,995 were serving sentences of twenty years or more, and 200,000 were serving "extremely long sentences" (Irwin and Austin, 1997).

The result of more people going to prison for longer periods of time is predictable. Between 1980 and 1992, the number of individuals incarcerated in jails and state and federal prisons increased from 330,000 to 883,000, constituting an increase of 168 percent. In 1987, 8.6 million people were admitted just to jails (Clear, 1994). In the federal system, the prison population jumped from 24,000 in 1980 to 95,000 in 1994 and to 145,416 by 2000 (Bureau of Justice Statistics, 1995b, 2008). In effect, the numbers of individuals under correctional supervision of any kind increased substantially. Even with more people in jails and state and federal prisons, the number of state and federal probationers still increased by 203 percent between 1975 and 1990. In 1980, 1.1 million offenders were on state and federal probation and 220,000 were on parole. By 1990, 2.5 million offenders were on state and federal probation and 457,000 were on state and federal parole or some other form of post-release supervision. This pattern continued, such that by 1998, the number of state and federal probationers totaled 3.3 million and the number of parolees totaled 694,787 (McCarthy et al., 2001).

One could argue that, as more offenders were admitted to some form of correctional supervision and to prisons for longer periods of time, the aims of incapacitation and therefore crime reduction were realized. However, with little forethought given to the consequences of getting tough in the absence of a dedicated funding source, the U.S. penal system nearly collapsed. Burgeoning prison populations reached unconstitutional levels, subjecting numerous states to lawsuits. By 1993, forty states and the District of Columbia were under court order to alleviate overcrowded conditions or to improve other substandard living conditions. On average, state correctional systems were operating at 31 percent over capacity, while the Federal Bureau of Prisons was operating at 46 percent over capacity. By 1994, eleven states' correctional systems exceeded their capacity by 150 percent, with only nine states operating below capacity. One-third (135) of the nation's jails were also under court order to relieve overcrowding (Irwin and Austin, 1997; Rothman, 1995a).

To accommodate the demands of escalating prison populations and constitutional requirements, federal, state and local governments embarked on costly prison-building campaigns. For example, California taxpayers would have to pay $4.1 billion to fund prison construction over an eight-year period (Morain, 1994). In New York State, 33,458 prison beds were constructed, with construction costs over the next thirty years estimated at nearly $6 billion (Correctional Association of New York, 1995). Between 1990 and 1994, the nation's prison capacity increased by nearly 200,000 beds. In 1994, federal legislation earmarked $7.9 billion to aid state prison construction (Edna McConnell Clark Foundation, 1995).

Adding operational expenses to the bill, the costs associated with managing offender populations grew beyond the reach of many state budgets. According to the 1992 *Corrections Compendium,* Connecticut,

Florida, Maine, Illinois, and Michigan were unable to operate newly constructed facilities because of insufficient funds (CEGA Services, Inc., 1992). Fiscal shortfalls forced five other states to delay institution openings, while other states could only use half the space available in the new facilities. This is not altogether surprising when one considers the expenses associated with staffing correctional facilities. According to the U.S. Bureau of Justice Statistics (1995a), the number of corrections personnel (including probation and parole) increased by 70 percent between 1984 and 1990, amounting to a total monthly payroll of almost $1.3 billion (ibid.). Ironically, by 1992, there were more than 500,000 correctional employees nationwide, which amounted to more than any Fortune 500 company other than General Motors (Beckett, 1997). The American Correctional Association membership doubled between 1982 and 1988, and even more startling is the increase in the number of criminal justice system employees: In 1965, there were 600,000 employees and there were more than 2 million by 1993 (ibid.). Altogether, correctional costs nationwide—including prison construction and maintenance, probation, and parole—increased from $6 billion in 1979 to $24.9 billion in 1990. Prior to 1979, correctional costs had increased at a much more gradual pace, growing from $2.3 billion in 1971, to $3.8 billion in 1975, and then to $6 billion in 1979 (Edna McConnell Clark Foundation, 1995).

Sentence Uniformity and "Doing Justice"

As for curbing unwarranted disparities in sentencing, the reforms of the past two decades merely shifted the discretion of judges and paroling authorities to prosecutors. In several states, prosecutors decide whether to invoke the mandatory laws and prosecutors decide whether to invoke the sentence enhancements permitted by habitual offender statutes in all states. Moreover, prosecutors (who are elected officials) decide whether or not to seek the death penalty.

The disparity in the enforcement of the laws is most evident with regard to the composition of the prison population. For example, Irwin and Austin (1997) pointed out that the rate of increase in the U.S. prison population is not the only remarkable feature of the "imprisonment binge"; the change in the composition of the prison population was equally dramatic. In 1982, one in 49 black males between the ages of 20 and 29 was incarcerated in a state prison, a ratio that is 8 times higher than that for whites. In 1989, nearly one-quarter of black males age 20 to 29 years old was under some form of correctional supervision (Mauer, 1990). In 1993, blacks comprised 44 percent of the state and federal prison population, but only 12 percent of the U.S. population. Moreover, 18 percent of the prison population was Hispanic, though Hispanics comprised only 10 percent of the U.S. population. Whites, on the other hand, constituted 74 percent of the U.S. population, but only 36 percent of the state and federal prison population (U.S. Bureau of Justice Statistics, 1995b).

The racial disparity in the prison population was inevitably a function of the selective focus of the war on drugs. Though survey data show that 13 percent of all monthly drug users are black, blacks constitute 35 percent of those arrested for drug possession, 55 percent of those convicted of drug possession, and 74 percent of those sentenced to prison for drug possession. When the Hispanic population is added, the percent of minorities sentenced to prison for drug possession increases to more than 90 (Beckett, 1997). This pattern of disparity is explained in large part by the fact that one gram of crack is the equivalent of one hundred grams of powdered cocaine in the eyes of the sentencing guidelines. Because the drug war focused on crack cocaine—which was mainly sold and used in inner-city communities—the overwhelming majority of offenders sentenced to prison for drug possession were poor blacks and Hispanics (Irwin and Austin, 1997).

Intermediate Punishment

Rather than helping to reduce prison overcrowding and corresponding costs, intermediate punishment programs often contributed to the very problems they were designed to alleviate. Few states or jurisdictions could claim true diversionary effects following their implementation (Blomberg, Bales, and Reed, 1993; Lucken, 1997). In Florida, the probability of a prison sanction actually increased following the implementation of the state's community-control program (Blomberg et al., 1993), though Baird and Wagner (1990) contended that prison overcrowding in Florida would have been worse in its absence. Georgia's intensive supervision program claimed a 10 percent diversion rate in the program's infancy (Petersilia, 1987), but was unable to sustain even this small diversionary result in the long term.

Not only were intermediate punishment programs generally implemented as supplements to incarceration, but also any initial diversionary effects likely were negated later by the prevalence of technical violations (Petersilia and Turner, 1993). Thus, whether intended as alternatives or supplements to incarceration during a period of crisis, intermediate punishments compounded the problem of institutional overcrowding. Jail and prison populations alike were aggravated by the recycling of technical violators who could not withstand the rigors of intermediate punishment. The "piled up sanctions" of substance abuse treatment, supervision fees, restitution, community service, anger management, drug tests, daily logs, and curfews often proved to be too onerous and costly for "socially disorganized" offenders (Lucken, 1997; Blomberg and Lucken, 1994b). In jurisdictions across the country, intensive supervision probation programs were producing nearly twice the number of technical violations as routine supervision did, though rates of reoffending for both programs were essentially equal (Petersilia and Turner, 1993). Georgia was even forced to prohibit returns to prison that were due to technical violations. Almost from the outset, then, intermediate punishment's success was jeopardized by its contradictory objectives. It was not possible to strictly enforce the conditions that made intermediate punishment more punitive than probation without also undermining the goals of reducing prison overcrowding and correctional costs.

Punishment Binge

Few dispute the fact that the 1980s were a triumph for upper America. Kevin Phillips, a Republican official in the Reagan administration, even concluded that the policies that shaped the distribution of wealth created a "nation of billionaires and homeless" (Phillips, 1991). Philosopher and criminologist Jeffrey Reiman (1990) took this assessment a step further by declaring that the "rich got richer and the poor got prison."

Without question, the war on crime involved a mass mobilization of resources that were narrowly focused on low-level drug offenders and street criminals. Getting tough on "them" was the bread and butter of local, state, and federal political campaigns. Entertainment and news programming fueled the frenzy by flooding the airwaves with criminal profiles and crime reports. Media coverage of crime stories tripled from 632 stories reported in 1991 to 1,949 stories in 1994. Surprisingly, 63 percent of respondents in a public opinion poll indicated that the media accurately depicted the crime problem in this country.

Though crime levels in the 1980s and early 1990s were much higher than they were in 1964, crime rates were not increasing categorically. Between 1973 and 1991, robbery and household burglary rates declined by 17 and 42 percent, respectively. Household larceny dropped as well. The murder sprees and drive-by shootings that fed the national hysteria

Table 11-1
Adult Correctional Population, Adult Population, and Crime Rates, 1980–1994

	1980	*1994*	*% Change*
Adult Correctional Population	1,832,350	5,196,505	184%
Probation	1,118,097	2,962,166	165%
Jails	163,994	490,442	199%
Prison	329,821	1,053,738	219%
Parole	220,438	690,159	213%
Adult U.S. Population	162,800,000	192,600,000	18%
Crime Rates			
Adult arrests	6,100,000	8,900,000	46%
Reported index crimes	13,400,000	14,000,000	4%

Source: Irwin and Austin (1997).

indeed augmented murder rates, but these incidents were highly isolated and confined to a few areas in a just a few cities. The urban wastelands of Washington, D.C., New York City, and Los Angeles bore the brunt of this violence (Walker, 1985), not the nation as a whole. Between 1980 and 1993, murder, robbery, and burglary rates across the nation were stable and, in some instances, declining (Blumstein, 1995). Nevertheless, the nation readily accepted the claim that unprecedented levels of serious crime justified the unprecedented levels of punishment.

The offenders who entered the penal system during this get-tough period were frequently new offenders caught in the drug-enforcement crackdown. For example, 45 percent of Florida's prison admissions had no prior prison commitments and another 23 percent had only one prior commitment (Florida Department of Corrections, 1994). Nationally, a number of repeat offenders were remanded to prison under the tough new laws, but a sizable proportion of these admissions to state and federal prisons came from parole violations. In 1983, 20 percent of prison admissions were returning parolees. This figure increased to 26 percent in 1987 and to 35 percent by 1997. Yet, many of the parole returns were generated by technical violations rather than new offenses (Holt, 1998). For example, roughly 35 percent of prison admissions in 1998 Pennsylvania were due to parole violations, 40 percent of which were due to technical violations rather than new offenses committed (Micek, 2005).

If more serious and increasing crime rates did not drive the punishment rates (see Table 11-1), then what did? To explain this unparalleled punitive trend, Scheingold (1984) and Beckett (1997) looked at the close dynamic between the media and the political juggernaut. They contended that politicians exploited the easy non-contentious issue of crime to gain broad public support, while the media reported the "problem" in earnest. In effect, the public was manipulated into believing that crime was an urgent problem and eventually ranked it as a top national priority. This essentially manufactured preoccupation with crime was subsequently used as cause for advancing a punitive agenda.

Other scholars put forth a different explanation for these punitive trends. Some surmised that, when the rehabilitative ideal failed to materialize, crime-control policy was governed by frustration rather than reason. The sense of resignation and confusion that followed is perhaps best reflected in the fact that incapacitation, deterrence, and retribution all were embraced in the same generational breath. For example, reliance upon increasingly severe punishment indicated an abiding public faith in the logic of deterrence—despite public awareness of its uncertain effectiveness. The logic of retribution, on the other hand, counters the assumption of needing to find something that "works" or is effective. Consequently, the goal of retributive strategies was not offender "correction," but justice through sentences that were evenly applied and proportionate to the harm committed. Incapacitation-based strategies also avoided the effectiveness question by entirely redefining success. Reductions in crime no longer were dependent upon the inexact science of offender reformation; they could now be achieved through the "failproof" practice of offender containment.

While scholars continue to grapple with the reasons for and likely future of law-and-order punishment, the effects of these policies continue unabated. The consequences of getting tough extend beyond what has been described here and include a host of bleak conditions. Many of these consequences are associated with the incarceration of "special" inmate populations (e.g., women, the elderly, and the mentally ill), whose presence in the penal system had previously been negligible. The substantial growth in these special inmate populations of late, however, has created new and more challenging burdens for the correctional system. The following chapter examines these populations and the controversies that have emerged in response to their increased presence in the penal system.

Note

1.   The states that abolished discretionary parole under all circumstances are Arizona, Delaware, Florida, Illinois, Indiana, Kansas, Maine, Minnesota, North Carolina, Ohio, Oregon, Washington, and Wisconsin.

12

Penal System as Surrogate Institution for Special Populations

The composition of the prison population has changed as a number of societal shifts have converged with law-and-order policies. This change in composition has also brought about a change in the look and function of the prison. The needs and risks of younger male offenders have always dictated the demands on the penal system and, overwhelmingly, still do. However, the needs and risks of females, the elderly, the diseased, and the mentally ill are adding to those demands, making correctional supervision in the prison and community a more costly and challenging process. Clearly, these "special populations" are not new to the correctional system, as women, the elderly, and the mentally ill have always been a part of our penal history. However, their presence is unprecedented of late due to the rate of increase in these populations and the total numbers involved. More than ever before, the correctional population consists of mothers, the mentally disordered, the infirm, and the dying.

Traditionally, penal systems have been highly resistant to change, but the needs and risks of special inmates have made change unavoidable. Policies governing inmate programming, health care, mental health, childcare, safety, and privacy have all been reexamined and modified accordingly. For example, policy must now specify whether women who give birth in prison should be permitted to keep their children. Of equal concern is whether dying inmates should be granted early release and whether elderly and mentally ill inmates should be separated from the general inmate population and housed in separate facilities.

These particularly difficult issues have been subjects of debate for correctional administrators and legislators for the past two decades.

Some states have adopted innovative programming in response to these special population needs, while others have maintained a more "business as usual" or "wait and see" approach. In many instances, change has only come about as a result of lawsuits. This chapter considers how the increasing incarceration of these various special populations has not only altered the responsibilities of the penal system and the prison more specifically, but also what the incarceration, release, and supervision of such offenders means for society.

Women and Mothers

There is no disputing that, "In the drama of criminal justice, most leading players have been men" (Friedman, 1993: 211). Women offenders have always been far fewer in number and it is their relative absence in the system that has dictated their treatment by the system. Historically, the scarcity of women in the penal system has worked to their gross disadvantage (Belknap, 1996). Because women offenders are in short supply, so to speak, resources devoted to their needs are also in short supply.

Up until the twentieth century, women were typically imprisoned in male facilities; specifically, they were housed in adjoining units in the same facility. Because of the close proximity, female inmates were often raped and prostituted at the hands of their keepers and other male inmates. It is no surprise then that prison pregnancies were a recurrent scandal early on (Friedman, 1993; Zedner, 1995). By sharing the facilities and resources of male inmates, female inmates' access to physicians and chaplains also was restricted. The ill effects of confinement were more exaggerated for female inmates as well, given that indoor domestic chores left little reason or opportunity to participate in outside activities. Additionally, there was greater oversight of female behavior. To instill proper social behavior, correctional officials intensely scrutinized the language, conversation, purity, and femininity of female inmates. As a result, female inmates were punished for rule infractions involving behaviors that were overlooked regularly among male inmates.

In light of this history, Carlen and Tchaikovsky (1985) concluded that, with regard to women, the prison tends to "discipline, infantilize, feminize, medicalize, and domesticize." While conceding that the prisoner and civil rights movements sparked modest reform in prison programming, they still contended that women remain something of an afterthought in the penal system. Although this generally still holds true, the spike in female incarceration rates has improved the environment for incarcerated women.

The Number of Incarcerated Women

Between 1981 and 1991, the increase in the overall incarceration rate for women surpassed that of men. During this time, female incarceration rates rose 254 percent, compared to a 147 percent increase for men (ibid.). In 1980, there were 12,331 women incarcerated in federal and state facilities. There was 40,566 by 1989 and 87,000 by 1991 (Bloom and Steinhart, 1993). Between 1984 and 1989, the average daily population of women in local jails rose by 95.3 percent, compared with only 50.9 percent for men (Bureau of Justice Statistics, 1990). Between 1985 and 1998, there were pronounced increases in the number of adult women under any form of correctional supervision. For example, in 1985, one in 227 women were under some type of correctional supervision (including jail, prison, probation, or parole); one in 267 was on probation; one in 4,762 was on parole; one in 4,762 was in jail, and one in 4,167 was in prison. By 1998, one in 109 women was under some form of correctional supervision; one in 144 was on probation, one in 1,262 was on parole, one in 1,628 was in jail, and one in 1,230 was in prison (Greenfeld and Snell, 1999).

Predictably, these increases resulted in a noticeable surge in the construction of female facilities (see Figure 12-1). It is important to note, however, that the rapid growth in the incarceration and community-supervision rates of women offenders were not the results of an emerging violent predatory breed of female criminal: Most women admitted to prison during this period were non-violent, petty property offenders or drug offenders. Moreover, incarcerations for murder almost always involved the killing of an abusive spouse or significant other. Far from being criminal predators who posed a great risk to public safety in general, female offenders were typically indigents, drug addicts, victims of sexual or domestic violence, and mothers (Belknap, 1996; Bloom and Steinhart, 1993; Immarigeon and Chesney-Lind, 1992).

Motherhood, Pregnancy, and Health Care

While a history of poverty, addiction, and prior abuse is hardly unique to women offenders, the issue of motherhood and child custody does distinguish them from their male counterparts. On any given day, ap-

Figure 12-1
Creation of State Prison Facilities for Women, 1930–1990

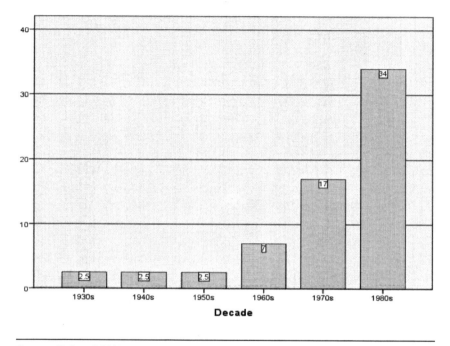

Source: Rafter (1990).

proximately 80 percent of women entering prison are mothers. Each incarcerated woman has, on average, two or three dependent children (American Correctional Association, 1993), many of whom were in their custody prior to their incarceration. Among incarcerated men, 60 percent are fathers, with less than half having had custody of their children at the time of their incarceration (Belknap, 1996). In 1986, it was estimated that more than 37,000 children had mothers who were incarcerated. In 1989, more than 52,000 children had mothers who were incarcerated (Bloom and Steinhart, 1993). The National Council on Crime and Delinquency estimated that, on any given day in 1991, approximately 167,000 children had mothers who were incarcerated in prisons or jails. Approximately 90 percent (or more than 125,000) of these children were under eighteen years old. By 1997, the number of children with incarcerated mothers jumped to 194,000 (Greenfeld and Snell, 1999).

The profile of incarcerated mothers provided in Table 12-1 shows that women pose a relatively low security risk but still possess a number of psychological, economic, and physical needs. However, as Zedner (1995) argued, penal accommodations are consistently guided by the principles of least effort and least expense. Consequently, the degree to which women's needs are met in the areas of motherhood and pregnancy is highly variable and, in some circumstances, completely inadequate.

The legal and policy questions associated with inmate motherhood are many, beginning with the care and custody of existing children and conditions surrounding visitation arrangements and the maintenance of family ties. The issue of maintaining family ties looms large, since children experience psychosocial problems as a result of separation (Gabel, 1992). A Justice Department study of women incarcerated in state and federal facilities found that fathers rarely assume custody of their children. Only 28 percent of mothers in the study indicated that their child's father was the primary caregiver during their period of incarceration (Handwerk, 2004). More than half of the women indicated that the grandparents

Table 12-1
Profile of Inmate Mothers (in percentages)

Ethnicity		*Employment/Public Assistance*	
African American	39	Not employed	65
White	34	Employed	35
Hispanic	16	Not on AFDC	58
Native American	8	On AFDC	42
Other	3		
		Annual Income	
Marital Status		Less than $10,000	64
Never married	33	$10,000–$25,000	28
Married	19	More than $25,000	9
Divorced	18		
Separated	13	*History of Abuse*	
Common law	11	Physical	53
Widowed	6	Sexual	42
Education		*Offense of Conviction*	
8th grade or less	11	Drugs	39
9th–11th grade	44	Felony/property	23
High school graduate	34	Serious/violent	15
Some college	11	Child abuse	2
		Other	21

Source: Bloom and Steinhart (1993).
Note: AFDC = Aid to Families with Dependent Children.

assumed the parenting responsibilities, while others reported that the children went with other relatives or into foster care (ibid.).

Regardless of who assumes the role of parent, maintaining contact is difficult and studies have shown that the frequency of mother–child visits is exceedingly low. For example, Snell and Morton (1994) and others (Bloom and Steinhart, 1993) have found that approximately 52 percent of incarcerated women are never visited by their children. Snell and Morton (1994) further found that only one in five mothers ever receives mail, while one in four never even speaks with their children. Other studies indicate that only 10 percent of mothers see their children on a weekly basis, 17 percent see them once a month, and 12 percent see them only once every four to six months (Bloom and Steinhart, 1993).

A number of factors can account for this lack of communication between mother and child. In some instances—approximately 25 percent of cases—the parent had not been regularly taking care of the child prior to incarceration (McCarthy, 1980). However, the conditions surrounding visitation are more likely to blame for the infrequency of family visits. Most families must travel hours to reach the facility, only to wait several more hours before the actual visit can begin. This coupled with callous treatment by prison officials and invasive searches for contraband often make the visit unpleasant. Moreover, the visitation atmosphere is not particularly conducive to meaningful interaction. In the majority of facilities (approximately 66 percent), visitation typically occurs in a common open area. In other facilities (approximately 9 percent), visitation occurs through partitions. Despite the long distances traveled by families, only 12 percent of facilities permit overnight stays (Bloom and Steinhart, 1993).

From a correctional administrator's standpoint, the policy questions surrounding motherhood become even more complicated when dealing with the care of pregnant inmates. What services or care should be made available during the pregnancy? Should prison officials grant requests for abortion? Should inmates be allowed to retain custody of their newborn infants? Approximately 6 percent of women at prison intake and 4 percent of women at jail intake are pregnant (Bloom and Steinhart, 1993). In 1987, there was an estimated 1,265 pregnant inmates in thirty-eight facilities (Ayers, 1999). A 1992 survey of jailed and imprisoned women revealed that approximately 9 percent of them gave birth while incarcerated. By 1997, the number of pregnant women at intake had remained fairly constant, with 6 percent of females admitted to jail being pregnant, compared with 5 percent admitted to state prison (Greenfeld and Snell, 1999).

The treatment of pregnant inmates has perhaps drawn the most criticism. The absence of twenty-four-hour medical and gynecological care, special diets, nutrition, maternity clothes, and prenatal classes are among the concerns most frequently cited by critics. The non-sterile searches of pregnant (and non-pregnant) inmates—which can lead to damaging infections to mother and fetus—also have come under attack (Holt, 1982). Equally troubling to critics is the indifference shown to the particular needs of the pregnant inmate who is also a drug addict. In the absence of proper obstetric and health care, officials generally overlook the fact that the fetus experiences the same symptoms of drug withdrawal as the mother (Ryan and Grassano, 1992). However, it is the use of shackles and restraints during transport to hospitals and child delivery that has most outraged Amnesty International and other offender advocacy groups. As a result of these various advocacy efforts, five states and the District of Columbia have forbidden the use of restraints during labor and delivery.

The problems associated with pregnant inmates are further compounded by the prevalence of HIV and AIDS among female offenders. In a study conducted by the Centers for Disease Control and Prevention (CDC) and the Johns Hopkins School of Public Health, it was found that rates of HIV infection in jails and prisons ranged from 2.5 to 14.7 percent for female inmates, compared with 2.1 to 7.6 percent for male inmates (Lawson and Fawkes, 1993). In 90 percent of the facilities surveyed, the infection rate for women—particularly women under the age of twenty-five—was two times higher than the rate for males. The same pattern emerged in a 1994 study, which found that 3.9 percent of women in state prisons were infected with the virus, compared with 2.4 percent of men in state prisons (Chesney-Lind, 1997). Between 1991 and 1994, the number of female inmates with AIDS increased by 69 percent, versus a 22 percent increase for males (ibid.). Although AIDS is not necessarily passed on to all babies, approximately 51 percent of newborns do acquire the disease from their mother (Lawson and Fawkes, 1993).

The correctional system also has been confronted with the predicament of unwanted pregnancies. While current law does not prevent abortion (except under certain circumstances) the problem for incarcerated women is gaining access to the necessary resources so their abortion right can be exercised. Because incarcerated individuals must rely on the state to meet their needs, ranging from the trivial to the vital, a key legal question that arises is whether the state—which is not required to fund abortions for free, indigent women—should be required to fund abortions for incarcerated women. To make this determination, one must consider that the incarcerated woman has in fact become a ward of the state and is therefore unable to raise the resources needed to pay for an abortion. Moreover, because the female inmate must rely entirely on the state to make the arrangements, Vitale (1980) has argued that failure to do so might violate the right to have an abortion.

This very issue has arisen in jails and prisons across the country, most notably in legal cases involving inmates in Pennsylvania, Missouri, and Arizona. For example, in 2005, a Pennsylvania inmate approached prison officials and said that she wanted an abortion. At the time, the prison board did not have a policy on the issue of abortion and instead recommended that no such policy be developed, believing it was best to make such decisions on a case-by-case basis and by order of a judge (Finnerty, 2005). The county's District Attorney indicated that, unless it was a life-threatening situation, he would consider the abortion to be elective surgery. However, the warden indicated that elective surgeries were not permitted during the term of incarceration, but that he would ultimately defer to any court order. Ultimately, the inmate did not have the abortion and has since been released. In 2008, however, the U.S. Supreme Court did rule that the Maricopa County Jail in Arizona had to provide pregnant inmates the transportation—at the taxpayers' expense—to facilities where abortions could be performed. Following this ruling, the American Civil Liberties Union filed and won a class action lawsuit on behalf of female inmates in Missouri who had been denied transportation to abortion facilities (Ertelt, 2008).

Vitale (2008) also argued that forcing an inmate to have an unwanted child is tantamount to cruel and unusual punishment. He contended that a forced pregnancy violates the Eighth Amendment on two different grounds. First, it imposes an unnecessary and wanton infliction of pain, and second, it constitutes a failure to treat medical needs. Vitale went on to argue that, if the prison must treat dental conditions, sinus conditions, ulcers, fevers, and varicose veins, then an unwanted pregnancy surely qualifies as a health condition deserving of attention. Moreover, the state's termination of the pregnancy in no way undermines the state's custody or punishment interests. Similar arguments were made in the Missouri and Arizona cases; namely, that security interests are not jeopardized by the transportation of inmates to abortion clinics, nor is the expense of the transportation any greater than to transport inmates for other required off-site medical procedures.

Should the pregnancy proceed, yet another controversial government decision emerges: Should the mother be permitted to keep the child for a limited period of time? Historically, this was not as unreasonable an expectation as it is today. Prison population reports from Maryland, Massachusetts, New York, and Pennsylvania between 1800 and 1840 documented the presence of children (Craig, 2009). And though the conditions at that time were completely unsuitable for children—at Sing Sing, for example, most babies died (ibid.)—the presence of children was viewed as an important rehabilitative tool for wayward women. This was especially the case during the era of reformatories. Records from a New York house of refuge operating between 1894 and 1931 specified that prison-born babies were allowed to stay with their mothers up to age two (ibid.). This was a typical policy in most reformatories and at the federal female prison between 1930 and 1960 (ibid.). While there was concern over the impact of the prison environment on the child, such as lack of stimulus from the real world (Zedner, 1995), the promise of re-socializing deviant women took priority.

Given that a punitive rather than a rehabilitative philosophy is emphasized today, the child is taken away from its mother in nearly all states within twenty-four to forty-eight hours. Consequently, prison nurseries are an anomaly rather than a fixture. Prior to 1981, Florida law allowed a female inmate to retain her child within the institution until the child was eighteen months old; however, this provision was repealed in *Delancy v. Booth* (1981) on the grounds that the mother had no constitutional or statutory right to raise the child in prison (Schupak, 1986). Since 1929, California law allowed a child to remain with the mother until the child was two years old, but California repealed this law as well in 1978. As an alternative, California created the Community Prisoner Mother–Infant Care Program (i.e., halfway-house), but the program was grossly underfunded (ibid.): In 1992, there were approximately five thousand mothers in prison but only one hundred community-based mother–infant care beds (Bloom and Steinhart, 1993).

The Federal Bureau of Prisons recently implemented a similar program called Mothers and Infants Together (MINT). The program allows qualifying pregnant women to spend three months prior to delivery and two months post-delivery in a halfway house. Here, the women are expected to improve their parenting skills and form bonds with their newborns (Handwerk, 2004). The Louisiana Correctional Institute for Women—one of the largest female facilities in the country—allows women to spend either a Saturday or Sunday afternoon with their children. Other states are experimenting with similar programs to foster the mother–child bond (ibid.). However, only New York and Nebraska allow children to remain with the mother. In these two states, children are permitted to stay on the premises until the age of eighteen months to two years. The state retains the right to revoke this privilege if the mother has a history of separation from the child or is facing multiple and lengthy sentences (Holt, 1982).

The problems associated with incarcerating women are many, including child custody issues, pregnancy, the transmission of HIV to unborn children, drug-withdrawal effects on the unborn, and specialized (obstetric) health care. State facilities have been slow in responding to these problems, making it apparent that the historical problems of inadequate programming, poor health care, and even rape still exist in the modern women's prison. As costs associated with expanding facilities for males have dominated correctional budgets, programs that are vital to women have been cut, even though they were substandard to begin with. A more comprehensive system of medical and social services is provided at the federal level, however. Birth control and abortions are available and newborns are not permitted to return to the institution except as a visitor. Additionally, the inmate is responsible for the child's placement (Holt, 1982).

Elderly

The elderly inmate, like the female inmate, still represents a comparatively small portion of the overall inmate population, but the presence of elder inmates has grown dramatically in the past two decades. They now represent the fastest-growing segment of the inmate population (Wheeler, 1999), giving rise to the popular colloquialism "the graying inmate population."

The Graying of Inmates

Between 1981 and 1991, the number of inmates past the age of fifty-five increased by 50 percent (Flynn, 1993). Between 1992 and 2001, the number of elderly inmates in state and federal facilities increased 173 percent, from 41,586 to 113,358 (Anno et al., 2004). In the year 2000, 125,000 of the nation's inmates were beyond the age of fifty and another 40,000 to 50,000 were past the age of sixty-five. Between 2000 and 2005, the number of elderly inmates nationwide increased by 33 percent. The increase in the elderly population has been particularly pronounced in the South, where sentences tend to be longer and more elderly tend to reside. For example, Florida has the third largest inmate population past the age of fifty in the country. In 1982, there were only 895 inmates older than fifty. By 1990, that number had reached 2,064—an increase of 131 percent. During the same period, the overall inmate population increased by only 68 percent (Rosseli, 1991). As of 2007, the number of inmates in Florida past the age of 50 had reached 12,658. The Ohio Department of Corrections projected equally high numbers: By the year 2025, it estimated that a full 25 percent of the inmate population will be older than 50 (Anno et al., 2004).

Like the rise in the number of female inmates, the growth in the number of elderly inmates does not stem from an outbreak in elderly crime. Flynn (1993) argued that, while absolute numbers of the elderly in prison are indeed increasing, the percentage of crime committed by the elderly is not. Even though some scholars argue that age-specific crime has increased somewhat, they acknowledge that this increase is disproportionate to the increases in the incarceration rate (Burnett and Chaneles, 1989). The answer to the question of growth does not lie solely with the types of offenses committed either. Fifty-three percent of all elderly arrests are for drunkenness, DUIs (driving under the influence), larceny/theft, and other offenses directly related to alcoholism (Feinberg, 1984; Wilbanks, 1984). The greatest increases in crime among this population have been in drug and property offenses (Feinberg, 1984; Wilbanks, 1984). For example, in Florida, there were only seventy-three elderly incarcerated for drug offenses in 1983–1984. Beginning in 1986–1987, drug offenses became the primary offense of incarceration for those past fifty years of age. Consequently, by 1989–1990, there were 312 elderly imprisoned for drug offenses (Rossell, 1991).

Of course, this does not mean that offenses committed by the elderly rarely are violent or serious, but evidence regarding the nature of their criminal behavior is mixed. For example, the second most common offense of the incarcerated elderly in Florida is illicit sexual conduct, followed by theft and forgery (ibid.). McShane and Williams (1990) found that 60 percent of an elder inmate cohort was violent, yet other studies reveal the opposite to be true. Kratcoski and Pownali (1989) found that only 13 percent of elderly inmates were violent and Soderstrom (1999) reported that offenders over the age of fifty were responsible for only 3.6 percent of violent crime.

While the source of the increased number of elderly inmates cannot be determined precisely, what is certain is that prison is a microcosm of society; just as there are many more elderly present in the population as a whole, their presence in prison can be expected to increase as well.

Equally evident is the effect of get-tough legislation that sentences more offenders to prison for longer periods of time without the possibility of parole or some other form of early release. In 1991 alone, 11,759 inmates across thirty-two prison systems were serving natural life sentences (Flynn, 1993). In forty-four U.S. jurisdictions, 44,541 inmates were serving life sentences and, across forty-seven systems, 105,881 were serving sentences of twenty years or more. As of 2003, 127,677 state and federal inmates—or one in 11—were serving life sentences (Butterfield, 2004).

Health Care and Housing Accommodations for the Elderly and Dying

Growing concern with the elderly inmate population is rooted in the prohibitive costs associated with their incarceration. It is estimated that the annual physical and mental health costs for an elderly inmate is approximately $70,000, compared with $23,000 for a non-elderly inmate (Durham, 1994; Rossell, 1991). The health care needs that contribute to these costs are numerous. Many of these offenders have a long history of substance abuse, alcoholism, depression, poor health habits, and untreated medical conditions. Consequently, they enter the system in a state of health that is far worse than their non-offending counterparts. In fact, it has been suggested that a fifty-year-old inmate is the physical and emotional equivalent of a non-offending sixty-year-old (Kratcoski and Pownali, 1989). Health care issues that arise throughout an elderly inmate's stay only compound the costs associated with pre-existing conditions. While their health issues are not unique (e.g., incontinence, respiratory difficulties, cancer, heart, arthritis, ulcers), it is estimated that the aging process of an inmate is accelerated by nearly twelve years due to poor health history and prior risky behaviors (Anno et al., 2004). Approximately 80 percent of those past the age of sixty-five will acquire at least one chronic illness requiring some form of long-term care. Recent figures from the Federal Bureau of Prisons indicate that 18 percent of its inmate population is under care for a chronic serous illness (ibid.).

While it is often serious chronic health care needs that draw the most attention, accommodations for the elderly do not always involve the critical care associated with hospitalization or round-the-clock nursing. Rather, it is the day-to-day "normal" accommodations for the elderly that require the most adjustments on the part of prison officials. Prosthetic devices, glasses, dentures, hearing aids, ambulatory equipment, special shoes, or wheelchairs are what shape the daily existence of the elderly inmate. Structural modifications also may be required, such as changes in lighting, the installation of hearing devices in telephones, and the installation of grab bars and guard rails. For those inmates who are disabled or in wheelchairs, cells must be enlarged and beds need to be fixed at different heights.

It is this collection of needs and accommodations that has partly prompted the question of whether elderly inmates should be housed in facilities apart from the general inmate population. At present, the establishment of separate facilities has not been the standard policy. Fifteen state systems have all elderly inmates housed in a single facility, while twenty-three state systems house terminally ill inmates in a single location (Anno et al., 2004). A nationwide survey revealed that most states make their housing determinations at the point of classification (Aday, 1994). In other words, custody classification, medical classification, housing, and release decisions are not based on age alone. Most assignments to specialized housing are for health-related reasons, not purely age considerations. For example, the Federal Bureau of Prisons designed geriatric units for only those elderly who are no longer able to function without constant, specialized medical care. Within these units, specialized diets are provided in addition to ongoing monitoring of health problems such as diabetes and cardiovascular dysfunction. Work and leisure programs also are modified in accordance with declining vision and hearing as well as bone deterioration and facilities are designed to accommodate walkers and wheelchairs.

Though the standard practice is to integrate elderly inmates within the general population, several other arguments for creating separate housing and programming exist. One major reason is that elderly inmates are vulnerable to abuse and predation by other, usually younger, inmates. The elderly also prefer separate housing because of difficulty coping with the fast-paced, noisy, and abrasive prison environment. Additionally, distance and confusing institutional design can pose problems for elderly inmates trying to find their way to common areas (e.g., infirmary, dining hall, canteen, recreation areas). The difficulties they encounter navigating the prison environment often force elderly inmates into isolation (ibid.). Moreover, they are not often part of the inmate subculture and, thus, rely on staff for their institutional adjustment (Kratcoski and Pownall, 1989). Their isolation is further aggravated by the fact that most elderly inmates have been abandoned by their families and, thus, have few or no visitors or ties to the community. They generally enter and leave the prison system single, widowed, separated, or divorced.

Physical activities—and the daily regimen as a whole—are also typically ill-suited. The elderly generally refrain from recreational activities designed for younger inmates out of frustration or embarrassment. Notably missing are programs geared toward rehabilitation, re-entry, and vocational training. Given that elderly inmates are not likely to return to the workforce, prison officials may discourage them from participating in educational and vocational programs so younger offenders can use them (Rossell, 1991). Prison programs simply are not geared to the survival issues that shape the elderly inmate's day, including death, illness, and simply remaining alert.

Special programs for the elderly are few in number, with the exceptions of compassionate leave programs and hospice units. While state policies vary, compassionate release generally applies to inmates who have six months or less to live. As of 2004, compassionate release provisions were available in forty-three states, but they were rarely utilized. Nationwide, the average number of annual requests for compassionate release is eighteen, with an average of eight being granted. In Florida, sixteen inmates were released early for medical reasons in 1994–1995. Texas reported the highest number of requests (115) and therefore the highest number of releases awarded (49) (Anno et al., 2004). Aside from political reasons, one impediment to release is that nursing homes are frequently unwilling to accept individuals with a prior record.

Hospice care is the major alternative to compassionate release. The need for hospice care inside prison has accelerated in the past two decades, as evidenced by the formation of The National Prison Hospice Association in 1991. The latest reports by the GRACE Project indicate that twenty-five of forty-nine state correctional systems operate a hospice program. Some of these are housed in separate units or buildings, while others are part of the regular inmate infirmary. Only one operates on an outpatient basis. Another nineteen states have identified use of formal end of life programs.

As with other correctional populations, the problem in dealing with elderly inmates lies in the scarcity of resources. For example, the Southern Center for Human Rights filed a federal class action lawsuit on behalf of a group of Alabama inmates with dementia and Alzheimer's cases who had to wait several months or more to receive treatment ("Aging Inmates," 2007). In 2006, a federal judge appointed an ombudsman to oversee the California Department of Corrections when it was discovered that at least one inmate per week—a total of sixty-six in one year—died from neglect or malpractice (ibid.). While prison health care facilities may be equipped to deal with acute illnesses and injuries of all kinds for all ages, they are just now beginning to deal with the management of the regular, chronic, long-term health problems associated with aging and dying.

Mentally Ill

In the 1960s and 1970s, decentralization efforts led to the closing of most state hospitals for the mentally ill. Though the federal government had little or no role in erecting state hospitals, it played a critical role in their closing through the passage of the Community Mental Health Act of 1963 (Gottschalk, 2008). Under this act, local governments became eligible for grants to create alternatives to state mental hospitals (ibid.). This spawned the development of community mental health centers in a relatively short period of time. While fiscal crises served as the prime motivation for the closings (Scull, 1977), the decarceration of mental hospitals was publicly justified on humanitarian grounds. It was held that the mentally ill could be better served at the local level, under the auspices of non-stigmatizing community centers. These centers were to dispense symptom-relieving psychotropic drugs and monitor the mentally ill on an outpatient basis. However, local jurisdictions often failed to develop these centers in sufficient number. Consequently, patients either were transferred to other facilities or were simply released and, if the latter, were eventually caught up in the criminal justice system.

In 1939, European scholar I. Penrose declared, "As a general rule, if the prison services are extensive, the asylum population is relatively small and the reverse also tends to be true" (quoted in Steadman et al., 1984: 474). What Penrose was attempting to communicate is a process that would later be termed "transinstitutionalization." Transinstitutionalization refers to the purported interdependent relationship between mental hospitals and prisons. Penrose proposed that the two institutions directly share and/or exchange populations based upon the relative allocation of resources. While transinstitutionalization did not occur in the United States exactly as Penrose envisioned, the effect of the decarceration movement of the 1960s and 1970s on the correctional system came awfully close.

The Effects of Decarceration and Getting Tough

The process of decarcerating the mentally ill was gradual, but the drop in the numbers of patients served was noticeably precipitous. In

1955, the state mental health population totaled approximately 559,000, which was nearly as large on a per capita basis as the prison population is today (Gottschalk, 2008). By 1965, there were 451,000 beds in public and private mental hospitals, which decreased to 177,000 beds in 1985. In roughly that same twenty-year period, state and federal prison populations increased from 210,000 to 420,000. By 2000, the state mental health population had fallen further to 100,000 (Gottschalk, 2008). California provides a particularly interesting case study of this phenomenon. In 1966, there were 27,000 individuals in California's state mental hospitals and 27,000 people incarcerated in the state's jails and prisons. By the end of the twentieth century, there were only 4,500 state hospital beds and 160,000 incarcerated in California's prisons (California Mental Hospitals, 1999).

In the nation as a whole, the mental hospitals that have remained open are largely empty and reserved for the most dangerous of the criminally insane. Those who do not qualify for these facilities often cycle in an out of the criminal justice system. The increased presence of the mentally ill in the criminal justice system then can be attributed not only to the paucity of community-based mental health centers, but also to laws that have made involuntary confinement of the mentally ill illegal unless their freedom poses an immediate and genuine threat to the community or to the afflicted individual. Consequently, the penal system—local jails in particular—receives the less dangerous mentally ill who no longer qualify for civil commitment (Steadman et al., 1984). According to the National Coalition for the Mentally Ill in the Criminal Justice System, there are approximately 33 percent more mentally ill individuals in jails than in mental hospitals.

The increased presence of the mentally ill in jails has been facilitated, in part, by the long reach of get-tough policies. "Broken windows" theory and urban gentrification projects prompted police departments and city officials to crack down on public disorder and nuisance crimes (e.g., panhandling, jumping subway turnstiles, disturbing the peace, trespassing, vagrancy), usually committed by the homeless and the mentally ill. Congressman Ted Strickland relayed the effects of these crackdowns before a House subcommittee in September of 2000: "On any given day, at least 284,000 schizophrenic and manic depressive individuals are incarcerated, and 547,800 are on probation. We have unfortunately come to accept incarceration and homelessness as part of life for the most vulnerable population among us" (quoted in Berkowitz, 2003).

Well before the Congressman acknowledged this reality, Teplin (1990) had found that, among 728 randomly sampled inmates in Chicago's Cook

County Jail, almost 6.4 percent manifested some form of psychosis (e.g., schizophrenia, mania, or severe depression), compared with a 1.8 percent prevalence rate in society at large. Research on the San Diego County Jail also found that 14 percent of the 4,572 male inmates and 25 percent of the 687 female inmates were on psychotic medication (Torrey, 1995). In Seattle's King County Jail, it was estimated that, on any given day, 160 of the 2,000 inmates are severely mentally ill. In the Travis County Jail in Austin, Texas, approximately 14 percent of inmates are afflicted with a serious mental illness. Dade County Jail in Miami separately houses approximately 350 inmates with mental illness, which is more than any state mental hospital in the country. In the Los Angeles County Jail, 3,300 of its 21,000 inmates require mental health services on a daily basis (ibid.). It was estimated that 100,000 people in jail required treatment for serious mental illness in 1988.

These figures are rendered even more troubling when one considers that research has shown that the mentally ill often spend three to four months in jail without trial, though the crimes they commit are commonly related to survival needs (e.g., sleeping/lying down, trespassing, panhandling, "dine and dash") or their mental illness (e.g., disorderly conduct). Because the mentally ill rarely post bail or qualify for other forms of release, they also remain in jail at least twice as long as the average inmate (Torrey, 1995). In Idaho, it was estimated that approximately three hundred mentally ill were jailed in 1990 for an average of five days without criminal charges. A 1992 survey revealed that this pattern of incarcerating the mentally ill occurs in roughly 29 percent of the nation's jails.

State and federal facilities also bear the burden presented by mentally ill offenders. In fact, the Human Rights Watch report *Ill-Equipped: U.S. Prisons and Offenders with Mental Illness* indicates that there are three times as many men and women with mental illness in U.S. prisons as in mental health hospitals (Berkowitz, 2003). Indeed, on any given day, Florida's prison system houses more than two times as many mentally ill as state mental hospitals (Wickham, 1999). More specifically, it is estimated that between 10 and 35 percent of inmates held in U.S. prisons have significant mental disorders (McCorkle, 1995), while an additional 17 percent have less severe but still serious mental illness (Edna McConnell Clark Foundation, 1995). In California, 8 percent of the state prison population has had at least one of four major mental disorders. More recent figures from the National Commission on Correctional Health Care indicate that the number of inmates suffering from severe mental illness (i.e., schizophrenia, schizoaffective disorder, bipolar disorder, and major depression) ranges from 10 to 19 percent in jails, 18 to 27 percent in state prisons, and 16 to 21 percent in federal prisons (Lamb et al., 2007).

The mentally ill in prison are more likely to be incarcerated for violent offenses, including robbery, assault, and murder (Ditton, 1999). Yet, in instances in which the crime committed is more serious and requires some degree of planning, it becomes hard to tell the difference between a criminal who happens to have a mental disorder and a person who has a mental disorder that causes him or her to commit crime (Kagan, 1990). It is also unclear whether the increase in the number of the mentally ill in prison is due more to the war on drugs or to an increase in the mentally ill population in society. For many mentally ill offenders, extended drug use creates neurological damage; for others, drug use can serve as a way of escaping the realities of mental illness.

The Care and Custody of the Mentally Ill

The realities of mental illness are what make the jail and prison system ill prepared to house this population. Suicidal tendencies are greater, as is the potential for security threats because of unruly behavior. The mentally ill are often reluctant to come out of their cells because they view their cells as safer and less stressful. They are also more prone to expressing their outrage through destruction of property (Adams, 1986), or injuring themselves by slamming their bodies to the floor, gouging their skin or genitals with nails, bashing their heads on stainless steel toilets, and smearing feces on themselves or their cells.

Furthermore, mentally ill inmates are more likely to have escape histories and to incur assault infractions and prison punishments. Though the incidence rate for these problems is very low, disciplinary measures may be precipitated by overreaction on the part of guards. When they know an inmate has a mental health history, they often tend to view him or her as inherently more dangerous (Adams, 1983). There is some truth to this perception: The mentally ill do in fact tend to be more violent toward fellow inmates, staff, and themselves (Baskin, Sommers, and Steadman, 1991), thereby inciting physical and verbal abuse by guards and other inmates (Hartstone et al., 1984; Steelman, 1987; Toch, 1977). However, the reverse is equally true. The Human Rights Watch report indicated that the mentally ill in prison are easy prey and are likely to be "picked on, physically or sexually abused, and manipulated by other inmates, who call them 'bugs'" (quoted in Berkowitz, 2003). As one California official aptly noted, the "mad" and the "bad" do not mix well (Torrey, 1995).

Clearly, the penal system enters perilous territory when dealing with the problems posed by the severely mentally ill. In fact, inmates provided their own mental health services for much of the twentieth century (Ferrara and Ferrara, 1991). Services provided by institutional staff were limited to crisis intervention, thus leaving other inmates to act as providers of counsel, restraint, and even medication. It was not until the prisoner rights movement that courts abolished this practice and began dictating the nature and scope of required mental health services. It is this court-driven treatment model that governs most mental health policies in institutions today. For example, the same Human Rights Watch report further indicated that litigation or the threat of it is still the primary vehicle for improvements. This was certainly the case in sixteen states wherein change came about only as a result of class action lawsuits.

Under the threat of violations of the Eighth Amendment and the Fourteenth Amendment, most institutions now provide services that focus on the prevention and relief of pain and suffering. In other words, tranquilizers, barbiturates, and sedative–hypnotic drugs help avert crises by serving as "chemical straightjackets" for controlling—rather than treating—aberrant behavior (Sommers and Baskin, 1990). Fifty percent of mentally ill inmates in state and federal facilities reported having taken prescription medicine, while only 44 percent reported having received counseling (Ditton, 1999). However, only trained and licensed professionals are permitted to provide treatment of any kind (Ferrara and Ferrara, 1991). Federal guidelines also have established policies overseeing patient-to-staff ratios and the use of psychotropic medication. The guidelines are additionally intended to prevent the denial of equal access to work, recreation, and other programs, as well as the use of segregated confinement as a housing practice for the mentally ill.

Even with these guidelines, confusion, mishap, and negligence in the treatment of the mentally ill still exist. The deaths of mentally ill inmates at a California medical prison in 1991 illustrate this point (Specter, 1994). In one weekend, three inmates died from heatstroke caused by a combination of extreme temperatures in their cell blocks (over 108 degrees) and psychotropic medication that inhibited the body from dissipating heat. The risk of heatstroke from these particular medications was well documented in the literature and well known to prison officials; a few years earlier, another prisoner on the same medication suffered extensive brain damage for the same reason. Other inmates had been left without their medication entirely, prompting a $3 million study of the California prison system's treatment of the mentally ill. Though the conclusions of the study were resolute in their denunciation of the care provided, the California prison system ignored the recommendations of three commissioned studies (ibid.).

In 1999, the Florida Department of Corrections was still grappling with the housing and treatment needs of the mentally ill. The one facility that was designed to house the state's most chronically mentally ill inmates was closed. Upon its closing, the inmates were transferred to a facility that had been cited with eighteen deficiencies in its treatment of the mentally ill. Some of the most severe citations were for nurses dispensing prescription drugs without a licensed pharmacist on duty, failure to ensure that inmates would receive the necessary treatment, and large numbers of mental health evaluations that were never conducted on the most severely mentally ill inmates. Nationwide, few states have gone beyond the basic minimum requirements. Consequently, there is little programming that involves case management. Moreover, only a handful of states have incorporated rehabilitative strategies aimed at bringing the individual to optimal functioning in anticipation of release.

Many states concentrate their mental health services at high-security facilities. Consequently, the mentally ill are often over-classified, when in fact their true risk or dangerousness level does not warrant the upgrade (Adams, 1993). Other states have since created specialized mental health facilities. As of 2001, 12 state prison facilities reported that mental health/psychiatric confinement was their primary specialty. Another 143 state facilities reported that mental health confinement was just one of many functions. About two-thirds of all state inmates receiving therapy or medications for mental illness were housed in regular prison facilities (Beck and Maruschak, 2001).

The community corrections system is equally distressed by the presence of mentally ill offenders, although the potential for abuse and mistreatment is less likely given the environment. Skeem and Louden (2006) claimed that mental illness and co-occurring substance use disorders are at least as prevalent among probationers as jail detainees. They estimated that at least half a million individuals with mental illness are placed on probation or parole each year. In 1998, approximately 547,800 mentally ill offenders were under probation supervision (Ditton, 1999). Compared with probationers without mental illness, those with mental illness are highly likely to fail on supervision. Specifically, parolees with mental illness are twice as likely as those without mental illness to have their parole suspended (65 percent compared with 30 percent) (Skeem and Louden, 2006). Research has shown that probationers with mental illness have been significantly more likely to be rearrested as well (54 percent compared with 30 percent) (Dauphinot, 1996).

More progressive measures have been implemented at the local level through various mental health courts and police diversion programs. Initially, mental health courts were established for mentally ill persons charged with misdemeanors, but in recent years, courts are now hearing non-violent felony cases as well. Some mental health courts are even willing to process cases involving violent felonies (Lamb and Weinberger, 2008). What distinguishes these courts from regular courts is that mental health professionals are part of a non-adversarial process and all members of the courtroom workgroup have training in mental health issues and available community resources. Adherence to conditions is monitored in addition to providing access to support services and treatment.

In the past decade, the number of mental health courts in the United States has grown from 4 to 120. This growth in specialty courts has been accompanied by a growth in diversionary strategies, programs, and services at the time of arrest, bail, and sentencing (Kuehn, 2007). However, many of these efforts do fall short of the elements needed to truly divert and serve the mentally ill, such as multi-agency participation, regular meetings between participating agencies, and non-traditional case management (Steadman et al., 1999).

Inmates with AIDS and Tuberculosis

The factors that put one at risk of contracting AIDS and TB are often the same factors that put one at risk of being incarcerated. Poverty and its associated problems of overcrowded living arrangements, poor health care, and drug use are among these factors. As these various public health problems merge in the prison, the problems of AIDS and TB are greatly magnified. This fact has rendered the safety of the prison environment even more precarious.

Tuberculosis Cases in Prison

Though TB had been nearly eradicated worldwide, its resurgence has been responsible for more deaths globally than any other disease. The rise in TB infections in the United States can be attributed in large part to increases in poverty, homelessness, drug use, and immigration from countries with high TB infection rates. The spread of TB also has been facilitated by the spread of HIV/AIDS, as an HIV infection is likely to move TB from less active and dangerous stages to more active and deadly stages. Once TB progresses from the infection stage to the disease stage, symptoms are displayed and the disease becomes highly contagious. Consequently, the 5- to 10-percent lifetime risk of disease increases to an 8-percent risk, per year (Blumberg and Langston, 1995). HIV also contributes to the spread of TB because it makes the diagnosis of TB more difficult. Thus, the infection accelerates without treatment.

Because TB tends to flourish in overcrowded and impoverished settings—where health care is deficient—it is only natural that penal systems would inherit this problem. Prisons are overcrowded, suffer from poor ventilation, and house individuals whose health and drug habits make them particularly vulnerable. Not surprisingly, the rate of TB among inmates is much higher than that of the general population. In one California prison, 30 percent of inmates are infected with TB, a rate that is ten times higher than the statewide average (ibid.). In New York, 27 percent of the inmate population is infected with TB, and a drug-resistant strain developed between 1990 and 1992 that killed thirty-six inmates and a correctional officer. Penal systems throughout the country have reported forty-five current and 140 cumulative cases of drug-resistant strains that strike inmates as well as staff.

As of 1996–1997, the total number of TB-infected inmates at intake in all U.S. facilities was 20,226. The total number infected with TB detected at points other than intake was 7,668. With 4,233 cases detected at intake, Illinois had the highest number of TB infections of any state (Criminal Justice Institute, 1997). At 1,514, Florida had the highest number of inmates with TB infections detected at times other than intake. New York had the highest number of inmates with active TB at intake (14), and Texas had the highest number of inmates with active TB detected at times other than intake (51) (ibid.).

Because TB is highly contagious, the methods of containing the spread of the disease are costly. The CDC recommended mass screening and mandatory segregation for those inmates with active cases of TB (Blumberg and Langston, 1995). Ninety-six percent of all correctional systems have followed these recommendations. For example, to accommodate their active TB cases, New Jersey and New York were forced to build 150 isolation units. The ability of the system to detect and treat the disease before it progresses to dangerous levels is important when one considers the following projection. According to the CDC, in one year, as many as

133,000 persons with TB may be released from state and federal facilities into the community (Hammett, Harold, and Epstein, 1998).

The Prevalence of HIV/AIDS in Prison

While HIV/AIDS poses a lesser problem than TB in terms of prevalence and ease of transmission, HIV/AIDS introduces controversies over prevention and regulation that TB clearly does not. In 1991, 16,921 inmates in state facilities were known to be HIV positive (Brien and Beck, 1998). In 1994, there were 21,749 HIV-positive inmates in state facilities. Between 1991 and 1994, the number of HIV-positive inmates in the Federal Bureau of Prisons increased by 53 percent, from 630 to 964. By 1997, that figure had increased to 1,030 (Maruschak, 1999). In terms of absolute numbers incarcerated, New York and Florida house the largest number of HIV-positive inmates in the country. Together, these two states house nearly half of all HIV-positive inmates in the nation (Brien and Beck, 1998). Texas and North Carolina, however, witnessed particularly large growth rates. Between 1991 and 1994, the number of HIV-positive inmates in Texas increased from 615 to 1,584, and 351 new HIV-positive cases entered the North Carolina penal system.

As with the other special needs populations, inmates who are HIV positive or have full-blown AIDS constitute a relatively small proportion of the prison population. Nationally, HIV/AIDS-infected male inmates constituted only 2.2 percent of the state prison population in 1991 and 2.4 percent in 1994. From 1997 to 2002, these figures remained relatively unchanged at around 2 percent (see Table 12-2). The prevalence of HIV/AIDS infection among female inmates in state prisons also remained unchanged and consistently twice that of males. In select states, the prevalence rates in general are more wide ranging. For example, in twenty-six states, HIV-positive inmates constituted only 1 percent of the overall inmate population (Brien and Beck, 1998). The highest percentages were found in New York (10.8), Florida (3.6), Connecticut (5.1), Maryland (3.5), and New Jersey (3.4). The prevalence rate in the federal system has been approximately 1 percent for every year between 1991 and 1997 (Maruschak, 1999).

Though research indicates that institutional transmission rates are low (Blumberg, 1990; Hammett et al., 1998; Vlahov, 1990), preventing the spread of the disease remains a paramount concern. Tattooing, needle sharing, and unprotected sex are commonplace. Further, it is estimated that 131,000 men are raped each year in prison (Donaldson, 1994; Dumond,

Table 12-2
Percentages of Male and Female State Prison Inmates Infected
with HIV/AIDS, 1991–2002

Year	Male	Female
1991	2.2	3.0
1992	2.6	4.0
1993	2.5	4.2
1994	2.4	3.9
1995	2.3	4.0
1996	2.3	3.5
1997	—	—
1998	2.2	3.8
1999	2.2	3.5
2000	2.1	3.4
2001	1.9	3.1
2002	1.9	2.9

Source: Franklin, Fearn, and Franklin (2005).
Note: Data for 1997 were not reported.

1992). As a result, the manner in which penal systems seek to prevent and contain the spread of the disease has implications for the institutional environment as well as society at large.

Correctional Policies for HIV/AIDS-Infected Inmates

The initial response to the HIV/AIDS "crisis" in prisons was to engage in mass screening and mandatory segregation. However, these policies quickly became subject to judicial review. Constitutional attacks on testing and segregation policies were primarily grounded in the First, Fourth, Eighth, and Fourteenth Amendments and the notion of the right to privacy. Lawsuits also reflected two different concerns: Inmates who were HIV positive claimed that testing and segregation policies are discriminatory and invade privacy, while non-infected inmates claimed that the absence of such policies would violate their constitutional rights (Haas, 1993).

In *Occoquan v. Barry* (1986), a federal court held that the failure to test for HIV could constitute a violation of the Eighth Amendment for non-infected inmates—if it could be shown that the failure to test demonstrated a "deliberate indifference" to the health of the inmate population (ibid.). Support for testing and segregation was affirmed and strengthened with the decision in *Turner v. Safley* (1987). This decision gave prison officials the right to enact any policy that could be shown to be reasonable and have a rational relationship to penological purposes. The standard established by the Turner decision was affirmed in *Harris v. Thigpen* (1993) when the courts upheld Alabama's practice of forced mass screening and segregation of HIV inmates. *Walker v. Sumner* (1990) stands alone as one of the few cases that ruled against testing, but not because of a blanket objection to the policy in and of itself. Rather, the courts declared that prison officials could not test inmates because the penal system in question had failed to demonstrate why the screening was necessary. In effect, prison officials must be able to articulate clearly what they plan to do with the test results.

The courts have overwhelmingly sided with prison officials and non-infected inmates on the matters of mandatory testing and segregation policies. Inmates seeking to challenge these policies have found little relief, particularly if the expectation of relief is linked to the Fourteenth Amendment right to equal protection. Most Fourteenth Amendment claims have failed because they require inmates to first establish that they are "similarly situated." In *Cordero v. Coughlin* (1984), the court established that HIV-positive inmates were not similarly situated, and, even if they were, the policy of segregation was reasonable for the protection of all involved.

The most successful attacks against testing and segregation have been launched under the notion of the right to privacy. Courts have generally agreed that one has a right against unauthorized disclosure of one's medical condition and records. Because segregation necessarily discloses one's condition, segregation policies have been successfully reversed on privacy grounds. In *Dough v. Coughlin* (1988), it was established that segregation is not permitted if treatment is not received. The court ruled that segregation is only permissible for the purpose of diagnosis and that release back to the general population must follow (ibid.).

Though the courts have cleared the path for mandatory testing and segregation, the majority of states have opted not to implement mandatory testing and segregation. It is recognized that testing may be a dubious policy given the indeterminable incubation period associated with HIV antibodies. Consequently, testing may do little more than produce false negatives and a corresponding false sense of security. Unless the penal system engages in ongoing periodic testing of all its inmates (such as how the Federal Bureau of Prisons, Alabama, Missouri, and Nevada conduct tests upon release as well), the benefits to such a policy are limited. Because early detection is important, inmates with high-risk behavior are often encouraged to submit voluntarily to testing. Most states require testing if the inmate is pregnant, when clinical tests have raised suspicion, or if an exchange of bodily fluids has occurred. Currently, only seventeen state prison systems and the Federal Bureau of Prisons conduct testing across-the-board.

Because few states conduct mass screening, it follows that few states segregate. Unless the inmate has full-blown AIDS and his or her medical condition requires separate housing, most states house HIV-positive inmates with the general population. Not only is it costly to erect separate facilities, it is likely that fewer inmates will volunteer for testing if they know they will be placed apart from the rest. The integration strategy of present has not always been the preferred one. In 1985, forty-two state systems, the federal system, and 60 percent of jails maintained segregation policies. By 1992, only 8 percent of state systems had segregation policies. Alabama and Mississippi are now the only states to isolate all known cases regardless of whether the inmate is asymptomatic. As of 1997–1998, only 278 inmates with confirmed AIDS were housed in separate medical facilities, while 354 were housed in non-medical facilities (Criminal Justice Institute, 1997).

Education, as opposed to testing and segregation, is regarded as the more effective way of preventing the spread of the disease. There is little controversy over the utility of education programs for both staff and inmates, and thus all states provide some form of education to both groups. A promising educational format that has proven successful is peer education. Peer education programs use HIV-positive inmates to teach other inmates about the disease. However, between 1990 and 1994, the number of such peer education programs in the United States declined significantly. Most systems, particularly local jails, rely on video instruction and written materials to educate inmates.

A far more controversial method of prevention is state-sanctioned condom distribution. To date, six correctional systems distribute condoms: Mississippi, New York City, Philadelphia, San Francisco, Vermont, and the District of Columbia. New York City and Vermont allow inmates one condom per medical visit. In Mississippi, an unlimited number of condoms may be purchased at the canteen. San Francisco makes condoms available only as part of its education program. The District of Columbia has a similar policy but also makes condoms available at the infirmary, while Philadelphia provides condoms as part of its counseling program (Blumberg and Langston, 1995).

Prison as Nursery, Hospital, and Asylum

The circumstances of these special populations raise a number of important policy questions. Most incarcerated women are nonviolent property or low-level drug offenders with a history of physical and sexual abuse, chemical dependency, and poverty. Moreover, some are pregnant and nearly all are mothers who must relinquish custody of the children that many of them provided care for prior to their incarceration. This does not mean, of course, that women should be given preferential treatment for these reasons. It does mean, however, that—given the totality of circumstances surrounding their incarceration—the need for incarceration becomes questionable. For example, research continues to explore the collateral effects of maternal incarceration on juvenile and adult offspring (Huebner and Gustafson, 2007). In addition to numerous studies showing the negative effects of parental incarceration on child delinquency (Bloom and Steinhart, 1993; Boswell and Wedge, 2002; Gabel and Shindledecker, 1993; Sharp and Marcus-Mendoza, 2001), research is examining the stigmatizing effect of parental incarceration status on the juvenile court processing of the children (Leiber and Mack, 2003).

Questions regarding the allocation of prison resources also pertain to the elderly, especially those who have aged in prison for a violent offense committed at a young age. Research consistently shows that criminal behavior declines dramatically with age, yet the release of most of these elders is not forthcoming. What is forthcoming are the exorbitant costs associated with their continued incarceration, with very little yield in terms of crime relief. For those offenders who have entered prison late in life, a different set of policy questions emerges, such as how their stay should be accommodated. While policies that emphasize separate housing are reasonable for a number of reasons, Soderstrom (1999) argued against a policy of separate facilities, claiming that the elderly have a stabilizing influence on the prison environment and are actually less likely than younger inmates to be victimized. However, new research on dying in prison suggests that housing issues may be beside the point: For those who are facing death in prison, a host of other dignity issues becomes paramount.

The ability of the prison and community-based alternatives to adapt and respond to the particular circumstances of the mentally ill is equally troublesome. Though modest improvements in mental health services have taken place in the institutional setting, such improvements have been hard to come by and, in budget-crisis times like we now face, are likely to be the first to go. For example, Michigan—a state once praised for its improvements—cut 50 mental health positions in 2002. In the area of community supervision, agencies have developed specialized mental health courts and caseloads, but again, community-based programs have been grossly under-funded as prison budgets consistently consume the bulk of correctional funding. The mentally ill may also find the community corrections system complicated and frustrating in its own right, with its highly structured regimen and numerous conditions. This problem is exacerbated by the absence of laws that mandate medication compliance.

For inmates who are HIV positive or afflicted with full-blown AIDS, the prison system is no longer in crisis mode. Rather, the focus has shifted to the longer-term concerns of housing, programming, and medical care (Lawson and Fawkes, 1993). In the past few years, several correctional systems (e.g., Florida, South Carolina) have addressed the problem of medical costs by permitting researchers and pharmaceutical companies to conduct experiments and to perform drug studies on inmates. This new "brand" of privatizing prison health care may well be extending to the treatment of other illnesses as well, such as asthma and hepatitis. The potential for private industry (i.e., pharmaceutical companies and researchers) to assist in the management of the needs of each of the special inmate populations is both real and potentially disturbing because it is proceeding with little to no objective oversight.

Discussion of special inmate populations again begs the question of the appropriate role of the prison in society. The limitations of law-and-order punishment and the over-reliance on prison become more glaring when one contemplates the incarceration of nonviolent mothers, the mentally ill, geriatrics, the sick, and the terminally ill. Recognizing that resources are limited—even without the added burdens of special populations—one must ask the questions, Who should be incarcerated and what can be reasonably expected of the prison in dealing with these populations? Will their increasing numbers lead to a more sustained effort at specialized community alternatives to prison? Or, will these populations prompt the development of new and more specialized systems of confinement, as is the case in Florida where the elderly, the mentally ill, and those with infectious diseases are being transferred to separate facilities? Although we may question who should be incarcerated and how, the next chapter documents that we still continue to incarcerate more and more of the overall population, which inevitably will result in still other special prison populations.

13

Punishment in the Millennial Age

It is difficult to comment on the social context and penal trends of a particular time period while it is still unfolding. Without the benefit of hindsight, one may under- or overstate the relevance and effects of particular events. As the penal ideas and practices of the past decade are discussed here, we keep in mind that the "era" of punishment since the year 2000 is still in the making.

In attempting to make sense of this latest historical moment, what is clear is that—in the arena of punishment—much remains the same. Unprecedented correctional costs and numbers of Americans under correctional supervision are undeniable constants. Because these conditions have prompted a continuing correctional fiscal crisis, the ongoing trend of privatization is examined. As private sector involvement in corrections has taken root, the capacity of the private sector to deliver on its promises of cost savings and quality programming deserves closer scrutiny. Other practices also indicate that an expensive get-tough mentality persists, especially for certain offender groups. For example, supermax prisons and sex offender statutes have accelerated in popularity over the past decade. These penal efforts are similar in that both employ unparalleled measures of monitoring and confinement for two different classifications of violent offenders. They are also similar in that both enjoy mainstream support, but also they have amassed considerable opposition from the mental health and legal communities.

There are also trends and movements afoot in the new millennium that point to a retreat from this traditional punitiveness. Patterns in the use of capital punishment, for instance, suggest that harshness and severity are becoming less appealing. A surge in the use of the death penalty typified the 1980s and 1990s but, entering into the twenty-first century, resistance to the death penalty has been increasing. Much of this resistance has emerged in response to numerous findings of innocents sent to death row. Another example of a new "softer" stance can be seen in the reentry movement: Guided by the notion of "second chances," this latest movement perhaps is one of the most definitive shifts in penal practice.

Overall, this contradictory or—depending on one's interpretation—multi-faceted penal approach reflects the fact that an overarching narrative for crime control is lacking. Several contrasting theories of crime, penal philosophies and practices are operating concurrently, with no single explanation, justification, or strategy emerging as predominant. Consequently, free will, social structure, rehabilitation, retribution, deterrence, incapacitation, get tougher, get softer, the public sector, and the private sector all have a seat at the policy table.

Postmodern Society

The "postmodern" concept has been injected frequently into the academic literature as a metaphor for the condition of post-World War II society. As a result, the concept has been widely used as an interpretive framework in the realms of philosophy, economics, history, religion, education, politics, and law. In its simplest form, the concept implies a break with the "modern" past, with modernity constituting the time period roughly between the Enlightenment and 1960. If modernity is foremost characterized by the use of reason and science to discover absolute truths in all areas concerning man, society, and the universe, then postmodernity is characterized by the assumption of diverse subjective truths. Some of the intellectual and material conditions associated with postmodern society therefore include eclecticism, pluralism, fragmentation, relativism, and ambivalence.

Gross's (1997) observations help illustrate some of the purported conditions of postmodern society. He concluded that disorder and irrationality are pervading all institutions of society, including art, the military, higher education, churches, the workplace, and criminal justice. Sarup (1993) added to this understanding of postmodern society when he stated that cybernetics, computer technology, and "sound bite" communications have generated a refusal to think historically. Jameson (1981) similarly claimed that postmodern society has lost its capacity to retain its own past and has begun to live in a perpetual present.

Whether one agrees or disagrees with the validity of postmodern arguments, the framework does provide a way of conceptualizing the developments occurring in American penology—not the least of which is, ironically, reform without change. The ahistorical and eclectic tendencies of a purportedly postmodern society are particularly helpful in interpreting the state of current criminological theory and penal practice.

Integrated Theories of Crime

An assumption underlying efforts to develop integrated theories of crime is that previous theoretical accounts of crime—including biological, culture conflict, strain or anomie, learning, and labeling—have only some degree of explanatory support. That is, elements of particular theories are capable of explaining only certain aspects or variations of crime. As a result, it is believed that combining (or integrating) individual theories provides more comprehensive and compelling explanations of crime.

The integration of theoretical perspectives is not completely unprecedented. But where current integrative efforts depart from previous attempts is in the degree of specificity and sophistication of the causal models. The relationships between the multiple relevant variables are more clearly delineated and measured. While recent attempts to integrate theories of crime have varied, several common approaches have emerged.

Cullen and Agnew (1999) argued that the most common approach to theory integration is the "end-to-end" strategy that seeks to identify the temporal ordering of variables contributing to criminal behavior. For example, such a temporal-ordering approach could argue that high levels of culture conflict and associated strain (or anomie) lead individuals to develop and/or join delinquent subcultures which, in turn, lead to criminal behavior (ibid.). Thus, the essential task in end-to-end theory integration is to forge relationships between theories that capture the temporal ordering, or the sequence of events and conditions, that culminates in criminal behavior.

More broadly based efforts to develop integrated theories of crime involve "interdisciplinary integration." Such approaches include combining elements of biology, psychology, and sociology. Various biopsychological and biosocial theories contend that certain individual-level characteristics predispose individuals either toward criminal behavior or toward learning criminal behavior. These theories acknowledge that biological factors—be they genetic or not—shape individual traits that, in turn, influence the learning process. These types of integrated theories acknowledge the fundamental role of the social environment in shaping the learning process, particularly early family circumstances (see Wilson and Herrnstein, 1985).

Other examples of theoretical integration have involved more micro-level efforts to integrate two or more theories to explain specific instances of individual criminal behavior (Tittle, 1995; Catalano and Hawkins, 1996). Conversely, macro-level theory integration has attempted to explain group crime rates. For example, Rosenfeld and Messner's (1999) institutional anomie theory combines Merton's (1938) cultural emphasis on the pursuit of money with social disorganization's focus on the inability of institutions to provide effective social control. Moreover, there has been interest in combining macro- and micro-level theories. Cullen and Agnew (1999) concluded that these particular integration efforts involve descriptions of the ways in which macro-level variables affect the behavior of individuals which, in turn, affects crime rates.

Still another variant of integration is theoretical elaboration, in which original crime theories rooted in, for instance, economic strain are expanded to include several types of strain—psychological, social, or otherwise. For example, general strain theory holds that crime and deviance are potential adaptive coping responses to any adverse negative condition (Agnew, 2006)

The development of integrated theories of crime has enjoyed major interest and popularity, but still our understanding of criminal behavior has only modestly improved. Even as efforts to achieve empirical validation are ongoing, there is a sense that such efforts are proceeding in vain. Surely, any postmodern cynic would contend that, if everything explains crime, then nothing explains crime. Because multiple causes of crime can now be reasonably assumed, theory has only a loose and indirect influence on current penal policy. As Gordon (1990) contended, eclectic is probably the best description of the theoretical underpinnings of the current penal system. While previous phases of crime control also exhibited ideological inconsistencies (e.g., classicism allowed some determinism, positivism allowed some punishment) there was at least a dominant set of ideas from which departures could be noticed. Now, "In the cheerless anti-theoretical realism of contemporary crime-control ideology, anything goes" (Cohen, 1985: 158–159).

"Anything Goes" Penal Strategies

Though it has been argued that the search for the causes of crime has given way to the search for identifying "what works" (ibid.), it is questionable whether program evaluation research can be any more incisive than crime causation research. If crime is attributed to some imprecise combination of everything, then an imprecise combination of everything will be applied to the problem of crime. Indeed, as policy makers and researchers experiment with different ingredients and dosages of penal policy, a diversified approach has evolved that recognizes the virtues of retribution, incapacitation, deterrence, and rehabilitation. Strategies for realizing these varied objectives run the gamut, including (though not limited to) mandatory minimums, three-strikes laws, the death penalty, intermediate punishment, restorative justice, sex offender registration and notification, offender re-entry programming, institutional and community-based substance abuse treatment and employability training, and different private- and public-sector schemes for administering these programs, sanctions, and services.

Supermax Prisons

The mandatory minimums, three-strikes, and truth-in-sentencing laws of the 1980s and 1990s essentially reduced punishment to the quantitative question of how much time in prison is needed before the requisites of retribution, deterrence, and incapacitation are satisfied. The qualitative question of *how* one spends their time in prison is an equally important policy question but, at the time, this issue was being either neglected or summarily answered with the rhetoric of severity. The importance of how one does their prison time dates back to the controversy between the Auburn and Pennsylvania prison systems. Both systems advocated a stark environment of silence and separation for the noble purpose of reform, regardless of the length of the sentence. The regimen of silence and isolation was soon denounced, however, because of the "semi-fatuous condition" in which it left the prisoners (1890 U.S. Supreme Court, cited in Kluger, 2007).

Given this historical precedent, it is somewhat alarming that austere institutions and inmate solitude have made a comeback in the form of supermax prisons. Even more troubling is the fact that the former beneficent rationale for isolation—reform and repentance—has been replaced by the Spartan aims of control and punishment. Marked by conditions of extreme deprivation, supermax prisons add another level of security to what previously had been a three-tier institutional classification system. These prisons, or units within prisons, are intended to be used for a different kind of criminal offender; namely, those deemed to be "super" threats to institutional safety and security. As of 1998, approximately 20,000 inmates were being housed in thirty-one supermax facilities nationwide

(King, 2006). Although the National Institute of Corrections warned corrections departments that the constitutionality of supermax programs is uncertain and that they should proceed with caution with regard to their use (King, 2006), more states have come to rely on this form of close custody institution. As of 2004, forty-four states had supermax facilities housing approximately 25,000 inmates (Mears, 2006).

While there is no common definition of the supermax prison, the National Institute of Corrections has identified three essential elements: (1) accommodation that is physically separate, or at least separable, from other units or facilities; (2) a controlled environment emphasizing safety and security through separation from staff and other prisoners and restricted movement; and (3) prisoners who have been identified through an administrative rather than a disciplinary process as needing special control on the grounds of their violent or seriously disruptive behavior in other high-security facilities (King, 1999). Prison administrators claim the facilities house the highest risk inmates, who have repeatedly exhibited violent behavior inside prison (Gavora, 1996). In effect, supermax prison administrators claim to house the so-called "worst of the worst," who cannot be effectively managed in the general prison populations.

A fairly standard regimen and structure can be found in all supermax facilities. Inmates are locked alone in a roughly seven-by-twelve-foot (often windowless) cell for as long as twenty-three hours a day to keep them isolated from the staff and other prisoners. The design of the facility separates inmate and staff routes throughout the prison. Inmates are always shackled while being escorted outside their cells. All meals are delivered to the inmates in their cells. Inmates are allowed only three showers a week and one hour a day in which to leave their cell and use a small exterior exercise area. Video surveillance cameras are positioned throughout the facility and cells, and security doors are computer-operated (Sheppard, 1996).

Despite claims of high-tech innovation and "robust" construction by supermax advocates, the constitutionality and effectiveness of supermax prisons are highly suspect. The use of these facilities has been opposed by some correctional administrators and courts, but such facilities have been condemned fully by the United Nations, Amnesty International, American Civil Liberties Union, and Human Rights Watch. These and other critics contend that supermax conditions constitute a form of "no-touch torture" (Alfred McCoy, cited in Kluger, 2007) that violates the International Covenant on Civil and Political Rights (which the United States ratified), as well as the United Nations Standard Minimum Rules for the Treatment of Prisoners, the Body of Principles for the Protection of All Persons Under Any Form of Detention or Imprisonment, and the Basic Principles for the Treatment of Prisoners, which were passed by the U.N. General Assembly (King, 1999). The only legal relief provided to inmates thus far has been a 2005 U.S. Supreme Court ruling holding that supermax isolation imposes such an "atypical and significant hardship" that inmates must have a formal opportunity to contest their reclassification and assignment to such a facility (Justice Kennedy, quoted in Kluger, 2007).

One need only look at the words contained in the diaries of de Beaumont and de Tocqueville during their tour of the U.S. penitentiary system in 1833 to understand why modern-day observers have also spoken out against this practice: "This trial, from which so happy a result had been anticipated, was fatal to the greater part of the convicts: in order to reform them, they had been submitted to complete isolation; but this absolute solitude, if nothing interrupts it, is beyond the strength of man; it destroys the criminal without intermission and without pity; it does not reform, it kills" (quoted in Marquart and Sorenson, 1997: 49). Haney's (1993) study of the Pelican Bay Supermax Facility in California confirms these nineteenth-century observations on solitary confinement. Haney noted that not all inmates experience the same degree of psychological damage, but that few emerge unscathed. For example, Haney observed that prisoners placed in supermax units went from being starved for social contact to being frightened of any social contact. Others acted out in ways simply to prove that they still actually existed—even if they knew their actions would elicit negative responses by correctional officers. Other supermax inmates became psychotic, filled with a perpetual fear of the correctional officers who "extracted" them from their cells for the slightest rule infraction. Still others engaged in suicidal or self-mutilating behavior: One inmate in Haney's study reported that he had been slicing his arms several times a day for years just to see the blood flow.

Despite the mental hardship and deterioration wrought by supermax confinement and the fact that the overwhelming majority of inmates housed in these facilities will be directly released to society, officials continue to view supermax facilities as a necessary tool. The supermax prison may even be embraced as the preferred construction alternative when there is a need for more prison cells (Franklin, 1998). Some states, once committed to providing some supermax accommodations, build more than is necessary because it is cheaper to build a five-hundred than a one-hundred bed facility. Once the beds are available, they are filled, regardless of whether the inmate's behavior truly warrants placement in the facility. The overall economic feasibility is still in question, however, as their effectiveness as a management tool is dubious. For example, supermax prisons cost two to three times as much to build and operate as do traditional maximum security facilities, and there is little agreement among wardens as to whether supermax facilities actually decrease riots, the influence of gangs, or escapes (Mears, 2006). Moreover, states generally have not conducted cost-benefit analyses prior to or after their implementation (ibid.).

Sex Offender Registration and Notification, Civil Commitment, and Residency Restrictions

Crime legislation in the past decade has become increasingly focused upon sex offenders, both juveniles and adults (Zimring, 2004). As support for the war on drugs has waxed and waned under charges of ineffectiveness and drug proliferation, high-profile stories of child murders and abductions has captured the attention of the media and outraged the public. One could even argue that the war on sex offenders has supplanted the war on drugs, at least in terms of the vigorous efforts to pursue more convictions and severe penalties. Indeed, increased conviction rates and longer prison sentences have resulted from national efforts to get tough on perpetrators of sex crimes. Overall, the number of sex offenders in prison increased by 74 percent between 1993 and 2002, compared with a 49 percent increase in the total state prison population (Bureau of Justice Statistics, 2002).

The hardened stance toward sex offenders is seen most visibly in the proliferation of sexual predator statutes. These various state statutes differ from the more traditional approaches to deterring crime (e.g., increases in convictions and prison terms) by responding to the problem of sexual violence in a way that is unparalleled for non-sexual violent offenses. Most notable among these statutes are the sex offender notification/registration (SONR), civil commitment (SOCC) and residency restrictions (SORR) laws that have been implemented nationwide.

Under financial encouragement from the federal government, every state has enacted SONR laws. The federal Violent Crime Control and Enforcement Act of 1994 contains provisions requiring sex offenders to register their whereabouts with law enforcement while states are required to develop sex offender registries or they risk losing federal funding for state and local law enforcement (Terry, 2006). In general, state laws require that persons convicted of sex offenses register with local police departments and that citizens be notified (or have the means of knowing) when a sex offender resides in their community. There is, however, considerable state-by-state variation in the registration and notification requirements and guidelines. These variations exist with respect to a number of features, such as whether juveniles can be registered, length of registration, the possibility of removal from the registry, the registering agency, methods of community notification, sanctions for failure to register, risk assessments to determine the type and level of community notification, and time period in which to register (Terry, 2006).

Given the negative implications of SONR, considerable controversy has erupted over the enactment of these laws. Many critics have questioned the constitutionality of such requirements, arguing that they violate rights related to privacy, double jeopardy, cruel and unusual punishment, and retroactive application of a state action (ibid.). Nevertheless, the Supreme Court ruled in *Connecticut v. Doe* (2003) and *Smith v. Doe* (2003) that registration and notification laws do not constitute a deprivation of liberty nor do they qualify as punitive in nature. SONR has been seen as problematic for extra-legal reasons as well. Some argue that the ability to obtain information on the residence of sex offenders leads to the possibility of lower real estate values in the neighborhoods and communities in which they reside. The laws are further seen as detrimental in that they increase the potential for vigilantism and offender ostracism, which serves to counteract any benefits that might be gained from sex offender treatment. Specifically, stigmatization and harassment may lead the sex offender to abscond from supervision and their authorized place of residence.

An equally controversial get-tough measure aimed at sex offenders is SOCC. SOCC laws have been enacted in sixteen states, with twenty other states also considering civil commitment laws.[1] In brief, SOCC permits the incarceration of certain sex offenders in the prison *and* mental health systems when commitment to prison alone is the presumptive sentence for offenders deemed competent to stand trial. For sex offenders evaluated and found to possess a "mental abnormality" that predisposes them to recidivating (i.e., a sexually violent predator), SOCC authorizes indeterminate custody in a separate treatment facility after the prison sentence has been served. As of 2007, approximately 2,700 sex offenders nationwide were being confined in these treatment facilities indefinitely. More can be expected, however, as several states plan to expand their number of civil commitment beds. California completed a $388 million facility to hold 1,500 sex offenders, while Florida, Minnesota, Nebraska, Virginia, and Wisconsin also plan to increase their number of beds (ibid.).

SOCC laws are based on two dubious assumptions. The first is that sex offenders suffer from a mental abnormality that makes them more likely to recidivate than non-sex offenders. The second is that sex offenders as a group can be conclusively differentiated by risk. While legislators have been quick to accept the direct sexual-violence–mental-disorder–recidivism-relationship, many experts have rejected or expressed reservations about this premise and therefore the promise of SOCC (Alexander, 1995; Schopp and Sturgis, 1995; Winick, 1998). For many critics, the key question is whether the evaluations of behavioral science can function as adjudicators of fact (Janus, 2000), when experts are debating how best to assess the risk that earns one the label of "sexual predator," and whether such a label even is justified from a clinical or legal perspective (Lucken and Bales, 2008).

Risk assessments employed in the SOCC process have been informed largely by the sex offender recidivism research. While a substantial body of research shows that sex offenders are no more likely to recidivate or to be specialists than are non-sex offenders (Beck and Shipley, 1989; Langan and Levin, 2002; Sample and Bray, 2003; Scheingold, Olson, and Pershing, 1992; Miethe et al., 2006), the burden of risk assessment in SOCC is to differentiate one sex offender from another. The notion of inter-group distinctions has received strong support in the research literature, yet the research has generated varying results. While the results of these various studies support one assumption underlying SOCC—namely, that sex offenders as a group exhibit varying patterns of recidivism—the findings are neither simple nor absolute. The formula for predicting sex offender recidivism is complicated not only by the controversy over which risk factors should be included, but also by the relative priority of these factors and the manner in which they should be organized and interpreted (Lucken and Bales, 2008).

For example, Janus and Walbek's (2000) study of sex offender commitments in Minnesota shows a "striking degree of variability" with respect to offender demographic characteristics, criminal record, victim demographics, and the clinical and institutional histories of sex offenders. The authors reported substantial variation in the characteristics of committed offenders in any given year. This led them to conclude that, while Minnesota's statute is explicitly aimed at the "most dangerous," the high variability in factors associated with recidivism indicates there may be high variability in the risk of recidivism among those committed. While

they found that the number of commitments and the age of those committed had increased over time and that commitments were more likely to
have substantial and serious criminal health histories unrelated to mental
health problems, it was unclear whether a core set of predictor variables
was consistently indicated in the referral decision process. However, in
a study of Florida's SOCC process, Lucken and Bales (2008) found that,
despite considerable discretion given to evaluators in assessing risk, there
were substantial and salient group differences between sex offenders
that were released and referred, and that the primary factors informing
referral decisions were consistent with legislative intent, actuarials, and
sex offender recidivism research (see also Levinson, 2004).

Whether the recidivism and mental health assumptions about sex offenders are flawed or accurate, SOCC laws are still deemed controversial
for a number of other legitimate reasons. First and foremost, they apply
to offenders that have already served their time for a given sexual offense
and to sexual offenses that are not the current offense of conviction and
incarceration. In other words, an offender may qualify for SOCC even
if the sex offense occurred several years ago and already was successfully adjudicated and punished. Moreover, the evaluation process that
determines whether someone is a "sexually violent predator" does not
begin until the offender is nearing release. Consequently, an offender
may remain confined after the conclusion of the sentence awaiting a
"sexual predator" designation that might not occur. Treatment that could
be provided at the outset and throughout the term of prison incarceration,
furthermore, is postponed until the offender is transported from prison to a
different facility—at the substantially added annual cost of approximately
$100,000 per offender (Davey and Goodnough, 2007). This is about four
times the cost of regular imprisonment.

For these reasons, legal scholars have been decidedly critical in their
assessment of SOCC laws. In particular, many claim these laws are dis-
ingenuous in their intent. For example, Boruchowitz (1992) and others
(Reardon, 1992; Becker and Murphy, 1998; Erlinder, 1993; Schopp and
Sturgis, 1995; Wettstein, 1992) claimed that vague terms such as "mental
abnormality," "psychopathic personality," and "personality disorder"
have enabled the civil system to accomplish what could not be done
lawfully in the criminal justice system. Many legal scholars also have
interpreted the courts' willingness to accept this ambiguous terminology
as being a new and dangerous form of control that threatens a number of
constitutional protections (Alexander, 1995; Falk, 1999; King, 1999; La
Fond, 1992; Smith, 1995). A number of lawsuits have charged that SOCC

violates double jeopardy, due process, and self-incrimination rights (e.g., *Foucha v. Louisiana*, 504 U.S. 71 (1992); *Allen v. Illinois*, 478 U.S. 364 (1986); *In re Blodgett*, 490 N.W. 2d 638, 647 (Minn. App.1992); *Kansas v. Hendricks*, 521 U.S. 346 (1997). However, the courts have yet to side with the claimants on these legal issues.

SORR adds another level of punishment, surveillance, and stigma for offenders supervised in the community or who are released from either prison or civil commitment facilities. SORR, which generally prohibits all sex offenders (not just pedophiles) from living within a specified distance of places inhabited by children (e.g., schools, day care, parks), have been implemented in eighteen states. Some of these laws are jurisdictional while others are statewide. For example, Iowa passed a law barring sex offenders from living with in 2,000 feet of schools or day care facilities in 2002. In Miami Beach Florida, a 2,500-foot buffer zone was established around schools, parks, and day care facilities (Davey and Goodnough, 2007).

SORRs are problematic in that authorities often encounter extreme difficulty in locating housing for released sex offenders. Sometimes sex offenders (and their families) are forced to move out of their established homes, or are relegated to essentially centralized housing with other sex offenders. Predictably, the application of such restrictions leads to isolation, financial and emotional stress, and decreased stability—all of which serve as powerful triggers for sexual reoffending (Levenson and Cotter, 2005)

Death Penalty

Significant changes and new debates have emerged with respect to the use of capital punishment. In 1999, the number of executions in the United States reached a peak of 98 (see Figure 13-1). Since that time, the number of executions has consistently declined, with 37 executions taking place in 2008. Particularly noteworthy is the decline in the number of death sentences imposed since 1999. Between 1993 and 1999, the number of death sentences imposed remained relatively consistent, hovering between a low of 281 and a high of 328 (Death Penalty Information Center, 2009). Since 1999, when the number was at 284, the number has dropped each year, reaching only 115 in 2007 and a (projected) 111 for 2008 (Bureau of Justice Statistics, 2007). While it is not entirely clear why this decline has taken place, it certainly is due in part to declining public and public official support, discoveries of innocent death row inmates, and continued findings of racial bias.

Figure 13-1
U.S. Execution Rates, 1977–2009

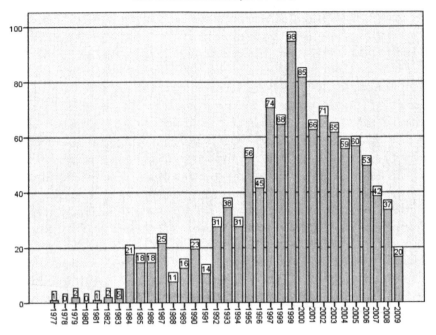

Source: Death Penalty Information Center (2009).

A 2006 Gallup Poll found that overall support for the death penalty was at 65 percent, down from 80 percent in 1994 (Death Penalty Information Center, 2009). The same poll revealed that, when given the choice of life without parole as an alternative sentence, more respondents preferred life without parole to death. A 1995 poll found that even police chiefs did not believe that the death penalty was an effective means of controlling crime (ibid.). Specifically, the police chiefs ranked the expansion of the death penalty last as a means of reducing violent crime, far behind crime-control strategies like reducing drug abuse, improving jobs and the economy, adding police officers, imposing longer prison sentences, and reducing the availability of guns (ibid.). Some prison wardens even have reversed their stance and actively spoken out against its use as well. For example, a former Florida prison superintendent and supporter of capital punishment became a vocal advocate of abolishing the death penalty in 2007, claiming that "vengeance dehumanizes, and the death-penalty ritual is state-sponsored theater designed precisely to achieve that objective" (Berlow, 2007). In 2005, conservative Republican U.S. Senator Rick

Santorum from Pennsylvania also announced that he was questioning his once-unyielding support for the death penalty (Badkhen, 2005). Senator Sam Brownback, an equally conservative U.S. senator from Kansas who has voted against measures to make it easier for inmates to appeal their cases, has now expressed his opposition to the death penalty. Specifically, he recently claimed that the death penalty is not consistent with a broader "culture of life" perspective and that taxpayer funding for (abortion and) capital punishment should be abolished (ibid.). A 2005 poll also showed that support for the death penalty among Catholics had dropped 20 percentage points. Similarly, a 2004 poll showed a drop in support (i.e., a decrease from 82 to 59 percent) among evangelical Christians (Badkhen, 2005).

Certainly, a major factor in the movement away from the death penalty is the number of death-row inmates who have been released due to findings of innocence. The Innocence Project at Cardoza Law School in New York—followed by scores of other innocence projects housed in law schools and defense attorney associations across the country—has played a major role in bringing justice to wrongfully convicted inmates. Because of these efforts, there has been an average of 5 exonerations per year between 2000 and 2007, compared with 3.1 exonerations per year between 1973 and 1999 (Death Penalty Information Center, 2009). In Florida alone, 22 death row inmates have been exonerated since 1973, with Illinois running a close second at 18 (ibid.).

Waning public support and findings such as these have prompted a number of legislative debates, state moratoriums, and bans on the death penalty. The high number of releases from death row in Illinois prompted the governor to appoint a commission to study the death penalty. One of the recommendations of this commission was that the death penalty be abolished. However, until then, they proposed a moratorium on the death penalty so that major reforms could be implemented. Other recommendations included limiting the influence of testimony from jailhouse snitches, requiring the videotaping of confessions to ensure suspects were not coerced, and mandating special training for prosecutors and judges. In 2005, Connecticut lost a close battle to abolish the death penalty and an attempt to reinstitute the death penalty in New York failed. More significantly, the U.S. Supreme Court in *Atkins v. Virginia* (2002) held that it is unconstitutional to execute defendants with mental retardation. The American Psychiatric Association, the American Psychological Association, the National Alliance for the Mentally Ill, and the American Bar Association each have called for a similar ruling in the case of the mentally ill. And in *Roper v. Simmons* (2005), the U.S. Supreme Court also struck down the use of the death penalty on juveniles (Death Penalty Information Center, 2009).

Despite these various challenges and reforms, one of the enduring issues in the death penalty dilemma has been the continued role of race: Several studies continue to show various disparities in this regard. For example, a report to the American Bar Association showed that, in 96 percent of states in which there have been reviews of race and the death penalty, a pattern of race-of-victim or race-of-defendant discrimination is present (ibid.). Another study showed that 98 percent of chief district attorneys in death penalty cases are white (Pokorak, 1998). Finally, a study of the death penalty in North Carolina found that the odds of receiving death increase by 3.5 times for defendants with white victims (Boger and Unah, 2001). A California study similarly found that offenders with white victims are more than 3 times more likely to be sentenced to death than are those who kill blacks (Pierce and Radelet, 2005).

Offender Re-Entry

The costs associated with the war on crime, such as those reported in the previous two chapters, have been a dominant theme in the criminological literature for nearly three decades. Research has long documented the unprecedented number of individuals under correctional supervision, as well as the human and financial toll of twenty years worth of get-tough strategies. The strain of these strategies on state budgets, offenders, their families, and communities has been especially noted in the critical debates on punitive justice.

In the past few years, the urgency in addressing these various costs has reached a critical juncture. As shown in Table 13-1, it is estimated that more than 600,000 offenders leave state and federal prisons each year, with poor communities often disproportionately bearing the burden of their re-entry (Lucken and Ponte, 2008). Of the offenders leaving prison, only one-third receives vocational or educational training and one-fourth participates in substance abuse programming (Petersilia, 2003). Less than ten percent participates in a pre- or post-prison release program and two thirds will likely remain unemployed for up to three years after their release (Saxonhouse, 2004). As the previous chapter demonstrated, many more leave prison afflicted with mental illness and infectious diseases, with little or no assistance in accessing community support services.

Table 13-1
Number of Sentenced Prisoners Admitted and Released from State and Federal
Jurisdictions During the Calender Year, 2000-2006

Year	Admissions			Releases		
	Total	Federal	State	Total	Federal	State
2000	625,219	43,732	581,487	604,858	35,259	569,599
2001	638,978	45,140	593,838	628,626	38,370	590,256
2002	661,082	48,144	612,938	630,176	42,339	587,837
2003	686,437	52,288	634,149	656,384	44,199	612,185
2004	699,812	52,982	646,830	672,202	46,624	625,578
2005	733,009	56,057	676,952	698,459	47,981	650,478
2006	749,798	57,495	692,303	713,473	47,920	665,553

Source: Sabol and Couture (2008).
Note: Totals exclude transfers, escapes, and offenders absent without leave.

Attempts to address deficiencies in transition programming and the ensuing threats to public safety can be seen in the latest reform movement known as offender re-entry. Offender re-entry has become an umbrella term for various strategies that aim to transition offenders successfully from prison to the community through the coordinated efforts of criminal justice and social service agencies (Lucken and Ponte, 2008). In marked contrast to the get-tough rhetoric of the 1980s and 1990s, re-entry initiatives have invoked the much softer language of "redemption" (Lattimore, 2006) and "land of second chances" (2004 Presidential State of the Union Address; State of Florida, 2005). Federal, state, and local re-entry programs are beginning to emerge and will proliferate further with the recent passage of the federal Second Chance Act (2008).

Given that virtually everything about corrections ultimately relates to offender re-entry—that is, 93 percent of all prisoners will be released (Petersilia, 2003)—the range of programs and services that falls within the parameters of re-entry is broad indeed. Re-entry efforts include short- and long-term jail and prison pre-release programs, post-prison residential and non-residential programs, re-entry courts, one-stop drop-in centers, and assorted criminal justice and human services partnerships (see Cadora, Swartz and Gordon, 2003; Rossman, 2003; Gaes and Kendig, 2003). The content of re-entry programs is varied as well, including educational, vocational, employment, housing, and/or substance abuse assistance. Re-entry programming also may be administered on a mandatory or a voluntary basis. For example, Petersilia (2003) framed re-entry primarily in the context of parole supervision, or what amounts to a control risk-based narrative. She contended that policy reform needs to occur by altering the in-prison experience by adding more rehabilitative opportunities, and also by instituting a system of discretionary parole release with guidelines and improving parole supervision classification systems. Others (see Travis and Waul, 2003) have defined re-entry more in terms of the effects of incarceration and re-entry on children, families, and communities, a definition that constitutes more of a service, needs-based narrative. Here the focus may be on developing skills sets and meeting the health care needs of released offenders (Gaes and Kendig, 2003) or on maintaining family ties while incarcerated through parenting programs and policies that are attentive to prison location, prison alternatives, and funding for family programs and services (Hairston, 2003; Braman and Wood, 2003).

Legislation calling for the reversal or tempering of collateral sanctions affecting felony offenders has come under the umbrella of re-entry as well. Collateral sanctions or what have been termed "invisible punishments" (Travis, 2002) have emerged as a key issue in the national dialogue on offender re-entry. Travis has employed the term "invisible punishments" to refer to the collection of laws and regulations that operate outside the jurisdiction of sentencing judges, yet diminish the rights and privileges of those who have been convicted of a felony offense. Included among these collateral sanctions or invisible punishments are various regulatory and statutory sanctions that restrict or prohibit offender eligibility for civil rights (e.g., voting, holding public office), numerous licensed and public sector occupations, state and federal benefits (e.g., welfare assistance, food stamps, social security income, student loans), and public housing. Approximately 59 million Americans have a criminal history file on record (Bureau of Justice Statistics, 2001), and between 13 and 18 million Americans may be subject to some form of temporary or permanent social exclusion due to prior convictions for drug and other felony offenses (Uggen et al., 2002).

The consequences of invisible (or collateral) sanctions on offender re-entry are profound, especially when one considers the effect of these sanctions and a prior record on job attainment. A national survey of 600 businesses participating in the Welfare-to-Work Partnership showed that 8 percent of employers would never hire anyone with a criminal record, while 40 percent would never hire anyone with a felony drug conviction. Forty-three percent of surveyed businesses indicated that they would never hire anyone with a violent felony conviction (Petersilia,

2003). A study of 3000 employers in Atlanta, Boston, Detroit and Los Angeles further revealed that more than 60 percent of employers who had recently hired low-skilled workers would "probably not" or "definitely not" hire an applicant with a criminal record (Holzer, 1996). Holzer and colleagues (2002) also found that employers are least likely to hire former prisoners when compared with other disadvantaged groups, such as welfare recipients. While employers are more likely to hire ex-offenders in manufacturing and construction positions—as opposed to service and retail sector positions—such jobs constitute only 15 percent of all employment (Bania et al., 2000; Solomon et al., 2004).

Various states have been engaged in proposals to mitigate the effects of a felony record on subsequent employment. However, these types of re-entry initiatives have been concentrated on the less risky strategies of job preparedness and locating employment, without fully adjusting the statutory and regulatory impediments that restrict and disqualify ex-offenders from a sizable portion of the labor market (Lucken and Ponte, 2008). Those states that have attempted such extra adjustments have witnessed legislative efforts fail, stagnate, or offer only limited relief to select minor offenders (ibid.).

The ultimate task of evaluating re-entry efforts as a whole is likely to be complicated because the concept has such broad application. Though Visher claimed that "literally hundreds of re-entry programs are underway that could be assessed for possible evaluation" (2006), what constitutes a re-entry program is largely left to the researcher's interpretation. As a result, distinctions between "traditional" rehabilitative (i.e., substance abuse, education, and other forms of behavioral treatment) and "new generation" re-entry programs (e.g., employment preparation, housing, social services) have been blurred. Lynch highlighted this tendency to blur when claiming that a danger of re-entry is "giving names to agglomerations of things and then treating them as a single phenomenon by referring to them by that name" (2006). He stated, "Terms like 're-entry program' or 'aftercare' are names that are applied uniformly to very different classes of events, and this heterogeneity can affect the ability to detect the effects of different factors on the dependant variable" (2006: 403).

What we know about re-entry so far is limited and is based on programs that are very different in structure. Much of the existing research also assesses programs operating prior to the current efforts of legislators and government agencies to institute and fund re-entry programs. For instance, a Vera Institute of Justice study of a thirteen-week self-help, pre-release program (i.e., 99 Days & a Get Up) found that families seldom participated in a pre-release activity component and that most inmates returned to the community without many ties (Nelson, Dees, and Allen, 1999). An evaluation of the eight-week pre-release Greenlight Re-Entry Program found that participants performed significantly worse on multiple measures of recidivism after one year, despite program components that were comprehensive and consistent with best practices principles (i.e., cognitive skills, life skills, employment searches, job interviews, housing, drug relapse prevention, links to the community, and job readiness training) (Wilson and Davis, 2006). The researchers attributed the negative findings mostly to low offender involvement with the cognitive component, too short an intervention period for higher risk offenders, and weak planning for post-release services. Turner and Petersilia (1996) also found that a community-based non-profit program providing jobs as well as housing and social support for released offenders had a recidivism rate of less than 5 percent for its work release participants. Saylor and Gaes (1992) found that participation in prison-based work programs had a positive effect on post-release success. Finally, Dion and associates (1999) found that New York City's Center for Employment Opportunities placed 70 percent of its participants in day-labor work-crew jobs between 1992 and 1996. Job retention in 1996 was 75 percent after one month, 60 percent after three months, and 38 percent after six months. The success of the program was attributed partially to the fact that the average pay well exceeded minimum wage, benefits were often included, and participants were required to enroll as a condition of parole.

Privatization

The private sector, both for profit and non-profit, has played a significant role in the administration of punishment for the past two decades and will play a key role in the administration of various re-entry programs as well. While private sector involvement in the penal system is hardly new—after all, the private sector was tied to the transportation of convicts to the colonies, labor in the penitentiaries, the convict lease system in the post-Civil War South—a powerful re-engagement of the private sector occurred in the late 1980s. Recall that the get-tough approach of the 1980s and 1990s led to unprecedented incarceration rates that cost the nation nearly thirty billion dollars a year (Smalley, 1999). This fiscal crisis has encouraged states and the federal government to accept greater private sector control in the management of penal systems.

There are approximately twenty large companies that operate prisons and jails in the United States, and private-controlled facilities are growing at four times the rate of government facilities (Lippke, 1997). In Florida alone, private companies are responsible for the care of more than 80 percent of the state's more than ten thousand youth held in juvenile justice facilities. In 1997, a private company made a proposal (which was ultimately rejected) to Tennessee to assume full responsibility for the state's entire prison system (Kyle, 1998). At the end of 2007, privately operated prison facilities housed 87,860 state inmates nationwide (Sabol and Couture, 2008). In 2002, 73,497 state prison inmates were housed in 31 states (Harrison and Beck, 2003), compared with 67,380 in 1999 (Beck, 2000). Although, the total state inmate population increased by 4.1 percent from 1999 to 2002, the number of offenders housed in private facilities grew 9.1 percent and accounted for 12.7 percent of state prison population growth over these three years (Bales et al., 2005). Table 13-2 identifies the growth in the number of federal and state prisoners held in private facilities between 2000 and 2007. Of particular interest is the fact that the number of federal prisoners held in private facilities has doubled during this time.

Opponents of privatization assert that only state and federal government should be allowed to punish citizens (Gowdy, 1997)—regardless of private sector claims to be able to oversee punishment systems more effectively. Opponents also claim that the bottom line of the private sector—namely "doing well"—always will interfere with the public mandate of "doing good" (Robbins, 1987). For example, a number of private

Table 13-2
Prisoners Held in Private Facilities, 2000–2007

Year	Number of Prisoners			Percent of All Prisoners
	Total	Federal	State	
2000	90,542	15,524	75,018	6.5
2001	91,953	19,251	72,702	6.5
2002	93,912	20,274	73,638	6.5
2003	95,522	21,865	73,657	6.5
2004	98,901	24,768	74,133	6.6
2005	101,720	26,544	75,176	6.9
2006	112,134	27,108	85,026	7.2
2007	118,239	30,379	87,860	7.4

Source: Sabol and Couture (2008).

prison facilities have been found to have cut costs by not properly training their personnel, maintaining only bare-minimum staff, reducing inmate programs, and reducing health care and food services (Smalley, 1999). In 1999, the largest private sector company, Corrections Corporation of America, settled a class action lawsuit brought by inmates because of inadequate medical care and abusive guard behavior (ibid.). It is also the case that shareholder interests often supersede public and institutional safety, especially when escapes, riots, and other problems occur in private facilities. Dyer (2000) reported that, in the wake of a publicized riot at a private New Jersey facility, stock prices for the company plummeted from $20 to $7 a share. He claimed that this incident sent "shockwaves" through the private prison business community, prompting reluctance on the part of private corrections corporations to report problems within institutions. This reluctance to report and address problems is aggravated by the fact that wardens and correctional officers are offered stock in the prison company as ways of reducing staff turnover and compensating for little or no benefits.

Dyer (2000) also noted that private companies can avoid accountability through the practice of housing inmates that are not from the state where the facility is located. To illustrate, states set minimum standards for the care and custody of inmates housed within their own state public facilities. A private facility in Texas, however, can house inmates from Colorado and thereby avoid the standards set by Texas. Compounding the problem of auditing private prisons that house only out-of-state inmates is the fact that private corporations are exempt from the freedom-of-information process (Dyer, 2000).

Given the billions of dollars involved in privatized corrections, private companies have developed sophisticated lobbying efforts that wield substantial influence in penal policy making. Opponents claim private companies will promote the escalated use of prisons and jails while denouncing other forms of viable and less costly punishment. These opponents contend that a private company's concern for profit and the associated need for more prisoners to fill their prison and jail beds will lead the companies to lobby for harsher punishments to keep prisoners as long as possible (ibid.). As Lippke (1997) suggested, the growth in private prisons indicates that, to some extent, governments are willing to modify their traditional roles in relation to legal offenders, though the U.S. Government Accounting Office has reported that there are relatively few differences in operating costs for public and private facilities over time (Robbins, 1987). Not only has privatization failed to yield meaningful cost savings, but also the most recent and rigorous research suggests that privatized efforts have failed to affect recidivism, which was a part (albeit a smaller part) of the impetus for privatization (Bales et al., 2005).

While jails and prisons have been at the center of the literature and controversy on privatization, the involvement of the private sector has assumed a number of other and more prolific forms. For example, though less attention has been given to the phenomenon, the private sector reaches more offenders through community-based corrections (Lucken, 1997). Offenders on diversion, probation, parole, and intermediate punishment are routinely referred to private agencies that evaluate and provide treatment for anger management, domestic violence, substance abuse, and mental health problems as a condition of supervision. Once referred to these private agencies—most of which depend entirely upon offenders for clientele and hence survival—offenders are fully subject to the discretionary judgments of these agencies regarding such matters as the type, cost, and duration of treatment. Failure to comply with the various stipulations of private treatment programs translates into a failure to comply with community supervision (Lucken, 1997).

Other forms of private sector involvement include contracts for the provision of prison goods and services (e.g., food, health care, education, treatment), the operation of community-based residential facilities (e.g., halfway houses, work release centers), and the production and sale of various technologies and materials to support the penal industry. Thus, whether it is in the area of construction, operation, or providing various services or technologies to facilitate the more efficient control, treatment, and surveillance of offenders, the private sector has become fully entrenched in the penal system. Its level of involvement has become so embedded that it has been likened to an "iron triangle" or a "corrections commercial complex" (Lilly and Knepper, 1993). These two terms refer to the all-too-common fact that the vested parties in penal decision making (e.g., legislators, lobbyists, private industry personnel, corrections professionals) all work together to their own benefit, with little or no public scrutiny.

Of course, this is not to say that privatization has no role in corrections; it is absolutely necessary in many respects. It only becomes problematic when the degree of involvement creates a blurring of private and public interests, which has been demonstrated to be the case on several occasions in the operation of privatized prisons. More generally, it is problematic when profit-motivated actors begin to control definitions of who should be punished and the type or degree of punishment received. This type of infringement has subtly taken form already in the domain of treatment services in community corrections (Lucken, 1997). Indeed, even privatization advocate Charles Thomas (1991) concurred that such control of this kind would "create the possibility for an abuse of the punishment process in the service of profit."

Blending Soft and Tough Punishment

We have portrayed American penology in the millennial age by examining some of the more striking, stable, and well-researched trends and movements. No doubt, the issues of supermax prisons, sex offender statutes, capital punishment, offender re-entry, and privatization do not capture the full range of contemporary penal happenings. For example, in 2005, the U.S. Supreme Court ruled that federal judges are no longer bound by mandatory sentencing guidelines. This is a significant decision that will influence the sentencing of all federal offenders and the federal correctional system, though the effects of this change have yet to be examined. Also, boot camps—a widely popular get-tough panacea for youthful offending in the late 1980s—have all but disappeared in the past decade.

Capturing the course of penal events is no easy task, especially when the process of reform appears more volatile and faster paced than ever. The life span of a particular policy seems shorter, and the advent of new policies more rapid. This may be due to ongoing research identifying what does and does not work and/or media reports that quickly and intensely focus on the few, but grave, mishaps of any strategy. Though the research may be tentative and media reports unreflective of the whole, the dissemination of any bad news is wide and powerful in effect, prompting legislators to respond in kind.

The number of people under correctional supervision is certainly one of the most salient aspects of American penology today. We therefore close this chapter with two parting snapshots of the statistical state of punishment. These concluding figures are not meant to be thought of as mere addendums to the above main events, but as the culmination of many events over many years. The first statistical picture shows that the growth rate in the state and federal prison and jail population between 2000 and 2007 has slowed relative to what it was in the 1980s and 1990s. Nevertheless, there is still a 2.6 percent growth rate, which has resulted in 2.3 million people being in custody as of 2007. The second set of figures is perhaps more grim in that it shows that, as of 2007, one in 31

Americans were under some form of state correctional supervision on any given day: 780,581 were in jail; 4,293,163 were on state probation; 824,365 were on state parole; and 1,512,576 were in prison (Pew Center on States, 2009).

Note

1.   States with SOCC laws are Arizona, California, Florida, Illinois, Iowa, Kansas, Minnesota, New Jersey, North Dakota, South Carolina, Washington, District of Columbia, Missouri, Virginia, Massachusetts, Wisconsin, and Texas. In Texas, civil commitment operates on an outpatient basis.

14

Conclusion

The final chapter of a book bears a unique burden, as the measure of any good story is its ending. Readers may judge the ending as unexpected, predictable, provocative, or even unsatisfying for having raised more questions than answers. Nevertheless, because the ending likely may be what the reader most remembers, the impression left is important. In this final chapter, several of the book's themes will be reviewed to help inform the reader about the future of American penology, including the potential role of criminologists and citizens in helping shape that very future.

Past and Present Penal Practices

Today's penal practices reflect not only the latest in American penology, but also they provide a connection between penology's past and future. Sex offender identification and community residency restrictions, "tough" and "soft" punishment, supermax prisons, the death penalty, offender re-entry, and privatization demonstrate that many of our current penal approaches are—in some ways—a reconstruction of past ideas and practices. For example, current identification and community residency restrictions for sex offenders and public access to their criminal records are reminiscent of colonial practices involving the public display of criminal offenders and the "warning out" and banishment of other undesirables and offenders from the community altogether. In the period of transition, crime was understood as a function of rational thought or free will. Consequently, it was also assumed that the threat of long-term incarceration would deter rational individuals, particularly when applied in a uniform, swift, and certain manner. Then in the nineteenth century, crime was considered to be a moral disease caused by the breakdown of the family and a vice-ridden community. Confinement in a well-ordered asylum—known as the penitentiary—was thought to provide a means to contain the spread of disease and to cure its victims; namely, criminal offenders. And for more than half of the twentieth century, crime in Progressive America was considered to be a consequence of an offender's social or psychological circumstances. It was believed that these circumstances could be overcome with targeted and individualized treatment, provided through prisons, parole, probation, and the juvenile court and youth reformatories for trouble youths. In the 1960s and 1970s, the dominant belief was that it is not so much the offender to blame for crime but rather society and the criminal justice system's responses to the offender that cause, perpetuate, and intensify criminal behavior. This was also a period of widespread distrust of the government and the expansion of individual rights, a time Friedman (1993) characterized as the "culture of rights." Accordingly, penal practices were focused upon decentralization and diversion with the goal of minimizing if not avoiding criminal labeling and formal justice system contact altogether. By the 1980s, a modified version of free will dominated the thinking on crime once again: Because offenders were believed to exercise "rational choice" in committing their crimes, all that was needed were strategies like those in the period of transition; prison needed to be seen as too costly for rational-thinking individuals who may otherwise be predisposed to crime.

The current penal system offers an array of strategies that are certainly reminiscent of the past and include—but are not limited to—fines, pretrial intervention, arbitration, restitution, community service, teen and juvenile courts, victim–offender meeting programs, citizen panels, pretrial release, work release, probation and restitution centers, halfway houses, probation, parole, day-reporting centers, intensive supervision probation, boot camps, home confinement, electronic monitoring, jail, prison, supermax prisons, and various other community-based residential facilities and re-entry programs. Perhaps the most notable difference in penology today from that of the past (that will, no doubt, accelerate in the future) is the increasing reliance upon technology in offender surveillance and control, such as satellite global positioning systems.

In the effort to explain the relationship between penology's past, present, and future, the concepts of "social amnesia," "illusion of knowledge," and "net widening" are helpful. Social amnesia refers to the tendency of American penology to ignore history when responding to the present or informing the future. That is, discarded ideas and practices are reinvented and repackaged; at the same time, however, the expectations for these practices remain the same—namely, that the recycled strategies will yield more effective crime control. Not surprisingly, social amnesia also involves the tendency of reformers and observers to interpret past events not necessarily as they were, but as they choose to remember them. Our interpretations of the past tend to be informed by current events and perspectives rather than how historical events actually unfolded. For example, the assumption that "nothing works" in rehabilitation is generally based on a flawed view of how rehabilitation was implemented in the first place. Specifically, we do not know if specific rehabilitation programs actually worked or not because the programs were seldom implemented as intended. Additionally, patterned declines in serious crime during the late 1990s and into the early 2000s have routinely been credited to various get-tough measures rather than to the then-robust economy, low unemployment, and reduced populations at risk of committing crime. As a result, many citizens and policy makers truly believe that getting tough on crime is the ultimate solution. Such broadly held beliefs continue to fuel new and more imaginative get-tough penal strategies, which in turn are generating far-reaching consequences that extend well beyond criminal offenders. Yet, today in 2009, we face a major economic downturn that is beginning to spark the search for less costly and softer crime-control methods that may possibly reverse—or at least temper—America's traditional reliance on ever increasing incarceration.

This pattern of social amnesia also reveals that we operate under a recurring and broadly held illusion of knowledge. What this notion suggests is that each generation of reformers thinks it knows what causes crime and therefore believes it knows precisely how best to control it effectively. In the book, *The Discoverers: A History of Man's Search to Know His World and Himself* (1983), Boorstin chronicled man's historical quest for progress and found that, throughout history, the biggest impediment to progress has been what he termed the illusion of knowledge. Boorstin concluded that mankind's progress rests not so much in knowing, but—quite the opposite—in recognizing how little we do know. Recognition of ignorance, then, is the fundamental first step to progress. However, where in the history of American penology can we identify a point at which recognition of ignorance helped temper penal ideas, reforms, and practices?

Not only have we generally suffered from social amnesia and failed to recognize our ignorance in the promotion of penal reforms and practices, but also we have not done or accomplished what we say we are going to do and accomplish. As Cohen (1985: 359) summarized, "Consequences so different from intentions; policies carried out for reasons opposite to their stated ideologies; the same ideologies supporting quite different policies; the same policy supported for quite different ideological reasons. And any possible correspondence between ideas and policies will become even harder to locate." Various theoretical models including implementation impediments, organizational convenience, professional and ideological contradictions, and the political economy have tried to account for this failed record of outcomes (Austin and Krisberg, 1981; Blomberg, 1987; Cohen, 1985; Feeley and Simon, 1992; Klein, 1979). But regardless of the interpretation, the conclusion about American penal reform history has been gloomily punitive and repetitive. The persistent disparity between ideas and practices, while problematic in its own right, has contributed to the ongoing history of net widening in penological reform efforts. As a result, more and more of the base population have become subject to some form of penal control—with frightful predictions for even more technologically driven control and surveillance looming in the near future, and well beyond the walls of prisons and into our civic communities.

To illustrate this historical pattern of net widening, Figure 14-1 provides the combined federal and state prison incarceration rates from 1850 to 2007. The rate of incarceration increased from 29 per 100,000 individuals in 1850 to 756 per 100,000 individuals in 2007. The rapid and unprecedented increase of the 1990s is noteworthy in light of the steady decline in crime during this particular period. In other Western countries, between 50 and 135 residents per 100,000 are in prison. Thus, the U.S. incarceration rate is between 6 and 12 times higher than other Western countries.

Further illustrations of net widening appear in Table 1. The table provides figures for the total population subject to correctional control, as well as the number of adults on probation and parole and held in jails and prisons. Between 1980 and 2006, when prison populations more than quadrupled, probation populations increased from slightly more than 1 million to more than 4 million, while parole increased from 220,438 to just more than 800,000. In 2006, more than 7 million people were subject to either probation, jail, prison, or parole (U.S. Bureau of Justice Statistics, 2006). However, it is important to recognize that these alarming statistics are only a portion of the true extent of penal control: Most of the locally operated community-based programs are not included in these figures. Nor do these figures take into account changes in the character of the control, such as the "piling up of sanctions" in the community, the imposition of "collateral consequences" such as housing and

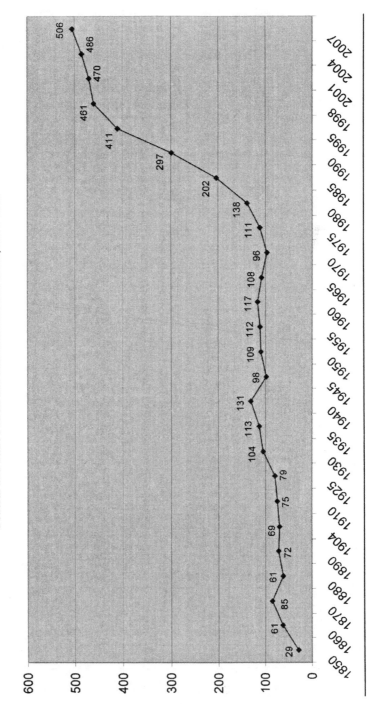

Figure 14-1
Federal and State Prison and Jail Incarceration Rates, 1850–2007

employment restrictions, and the increased punitiveness and duration of institutional confinement.

These figures also fail to capture the more expansive and changing technological character of penal control. A prime example of this change is the recent implementation of satellites to track probationers throughout Florida: Crime Trax (Rosica, 2000). The Crime Trax system employs twenty-four satellites circling twenty thousand miles overhead to follow the state's 143,000 people on any form of court-ordered probation. Each offender wears a wristlet that records his or her location once every

Table 14-1
Adults on Probation, in Jail or Prison, and on Parole, 1980–2006

	Total Estimated Correctional Population	Probation	Jail	Prison	Parole
1980	1,840,400	1,118,097	182,288	319,598	220,438
1981	2,006,600	1,225,934	195,085	360,029	225,539
1982	2,192,600	1,357,264	207,853	402,914	224,604
1983	2,475,100	1,582,947	221,815	423,898	246,440
1984	2,689,200	1,740,948	233,018	448,264	266,992
1985	3,011,500	1,968,712	254,986	487,593	300,203
1986	3,239,400	2,114,621	272,735	526,436	325,638
1987	3,459,600	2,247,158	294,092	562,814	355,505
1988	3,714,100	2,356,483	341,893	607,766	407,977
1989	4,055,600	2,522,125	393,303	683,367	456,803
1990	4,350,300	2,670,234	405,320	743,382	531,407
1991	4,535,600	2,728,472	424,129	792,535	590,442
1992	4,762,600	2,811,611	441,781	850,566	658,601
1993	4,944,000	2,903,061	455,500	909,381	676,100
1994	5,141,300	2,981,022	479,800	990,147	690,371
1995	5,342,900	3,077,861	507,044	1,078,542	679,421
1996	5,490,700	3,164,996	518,492	1,127,528	679,733
1997	5,734,900	3,296,513	567,079	1,176,564	694,787
1998	6,134,200	3,670,441	592,462	1,224,469	696,385
1999	6,340,800	3,779,922	605,943	1,287,172	714,457
2000	6,445,100	3,826,209	621,149	1,316,333	723,898
2001	6,581,700	3,931,731	631,240	1,330,007	732,333
2002	6,758,800	4,024,067	665,475	1,367,547	750,934
2003	6,883,200	4,073,987	691,301	1,390,279	774,588
2003 revised	6,924,500	4,120,012	691,301	1,390,279	769,925
2004	6,995,100	4,143,792	713,990	1,421,345	771,852
2005	7,051,900	4,166,757	747,529	1,448,344	780,616
2006	7,211,400	4,237,023	766,010	1,492,973	798,202

Source: Sourcebook of Criminal Justice Statistics Online (albany.edu/sourcebook/pdf/t612006.pdf).

minute by bouncing a signal off one of the twenty-four satellites circling overhead. At night, the wristlet acts as a remote control that transmits its information to a black box receiver located in the probationer's home. This box transmits the information through secure telephone lines to a state law-enforcement computer. Simultaneously, law-enforcement agencies throughout the state transmit the day's crime and incident information, including times and addresses, to this same state law-enforcement computer. The computer, in turn, maps all the reported crime data and probationers' movement data to identify potential matches in time, place, individual probationer, and crime incidents. Florida previously used this technology for several years to monitor high-risk probationers in the community, but has now substantially expanded its uses to all probationers.

Together, these incarceration and community surveillance trends not only render an ever-increasing proportion of America's population subject to some form of penal control, but also these trends impose a form of control that is more complete and encompassing. Added to the increasingly punitive penal measures employed with juvenile offenders as well as the various other quasi-formal and informal public and private penal programs, it seems that we are indeed approaching a "medium-secure society" in which all of us are becoming subject to elements of prison-like surveillance, regulation, and control in the communities where we live and work.

Culture of Control

While any discussion of the future must be viewed with considerable caution, there is mounting evidence that American life in the new millennium will be subject to new and more far-reaching levels of control. Clearly, we all have witnessed these increased levels of control since 9/11. Over a period of several centuries, we have effectively built a community of corrections that normalizes the presence of formal control, and even informal control, in the larger civic society. As Foucault suggested, perhaps the most important consequence of this community of corrections "is that it succeeds in making the power to punish natural and legitimate, in lowering at least the threshold of tolerance to penality" (1977). As this dispersal of control continues and becomes more widespread—particularly since 9/11—the question that arises is: Are we experiencing a transformation in the character of crime control, in which the penal system is only a part of the larger culture of control? Staples

(1997: 1) identified several examples of the increased blurring between penal control and the fast-developing culture of control:

> Today, nearly ninety percent of U.S. manufacturers are testing workers for drug use.... In California and Texas, every citizen wishing to be issued a driver's license must have their thumbprint computer scanned.... In Kansas, school children are identified with "bar codes" so that a teacher can use a computer to track their daily behavioral and academic performance.... In Maine, a police officer whose name is simply raised in a local sex-abuse case is told he has to submit to a test designed to measure his sexual desire.... In Arizona, a "welfare mother" has a court-ordered contraceptive device surgically implanted in her arm.... And, in nearly every state in the country, convicted felons are placed under "house arrest," their movements monitored electronically by a transmitter attached to their ankles.

Today, technologically integrated profiles of individual citizens can provide detailed portraits of our lives, circumstances, and patterns, including our daily e-mails and telephone conversations. Information technologies can access various data on individual finances, employment history, medical history, marital status, consumer preferences, telephone records, welfare eligibility, nationality, ethnic background, religion, group associations, educational records, and criminal histories. Moreover, these databases and information systems enable the compilation of individual "profiles" that can be used in time-series analyses from which various predictions can be made about our future health, life span, earning capacities, consumer preferences, terrorist risk, and other future behaviors. For example, in late 1999, major newspapers throughout the country reported that data from a couple's premarital arguments could be used to accurately predict whether particular marriages would succeed or end in divorce.

Corbett and Marx (1991) suggested that these new technologies and their applications mean that we are living in a society that is becoming increasingly characterized by an implosion of previously accepted boundaries, resulting in the disintegration of the barriers that once offered individual sanctuary. Such "historic" or "modern" barriers as distance, darkness, time, walls, and even skin—which have all been basic to conceptions of privacy and liberty—are fast becoming outmoded in the current technology-driven culture of control. The contention here is that our communities, homes, workplaces, and bodies are becoming increasingly glasslike, or transparent, and therefore can be more easily regulated and controlled.

We all appear to have reached a greater tolerance for control and its associated technologies. But why have we become more accepting of this expanding control? Clearly, it has not occurred because of a totalitarian takeover or collapse of worldwide democracy. Could it be the result of a quiet revolution in technology? With "an invention here and a new computer application there," American culture is nearing the point forewarned by those who feared technology could breed a new kind of oppression" (Staples, 1997: 128). It is these new social control technologies and methods applied to the individual, the home, the workplace, the community, and other public places that—while appearing minor, necessary, and even useful—are providing an infrastructure for a system of control that has significant intrusive and punitive capacities.

The interesting paradox according to Staples is "that the gaze is increasingly secured through the very products and services that we all are seduced into consuming. Portable phones are easily listened in on, and inexpensive video technology ensures that cameras and their tapes abound; meanwhile, emerging computer networks make our activities and correspondence easier to monitor" (ibid.: 57). As summarized by Lyon (1994), this is all merely "pleasurable social control"—or perhaps even expedient social control. In Florida, for example, state police asked citizens with cell phones to help monitor Florida's highways; the response was so great, however, that the police had to instruct citizens not to report all minor infractions because they did not have enough resources to respond to all the calls they received ("Thousands of Eyes," 1994).

So, who then is behind this developing culture of control? Staples (1997: 129–130) convincingly argued that there is no "Big Brother," but rather, we, the citizenry, are an integral part of the culture of control:

> Rather than having appeared simply "from the top down" or having originated from a small group of identifiable individuals or even a particular organization, disciplinary power has and is advanced, directly or indirectly, by all of us. It is not orchestrated by only a few or part of some master plan that is simply imposed on us; rather, disciplinary power is "bi-directional," flowing from top to bottom and vice versa. So, while [the President] can issue an executive order that [requires] all federal workers be tested for drugs, an ex-auto mechanic can start marketing and selling video cameras to school districts for their buses. While the FBI can help push a wiretap bill through Congress, an employee in your hometown may initiate "integrity" testing of all job applicants. A government agency or giant corporation may set out to create a new surveillance gadget, but it seems just as likely that a university professor will develop one—or, importantly, the basis for a potential one—for no other reason than curiosity or to get a promotion. A young computer software designer may develop a new program because its capabilities are "cool," rather than seeing it as an employee monitoring tool.

The growth of surveillance technologies and their broad application, however, have not been without some setbacks and instances of protest and resistance. For example, Michigan welfare recipients challenged a law that required them to submit to drug tests to prove they were drug free before they qualified for welfare funds. Further, media stories routinely report on the uncharted and potentially dangerous future of more broadly administered DNA tests for all arrestees, the developing medical technologies and the availability of individual test results, and the information technologies and databases that hold numerous data on individual citizens. Nonetheless, and despite these protests and media calls for restraint, the development of DNA profiles from blood samples for all sex offenders has been implemented. Since 2000, DNA profiles have been developed for all jail and prison inmates, and there are future plans to generate DNA profiles of every American citizen to facilitate solving any crime involving blood or other DNA evidence.

As this larger culture of control continues to grow, the ultimate question is, Will the culture of control that we all appear to be contributing to and are victims of result in a ceiling, or will it continue until democracy, privacy, and other individual rights become irrevocably weakened or disappear altogether? In his important book, *An Inquiry into the Human Prospect* (1980), Heilbroner argued that the worldwide runaway population, coupled with accelerating declines in natural resources, does indeed signal the demise of both conspicuous consumption by some countries like the United States and also of democratic values associated with individual rights, freedom of choice, and rights to be different. Heilbroner contended that the public interest must—and will—take precedence over individual rights, which will result in increasing government regulation over our private lives. Clearly, we do appear to be undergoing this very transition from democracy and primacy of individual rights to some vaguely defined goals of order and public interest, particularly with today's threats of terrorism.

The historical quest by governments for preserving order while maintaining enough individual freedom to avoid tyranny appears particularly applicable to the current culture of control and escalating conditions of economic uncertainty. While several arguments have been circulated about what may temper the culture of control in the future, most futurists acknowledge that increasing control over the lives of all citizens will be forthcoming in a manner consistent with what we have all experienced since 9/11. Further, it appears safe to suggest that Americans are unlikely to stop wishing for the greater convenience, predictability, comfort, safety, and order that is associated with these various technological advances. However, as we become more experienced with these modern technologies, their advances, and new levels of control, perhaps we will become less careless, less open, and less trusting. Such awareness could result in each of us becoming more careful and skillful in what we disclose and agree to provide, not provide, or participate in. Additionally, it can be reasoned that, as we become more cognizant of the questionable prospects and problems associated with the culture of control, we may become involved in more direct action, since much of this control originates in our local communities rather than in state capitals or the nation's capital.

Criminology and Public Policy

Over the past several decades, a series of criminological arguments have been proposed regarding the continuous changes and resulting expansions in penology and social control. These developments include the use of such metaphors and theoretical abstractions as net widening, dispersal of discipline, transcarceration, carceral society, maximum-security society, the new penology, and the culture of control. Among the concerns addressed by these metaphors and theoretical interpretations has been the repeated disparity between the ideas and practices of different penal reforms and the resulting pattern of expanding control and other unintended and negative consequences. However, the question remains as to what can be done in the future to alter or mitigate the historically repetitive outcomes that have been chronicled in this book's preceding chapters.

What is certain today is that our fast-developing technology makes it possible to control subjects more completely. However, and seldom, if ever, discussed in the penology literature is that this same technology makes it possible to control subjects in more discerning ways. Stated differently, emerging technologies need not always result only in more expansive and punitive control and associated unintended consequences. Rather, current and emerging technologies are capable of producing more refined and even liberating control. However, such criminological arguments as net widening, transcarceration, new penology, and culture of control generally lump these strategies together suggesting that electronic monitoring, for example, results only in ineffective intrusions into basic individual rights and liberties. Clearly, from a public policy perspective, there is much to be concerned about regarding the future of penology in particular and of control more generally. To illustrate, Downes (2006) suggested that there is a fundamental value issue surrounding how far an already criminogenic society may go in ceasing to care about what motivates offenders if these offenders can be controlled ever more effectively and cheaply by emerging technology.

We all have witnessed how the post-9/11 threat significantly elevated the quest for more control. Moreover, the resulting culture associated with this ever-expanding technology, surveillance, and control now pervades our everyday lives. Whether driving through intersections, entering public restrooms, shopping, banking, eating at restaurants, traveling, or conducting other routine and everyday activities, the level of surveillance, monitoring, and video recording of these activities is continuous and generally unquestioned. It is as if we have little choice other than to accept the cameras, surveillance, and monitoring. Moreover, our children are accustomed to computers, video games, play stations, and a host of other technologies. In fact, it was reported in a recent research study that eight of ten U.S. children up to age six watch television, play video games or use the computer at least two hours per day (Kaiser Family Foundation, 2006). The study found that most parents view the frequent use of media by their children as a positive educational experience. Indeed, this is our evolving culture and it extends throughout our daily life experiences and perceptions of normalcy.

Certainly, the future promises more integrated and technologically driven social control, and this escalating web of control is being facilitated by a responsive public and culture that both supports these changes and considers them to be necessary and inevitable. Social control changes are being promoted and understood as responsive to the challenges of terrorism, crime, globalization, and economics.

Still, one must ask: Is this ever-escalating pattern of control necessary, and is there something criminologists can do to more effectively address these patterns and associated public policy questions? What is now occurring in both sociology and criminology is an unprecedented recognition and associated effort to directly address important public policy issues with more accessible empirical research. While not all sociological and criminological scholars agree that they should assume any sort of public policy role, it appears that a growing number of scholars are committed to an active public policy role (for examples, see Clear and Frost, 2001; Burawoy, 2005).

The traditional divide between penology/social control scholarship and public policy needs to be seriously questioned if we are to help guide, temper, and understand what now appears to be a potentially ominous future. The issue need be not only what works in penology but also what kind of future do we seek and at what price? Moreover, is now the time for penology and social control scholars to move beyond negative analyses and forecasts toward a more public policy purpose that recognizes the need to reduce the suffering and misery of crime while, at the same time, not ignoring democratic values?

Such a public policy purpose creates a tension for scholars in terms of being accessible and dealing with immediate issues reflected in today's headlines, journalists' questions, and urgent e-mail inquiries, while also being simultaneously comprehensive, reflexive, and objective. To elaborate, objectivity requires scholarly work to be more nuanced and often impenetrable to the larger public and legislative and policy-making bodies. Moreover, beyond immediacy and accessibility are issues of commitment and values. Committed scholarship involves a delicate balance. Most importantly, it is not so much a matter of becoming embroiled in public debates by supporting one particular policy over another, but rather a matter of identifying and explaining what choices and likely consequences are involved in various policy options. Careful and objective analysis should never be trumped by advocacy or the "taking of sides" for some specific public policy.

Today, the question of what is the appropriate public role for criminological scholars is generating considerable dialogue, reflection, and associated disciplinary changes. For example, the American Society of Criminology began publishing the journal *Criminology & Public Policy* in 2001. The journal is aimed at bridging the traditional divide between criminological scholarship and public policy by disseminating state-of-the-art research and associated actionable public policy steps to a larger audience of academics and policy related personnel. *Criminology & Public Policy* is therefore devoted to building awareness of the importance of research-based objective and empirical evidence in guiding public policy, as opposed to the more theoretical or ideological concerns that commonly characterize academic literature. While debate and dialogue surely will persist over the appropriateness and value of a more public policy role and purpose for criminologists, it does appear that the public policy role of criminologists will continue to be clarified and advanced in the future.

Individualism, Rights, and the Culture of Control

The major events in the history of American penology have been reported before, with some contributions being more focused and others being more general. What this book has done is provide a middle ground that identifies and describes penal relationships and patterns emerging from several centuries of American experience. By examining distinct historical contexts and their associated ideas about crime that gave rise to particular penal practices, we have been able to identify several themes. These themes provide us with insights into the likely future of, not only penology, but also the larger culture of control in which we live every day. Throughout America's history of penal reform, various efforts to promote alternative practices have resulted in the implementation of supplements to previous practices that were in turn applied to an ever-growing proportion of America's base population. Today, we face a related but even more pervasive dispersal of control that is increasingly blurring the penal system and the civic society at large. This very system of penology and larger culture of control—while posing threats to democracy, freedom, and privacy—also has the potential to be guided in responsible ways that can simultaneously be effective in crime control and be liberating to offenders and citizens alike.

We certainly cannot be complacent or simply assume that the emerging culture and technology of control serves only positive goals, such as the need to control and prevent crime and terrorism, improve health and productivity, or advance the quality of our lives. Further, we must recognize how little we know about the full set of consequences of these continual technological advances and control capacities. Our notions of privacy and individual rights are quickly changing with far too little research, public and legislative attention, scrutiny, or understanding. As we come to recognize how little we do know, we must begin to address the ultimate question: Can we live with these new levels of technology and accompanying control while simultaneously maintaining our commitment to fundamental democratic values?

Advances in technology and control do not necessarily indicate an abrupt end to all life as we know it, nor do such advances represent merely another challenge that democratically minded Americans will overcome. While the future is complex and uncertain, advancing technology and control will, no doubt, provide society and the individual with both gains and losses. Precisely what these gains and losses will be remains to be seen. What is essential is that each individual recognizes these mixed gain and loss potentials and not assume that businesses, corporations, and/or the government will regulate or protect us from these fast-developing technologies. The message is clear: We cannot ignore our individual responsibilities—technology's spread applies to all of us. Neither fear nor complacency will suffice; we must play a part in confronting technology—be it through active education, greater awareness, or direct action. Nonetheless, while each of us may be able to temper some of the influences of technology on our daily lives, it should be evident from this book's recounting of America's penal developments and the emerging culture of control that the future does appear to hold more of the same; namely, more visibility, increased regulation, and expanded control. Our traditional values concerning the primacy of the individual and individual rights are becoming redefined. While the notion of American society becoming like a maximum-security prison is not imminent, it has become increasingly evident that autonomous individualism is fading. We can no longer be content to support and implement public policies that are without abundantly clear empirical justification. New partnerships between citizens, criminologists, legislators, policy makers, and practitioners can and must alter the historical pattern in American penology of "reform without change."

References

Adams, K. 1983. Former mental patients in a prison and parole system. *Criminal Justice and Behavior, 19*(3), 358–84.

Adams, K. 1986. The disciplinary experience of the mentally disordered inmate. *Criminal Justice and Behavior, 13*(3), 297–316.

Adams, K. 1993. Who are the clients? Characteristics of inmates referred for mental health treatment. *Prison Journal, 72,* 120–41.

Aday, R. H. 1994. Golden years behind bars: Special programs and facilities for elderly inmates. *Federal Probation, 58*(2), 47–54.

"Aging inmates clogging nation's prisons." 2007. *USA Today,* 29 September.

Agnew, R. 2006. *Pressured into crime: An overview of general strain theory.* Los Angeles: Roxbury.

Allen, F. 1964. *The borderland of criminal justice: Essays in law and criminology.* Chicago: University of Chicago Press.

Alexander, R. 1995. Employing the mental health system to control sex offenders after penal incarceration. *Law and Policy, 17,* 111–30.

Amatangelo, G. 2001. Andean Regional Initiative: A policy fated to fail. *Foreign Policy in Focus, 6*(29), July 1.

American Correctional Association. 1993. *Female offenders: Meeting needs of a neglected population.* Laurel, MD: Author.

Anno, B. J., Graham, C., Lawrence, J. E., & Shansky, R. 2004. *Correctional health care: Addressing the needs of elderly, chronically ill, and terminally ill inmates.* Washington, DC: U.S. National Institute of Corrections.

Ashford, N. 1990. The conservative agenda and the Reagan presidency. In J. Hogan (Ed.), *Back to the 1970s: The context of the Reagan presidency* (pp. 3–20). New York: Manchester University Press.

Austin, J., Clark, J., Hardyman, P., & Henry, D. A. 1999. The impact of "three strikes and you're out." *Punishment and Society, 7*(2), 131–62.

Austin, J., & Irwin, J. 2001. *It's about time: America's imprisonment binge* (3rd ed.). Belmont, CA: Wadsworth.

Austin, J., & Krisberg, B. 1981. Wider, stronger and different nets: The dialectics of criminal justice reform. *Journal of Research in Crime and Delinquency, 78*(1), 165–96.

Ayers, K. 1999. Should incarceration of pregnant women be avoided? In C. B. Fields (Ed.), *Controversial issues in corrections* (pp. 90–8). Needham Heights, MA: Allyn and Bacon.

Aylward, A., & Thomas, J. 1984. Quiescence in women's prisons litigation: Some exploratory issues. *Justice Quarterly, 1,* 253–76.

Badkhen, A. 2005. Pendulum begins swing away from death penalty. *San Francisco Chronicle,* 10 April.

Baird, C., & Wagner, D. 1990. Measuring diversion: The Florida Community Control Program. *Crime and Delinquency, 36*(1), 112–25.

Bales, W. D., Bedard, L. E., Quinn, S. T., Ensley, D. T., & Holley, G. P. 2005. Recidivism of public and private state prison inmates in Florida. *Criminology & Public Policy, 4*(1), 57–82.

Bales, W. D., & Dees, L. C. 1992. Mandatory minimum sentences in Florida: Past trends and future implications. *Crime and Delinquency, 38*(3), 309–29.

Bania, N., Coulton, C., & Leete, L. 2000. Welfare reform and access to job opportunities in the Cleveland metropolitan area. In M. Rich (Ed.), *Multi-city access to opportunity study*. Atlanta, GA: Emory University.

Barnes, H. E. 1972. *The story of punishment*. Montclair, NJ: Patterson Smith.

Baron, R. 1977. *Human aggression*. New York: Plenum.

Baron, R., Feeney, F., & Thornton, W. 1973. Preventing delinquency through diversion. *Federal Probation, 37*(1), 13–8.

Baskins, D., Sommers, I., & Steadman, H. 1991. Assessing the impact of psychiatric impairment on prison violence. *Journal of Criminal Justice, 19*, 271–80.

Bates, E. 1998. Private prisons. *Nation, 266*, 11–9.

Beccaria, C. [1764] 1963. *On crimes and punishment*. Translated with an introduction by Henry Paolucci. New York: MacMillan.

Beck, A. J., & Maruschak, L. M. 2001. Mental health treatment in state prisons, 2000. Washington, DC: U.S. Department of Justice.

Beck, A. J., & Shipley, B. E. 1989. *Recidivism of prisoners released in 1983*. Washington, DC: Bureau of Justice Statistics.

Becker, H. S. 1963. *Outsiders: Studies in the sociology of deviance*. New York: Free Press.

Becker, J. V., & Murphy, W. D. 1998. What we know and do not know about assessing and treating sex offenders. *Psychology, Public Policy, and Law, 4*, 116–37.

Beckett, K. 1997. *Making crime pay: Law and order in contemporary American politics*. New York: Oxford University Press.

Bedau, H. A. 1997. *The death penalty in America: Current controversies*. New York: Oxford University Press.

Belden, E. 1920. *Courts in the United States hearing children's cases*. Washington, DC: U.S. Children's Bureau.

Belknap, J. 1996. *The invisible woman: Gender, crime, and justice*. Belmont, CA: Wadsworth.

Bell, M. (Ed.) 1957. *Parole in principle and practice: A manual and report: The national conference on parole*. New York: National Probation and Parole Association.

Benekos, P. J., & Merlo, A. V. 1994. *Three strikes and you're out: The political sentencing game*. National Institute of Justice Research Report. Washington, DC: U.S. Department of Justice.

Bennett, W. J. 1994. *Index of leading cultural indicators*. New York: Simon and Schuster.

Bentham, J. 1789. *An introduction to the principles of morals and legislation*. London: T. Payne.

Berecochia, J. E. 1982. *The origins and early development of parole in California*. Ph.D. dissertation, University of California, Berkeley.

Berger, D. E., Lipsey, M. W., Dennison, L. B., & Lange, J. M. 1977. *The effectiveness of the sheriff department's juvenile diversion projects in southeast Los Angeles County*. Claremont, CA: Claremont Graduate School.

Berkowitz, B. 2003. Mad in the USA. *PrisonerLife.com*, 19 November. Retrieved 11 April 2005, from http://www.prisonerlife.com/articles/articleID=51.cfm

Berlow, B. 2007. *From prison warden to anti-death penalty advocate*. Denver, CO: Colorado Criminal Justice Reform Coalition.

Binder, A. 1976. *Diversion and the justice system: Evaluating the results.* Mimeograph. Irvine: University of California.

Birdsall, R. D. 1970. The second great awakening and the New England social order. *Church History,* 39, (September).

Bittenger, D. 1870. Sources of crime. *New York Evangelist,* 8 December, 41(49). Retrieved from the ProQuest: American Periodicals Series Online Database.

Blomberg, T. G. 1977. Diversion and accelerated control. *Journal of Criminal Law and Criminology, 68*(2), 274–82.

Blomberg, T. G. 1978. *Social control and the proliferation of juvenile court services.* San Francisco: R. and E. Research Associates, Inc.

Blomberg, T. G. 1987. Criminal justice reform and social control: Are we becoming a minimum security society? In J. Lowman, R. J. Menzies, & T. S. Palys (Eds.), *Transcarceration: Essays in the sociology of social control* (pp. 216–8). Aldershot, UK: Cower.

Blomberg, T. G., Bales, W., & Reed, K. 1993. Intermediate punishment: Extending or redistributing social control. *Crime, Law, and Social Change, 19*(2), 197–201.

Blomberg, T. G., & Cohen, S. (Eds.). 1995. *Punishment and social control: Essays in honor of Sheldon L. Messinger.* Hawthorne, NY: Aldine de Gruyter.

Bloom, B., & Steinhart, D. 1993. *Why punish the children: A reappraisal of the children of incarcerated mothers in America.* San Francisco: National Council on Crime and Delinquency.

Blumberg, M. 1990. *AIDS: The impact on the criminal justice system.* Columbus, OH: Merrill.

Blumberg, M., & Langston, D. 1995. The impact of HIV/AIDS and tuberculosis on corrections. In K. C. Haas & G. P. Alpert (Eds.), *The dilemmas of corrections* (3rd ed., pp. 572–84). Prospect Heights, IL: Waveland.

Blumer, H. 1969. *Symbolic interactionism: Perspective and method.* Englewood Cliffs, NJ: Prentice-Hall.

Blumstein, A. 1995. Stability of punishment: What happened and what next? In T. G. Blomberg & S. Cohen (Eds.), *Punishment and social control: Essays in honor of Sheldon L. Messinger* (pp. 259–74). Hawthorne, NY: Aldine de Gruyter.

Boger, J., & Unah, I. 2001. University study finds death penalty racially unfair. *University of North Carolina Gazette,* 25 April.

Bok, M. 1992. *Civil rights and the social programs of the 1960s.* Westport, CT: Praeger.

Bonomi, P. U. 1986. *Under the scope of heaven.* New York: Oxford University Press.

Boorstin, D. J. 1983. *The discoverers: A history of man's search to know his world and himself.* New York: Random House.

Bortner, M. A. 1984. *Inside a juvenile court: The tarnished ideal of individualized justice.* New York: New York University Press.

Boruchowitz, R. C. 1992. Sexual predator law—Nightmare in the halls of justice. *University of Puget Sound Law Review, 15*, 827–42.

Boswell, G., & Wedge, P. 2002. *Imprisoned fathers and their children.* Philadelphia: Jessica Kingsley Publishers.

Bradford, W. [1793] 1972. *Reform of criminal law in Pennsylvania: Selected inquiries 1787–1819.* New York: Arno.

Bradley, R. C. 1990. Judicial appointment and judicial intervention: The issuance of structural reform decrees in correctional litigation. In J. J. DiIulio (Ed.), *Courts, corrections, and the Constitution* (pp. 249–67). New York: Oxford University Press.

Braman, D., & Wood, J. 2003. From one generation to the next: How criminal sanctions are reshaping family life in urban America. In J. Travis & M. Waul (Eds.), *Prisoners once removed* (pp. 157–88). Washington, DC: Urban Institute Press.

Branham, L. S., & Krantz, S. 1994. *Sentencing, corrections, and prisoners' rights* (4th ed.). St. Paul, MN: West.

Brien, P. M., & Beck, A. J. 1998. HIV in Prisons. In T. J. Flanagan, J. W. Marquart, & K. G. Adams (Eds.), *Incarcerating criminals* (pp. 158–60). New York: Oxford University Press.

Brockway, Z. R. 1997. The American reformatory prison system. In J. R. Marquart & J. R. Sorensen (Eds.), *Correctional contexts*. Los Angeles: Roxbury. (Reprint of original from *Prison reform: Corrections and prevention* published in 1910.)

Bureau of Justice Statistics. 2001. *Use and management of criminal history record information: A comprehensive report, 2001 update*. Washington, DC: U.S. Department of Justice.

Bureau of Justice Statistics. 2007. *Capital punishment, 2007*. Washington, DC: U.S. Department of Justice.

Burgess, E. W., & Bogue, D. J. (Eds.). 1967. *Urban sociology*. Chicago: University of Chicago Press.

Burnett, C., & Chaneles, S. (Eds.). 1989. *Older offenders: Current trends*. New York: Haworth.

Butterfield, F. 2004. Almost 10% of all prisoners are now serving life terms. *The New York Times*, 12 May, A17.

Butts, A. C. 1888. Criminal anthropology: The physical indicia of the moral nature. *The Phrenological Journal and Science of Health,* April, 87(4). Retrieved from the ProQuest: American Periodicals Series Online Database.

Byrne, J. M., & Pattavina, A. 1992. The effectiveness issue: Assessing what works in the adult community corrections system. In J. M. Byrne, A. J. Lurigio, & J. Petersilia (Eds.), *Smart sentencing* (pp. 281–303). Newbury Park, CA: Sage.

Cable, G. W. 1884. The convict lease system in the southern states. *Century Illustrated Magazine,* February, XXVII(4). Retrieved from the ProQuest: American Periodicals Series Online Database.

Cahalan, M. W. 1986. *Historical corrections statistics in the United States, 1850–1984*. Washington, DC: U.S. Bureau of Justice Statistics.

"California mental hospitals filling up with criminals." 1999. *Orlando Sentinel*, 1 May.

"Capital punishment." 1846. *Prisoner's Friend,* 4 November, 1(44). Retrieved from the ProQuest: American Periodicals Series Online Database.

Carlen, P., & Tchaikovsky, C. 1985. Women in prison. In P. Carlen, J. Hicks, J. O. Dwyer, & D. Christin (Eds.), *Criminal women* (pp. 182–6). Cambridge, MA: Polity.

Carter, G. W., & Gilbert, G. R. 1973. *An evaluation progress report of the Alternatives Routes Project*. Los Angeles: Regional Research Institute in Social Welfare, University of Southern California.

Carter, R. M., & Wilkins, L. T. 1976. *Probation, parole, and community corrections*. New York: John Wiley.

Cashman, S.D. 1988. *America in the age of the titans: The Progressive Era and World War I*. New York: New York University Press.

Catalano, R. F., & Hawkins, J. D. 1996. The social development model: A theory of antisocial behavior. In J. D. Hawkins (Ed.), *Delinquency and crime: Current theories* (pp. 149–97). Cambridge, MA: Cambridge University Press.

CEGA Services, Inc. 1992. *Corrections compendium*. New York: Edna McConnell Clark Foundation.

Center for Research on Criminal Justice. 1975. *The iron fist and the velvet glove: An analysis of U.S. police*. Berkeley, CA: Author.

Chesney-Lind, M. 1991. Patriarchy, prisons, and jails: A critical look at trends in women's incarceration. *Prison Journal, 71,* 51–67.

Chesney-Lind, M. 1997. *The female offender.* Thousand Oaks, CA: Sage.

Cicourel, A. 1968. *The social organization of juvenile justice.* New York: John Wiley.

Clear, T. R. 1994. *Harm in American penology.* Albany, NY: SUNY Press.

Clear, T. R., & Cole, G. F. 1993. *American corrections* (3rd ed.). Belmont, CA: Wadsworth.

Clear, T. R., & Cole, C. F. 2000. *American corrections* (4th ed.). Belmont, CA: Wadsworth.

Clemmer, D. 1940. *The prison community.* New York: Holt, Rinehart, & Winston.

"Clinton orders new privacy rules for medical records." 1999. *Tallahassee Democrat,* 30 October, B3.

Cloward, R. A., & Ohlin, L. 1960. *Delinquency and opportunity: A theory of delinquent gangs.* Glencoe, IL: Free Press.

Coates, R. B., Miller, A. D., & Ohlin, L. E. 1978. *Diversity in a youth correctional system: Handling delinquents in Massachusetts.* Cambridge, MA: Ballinger.

Cohen, A. K. 1955. *Delinquent boys: The culture of the gang.* Glencoe, IL: Free Press.

Cohen, A. K., Lindesmith, A., & Schuessler, K. (Eds.). 1956. *The Sutherland papers.* Bloomington: Indiana University Press.

Cohen, L. E., & Felson, M. 1979. Social change and crime rate trends: A routine activities approach. *American Sociological Review, 44,* 588–608.

Cohen, S. 1985. *Visions of social control.* Cambridge, MA: Polity.

Cooley, C. H. 1902. *Human nature and the social order.* New York: Scribner's.

Corbett, R., & Marx, G. T. 1991. Critique: No soul in the new machine: Technofallacies in the electronic monitoring movement. *Justice Quarterly, 8*(3), 399–414.

Cornish, D., & Clarke, R. V. 1986. *The reasoning criminal: Rational choice perspectives on offending.* New York: Springer.

Correctional Association of New York. 1995. *Seeking justice: Crime and punishment in America.* New York: Edna McConnell Clark Foundation.

Corry, E. M. 1983. Receptive sites. In S. Kobrin & M. W. Klein (Eds.), *Community treatment of juvenile offenders* (pp. 120–35). Beverly Hills, CA: Sage.

Craig, S. C. 2009. A historical review of mother and child programs for incarcerated women. *The Prison Journal, 89*(Suppl. 1), 35S–53S.

Cressey, D. R., & McDermott, R. A. 1973. *Diversion from the juvenile justice system.* Ann Arbor: National Assessment of Juvenile Corrections, University of Michigan.

Criminal Justice Institute. 1997. *The corrections yearbook.* South Salem, NY: Author.

Cripe, C. A. 1990. Courts, corrections, and the Constitution: A practitioner's view. In J. J. DiIulio (Ed.), *Courts, corrections, and the Constitution* (pp. 268–86). New York: Oxford University Press.

Cullen, F. T., & Agnew, R. 1999. *Criminological theory: Past to present.* Los Angeles: Roxbury.

Dauphinot, L. L. 1996. *The efficacy of community correctional supervision for offenders with severe mental illness.* Unpublished doctoral dissertation, University of Texas at Austin.

Davey, M., & Goodnough, A. 2007. Doubts rise as states hold sex offenders after prison. *The New York Times,* 4 March.

de Beaumont, G., & de Toqueville, A. [1833] 1997. On the penitentiary system in the United States and its application in France. In J. M. Marquart & J. R. Sorensen (Eds.), *Correctional contexts.* Los Angeles: Roxbury.

Dean-Myrda, M., & Cullen, R. 1998. The panacea pendulum: An account of community as a response to crime. In J. Petersilia (Ed.), *Community corrections: Probation, parole, and intermediate sanctions* (pp. 3–18). New York: Oxford University Press.

Death Penalty Information Center. 2009. *Facts about the death penalty,* 16 March. Retrieved 18 March 2009, from http://www.deathpenaltyinfo.org

Dhami, M. K., Ayton, P., & Loewenstein, G. 2007. Adaptation to imprisonment: Indigenous or imported? *Criminal Justice Behavior, 34*(8), 1085–100.

Dickens, C. [1842] 1972. *American notes.* Harmondsworth: Penguin.

DiIulio, J. J. 1990. Introduction: Enhancing judicial capacity. In J. J. DiIulio (Ed.), *Courts, corrections, and the Constitution* (pp. 3–11). New York: Oxford University Press.

DiIulio, J. J. 1993. Well-governed prisons are possible. In G. F. Cole (Ed.), *Criminal justice: Law and politics* (pp. 438–46). Belmont, CA: Wadsworth.

Diner, S. J. 1998. *A very different age: Americans of the Progressive Era.* New York: Hill and Wang.

Dion, M. R., Derr, M. K., Anderson, J., & Pavetti, L. 1999. *Reaching all job-seekers: Employment programs for hard-to-employ populations.* Boston: Mathematica Policy Research.

Ditton, P. M. 1999. Mental health and treatment of inmates and probationers: Bureau of Justice Statistics Special Report, July 1999. Washington DC: U.S. Department of Justice, Office of Justice Programs.

Ditton, P. M., & Wilson, D. J. 1999. Truth in sentencing in state prisons: Bureau of Justice Statistics Special Report, January 1999. Washington DC: U.S. Department of Justice, Office of Justice Programs.

Donaldson, S. 1994. *Rape of incarcerated males in the U.S.A.: A preliminary statistical look* (5th ed.). Unpublished manuscript.

Driver, T. F. 2001. Drugs, oil and markets: Columbia's war. *The Christian Century, 118*(30), 14–5.

Duffee, D. E. 1989. *Corrections: Practice and policy.* New York: Random House.

Dugdale, R. [1877] 1979. The jukes: A study in crime, pauperism, and heredity. In J. E. Jacoby (Ed.), *Classics of criminology.* New York: MacMillan.

Dumond, R. W. 1992. The sexual assault of male inmates in incarcerated settings. *International Journal of the Sociology of Law, 20,* 135–57.

Durham, A. M. III. 1994. *Crisis and reform: Current issues in American punishment.* Boston: Little, Brown.

Dyer, J. 2000. *The perpetual prisoner machine.* Boulder, CO: Westview Press.

Edna McConnell Clark Foundation. 1995. *Seeking justice: Crime and punishment in America.* New York: Author.

Elkins, S., & McKitrick, E. 1993. *The age of federalism.* London: Oxford University Press.

Elliott, D. S., Dunford, F. W., & Knowles, B. A. 1978. *Diversion: A study of alternative processing practices.* Final Report Summary, NIMH. Boulder, CO: Behavioral Research Institute, University of Colorado.

Ellis, L., & Hoffman, H. 1990. *Crime in biological, social, and moral contexts.* New York: Praeger.

"The Elmira Reformatory." 1885. *Christian Advocate,* 30 July, 60(31). Retrieved from the ProQuest: American Periodicals Series Online Database.

Emerson, R. M. 1969. *Judging delinquents: Context and process in juvenile court.* Chicago: Aldine.

Empey, L. T. 1982. *American delinquency: Its meaning and construction.* Homewood, IL: Dorsey.

Erikson, K. T. 1966. *Wayward puritans: A study in the sociology of deviance.* New York: John Wiley.

Erlinder, C. P. 1993. Minnesota's gulag: Involuntary treatment for the politically ill. *William Mitchell Law Review, 19,* 99-113.

Ertelt, S. 2008. Missouri must take pregnant prisoner for abortions at taxpayer expense. *Lifenews.com,* 22 January. Retrieved 20 March 2009, from http://www.lifenews.com/state2805.html.

Falk, A. J. 1999. Sex offenders, mental illness and criminal responsibility: The constitutional boundaries of civil commitment after *Kansas v. Hendricks. American Journal of Law and Medicine, 25,* 117–47.

Feeley, M. M., & Hanson, R. A. 1990. The impact of judicial intervention of prisons and jails: A review of the literature. In J. J. DiIulio (Ed.), *Courts, corrections, and the Constitution* (pp. 12–46). New York: Oxford University Press.

Feeley, M. M., & Sarat, A. D. 1980. *The policy dilemma: Federal crime policy and the Law Enforcement Assistance Administration.* Minneapolis: University of Minnesota Press.

Feeley, M. M., & Simon, J. 1992. The new penology: Notes on the emerging strategy of corrections and its implications. *Criminology, 30*(4), 449–74.

Feenberg, A. 1986. Paths to failure: The dialectics of organization and ideology in the New Left. In A. Reed (Ed.), *Race, politics, and culture: Critical essays on the radicalism of the 1960s* (pp. 119–44). Westport, CT: Greenwood.

Feinberg, C. 1984. White haired offenders: An emergent social problem. In W. Wilbanks & P. Kim (Eds.), *Elderly criminals* (pp. 83–101). Lanham, MD: University Press of America.

Ferrara, M., & Ferrara, S. 1991. The evolution of prison mental health services. In W. Wilbanks & P. Kim (Eds.), *Elderly criminals* (pp. 198–203). Lanham, MD: University Press of America.

Feuer, J. 1995. *Seeing through the eighties: Television and Reaganism.* Durham, NC: Duke University Press.

Finnerty, J. 2005. Only court can order abortion. *The Daily Item,* 9 April. Retrieved 11 April 2005, from http://www.dailyitem.com.

Fishbein, D. H. 1990. Biological perspectives in criminology. *Criminology, 28,* 27–72.

Flanagan, T. J. 1980. The pains of long-term imprisonment. *British Journal of Criminology, 20,* 148–56.

Florida Department of Corrections. 1994. *1993–1994 annual report.* Tallahassee, FL: Author.

Flynn, E. 1993. The graying of America's prison population. *Prison Journal, 72,* 77–98.

Forward, J. R., Kirby, M., & Wilson K. 1974. *Volunteer intervention with court-diverted juveniles.* Boulder: University of Colorado.

Foucault, M. 1977. *Discipline and punish: The birth of the prison* (A. Sheridan, Trans.). New York: Pantheon.

Franklin, R. H. 1998. Assessing supermax operations. *Corrections Today, 60,* 126–28.

Friedan, B. 1963. *The feminine mystique.* New York: Norton.

Friedman, L. 1993. *Crime and punishment in American history.* New York: Basic Books.

Gabel, S. 1992. Children of incarcerated and criminal parents: Adjustment, behavior, and prognosis. *Bulletin on Academic Psychiatric Law, 20,* 33-45.

Gabel, S., & Shindledecker, R. 1993. Characteristics of children whose parents have been incarcerated. *Hospital Community Psychiatry, 44,* 656–60.

Gaes, G., & Kendig, N. 2003. The skill sets and health care needs of released offenders. In J. Travis & M. Waul (Eds.), *Prisoners once removed* (pp. 105–53). Washington, DC: Urban Institute Press.

Garland, D. 1990. *Punishment and modern society.* Oxford: Clarendon.

Garland, D. 1998. *Eight propositions about the present.* Plenary presentation at the 1998 Southern Conference on Corrections, Palm Beach, Florida.

Gavora, J. 1996. The prisoners' accomplice. *Policy Review, 79,* 6–9.

Gearan, A. 2000. Clinton pushes privacy rules. *Tallahassee Democrat,* 1 May.

Giallombardo, R. 1966. *Society of women: A study of a women's prison.* New York: Wiley.

Glaser, D. 1966. The effectiveness of correctional education. *American Journal of Correction, 28*(2), 4–9.

Goddard, H. H. 1912. *The Kallikak Family: A study in the heredity of feeble-mindedness.* New York: Macmillan.

Goddard, H. H. 1914. *The criminal imbecile: An analysis of three remarkable murder cases.* New York: Macmillan.

Goddard, H. H. 1915. *Feeble-mindedness: Its causes and consequences.* New York: MacMillan.

Goffman, E. 1961. On the characteristics of total institutions: The inmate world. In D. R. Cressey (Ed.), *The prison: Studies in institutional organization and change* (pp. 15–67). New York: Holt, Rinehart, & Winston.

Gomes, P. J. 1996. *The good book.* New York: William Morrow.

Gordon, D. 1990. *The justice juggernaut.* Newark, NJ: Rutgers University Press.

Gorringe, T. 1996. *God's just vengeance: Crime, violence, and the rhetoric of salvation.* Cambridge, MA: Cambridge University Press.

Gottschalk, M. 2009. Money and mass incarceration: The bad, the mad, and penal reform. *Criminology and Public Policy, 8*(1), 97–110.

Gowdy, V. B. 1997. Should we privatize our prisons: The pros and cons. *Corrections Management Quarterly, 7,* 56–63.

Graham, H. D. 1992. *Civil rights and the presidency: Race and gender in American politics, 1960–1972.* New York: Oxford University Press.

Greenberg, D. F. 1977. The dynamics of oscillatory punishment processes. *Journal of Criminal Law and Criminology, 68*(4), 643–51.

Greenfeld, L. A., & Snell, T. L. 1999. Women offenders: Bureau of justice Statistics Special Report. Washington, DC: U.S. Department of Justice, Office of Justice Programs.

Gross, D. 1986. Culture, politics, and lifestyle in the 1960s. In A. Reed (Ed.), *Race, politics, and culture: Critical essays on the radicalism of the 1960s* (pp. 99–117). Westport, CT: Greenwood.

Gross, M. L. 1997. *The end of sanity: Social and cultural madness in America.* New York: Avon.

Haas, K. C. 1993. Constitutional challenges to the compulsory HIV testing of prisoners and the mandatory segregation of HIV-positive prisoners. *Prison Journal, 73,* 391–422.

Hagan, J. 1973. Labeling and deviance: A case study in the sociology of the interesting. *Social Problems, 20*(4), 447–58.

Hairston, C. F. 2003. Prisoners and their families: Parenting issues during incarceration. In J. Travis & M. Waul (Eds.), *Prisoners once removed* (pp. 259–82). Washington, DC: Urban Institute Press.

Hammett, T. M., Harrold, L., & Epstein, J. 1998. Tuberculosis in correctional facilities. In T. J. Flanagan, J. W. Marquart, & K. G. Adams (Eds.), *Incarcerating criminals* (pp. 166–8). New York: Oxford University Press.

Handwerk, B. 2004. Mother behind bars: What happens to the children? *National Geographic News,* 30 January. Retrieved 12 April 2005, from http://news.national-geographic.com/news.

Haney, C. 1993. Infamous punishment: The psychological consequences of isolation. *National Prison Project Journal, 21,* 3–7.

Hansen, M. 1999. Going, going . . . gone: Support for minimum drug sentences hits new low. *American Bar Association Journal, 14*(1), 85–74.

Harrison, B., & Bluestone, B. 1988. *The great u-turn: Corporate restructuring and the polarizing of America.* New York: Basic Books.

Hart, H. 1910. *Preventive treatment of neglected children.* New York: Russell Sage Foundation.

Hartstone, E., Steadman, H., Robbins, P., & Monahan, J. 1984. Identifying and treating the mentally disordered prison inmate. In L. Teplin (Ed.), *Mental health and criminal justice* (pp. 279–96). Beverly Hills, CA: Sage.

Healy, W. 1915. *The individual delinquent: A textbook of diagnosis and prognosis for all concerned in understanding offenders.* Boston: Little, Brown.

Heilbroner, R. L. 1980. *An inquiry into the human prospect: Updated and reconsidered for the 1980s.* New York: W. W. Norton.

Helium, F. R. 1983. The deinstitutionalization of status offenders: The legislative mandate. In S. Kobrin & M. W. Klein (Eds.), *Community treatment of juvenile offenders* (pp. 19–38). Beverly Hills, CA: Sage.

Henderson, C. R. 1899. The relation of philanthropy to social order and progress: Proceedings of the National Conference of Charities and Corrections. In F. L. Faust & P. C. Brantingham (Eds.), *Juvenile justice philosophy* (pp. 24–35). St. Paul, MN: West.

Hensley, C., Tewksbury, R., & Koscheski, M. 2002. The characteristics and motivations behind female prison sex. *Women & Criminal Justice, 13*(2/3), 125–39.

Hibbert, C. 1963. *The roots of evil: A social history of crime and punishment.* Boston: Little, Brown.

Hochstetler, A., & DeLisi, M. 2005. Importation, deprivation, and varieties of serving time: An integrated-lifestyle-exposure model of prison offending. *Journal of Criminal Justice, 33*, 257–66.

Holt, K. 1982. Nine months to life: The law and the pregnant inmate. *Journal of Family Law, 20*, 523–43.

Holt, N. 1998. The current state of parole in America. In J. Petersilia (Ed.), *Community corrections* (pp. 28–41). New York: Oxford University Press.

Holzer, H. J. 1996. *What employers want: Job prospects for less-educated workers.* New York: Sage.

Holzer, H., Raphael, S., & Stoll, M. 2002. *Can employers play a more positive role in prisoner re-entry?* Paper presented at the Urban Institute's Reentry Roundtable, Washington, DC, 20–21 March.

Hood, W. M. 1831. Temperance. *Hazard's Register of Pennsylvania,* 23 July, 8(4), Retrieved from the ProQuest: American Periodical Series Online Database.

Huebner, B. M., & Gustafson, R. 2007. The effect of maternal incarceration on adult offspring involvement in the criminal justice system. *Journal of Criminal Justice, 35*, 283–96.

Hunter, R. [1904] 1965. *Poverty: Social conscience in the Progressive Era.* New York: Harper & Row.

Hutchison, K. B. 1999. The truth about the drug war. *The Washington Post,* March 9, A15.

Hylton, J. H. 1982. Rhetoric and reality: A critical appraisal of community correctional programs. *Crime and Delinquency, 28*(3), 341–73.

Immarigeon, R., & Chesney-Lind, M. 1992. *Women's prisons: Overcrowded and overused.* San Francisco: National Council on Crime and Delinquency.

Irwin, J. 1970. *The felon.* Englewood Cliffs, NJ: Prentice-Hall.

Irwin, J. 1980. *Prisons in turmoil.* Boston: Little, Brown.

Irwin, J., & Austin, J. 1997. *It's about time: America's imprisonment binge* (2nd ed.). Belmont, CA: Wadsworth.

Irwin, J., & Cressey, D. R. 1962. Thieves, convicts, and the inmate culture. *Social Problems, 10*(2), 142–55.

Jacobs, J. B. 1997. The prisoner rights movement and its impact. In J. W. Marquart & J. R. Sorenson (Eds.), *Correctional contexts* (pp. 231–47). Los Angeles: Roxbury.

Jacobs, J. B. 2004. Prison reform amid the ruins of prisoner rights. In M. Tonry (Ed.), *The future of imprisonment* (pp. 179–96). New York: Oxford University Press.

Jacoby, R. 1975. *Social amnesia: A critique of conformist psychology from Adler to Laing.* Boston: Beacon.

Jacoby, J. E. 1979. *Classics of criminology.* New York: MacMillan.

Jameson, F. 1981. *The political unconscious: Narrative as a socially symbolic act.* Ithaca, NY: Cornell University Press.

Janus, E. S., & Walbek, N. H. 2000. Sex offender commitments in Minnesota: A descriptive study of second-generation commitments. *Behavior Sciences and the Law, 18,* 343–74.

Kann, M. E. 2005. *Punishment, prisons, and patriarchy: Liberty and power in the early American republic.* New York: New York University Press.

Kagan, D. 1990. Landmark Chicago study documents rate of mental illness among jail inmates. *Corrections Today,* December, 164.

Kassebaum, G. 1972. Sex in prison: Violence, homosexuality, and intimidation are everyday occurrences. *Sexual Behavior, 2*(1), 39–45.

King, C. A. 1999. Fighting the devil we don't know: *Kansas v. Hendricks,* a case study exploring the civilization of criminal punishment and its ineffectiveness in preventing child sexual abuse. *William and Mary Law Review, 40,* 1427–69.

King, R. D. 1999. The rise and rise of supermax: An American solution in search of a problem? *Punishment and Society,* 7(2), 163–86.

King, R. D. 2006. The effects of supermax custody. In A. Liebling & S. Maruna (Eds.), *The effects of imprisonment* (pp. 118–45). Portland, OR: Willan Publishing.

Kitsuse, J. I. 1964. Societal reaction to deviant behavior: Problems of theory and method. In H. S. Becker (Ed.), *The other side* (pp. 87–102). New York: Free Press.

Klein, M. W. 1974. Labeling, deterrence, and recidivism: A study of police dispositions of juvenile offenders. *Social Problems, 22*(2), 292–303.

Klein, M. W. 1975. *Alternative dispositions for juvenile offenders.* Los Angeles: University of Southern California.

Klein, M. W. 1979. Deinstitutionalization and diversion of juvenile offenders: A litany of impediments. In N. Morris & M. Tonry (Eds.), *Crime and justice: An annual review of research* (pp. 145–201). Chicago: University of Chicago Press.

Kulger, J. 2007. The paradox of supermax. *Time, 169*(6), 52–3.

Kobrin, S., & Klein, M. W. (Eds.) 1983. *Community treatment of juvenile offenders.* Beverly Hills, CA: Sage.

Kratcoski, P. C., & Pownall, G. A. 1989. Federal Bureau of Prisons programming for older inmates. *Federal Probation, 53,* 28–35.

Ku, R., & Blew, C. H. 1977. *A university's approach to delinquency prevention: The adolescent diversion project.* Washington, DC: U.S. Government Printing Office.

Kuehn, B. M. 2007. Mental health courts show promise. *The Journal of the American Medical Association, 297*(15), 1641–3.

Kuntz, W. F. II. 1988. *Criminal sentencing in three 19th-century cities: Social history of punishment in New York, Boston, and Philadelphia, 1830–1880.* New York: Garland.

Kyle, J. 1998. The privatization debate continues. *Corrections Today, 60,* 88–93.

LaFond, J. Q. 1992. Washington's sexually violent predator law: A deliberate misuse of the therapeutic state for social control. *University of Puget Sound Law Review, 15,* 655–703.

Lamb, H. R., & Weinberger, L. E. 2008. Mental health courts as a way to provide treatment to violent persons with severe mental illness. *The Journal of the American Medical Association, 300*(6), 722–4.

Lamb, H. R., Weinberger, L.E., Marsh, J. S., & Gross, B. H. 2007. Treatment prospects for persons with severe mental illness in an urban county jail. *Psychiatric Services, 58*(6), 782–6.

Lamb, S. 1996. *The trouble with blame.* Cambridge, MA: Harvard University Press.

Langan, P. A., & Levin, D. J. 2002. *Recidivism of prisoners released in 1994.* Washington, DC: U.S. Department of Justice, Bureau of Justice Statistics.

Lattimore, P. 2006. Re-entry, reintegration, rehabilitation, recidivism, and redemption. *The Criminologist, 31*(3), 1–3.

Lawson, W. T., & Fawkes, L. S. 1993. HIV, AIDS, and the female offender. In American Correctional Association (Ed.) *Female offenders: Meeting needs of a neglected population* (pp. 43–8). Laurel, MD: Editor.

Leiber, M., & Mac, K. Y. 2003. The individual and joint effects of race, gender, and family status on juvenile justice decision making. *Journal of Research in Crime and Delinquency, 40*, 34–70.

Lemert, E. M. 1970. *Social action and legal change: Revolution within the juvenile court.* Chicago: Aldine.

Lemert, E. M. 1971. *Instead of court: Diversion in juvenile justice.* Washington, DC: U.S. Government Printing Office.

Lemert, E. M. 1981. Diversion in juvenile justice: What hath been wrought. *Journal of Research in Crime and Delinquency, 78*(1), 34–46.

Lemert, E. M. 1993. Vision of social control: Probation considered. *Crime and Delinquency, 39*(4), 447–61.

Levenson, J. S., & Cotter, L. P. 2005. The impact of sex offender residence restrictions: 1,000 feet from danger or one step from absurd? *International Journal of Offender Therapy and Comparative Criminology, 49*(2), 168–78.

Levinson, J. 2004. Sexual predator civil commitment: A comparison of selected and released offenders. *International Journal of Offender Therapy and Comparative Criminology, 48*(6), 638–48.

Lichtenstein, A. 1993. Good roads and chain gangs in the Progressive South: "The negro convict is a slave." *Journal of Southern History, 59*(1), 85–110.

Lieber, F. 1838. A popular essay on subjects of penal law and on uninterrupted solitary confinement. *The North American Review,* October, XLVII. Retrieved from the ProQuest: American Periodical Series Online Database.

Lieber, F., & Julius, N. H. 1835. Education and crime. *American Annals of Education, 5*(3), 129–34. Retrieved from the ProQuest: American Periodical Series Online Database.

Lilly, J. R., Cullen, F. T., & Ball, R. A. 1995. *Criminological theory: Context and consequences.* Thousand Oaks, CA: Sage.

Lilly, J. R., & Knepper, P. 1993. The corrections–commercial complex. *Crime and Delinquency, 39,* 150–66.

Lincoln, S. B. 1976. Juvenile referral and recidivism. In R. M. Carter & M. W. Klein (Eds.), *Back on the street: The diversion of juvenile offenders* (pp. 321–8). Englewood Cliffs, NJ: Prentice-Hall.

Lincoln, S. B., Teilman, K., Klein, M. W., & Labin, S. 1977. *Recidivism rates of diverted juvenile offenders.* Paper presented at the National Conference on Criminal Justice Evaluation, Washington, DC.

Lindsey, B., & Burrough, R. 1931. *The dangerous life.* London: Harold Shaler.

Lippke, R. L. 1997. Thinking about private prisons. *Criminal Justice Ethics, 16*, 26–39.

Lowman, J., Menzies, R. J., & Palys, T. S. (Eds.). 1987. *Transcarceration: Essays in the sociology of social control*. England: Gower Press.

Lucken, K. 1997. Dynamics of penal reform. *Crime, Law, and Social Change, 26*(4), 367–84.

Lucken, K. 1997. Privatization discretion: "Rehabilitating" treatment in community corrections. *Crime and Delinquency, 43*(3), 243–59.

Lucken, K. 1998. Analyzing penal reform: Can theory and policy ever meet? In J. T. Ulmer (Ed.), *Sociology of crime, law, and deviance: Volume I* (pp. 85–103). Greenwich, CT: JAI.

Lucken, K., & Bales, W. D. 2008. Florida's sexually violent predator program: An examination of risk and civil commitment eligibility. *Crime and Delinquency, 54*(1), 95–127.

Lucken, K., & Latina, J. 2002. Sex offender civil commitment laws: Medicalizing deviant sexual behavior. *Barry Law Review, 3*(1), 15–38.

Lucken, K., & Ponte, L. M. 2008. A just measure of forgiveness: Reforming occupational licensing regulations for ex-offenders using BFOQ analysis. *Law & Policy, 30*(1), 46–72.

Luke, T. W. 1986. The modern service state: Public power in America from the New Deal to the new beginning. In A. Reed (Ed.), *Race, politics, and culture: Critical essays on the radicalism of the 1960s* (pp. 183–205). Westport, CT: Greenwood.

Lurigio, A. J., & Petersilia, J. 1992. The emergence of intensive probation supervision programs in the United States. In J. M. Byrne, A. J. Lurigio, & J. Petersilia (Eds.), *Smart sentencing* (pp. 103–19). Newbury Park, CA: Sage.

Lynch, J. P. 2006. Prisoner re-entry: Beyond program evaluation. *Criminology & Public Policy, 5*(2), 401–12.

Lyon, D. 1994. *The electronic eye: The rise of surveillance society*. MN: University of Minnesota Press.

Mack, J. W. 1909. The juvenile court. *Harvard Law Review, 23*, 104–22.

Mahoney, R. 1974. The effect of labeling upon youths in the juvenile justice system: A review of the evidence. *Law and Society Review, 8*(4), 583–614.

Malabre, A. L. 1987. *Beyond our means*. New York: Random House.

Mannheim, H. 1940. *Social aspects of crime in England between the wars*. London: Allen and Unwin.

Marcus, D. L. 1999. File this under shock, future: Libraries enter the modern age. *U. S. News and World Report*, 12 July, 48–49.

Marquart, J. R., & Sorensen J. R. (Eds.) 1997. *Correctional contexts*. Los Angeles: Roxbury.

Martin, B. 1980. Massachusetts's correctional system. Treatment or an ideology of control? In T. Platt & P. Takagi (Eds.), *Punishment and penal discipline* (pp. 156–64). Berkeley, CA: Crime and Social Justice Associates.

Martinson, R. 1974. What works? Questions and answers about prison reform. *Public Interest, 35*(2), 22–54.

Maruschak, L. M. 1999. *HIV in prisons, 1997*. Bureau of Justice Statistics Bulletin. Office of Justice Programs, Washington, D.C.

Maruschak, L. M. 2004. *HIV in prisons, 2001*. Bureau of Justice Statistics Bulletin. Office of Justice Programs, Washington, D.C.

Marx, G. 1988. *Undercover: Police surveillance in America*. Berkeley: University of California Press.

Mauer, M. 1996. The truth about truth in sentencing. *Corrections Today, 58*, 51–9.

Mauer, M. 1990. *Young black men in the criminal justice system: A growing national problem.* Washington, DC: The Sentencing Project.

McCarthy, B. R. 1980. Inmate mothers: The problems of separation and reintegration. *Journal of Offender Counseling, Services, and Rehabilitation, 4*(3), 199–212.

McCarthy, B. R., McCarthy, B. J. Jr., & Leone, M. C. 2001. *Community-based corrections* (4th ed.). Belmont, CA: Wadsworth.

McCorkle, R. C. 1995. Gender, psychopathology, and institutional behavior: A comparison of male and female mentally ill prison inmates. *Journal of Criminal Justice, 23*(1), 53–61.

McDonald, D., & Carlson, K. E. 1992. *Federal sentencing in transition.* U. S. Bureau of Justice Statistics Special Report. Washington, DC: U.S. Government Printing Office.

McKelvey, B. 1936. *American prisons.* Chicago: University of Chicago Press.

McShane, M. D., & Williams, S. P. III. 1990. Old and ornery: The disciplinary experiences of elderly prisoners. *Journal of Offender Therapy and Comparative Criminology, 34*(3), 197–212.

Mead, G. H. 1934. *Mind, self, and society.* Chicago: University of Chicago Press.

Mears, D. P. 2006. *Evaluating the effectiveness of supermax prisons.* Washington, DC: The Urban Institute.

Mednick, S. A. 1987. Genetic factors in the etiology of criminal behavior. In S. A. Mednick, T. E. Moffitt, & S. A. Stock (Eds.), *The causes of crime* (pp. 74–91). New York: Cambridge University Press.

Melossi, D., & Pavarini, M. 1981. *The prison and the factory.* Totowa, NJ: Barnes & Noble.

Mennel, R. M. 1973. *Thorns and thistles: Juvenile delinquents in the United States, 1825–1940.* Hanover, NH: University Press of New England.

Merton, R. K. 1938. Social structure and anomie. *American Sociological Review, 3,* 672–82.

Merton, R. K. 1949. *Social theory and social structure.* Glencoe, IL: Free Press.

Micek, J. L. 2005. Parole violations landing more inmates back in jail. *The Morning Call,* 27 March.

Michael, J., & Adler, M. J. 1933. *Crime, law, and social science.* New York: Harcourt-Brace.

Miethe, T. D., Olson, J., & Mitchell, O. 2006. Specialization and persistence in the arrest histories of sex offenders. *Journal of Research in Crime and Delinquency, 43,* 204–29.

Miller, M. B. 1980. At hard labor: Rediscovering the 19th-century prison. In T. Platt & P. Takagi (Eds.), *Punishment and penal discipline* (pp. 79–88). Berkeley, CA: Crime and Social Justice Associates.

Miller, W. B. 1958. Lower-class culture as a generating milieu of gang delinquency. *Journal of Social Issues, 14*(3), 5–19.

Morain, D. 1994. California's prison budget: Why is it so voracious? *Los Angeles Times,* 19 October.

Morris, N. 1974. *The future of imprisonment.* Chicago: University of Chicago Press.

Morris, N., & Hawkins, G. 1976. Rehabilitation: Rhetoric and reality. In K. M. Carter & L. T. Wilkins (Eds.), *Probation, parole, and community corrections* (2nd ed., pp. 26–39). New York: John Wiley.

Mullen, J. 1975. *The dilemma of diversion: Resource materials on adult pre-trial intervention programs.* Washington, DC: U.S. Government Printing Office.

Nakell, B., & Hardy, K. A. 1987. *The arbitrariness of the death penalty.* Philadelphia, PA: Temple University Press.

Nelson, M., Deess, P., & Allen, C. 1999. *The first month out: Post-incarceration experiences in New York City*. New York: Vera Institute of Justice.

New York Times. 1999. War on crack is past, but problems remain. *The Orlando Sentinel*, 28 February, A6.

Newman, G. 1978. *The punishment response*. Philadelphia: I. B. Lippincott.

Norton, M. B. 1991. Gender, crime, and community in 17th-century Maryland. In J. A. Henretta, M. Kammen, & S. N. Katz (Eds.), *The transformation of early American history* (pp. 123–50). New York: Alfred A. Knopf.

O'Connell, J. P. Jr. 1995. Throwing away the key. *Spectrum: The Journal of State Government*, 68(1), 28–33.

O'Toole, P. 1998. *Money and morals in America*. New York: Clarkson Potter.

Obrien, K. E., & Marcus, M. 1976. *Juvenile diversion: A selected bibliography*. Washington, DC: U.S. Government Printing Office.

Pallas, J., & Barber, B. 1980. From riot to revolution. In T. Platt & P. Takagi (Eds.), *Punishment and penal discipline* (pp. 146–54). Berkeley, CA: Crime and Social Justice Associates.

Palmer, J. W. 1991. *Constitutional rights of prisoners* (4th ed.). Cincinnati, OH: Anderson.

Park, R. E., & Burgess, E. W. 1924. *Introduction to the science of sociology* (2nd ed.). Chicago: University of Chicago Press.

Parshall, G. 1998. Discovery: Makers of the 20th century. *U. S. News and World Report*, 17 August.

Paulsen, M. G., & Whitebread, C. H. 1974. *Juvenile law and procedure*. Reno, NV: National Council of Juvenile Court Judges.

Pessen, E. 1969. *Jacksonian America: Society, personality, politics*. Homewood, IL: Dorsey.

Petersilia, J. 1987. Georgia's intensive probation: Will the model work elsewhere? In B. R. McCarthy (Ed.), *Intermediate punishments: Intensive supervision, home confinement, and electronic surveillance* (pp. 15–30). Monsey, NY: Criminal Justice Press.

Petersilia, J. 2003. *When prisoner come home: Parole and prisoner reentry*. New York: Oxford University Press.

Petersilia, J., & Turner, S. 1990. Comparing intensive and regular supervision for high-risk probationers: Early results from an experiment in California. *Crime and Delinquency*, 36(1), 87–111.

Petersilia, J., & Turner, S. 1993. Intensive probation and parole. In M. Tonry (Ed.), *Crime and justice: A review of research, Vol. 17*. Chicago: University of Chicago Press.

Pew Center on the States. 2009. *One in 31: The long reach of American corrections*. Washington, DC: The Pew Charitable Trusts.

Pezman, T. C. 1963. Untwisting the twisted. *Probation, camps, ranches, and schools* (pp. 1–2). Sacramento: California Probation, Parole, and Correctional Division.

Phillips, K. 1991. *The politics of rich and poor*. New York: Random House.

Pierce, G., & Radelet, M. 2005. The impact of legally inappropriate factors on death sentencing for California homicides, 1990–1999. *Santa Clara Law Review, 46*, 1–41.

Pisciotta, A. W. 1994. *Benevolent repression: Social control and the American reformatory prison movement*. New York: New York University Press.

Platt, A. M. 1969. *The child savers: The invention of delinquency*. Chicago: University of Chicago Press.

Platt, A. M. 1977. *The child savers: The invention of delinquency* (2nd ed.). Chicago: University of Chicago Press.

Pokorak, J. J. 1998. Probing the capital prosecutor's perspective: Race of the discretionary actors. *Cornell Law Review, 83*, 1811–20.

Polk, K. 1971. Delinquency prevention and the youth service bureau. *Criminal Law Bulletin, 7,* 490–529.

Polk, K. 1981. *Youth service bureaus: The record and the prospects.* Mimeograph. Eugene: University of Oregon.

Powers, E. 1966. *Crime and punishment in early Massachusetts, 1620–1692: A documentary history.* Boston: Beacon.

Preyer, K. 1982. Penal measures in the American colonies: An overview. *American Journal of Legal History, 26,* 326–53.

"Prison abuses." 1881. *National Police Gazette,* 15 January, 37(173). Retrieved from the ProQuest: American Periodicals Series Online Database.

"Prison reform." 1872. *American Church Review,* 1 July. Retrieved from the ProQuest: American Periodical Series Online Database.

Radzinowicz, L. 1994. *Adventures in criminology.* New York and London: Routledge.

Rafter, N. 1990. *Women, prison, and social control.* New Brunswick, NJ: Transaction.

Ralph, P. H. 1997. From self-preservation to organized crime: The evolution of inmate gangs. In J. W. Marquart & J. R. Sorenson (Eds.), *Correctional contexts* (pp. 182–8). Los Angeles: Roxbury.

Ramirez, J. 1984. Prisonization, staff, and inmates: Is it really about us versus them? *Criminal Justice and Behavior, 11,* 423–60.

Reardon, J. D. 1992. Predators and politics: A symposium of Washington's sexually violent predator's statute. *University of Puget Sound Law Review, 15,* 507–877.

Reiman, J. 1990. *The rich get riche and, the poor get prison.* New York: MacMillan.

"Religion was 'salt that flavored' colonial life." 1998. *Orlando Sentinel,* 5 July, A7.

Rhine, E. 1990. The rule of law, disciplinary practices, and Rahway State Prison: A case study in judicial intervention and social control. In J. J. DiIulio (Ed.), *Courts, corrections, and the Constitution* (pp. 173–222). New York: Oxford University Press.

Rhode, D. L. 1989. *Justice and gender.* Cambridge, MA: Harvard University Press.

Rhodes, M. L. 1979. The impact of social anchorage on prisonization. *Dissertation Abstracts International, 40,* 1694A.

Richmond, M. 1917. *Social diagnosis.* New York: Russell Sage.

Ringel, C., Cowles, E., & Castellano, T. 1993. *The recasting of parole supervision: The causes and responses of systems under stress.* Paper presented at the Academy of Criminal Justice Sciences Conference, Kansas City, Missouri.

Robbins, I. P. 1987. Privatization of corrections: Defining the issues. *Vanderbilt Law Review, 40,* 813–28.

Rosenfeld, R., & Kempf, K. 1991. The scope and purpose of corrections: Exploring alternative responses to crowding. *Crime and Delinquency, 37*(4), 481–505.

Rosenfeld, R., & Messner, S. F. 1999. Crime and the American dream. In F. T. Cullen & R. Agnew (Eds.), *Criminological theory: Past to present* (pp. 141–50). Los Angeles: Roxbury.

Rosenheim, M. 1969. Youth service bureaus: A concept in search of definition. *Juvenile Court Judges Journal, 20,* 69–74.

Rosica, J. L. 2000. Eyes in the sky will keep cons square. *Tallahassee Democrat,* 8 May.

Rossell, N. R. 1991. *Older inmates.* Tallahassee: Florida House of Representatives.

Rossiter, C. 1971. *The American quest, 1790–1860: An emerging nation in search of identity, unity, and modernity.* New York: Harcourt-Brace.

Rothman, D. J. 1971. *The discovery of the asylum: Social order and disorder in the new republic.* Boston: Little, Brown.

Rothman, D. J. 1980. *Conscience and convenience: The asylum and its alternatives in Progressive America.* Boston: Little, Brown.

Rotman, E. 1995. The failure of reform: United States, 1865–1965. In N. Morris & D. J. Rothman (Eds.), *The Oxford history of the prison* (pp. 169–97). New York: Oxford University Press.

Rowe, D. C., & Osgood, D. 1984. Heredity and sociological theories of delinquency: A reconsideration. *American Sociological Review, 49,* 526–40.

Rubin, J. 1971. *We are everywhere.* New York: Harper and Row.

Rusche, G., & Kirchheimer, O. 1939. *Punishment and social structure.* New York: Columbia University.

Rutherford, A., & McDermott, R. A. 1976. *Juvenile diversion.* Washington, DC: U.S. Government Printing Office.

Ryan, T. A., & Grassano, J. B. 1992. Taking a progressive approach to treating pregnant offenders. *Corrections Today, 54,* 184–6.

Ryerson, E. 1978. *The best laid plans: America's juvenile court experience.* New York: Hill and Wang.

Sabol, W. J., & Couture, H. 2008. *Prison inmates at midyear 2007.* Washington, DC: U.S. Department of Justice.

Sample, L. L., & Bray, T. M. 2003. Are sex offenders dangerous? *Criminology & Public Policy, 3*(1), 59–82.

Sarri, R. C. 1983. The use of detention and alternatives in the United States since the *Gault* decision. In R. R. Corrado, M. LeBlanc, & J. Trepanier (Eds.), *Current issues in juvenile justice* (pp. 315–34). Toronto: Butterworths.

Sarup, M. 1993. *An introductory guide to post-structuralism and postmodernism* (2nd ed.). Athens: University of Georgia Press.

Sassoon, T. 1995. *Crime talk: Citizens construct a social problem.* Hawthorne, NY: Aldine de Gruyter.

Saxonhouse, E. 2004. Unequal protection: Comparing former felons' challenges to disenfranchisement and employment discrimination. *Stanford Law Review, 56,* 1597–638.

Saylor, W. G, & Gaes, G. G. 1992. Post-release employment project: Prison work has measurable effects on post-release success. *Federal Prisons Journal, 2*(4), 32–6.

Scheingold, S. A. 1984. *The politics of law and order: Street crime and public policy.* New York: Longman.

Scheingold, S., Olson, T., & Pershing, J. 1992. The politics of sexual psychopathy: Washington State's sexual predator legislation. *University of Puget Sound Law Review, 15,* 809–20.

Schlossman, S. L. 1977. *Love and the American delinquent: The theory and practice of "progressive" juvenile justice, 1825–1920.* Chicago: University of Chicago Press.

Schlossman, S. L. 1995. Delinquent children: The juvenile reform school. In N. Morris & D. J. Rothman (Eds.), *The Oxford history of the prison* (pp. 363–89). New York: Oxford University Press.

Schopp, R. F., & Sturgis, B. J. 1995. Sexual predators and legal mental illness for civil commitment. *Behavioral Sciences & The Law, 13,* 437–58.

Schulhofer, S. J. 1993. Rethinking mandatory minimums. *Wake Forest Law Review, 28,* 199–222.

Schupak, T. 1986. Women and children first: An examination of the unique needs of women in prison. *Golden State University Law Review, 16*(3), 455–74.

Schur, E. M. 1971. *Labeling deviant behavior: Its sociological implications.* New York: Harper and Row.

Schwendinger, H., & Schwendinger, J. R. 1974. *The sociologists of the chair: A radical analysis of the formative years of North American sociology (1883–1922).* New York: Basic Books.

Scull, A. 1977. *Decarceration.* New Brunswick, NJ: Rutgers University Press.

Seiter, R. P. 1998. A rebirth of rehabilitation: The responsibility model. *Corrections Management Quarterly, 2,* 89–92.

Sewall, G. T. 1997. *The eighties.* Reading, MA: Addison-Wesley.

Sharp, S. F., & Marcus-Mendoza, S. T. 2001. It's a family affair: Incarcerated women and their families. *Women and Criminal Justice, 12,* 21–49.

Shaw, C. R. 1930. *The jackroller.* Chicago: University of Chicago Press.

Shaw, C. R. 1931. *The natural history of a delinquent career.* Chicago: University of Chicago Press.

Shaw, C. R. 1938. *Brothers in crime.* Chicago: University of Chicago Press.

Shaw, C. R., & McKay, H. D. 1972. *Juvenile delinquency and urban areas* (rev. ed.). Chicago: University of Chicago Press.

Sheppard, R. A. 1996. Closed maximum security: The Illinois supermax. *Corrections Today, 58,* 84–8.

Simon, J. 1993. *Poor discipline: Parole and the social control of the underclass, 1390–1990.* Chicago: University of Chicago Press.

Sinclair, Upton. 1906. *The jungle.* New York: Bantam Books.

Skolnick, J. H. 1969. *The politics of protest.* New York: Baliantine.

Skolnick, J. H. 1995. Sheldon L. Messinger: The man, his work, and the carceral society. In T. G. Blomberg & S. Cohen (Eds.), *Punishment and social control: Essays in honor of Sheldon L. Messinger* (pp. 15–28). Hawthorne, NY: Aldine de Gruyter.

Smalley, S. 1999. Slamming the slammers: A stir over private pens. *National Journal, 31,* 1168–75.

Smart, C. 1976. *Women, crime and criminology: A feminist critique.* London: Routledge & Kegan Paul.

Smith, C. E. 2000. *Law and contemporary corrections.* Belmont, CA: Wadsworth.

Smith, R. C. 1995. Sex offender program planning and implementation. In B. K. Schwartz & H. R. Cellini (Eds.), *The sex offender, Vol. 1: Corrections, treatment, and legal practice* (pp. 7:1–7:13). Kingston, NJ: Civic Research Institute.

Snell, T. L., & Morton, D. C. 1994. *Women in prison.* Washington, DC: U.S. Bureau of Justice Statistics.

Soderstrom, I. R. 1999. Is it still practical to incarcerate the elderly offender? In C. B. Fields (Ed.), *Controversial issues in corrections* (pp. 72–80). Needham Heights, MA: Allyn and Bacon.

Solomon, A. L., Johnson, K. D., Travis, J., & McBride, E. C. 2004. *From prison to work: The employment dimensions of prisoner re-entry.* Washington, DC: The Urban Institute.

Sommers, L. & Baskin, D. R. 1990. The prescription of psychiatric medications in prison: Psychiatric versus labeling perspectives. *Justice Quarterly, 7*(4), 739–55.

Specter, D. 1994. Cruel and unusual punishment of the mentally ill in California's prisons: A case study of a class action suit. *Social Justice, 27*(3), 109–16.

Spierenburg, P. 1984. *The spectacle of suffering: Executions and the evolution of repression.* Cambridge, MA: Cambridge University Press.

Staples, W. G. 1997. *The culture of surveillance: Discipline and social control in the United States.* New York: St. Martin's.

Steadman, H. J., Dean, M. W., Morrissey, J. P., Westcott, M. L., Salasin, S., & Shapiro, S. 1999. A SAMHSA research initiative assessing the effectiveness of jail diversion programs for mentally ill persons. *Psychiatric Services, 50*(12), 1620–3.

Steadman, H. J., Monahan, J., Duffee, B., Hartstone, E., & Robbins, P. C. 1984. The impact of state mental hospital deinstitutionalization on U.S. prison populations, 1968–1978. *Journal of Criminal Law and Criminology, 75,* 474–90.

Steelman, D. 1987. *The mentally impaired in New York's prisons.* New York: Correctional Association of New York.

Stratton, J. G. 1975. Effects of crisis intervention counseling on pre-delinquent and misdemeanor juvenile offenders. *Juvenile Justice, 26,* 7–18.

Sutherland, E. H. 1947. *Principles of criminology* (4th ed.). Philadelphia: Lippincott.

Sykes, G. 1958. *The society of captives.* Princeton, NJ: Princeton University Press.

Sykes, G. 1995. The structural, functional perspective on imprisonment. In T. G. Blomberg & S. Cohen (Eds.), *Punishment and social control: Essays in honor of Sheldon L. Messinger* (pp. 77–84). Hawthorne, NY: Aldine de Gruyter.

Sykes, G., & Messinger, S. L. 1960. The inmate social system. In R. A. Cloward (Ed.), *Theoretical studies in the social organization of the prison* (pp. 5–20). New York: Social Science Research Council.

Tannenbaum, F. 1938. *Crime and the community.* New York: Columbia University Press.

Teplin, L. 1990. The prevalence of severe mental disorder among male urban jail detainees: Comparison with the epidemiologic catchment area program. *American Journal of Public Health, 80*(6), 663–9.

Terry, K. J. 2006. *Sexual offenses and offenders.* Belmont, CA: Thomson Wadsworth.

Thomas, C. W. 1975. Prisonization as resocialization: A study of external factors associated with the impact of imprisonment. *Journal of Research in Crime and Delinquency, 10,* 13–21.

Thomas, J. 1988. *Prisoner litigation.* Totowa, NJ: Rowman and Littlefield.

Thompson, R. 1986. Sex *in Middlesex: Popular mores in a Massachusetts county, 1649–1699.* Amherst: University of Massachusetts Press.

"Thousands of eyes for state police." 1994. *New York Times,* 19 May, A8.

Tittle, C. R. 1995. *Control balance: Toward a general theory of deviance.* Boulder, CO: Westview.

Toch, H. 1977. *Living in prison: The ecology of survival.* New York: Free Press.

Tonry, M. 1999. Why are U.S. incarceration rates so high? *Crime and Delinquency, 45*(4), 419–37.

Torrey, E. 1995. Editorial: Jails and prisons—America's new mental hospitals. *American Journal of Public Health, 85*(12), 1611–3.

Towner, A. 1886. The treatment of criminals, with some account of the reformatory at Elmira, N.Y.—Its history and system.

Travis, J. 2002. Invisible punishments: An instrument of social exclusion. In M. Mauer & M. Chesney-Lind (Eds.), *Invisible punishment: The collateral consequences of mass imprisonment* (pp. 15–36). Washington, DC: New Press.

Travis, J., & Waul, M. 2003. *Prisoners once removed: The children and families of prisoners.* Washington, DC: The Urban Institute.

Turner, S., & Petersilia, J. 1996. Work release in Washington: Effects on recidivism and corrections costs. *The Prison Journal, 76*(2), 138–64.

Uggen, C., Thompson, M., & Manza, J. 2002. *Crime, class, and reintegration: The scope and social distribution of America's criminal class.* Unpublished paper, University of Minnesota, Minneapolis.

U.S. Bureau of Census. 1975. *Bureau of Census Statistics.* Bulletin. Washington, DC: U.S. Government Printing Office.

U.S. Bureau of Justice Statistics. 1995a. *Prison sentences and time served for violence.* Washington, DC: U.S. Government Printing Office.

U.S. Bureau of Justice Statistics. 1995b. *Prisoners in 1994.* Washington, DC: U.S. Government Printing Office.

U.S. Bureau of Justice Statistics. 1996. *Correctional population in the United States, 1996.* Washington, DC: U.S. Government Printing Office.

U.S. Department of Justice. 1979. *Evaluation of the Des Moines community-based corrections replication programs: Summary report.* Washington, DC: U.S. Government Printing Office.

U.S. Department of Justice. 2003. *History of the federal parole system.* Washington, DC: Author.

U.S. Office of National Drug Control Policy. 1995. *National drug control strategy: Budget summary.* Washington, DC: Office of National Drug Control Policy, Executive Office of the President.

U.S. President's Commission on Law Enforcement and Administration of Justice. 1967a. *The challenge of crime in a free society.* Washington, DC: U.S. Government Printing Office.

U.S. President's Commission on Law Enforcement and Administration of Justice. 1967b. *Task force report: Juvenile delinquency and youth crime.* Washington, DC: U.S. Government Printing Office.

Unger, L., & Unger, D. 1977. *The vulnerable years: The United States, 1896–1917.* Hinsdale, IL: Dryden.

Vale, L. J. 2000. *From the Puritans to the projects: Public housing and public neighbors.* Cambridge: Harvard University Press.

"Vermont sterilized people." 1999. *Orlando Sentinel,* 8 August.

Visher, C. A. 2006. Effective re-entry programs. *Criminology & Public Policy, 5*(2), 299–302.

Vitale, A. 1980. Inmate abortions: The right to government funding. *Fordham Law Review, 48*(4), 550–67.

Vito, G. F. 1995. The penalty of death in the next century. In J. Klofas & S. Stojkovic (Eds.), *Crime and justice in the year 2010* (pp. 251–66). Belmont, CA: Wadsworth.

Vlahov, D. 1990. Co-infection with tuberculosis and HIV-1 in male prison inmates. *Public Health Reports, 705*(3), 307–10.

Vogelman, R. P. 1971. Prison restrictions, prisoner rights. In L. Radzinowicz & M. E. Wolfgang (Eds.), *Crime and justice series: The criminal in confinement, Vol. 3* (pp. 52–68). New York: Basic Books.

von Hentig, H. 1942. Degrees of parole violation and graded remedial measures. *Journal of the American Institute of Criminal Law and Criminology, 8,* 233–58.

von Hirsch, A. 1995. The future of the proportionate sentence. In T. G. Blomberg & S. Cohen (Eds.), *Punishment and social control: Essays in honor of Sheldon L. Messinger* (pp. 123–45). Hawthorne, NY: Aldine de Gruyter.

Wald, K. 1980. The San Quentin Six case: Perspective and analysis. In T. Platt & P. Takagi (Eds.), *Punishment and penal discipline* (pp. 165–75). Berkeley, CA: Crime and Social Justice Associates.

Walker, S. 1985. *Sense and nonsense about crime and drugs.* Belmont, CA: Wadsworth.

Wallace, D. H. 1992. *Ruffin v. Virginia* and slaves of the state: A non-existent baseline of prisoners' rights jurisprudence. *Journal of Criminal Justice, 20,* 333–42.

Wallace, D. H. 1994. The Eighth Amendment and prison deprivations: Historical revisions. *Criminal Law Bulletin, 30*(1), 5–29.

Walters, G. D. 2003. Changes in criminal thinking and identity in novice and experienced inmates: Prisonization revisited. *Criminal Justice and Behavior, 30*(4), 399–421.

Ward, D., & Kassebaum, G. 1965. *Women's prison: Sex and social structure.* Chicago, IL: Aldine Publishing Company.

Wellford, C. 1975. Labeling theory and criminology: An assessment. *Social Problems, 22*(3), 332–5.

Wettstein, R. M. 1992. A psychiatric perspective on Washington's sexually violent predators statute. *University of Puget Sound Law Review, 15,* 579–633.

"What has been done and what is to do." 1856. *Pennsylvania Journal of Prison Discipline and Philanthropy,* October, 11(4). Retrieved from the ProQuest: American Periodicals Series Online Database.

Wheeler, P. A., Trammell, R., Thomas, J., & Findlay, J. 1989. Persephone chained: Parity of equality in women's prisons. *Prison Journal, 69,* 88–102.

Wheeler, S. 1971. Socialization in correctional institutions. In L. Radzinowicz & M. E. Wolfgang (Eds.), *Crime and justice series: The criminal in confinement, Vol. 3* (pp. 97–116). New York: Basic Books.

Wheeler, W. M. 1999. Is it still practical to incarcerate the elderly offender? In C. B. Fields (Ed.), *Controversial issues in corrections* (pp. 72–80). Needham Heights, MA: Allyn and Bacon.

Wickham, D. S. 1999. Insane with no asylum: Mentally ill pack jails. *Orlando Sentinel,* 31 October, 18.

Wilbanks, W. 1984. The elderly offender: Placing the problem in perspective. In W. Wilbanks & P. Kim (Eds.), *Elderly criminals* (pp. 1–11). Lanham, MD: University Press of America.

Williams, D. E. 1993a. Life, last words, and dying confession of Rachel Wall, 1789. *Pillars of salt: An anthology of early American criminal narratives* (pp. 283–7). Madison, WI: Madison House.

Williams, D. E. 1993b. A faithful narrative of Elizabeth Wilson, 1786. *Pillars of salt: An anthology of early American criminal narratives* (pp. 271–81). Madison, WI: Madison House.

Williams, W. A. 1966. *The contours of American history.* Chicago: Quadrangle.

Wilson, J. A., & Davis, R. C. 2006. Good intentions meet hard realities: An evaluation of the Project Greenlight re-entry program. *Criminology & Public Policy, 5*(2), 303–38.

Wilson, J. Q., & Herrnstein, R. J. 1985. *Crime and human nature.* New York: Simon and Schuster.

Wilson, W. J. 1987. *The truly disadvantaged.* Chicago: University of Chicago Press.

Winick, B. J. 1998. Sex offender law in the 1990s: A therapeutic jurisprudence analysis. *Psychology, Public Policy, and Law, 4*(1/2), 505–70.

Winthrop, J. 1630. *A city upon a hill.* Retrieved 9 April 2009, from http://www.mtholyoke. edu/acad/intrel/winthrop.htm.

Wooldredge, J. D., & Masters, K. 1993. Confronting problems faced by pregnant inmates in state prisons. *Crime and Delinquency, 39,* 195–203.

Zedner, L. 1995. Wayward sisters, the prison for women. In N. Morris & D. J. Rothman (Eds.), *The Oxford history of the prison* (pp. 329–61). New York: Oxford University Press.

Index